Gateway 2nd Edition Book

Welcome	Introduction by David Spencer	p2
	Key concepts of *Gateway 2nd Edition*	pp2–3
Course components	Student's Book	pp4–10
	Digital Student's Book	p11
	Presentation Kit	p12
	Videos	p13
	Workbook	pp14–16
	Online Workbook	p17
	Teacher's and Student's Resource Centres	p18
	Testing and assessment materials	p19
Teacher support	Dave's top teaching tips	pp20–22
	Teacher development tips index	p23
	The CEFR and *Gateway 2nd Edition*	pp24–27

Teacher's notes	Unit 1	p28	Unit 6	p101
	Unit 2	p44	Unit 7	p117
	Unit 3	p60	Unit 8	p130
	Unit 4	p72	Unit 9	p145
	Unit 5	p87	Unit 10	p157

Audioscripts and answer keys	Class audioscript	p171
	Workbook answer key	p183
	Workbook audioscript	p197

Anna Cole

macmillan education

B2

Welcome
Introduction by David Spencer

Before I tell you about *Gateway 2nd Edition*, let me tell you a bit about myself.

After studying Modern Languages, I trained to be a secondary school teacher. And I'm still teaching in a secondary school now, over 25 years later. Being in the classroom every day is a great help when writing a course like *Gateway*. On the one hand, the daily contact with teenagers gives me ideas and inspiration. On the other hand, it keeps me realistic about what actually works in the classroom.

If you don't know *Gateway* already, the course is designed to lead teenage students to success in exams, particularly school-leaving exams. It's also designed to prepare students for further study and the world of work.

In *Gateway 2nd Edition* we've kept many of the features that have made *Gateway* so popular. Each unit has a clear, logical structure. The whole approach to grammar and vocabulary and to the development of the four skills is carefully staged to be both teacher- and student-friendly. Each level offers a wide range of strategies that will help students pass their exams.

But *Gateway 2nd Edition* has several exciting new features. Firstly there are the **Flipped classroom videos**, which bring grammar points from the Student's Book to life.

Then there is a whole new focus on **Life skills**, with a special section in each unit preparing teenagers for many, varied facets of life, complete with its own tailor-made video featuring British teenagers.

Meanwhile *Gateway 2nd Edition* offers brand-new, up-to-date texts to motivate you and your students. Reading texts include **Critical thinking** questions to get students reflecting on what they've just read. And for all these features, new and old, we've refreshed the design and made it even clearer and easier to use.

With *Gateway 2nd Edition* we want to support you in the classroom and in your professional development. Via the **Gateway Facebook page**, you can keep in direct contact with me and the *Gateway* team and with other teachers from around the world. We have news, teaching tips and occasional competitions, plus access to teaching videos and webinars. You can also find out about any upcoming *Gateway* talks in your part of the world. So far I've spoken in over 20 countries and hope to continue being able to share activities and ideas with you all.

I hope you and your students enjoy teaching and learning with *Gateway 2nd Edition*!

Dave

f www.facebook.com/macmillangateway

Key concepts of *Gateway 2nd Edition*

1 Preparation for school-leaving exams

Gateway 2nd Edition prepares secondary school students for both international and school-leaving exams. Throughout the units there are plenty of exam-style activities and preparation tasks as well as **Exam success** tips. These tips lead the students to more in-depth help in the Exam success section at the end of book. After every two units there are **Gateway to exams** pages which revise the exam techniques they have learnt and give them more practice in doing typical exam tasks. *Gateway 2nd Edition* is closely mapped to the CEFR and the course comes with both a **Test generator** and **printable tests**.

2 Content-based material and critical thinking

Gateway 2nd Edition provides material which helps to develop other areas of knowledge, as well as English-language skills. The most important criteria for choosing texts is that they should be genuinely interesting and appealing to students of the age group. Texts are then used to provide a realistic and meaningful context for the grammar and vocabulary to be studied within the unit. Students are also encouraged to think critically about what they have read, to question the content and personalise the topic of the text.

3 Life skills

We now have two pages at the heart of each unit which prepare students for life outside the classroom. We help students in areas as wide-ranging as personal and physical well-being, citizenship, social skills, money and finance, and the world of work. Each Life skills section has a motivating video with British teenagers demonstrating the topic and ends with students performing a **Life task**, an activity that has direct relevance to the students' lives outside the classroom.

4 The active role of the learners

Students are encouraged to participate actively in their own learning throughout the course. Here are just some of the ways this is done:

Exam success boxes in the Student's Book and **Study skills** boxes in the Workbook encourage students to reflect on the best way to learn before they are guided to the suggestions at the back of the book.

Students hypothesise about grammar rules before they are directed to the relevant information in the **Grammar reference** section at the end of each unit.

Students are invited to express personal reactions and/or think critically after reading or listening.

On the **Gateway to exams** pages which appear after every two units, there is a reference to the **'Can do' progress check** where students evaluate their own progress and decide what steps to take next to maximise their learning.

5 Grammar in context

The target grammar in each unit is given meaningful context through the reading and listening texts. The approach is one of guided discovery. Students are then directed to the **Grammar reference** section at the end of the unit to check their hypotheses.

An alternative approach to grammar presentation is now offered by the **Flipped classroom videos**.

After the grammar presentation stage, the students work through carefully graded exercises which help them to internalise the grammar, starting with exercises where students simply identify correct usage and ending with exercises where students use the grammar in active, oral communication.

The Grammar reference section appears directly at the end of the unit, providing a useful checkpoint for students when reviewing the unit. **Grammar revision** exercises facing the Grammar reference section make this part of the Student's Book interactive and ideal for self-study, for example for revision and self-testing before exams.

6 The Flipped classroom

In the traditional classroom, the teacher explains new content in the class and students do practice at home. The Flipped classroom refers to students learning new content outside the classroom, via video presentations, and then doing practice in the class. This makes it easier for the teacher to give more personalised help and attention during the practice stage. It also means students can go at their own speed during the presentation stage.

In *Gateway 2nd Edition* we have created a series of **Flipped classroom videos** to help you to find more time in lessons and to add variety to your teaching. The videos are short grammar presentations linked to one of each unit's **Grammar guides**. Students can watch the presentation at home, as many times as they want. There are interactive

tasks in the *Gateway 2nd Edition* Online Workbook or printable worksheets on the Resource centre to help the students to check that they've understood, and for you to check that they have actually watched the video.

The videos are a flexible teaching tool and can also be used for revision, or when students miss a class, or with the whole class in lesson-time, for variety. The Flipped classroom videos have the added bonus that they encourage students to take responsibility for their own progress and become independent learners.

7 Developing vocabulary

The course revises, extends and practises the most important lexical sets connected to typical topics that appear in school-leaving and international exams, so that students can talk and write about these topics with ease and will have less difficulty reading or listening to texts dealing with these topics. The course also develops the students' active vocabulary unit-by-unit by looking at 'systems' of vocabulary, such as word formation, collocation, phrasal verbs, and dependent prepositions. This approach is a key factor in helping students with Use of English tasks.

8 Developing skills

The emphasis of *Gateway 2nd Edition* is very much on developing the skills, not just testing them. In terms of speaking and writing, the approach taken is step-by-step preparation for the final, exam-style task at the end of the activity. Initial exercises are more receptive, working on a model text or dialogue. Students then analyse the words and expressions used and have guided, controlled practice of these before creating their own texts or performing their own dialogues. Words and expressions that are useful to complete these tasks successfully are highlighted in the **Speaking bank** and **Writing bank**. **Pronunciation**, an integral part of developing oral skills, is integrated into each unit at the most appropriate stage.

With reading and listening, there is attention to the strategies that help students to understand texts more easily. To develop reading and listening in a comprehensive way, there is a wide variety of text genres and task types.

Course components
Student's Book

The *Gateway 2nd Edition* Student's Book offers ten units with Grammar and Vocabulary reference and revision sections in the Language checkpoint at the end of each unit. Exam-style activities appear throughout, with consolidation and practice every two units in the Gateway to exams pages.

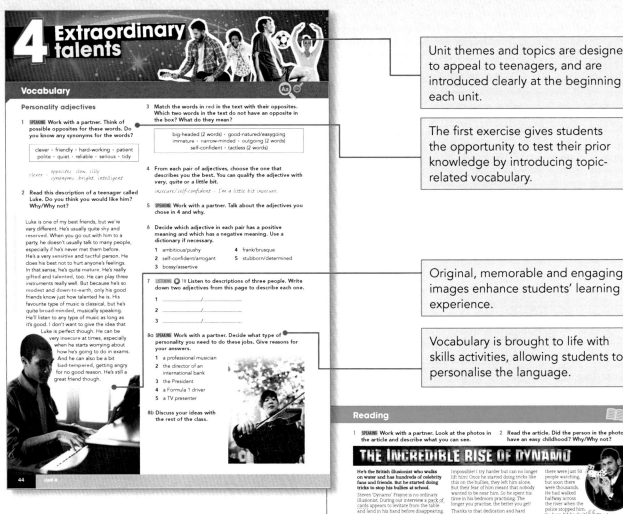

Unit themes and topics are designed to appeal to teenagers, and are introduced clearly at the beginning of each unit.

The first exercise gives students the opportunity to test their prior knowledge by introducing topic-related vocabulary.

Original, memorable and engaging images enhance students' learning experience.

Vocabulary is brought to life with skills activities, allowing students to personalise the language.

Reading tasks focus on stimulating topics using recognisable and relevant contexts.

Typical reading tasks include exam-style comprehension questions such as multiple-choice, True/False or inserting sentences into a text.

The **Critical thinking** activity embedded in every Reading lesson goes beyond traditional comprehension exercises to guide students towards the use of higher-order thinking skills. It also gives students the opportunity to develop analytical skills and use them in an authentically communicative way.

Grammar in context

Flipped classroom: watch the video on the Resource Centre or Online Workbook.

Comparative and superlative adjectives and adverbs

1a Look at the sentences. Which contain comparative forms and which contain superlative forms?

1 I try harder but can no longer lift him.
2 He grew up in one of the most dangerous areas in Bradford.
3 Even when you look more closely, it's impossible to know.
4 He is better than the rest.
5 My stomach hurts the least when I'm performing.
6 He practises the longest.
7 It's easier for him to do a trick than explain it.

1b Look at the sentences again. Which contain adjectives and which contain adverbs?

GRAMMAR REFERENCE ➤ PAGE 54

2 SPEAKING Work with a partner. Complete the table below and then explain the rules for the different groups of adjectives.

Adjective	Comparative	Superlative
long slow		
big thin		
friendly tidy		
ambitious hard-working		
good bad far little (determiner)	less	the farthest/the furthest

For one-syllable adjectives, add -er to make the comparative.

3a Match the rules and examples for comparative and superlative adverbs.

1 We usually make comparative and superlative adverbs with more and the most.
2 With some irregular adverbs we add -er and the -est.
3 Some comparative and superlative adverbs are irregular.

a well, bad, little
b carefully, quietly, easily, beautifully, often
c fast, hard, early, late, long, soon, near

3b Make the comparative form of the adverbs in 3a (a–c).

4 Rewrite the sentences using the correct comparative and superlative form.

1 In my opinion, Caleb is the friendlier person in this class.
2 I think Emma is slightly taller that Claire.
3 That is definitely the most silly thing I've heard today!
4 You can write much quicklier on a computer than by hand.
5 Sorry I couldn't come more soon.
6 Is it much more further to your house?
7 You need to try more hardly if you want to be a professional illusionist.
8 Houdini was one of the more famous illusionists in the world.
9 That film was terrible! It's the less interesting film I've ever seen.
10 She did more well than me in the test.

5a SPEAKING Work with a partner. Decide who in your class ...

1 talks the fastest.
2 shouts the loudest.
3 speaks the most quietly.
4 draws the best.
5 runs the furthest.
6 arrives the earliest.
7 writes the most neatly.
8 laughs the most often.

5b Say one of the names you chose in 5a. Can your classmates guess the description?

Other ways of making comparisons

6 Look at the sentences and answer the questions a–c.

1 I tried as hard as the others.
2 He was not as/so big as his classmates.
3 When he works, his stomach is less painful than when he rests.
4 We get older and older.
5 The longer you practise, the better you get.
6 The earlier you start, the easier it is.

a When do we use as ... as?
b When do we use not as ... as, not so ... as, or less ... than?
c How do you say 4–6 in your language?

GRAMMAR REFERENCE ➤ PAGE 54

46 Unit 4

---

7 Complete the second sentence so that it has a similar meaning to the first sentence, using the word given. Do not change the word given. You must use between two and five words, including the word given.

1 Liam enjoys surfing the Net as much as playing computer games.
   ENJOYABLE
   For Liam, surfing the Net _____ computer games.

2 Eating fruit and vegetables is healthier than eating fast food.
   LESS
   Eating fast food _____ eating fruit and vegetables.

3 When you walk at a higher speed, you get more tired.
   FASTER
   The _____ more tired you get.

4 Dylan thinks judo is better than karate.
   NOT
   For Dylan, karate _____ judo.

5 Olivia is quick when she writes, and so is Amy.
   AS
   Amy writes _____ Olivia.

6 Chinese is much harder to write than English.
   DIFFICULT
   English is _____ than Chinese.

7 Basketball becomes easier depending on your height.
   TALLER
   The _____ basketball becomes.

8 She's getting increasingly good at maths.
   AND
   She's getting _____ at maths.

8 SPEAKING Work with a partner. Match the halves of these common expressions. Check that you understand what they mean and then think of a situation when you might use them.

1 The sooner   a than done.
2 Better late   b to worse.
3 Easier said   c than never.
4 Better to be safe   d the harder they fall.
5 The more   e the merrier.
6 This is going from bad f the better.
7 The bigger they are   g than sorry.

The sooner the better. You use it when you want something to happen as soon as possible, for example the start of the holidays.

Developing vocabulary

Noun suffixes

1 Look at these words. Each one contains a noun suffix. Which of the nouns are for a person?

ability · actor · artist · difference · direction enjoyment · illness · performance politician · writer

2 Make nouns from these words using the suffixes in 1. You may need to change the spelling. Sometimes you can make more than one noun from each word.

act · appear · confident · create · different educate · electric · employ · happy · improve invent · investigate · mad · music relevant · science

3 Complete the text below with the correct form of the words given.

✓ EXAM SUCCESS

In this type of exercise, you may need to add a prefix or a suffix or both. Sometimes the word needs to be plural. Look at the context carefully to decide.
➤ EXAM SUCCESS page 145

Sometimes you can get the impression that (a) _____ (science) today spend all their time just improving high tech toys and phones. But just think of the (b) _____ (important) of some of the biggest inventions of the past. Take (c) _____ (electric), for example, or, more specifically, the electric light bulb. The (d) _____ (create) of the light bulb is one of the key moments in human progress. Its (e) _____ (invent) was the extraordinarily talented Thomas Edison. Edison's biggest skill was to take another person's idea and make (f) _____ (improve) to it. Electric light bulbs meant the (g) _____ (appear) of unsafe gas lighting. Before electric lights, people couldn't do much when it got dark at night. Edison gave people the (h) _____ (able) to see at night. What a (i) _____ (different) that made!

Unit 4 47

Annotations (preview callouts)

The **Grammar guide** box highlights sentences from the reading text. Students are asked to work out key information about the form and use of the grammar. The students are then referred to the **Grammar reference** section in the **Language checkpoint** at the end of the unit to check their ideas.

The **Flipped classroom** grammar presentation video provides a versatile and flexible learning tool, and an alternative grammar presentation which gives students greater control over their learning. Ideal for visual learners, research shows that the Flipped classroom can create a more effective language-learning environment.

Students progress to controlled grammar practice.

The Developing vocabulary section moves beyond the traditional lexical sets to focus on 'systems' of vocabulary. These include word formation, collocation and phrasal verbs, and often bridge the gap between vocabulary and grammar.

The final grammar activity asks students to use the new grammar in active, oral communication.

Students are given the opportunity to practise the language they have encountered in the activity.

Gateway to life skills offers three strands of lessons (Academic skills, Life skills, and 21st century skills) which equip students with the necessary transferable skills beyond school. The Life skills lesson allows students both controlled and freer language practice, using what they have learnt in previous lessons in a cumulative way.

The Life skills lesson is introduced to students with clear objectives.

Students are shown the key concepts of the Life skills lesson in a clear and concise form and have the chance to explore issues of universal interest and importance.

Engaging videos show a variety of different contexts including authentic interviews with teenagers and experts, vlogs, debates, lectures and role-playing.

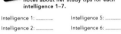

Students have many opportunities to give and share their opinions.

The lesson culminates in a productive task such as giving a presentation, creating a poster or making a plan. It gives students the opportunity to use language in an authentic and collaborative context while practising a useful and transferable Life skill.

Macmillan Life Skills winner of the ELTon award for Innovation in Teacher Resources!
Go to macmillanenglish.com/life-skills/resources to explore our collection of life skills resources.

Listening

Free climbing in the mountains

1 **SPEAKING** Work with a partner. Look at the photo and answer these questions.

1 Would you like to be in this situation? Why/Why not?
2 What type of people do you think normally do this type of activity?
3 How much training do you think you need to do this?

2 **LISTENING** 20 Listen to two people talking about a new TV series. Are these statements True (T), False (F) or is the information Not Mentioned (NM)?

1 For Sue Wilson, there wasn't much competition for best programme of the week. T/F/NM
2 She had the wrong idea about the programme *Hidden Talent* at first. T/F/NM
3 To make this programme, they invited people with special talents to do tests. T/F/NM
4 Maggie Reenan had always wanted to try rock climbing. T/F/NM
5 Being a nurse was possibly an advantage for Maggie when rock climbing. T/F/NM
6 Being able to detect lies is quite a common ability. T/F/NM
7 With the FBI, Brenda Chamberlain watched videos of suspects again and again. T/F/NM
8 Sue thinks that Maggie never knew about her talent before because she never had time for herself. T/F/NM

3 20 Listen again and answer the questions.

1 How many people did the tests for *Hidden Talent*?
2 How many tests did they do?
3 What do you know about Maggie's family situation?
4 How high was the rock she climbed?
5 What often makes the rock more difficult to climb?
6 How many people do they say have a strong ability for detecting lies?
7 What two things did the FBI teach Brenda?
8 What did the programme make Sue think?

4 **SPEAKING** What about you?

1 Would you like to watch this TV series? Why/Why not?
2 Would you like to do tests to see if you have a hidden talent? Why/Why not?

Grammar in context

Articles

1 **Read these sentences.**

1 There was a programme that stood out.
2 The programme was the first in the series.
3 [–] Nurses treat [–] patients in [–] emergencies.
4 You could be the best diver in the world.

2 **Match the sentence halves to make rules. Find an example of each rule in a sentence in 1.**

1 We use *a/an* ...
2 We use *the* ...
3 We use *the* ...
4 We use *the* ...
5 We use no article ...

a to talk about a singular countable person or thing for the first time, or to say that the person or thing is one of a number of people or things.
b to talk about a specific person or thing or a person or thing mentioned before.
c to talk about things in general in the plural.
d to talk about someone or something that is unique.
e with superlative adjectives, adverbs, *first* and *last*.

GRAMMAR REFERENCE ➤ PAGE 54

3 **Choose the correct alternative.**

1 In general, I think *the/[–]* teachers can help *the/[–]* young people to develop their talents.
2 Last night I saw *a/[–]* programme about *a/the* young girl who has *a/the* really good voice.
3 Did you read *a/the* book I gave you yesterday about *the/[–]* science?
4 I reckon she's *the/[–]* better than most TV presenters.
5 *A/The* biggest problem with *a/the* world today is that we are all too busy.
6 I've got *a/the* friend who trains *the/[–]* animals to appear in *the/[–]* films.
7 Last week I read *an/the* article about *the/[–]* first episode in *a/the* new comedy series.
8 I think *the/[–]* rock climbers do *the/[–]* most amazing things.

4 **Complete the text with *a*, *an*, *the* or *[–]*.**

I've got (a) _____ friend who has (b) _____ amazing talent. She has (c) _____ incredible memory. She's really good at remembering (d) _____ faces. She once met (e) _____ man for just a few seconds. When she saw (f) _____ man again six months later, she recognised him immediately, even though (g) _____ clothes he was wearing were completely different and now he had (h) _____ beard. I'm exactly the opposite. I think I have (i) _____ worst memory in (j) _____ world!

---

5 **Read the text and correct seven mistakes in the use of articles.**

One of the most interesting episodes of *Hidden Talent* was about a boy called James Whinnery. He was only 19. They discovered that the boy had a special talent for the languages. He learnt the Arabic in just 19 weeks. He did a test working in Turkish restaurant for a day, talking to the waiters in Arabic. Then, for his training, they say he learnt the new words – one hundred words each day! At the end of the episode, he travelled to Jordan and they interviewed him in Arabic on a special programme. Of course, nobody can really learn new language in just 19 weeks. But James learnt a lot of things in that time. It seems that sometimes the TV programmes can have positive effect on people and their lives.

so, such, too, enough

6 **Look at these sentences and complete the rules below with *so*, *such*, *too* or *enough*.**

a The weather is usually so bad that it can be a scary experience.
b She did it so well.
c It's such a difficult climb that you usually need many years of experience.
d It's such a pity.
e She's always been too busy to find the time.
f She was(n't) good enough to do it.

1 We use _____ to say if something is or isn't excessive. It comes before an adjective or adverb.
2 We use _____ to say if something is or isn't sufficient. It comes after an adjective or adverb.
3 We use _____ to intensify a noun (with or without an adjective). If the noun is singular we use *a/an* before the noun.
4 We use _____ to intensify an adjective or adverb.
5 We use *to* + infinitive after _____ and _____
6 We use that after _____ and _____

GRAMMAR REFERENCE ➤ PAGE 54

7 **Complete the sentences with these words. You can use the words more than once. If no word is necessary, put [–].**

a · enough · so · such · to · too

---

1 I'm 15, so I'm _____ young to vote in a general election.
2 It's such _____ beautiful day today.
3 She isn't tall _____ to get the book off the top shelf.
4 It's too late _____ say that you're sorry.
5 I have such _____ good memories of living by the sea.
6 The film was _____ exciting I watched it twice.
7 When you're 18, you're old _____ to drive in most countries.
8 Rebecca and Christine are _____ good friends that they seem like sisters.
9 I love that band. Their music is _____ good!

8 **Complete the second sentence so that it has a similar meaning to the first sentence, using the word given. Do not change the word given. You must use between two and five words, including the word given.**

1 That artist does such good pictures that everyone copies her. SO
That artist's pictures _____ copies her.
2 The water was so cold we couldn't swim. TOO
The water was _____ swim.
3 Her paintings are so good you could sell them. ENOUGH
Her paintings _____ sell.
4 It was so cold that day that they stayed at home. SUCH
It was _____ they stayed at home.
5 He's so insecure that he'll never be a good leader. SELF-CONFIDENT
He _____ be a good leader.
6 Kate doesn't sing very well so she won't become a professional singer. ENOUGH
Kate doesn't _____ to become a professional singer.

9a **Use your imagination to complete these sentences.**

1 They've got such a big house that ...
2 There was a woman who was so rich ...
3 My friend is so quiet ...
4 I knew somebody who was too lazy to ...
5 We aren't fit enough to ...
6 I'm such a good student that ...
7 My friend is so clever ...

9b **SPEAKING** Work in small groups. Compare your sentences in 9a. Choose the best ones and tell them to the rest of the class.

Students listen to a wide variety of realistic types of recording which include dialogues, radio programmes, adverts and interviews.

The second Grammar in context lesson functions in the same way as the previous one allowing students to discover grammar rules for themselves.

There is a wide variety of listening tasks, all of which appear in listening exams, such as True/False, completing notes and matching.

Students are given lots of opportunities to use new grammar in active, oral communication. This activity usually involves personalisation. Students work in pairs or small groups and find out new things about their classmates.

50 Unit 4

Unit 4 51

Developing speaking

Presentations - 1

💬 SPEAKING BANK

Useful expressions to structure a presentation
Beginning your presentation
- I'd like to begin by saying …
- To start with …
- The first thing I'd like to say is …
- I'm going to talk about …

Ordering your arguments
- First of all,
- Firstly,
- Secondly,
- Another thing is that,
- Furthermore,
- What's more,
- It's important to remember that …
- It's also true that …

Concluding your presentation
- In conclusion,
- Finally,
- To sum up,
- Last but not least,
- The point I'm trying to make is …
- In short,

1 SPEAKING Work with a partner. Talk about the people in the photos. Who are they and why are they famous?

2 SPEAKING How would you define a 'hero'? Would you call any of the people in 1 heroes? Why/Why not?

3 SPEAKING Work with a partner. Look at the presentation topic and discuss if you agree or disagree with the statement. Make notes of your ideas. Think of arguments to justify and explain your opinions.

'There are no heroes in today's world, just celebrities.'
Do you agree? Why/Why not?

4 LISTENING ⏺ 21 Listen to a student giving a presentation on this topic. What is their opinion? Do they mention any of your ideas in 3?

5 ⏺ 21 Listen again and tick (✓) the expressions in the Speaking bank that you hear.

6 Organise your notes from 3 in a logical order, with an introduction and a conclusion.

7 SPEAKING Work with a partner. Read the advice in Exam success. Take it in turns to give a presentation with your opinion. Remember to use expressions from the Speaking bank. When you finish, discuss how well you did your presentations.

✔ EXAM SUCCESS

When you give a presentation remember that you can look at your notes, but don't just read them aloud. Don't forget to look at your audience to see if they understand you and are interested.
➤ EXAM SUCCESS page 145

PRACTICE MAKES PERFECT

8a SPEAKING Prepare a presentation about somebody that you admire. Give reasons why you admire them. It can be a famous person or someone in your life, for example a friend or relative.

8b Give your presentation to the class.

52   Unit 4

The Developing speaking lesson develops students' oral skills with a highly-structured and supportive approach to speaking.

The Speaking bank highlights and analyses key language for students to refer to during the productive phase of the speaking task.

There are two Exam success boxes in each unit. They ask students to reflect on the best way to do a specific exam task. Students can discuss the question in pairs and they are then directed to a special section at the end of the book where useful strategies and tips are explained.

Students are given extensive practice of the language they have learnt in the Practice makes perfect activity.

Developing writing

An article - 1

1 SPEAKING Work with a partner. Read this announcement and talk about people that you could write about and what talents they have.

Young journalist

Articles wanted
Extraordinary talents!

We want to know who you think are the most talented people in the 21ˢᵗ century!

Write about one famous person who you think has extraordinary talents. Describe them and what they do. It could be an actor, singer, musician, writer, artist … anyone with an amazing talent!

Send us your articles … now!

2 Read an article written about the singer Ed Sheeran. What talents does the writer of the article say that Ed Sheeran has? Make a list.

Ed Sheeran

A How many good singers are there today? Hundreds, maybe? But how many can write great songs? And how many can perform a whole concert on their own, without any other musicians? In my opinion, there's only one, and his name is Ed Sheeran.

B Apart from his red hair, Ed Sheeran doesn't look very special. Maybe that's also because he tends to wear normal clothes like jeans and t-shirts. But when he starts to sing, you can tell that he is in fact incredibly special. As for his personality, what I love about him is that he's modest, funny and friendly.

C One of Ed Sheeran's most important talents is that he can play and sing in lots of different styles. For example, he has some very romantic songs, but he also raps sometimes. Another of his great talents is being able to write lyrics. He usually writes about down-to-earth things that young people understand. He also makes brilliant videos. In one video, he shows that he's a talented dancer, too!

D Ed Sheeran is already a great singer and performer. But the most exciting thing is that he's still very young. Just watch how he gets better and better!

3 Match the paragraphs A–D to these topics.
- Brief conclusion _____
- The person's name/introductory information about them _____
- The person's main talent(s) _____
- The person's appearance and personality _____

4 Read the Writing bank and underline examples in the article in 2.

✎ WRITING BANK

Useful language in descriptions
- He/She seems …
- He/She looks …
- He/She is very/really/extremely + 'normal' adjectives (good, big …)
- He/She is completely/totally/absolutely/really + 'extreme' adjectives (fantastic, huge …)
- He/She is quite/rather + 'normal' adjectives
- He/She can be …
- He/She tends to …
- He/She has a … side.
- He/She shows that …
- What I like (most) about him/her is …

5 SPEAKING Use expressions in the Writing bank to talk about the people you chose in 1.

What I like most about Daniel Radcliffe is his sense of humour.

PRACTICE MAKES PERFECT

6a Choose one person and write your article. Follow the paragraph plan in 3 and use expressions from the Writing bank.

6b When you finish writing your article, check it carefully. Have you included the relevant information? Is it easy to understand the ideas and information? Are there any grammar or spelling mistakes?

WRITING BANK ➤ PAGE 153

Unit 4   53

Students are given help in planning and organising the information they need to use in their writing activities. Model texts give students realistic examples of different genres of written texts.

The Writing bank highlights and analyses the key language of the writing task and gives help in planning and organising the information they need to include. Students refer to it during the productive stage.

The Practice makes perfect activity gives students further practice and refers them to the Writing bank at the end of the book for more extensive support and guidance.

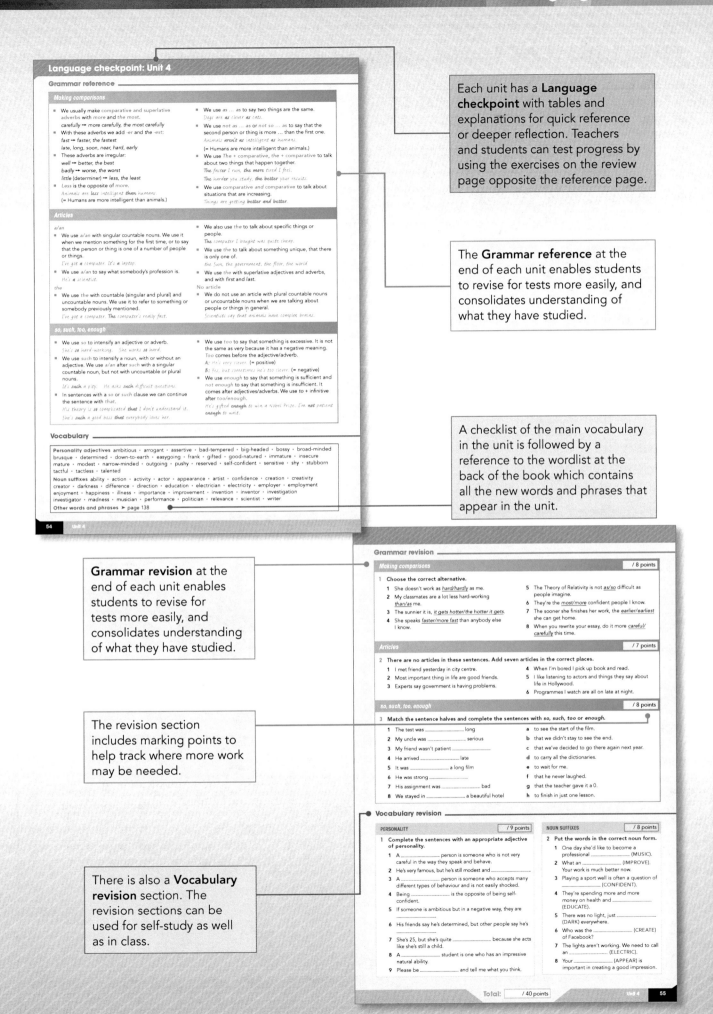

Each unit has a **Language checkpoint** with tables and explanations for quick reference or deeper reflection. Teachers and students can test progress by using the exercises on the review page opposite the reference page.

The **Grammar reference** at the end of each unit enables students to revise for tests more easily, and consolidates understanding of what they have studied.

A checklist of the main vocabulary in the unit is followed by a reference to the wordlist at the back of the book which contains all the new words and phrases that appear in the unit.

Grammar revision at the end of each unit enables students to revise for tests more easily, and consolidates understanding of what they have studied.

The revision section includes marking points to help track where more work may be needed.

There is also a **Vocabulary revision** section. The revision sections can be used for self-study as well as in class.

Every two units the **Gateway to exams** pages allow students to test their progress and at the same time develop their skills through targeted training tasks for exams.

Useful exam tips cover all of the skills – **Writing, Speaking, Listening, Reading** – and give guidance for **Use of English** tasks, providing invaluable reminders and hints for students to approach their exams fully prepared.

Students are referred to the **Exam success** pages at the back of the book for more detailed exploration of the skills they have been learning and the best way to approach a specific exam task.

The '*Can do*' progress check empowers students by encouraging them to measure their own progress against a checklist of tasks they are able to do successfully after every two units. It also acts as a useful summary of the language topics and skills covered so far.

Course components
Digital Student's Book

The *Gateway 2nd Edition* Digital Student's Book offers a content-rich interactive learning experience for your students, facilitating dynamic and engaging lessons.

Contains:

Interactive Student's Book activities

Complete class audio

Integrated video

Note-taking function

Automated marking

Gradebook

Students can work through interactive versions of the Student's Book exercises, developing their language skills through collaborative or individual learning.

Enhanced Student's Book pages are easy to navigate, and contain embedded audio and video, as well as interactive activities.

The Notes functionality enables students to put language into meaningful written practice, take presentation notes, or even add links for further research.

Completed exercises will be automatically marked and grades synced to your teacher Gradebook when online.

Course components
Presentation Kit

For teachers

Bring *Gateway 2nd Edition* to life in the classroom with your complete presentation and teaching tool.

Contains:

Interactive Student's Book activities

Complete class audio

Integrated video

Answer key feature

Note pad feature

Pages contain interactive versions of many of the Student's Book exercises with automated marking offering instant feedback.

Class audio and video can be played at the click of a button.

The built-in tools allow you to annotate and customise your presentations in advance.

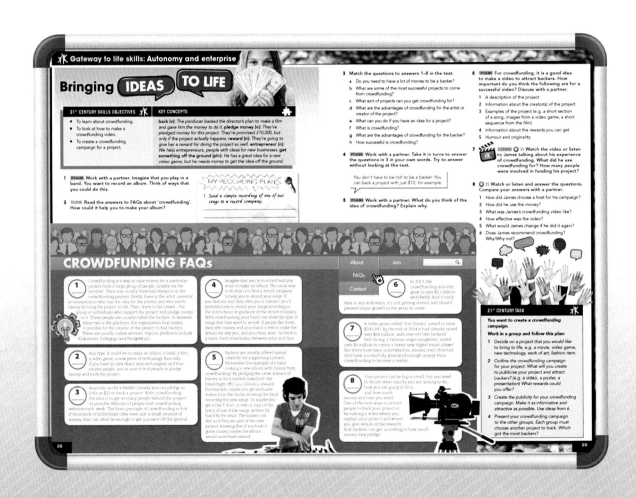

Course components
Videos

Gateway 2nd Edition offers a Flipped classroom grammar presentation video and a Life skills video in each unit. These integrate effectively into Student's Book lesson stages to enrich classes.

Use in class or for self-study

Flipped classroom videos

David Spencer, the author of *Gateway 2nd Edition*, delivers engaging grammar presentations that accompany one Grammar in context section for each unit. The presentations take a visual approach, introducing concepts and making new structures accessible through examples, timelines and diagrams.

Flipped classroom approach

By presenting the grammar outside the class, Flipped classroom allows more time for in-class practice. To find out more about the Flipped classroom approach, go to macmillangateway2.com

Flexible tool

The videos are a versatile and efficient resource for teachers which can also be used flexibly as a useful tool for mixed-ability groups or for revision.

Other ways of making comparisons

Unit 4

COMPARATIVE AND COMPARATIVE
- *situations that are increasing*
  e.g. bigger and bigger, more and more dangerous

The longer you practise, the better you get.

Gateway

Life skills videos

The Life skills videos form part of the Life skills lessons. They show British teens and subject experts demonstrating or discussing the topic in a way that has direct relevance to all students' lives. There are comprehension tasks on the Student's Book page and further exploitation exercises and activities for the video in the Resource Centre. The video formats are fun and appeal to teens, featuring:

- interviews
- debates
- school projects
- street interviews

After watching the video, students complete the task – a project or presentation in which they can apply what they have learnt during the lesson.

Bea

Team A: For citizen journalism

Team B: Against citizen journalism

The Workbook offers consolidation of the core language in the Student's Book, with extra listening, Study skills and a special cumulative Revision page in each unit.

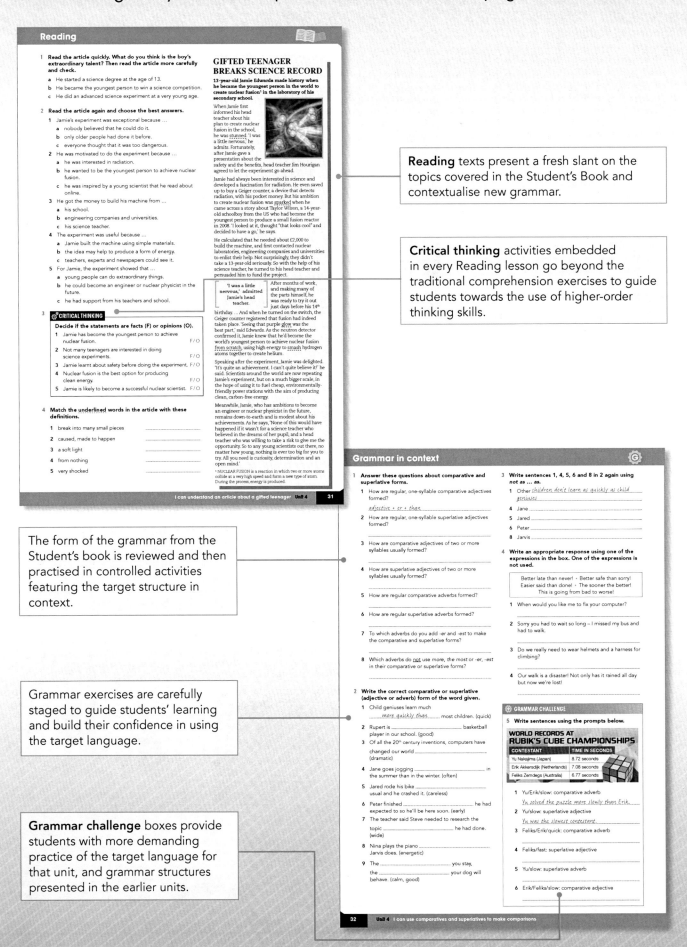

Reading texts present a fresh slant on the topics covered in the Student's Book and contextualise new grammar.

Critical thinking activities embedded in every Reading lesson go beyond the traditional comprehension exercises to guide students towards the use of higher-order thinking skills.

The form of the grammar from the Student's book is reviewed and then practised in controlled activities featuring the target structure in context.

Grammar exercises are carefully staged to guide students' learning and build their confidence in using the target language.

Grammar challenge boxes provide students with more demanding practice of the target language for that unit, and grammar structures presented in the earlier units.

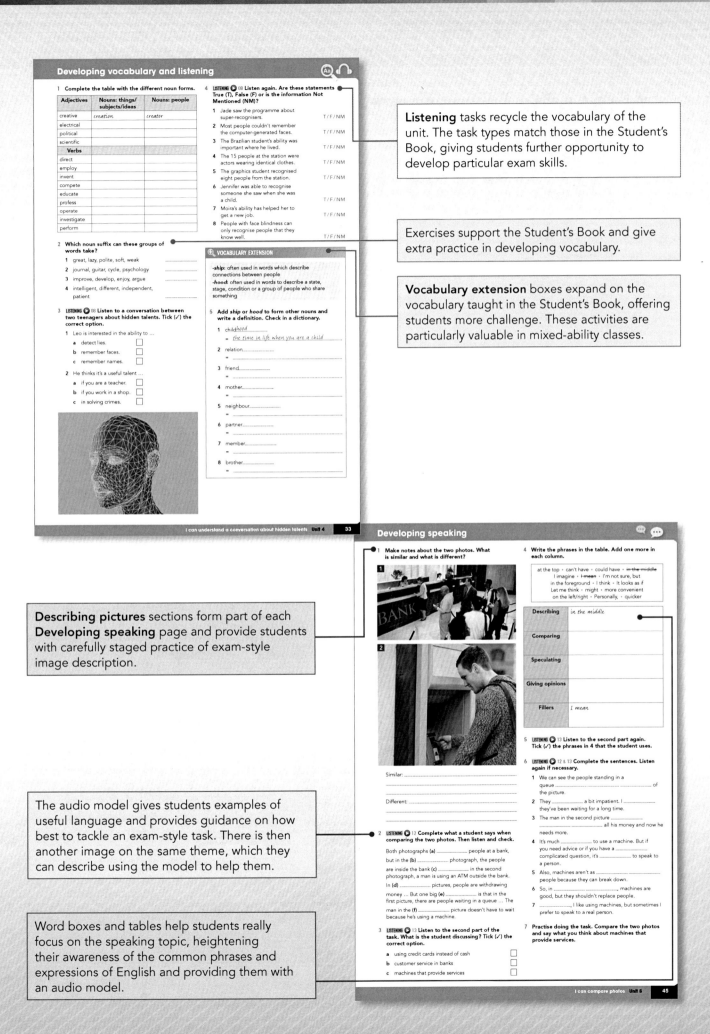

Developing vocabulary and listening

1 Complete the table with the different noun forms.

Adjectives	Nouns: things/subjects/ideas	Nouns: people
creative	creation	creator
electrical		
political		
scientific		
Verbs		
direct		
employ		
invent		
compete		
educate		
profess		
operate		
investigate		
perform		

2 Which noun suffix can these groups of words take?

1 great, lazy, polite, soft, weak ....
2 journal, guitar, cycle, psychology ....
3 improve, develop, enjoy, argue ....
4 intelligent, different, independent, patient ....

3 **LISTENING** ▶ 08 Listen to a conversation between two teenagers about hidden talents. Tick (✓) the correct option.

1 Leo is interested in the ability to …
   a detect lies. ☐
   b remember faces. ☐
   c remember names. ☐

2 He thinks it's a useful talent …
   a if you are a teacher. ☐
   b if you work in a shop. ☐
   c in solving crimes. ☐

4 **LISTENING** ▶ 08 Listen again. Are these statements True (T), False (F) or is the information Not Mentioned (NM)?

1 Jade saw the programme about super-recognisers. T / F / NM
2 Most people couldn't remember the computer-generated faces. T / F / NM
3 The Brazilian student's ability was important where he lived. T / F / NM
4 The 15 people at the station were actors wearing identical clothes. T / F / NM
5 The graphics student recognised eight people from the station. T / F / NM
6 Jennifer was able to recognise someone she saw when she was a child. T / F / NM
7 Moira's ability has helped her to get a new job. T / F / NM
8 People with face blindness can only recognise people that they know well. T / F / NM

VOCABULARY EXTENSION

-ship: often used in words which describe connections between people
-hood: often used in words to describe a state, stage, condition or a group of people who share something

5 Add *ship* or *hood* to form other nouns and write a definition. Check in a dictionary.

1 child*hood*
   = *the time in life when you are a child*
2 relation ....
   = ...
3 friend ....
   = ...
4 mother ....
   = ...
5 neighbour ....
   = ...
6 partner ....
   = ...
7 member ....
   = ...
8 brother ....
   = ...

I can understand a conversation about hidden talents **Unit 4** 33

Listening tasks recycle the vocabulary of the unit. The task types match those in the Student's Book, giving students further opportunity to develop particular exam skills.

Exercises support the Student's Book and give extra practice in developing vocabulary.

Vocabulary extension boxes expand on the vocabulary taught in the Student's Book, offering students more challenge. These activities are particularly valuable in mixed-ability classes.

Developing speaking

1 Make notes about the two photos. What is similar and what is different?

1
BANK

2

Similar: ....
....

Different: ....
....

2 **LISTENING** ▶ 12 Complete what a student says when comparing the two photos. Then listen and check.

Both photographs (a) .... people at a bank, but in the (b) .... photograph, the people are inside the bank (c) .... in the second photograph, a man is using an ATM outside the bank. In (d) .... pictures, people are withdrawing money … But one big (e) .... is that in the first picture, there are people waiting in a queue … The man in the (f) .... picture doesn't have to wait because he's using a machine.

3 **LISTENING** ▶ 13 Listen to the second part of the task. What is the student discussing? Tick (✓) the correct option.

a using credit cards instead of cash ☐
b customer service in banks ☐
c machines that provide services ☐

4 Write the phrases in the table. Add one more in each column.

| at the top • can't have • could have • in the middle |
| I imagine • I mean • I'm not sure, but |
| in the foreground • I think • It looks as if |
| Let me think • might • more convenient |
| on the left/right • Personally, • quicker |

Describing	in the middle
Comparing	
Speculating	
Giving opinions	
Fillers	I mean

5 **LISTENING** ▶ 13 Listen to the second part again. Tick (✓) the phrases in 4 that the student uses.

6 **LISTENING** ▶ 12 & 13 Complete the sentences. Listen again if necessary.

1 We can see the people standing in a queue .... of the picture.
2 They .... a bit impatient. I .... they've been waiting for a long time.
3 The man in the second picture .... all his money and now he needs more.
4 It's much .... to use a machine. But if you need advice or if you have a .... complicated question, it's .... to speak to a person.
5 Also, machines aren't as .... people because they can break down.
6 So, ... machines are good, but they shouldn't replace people.
7 ...., I like using machines, but sometimes I prefer to speak to a real person.

7 Practise doing the task. Compare the two photos and say what you think about machines that provide services.

I can compare photos **Unit 5** 45

Describing pictures sections form part of each **Developing speaking** page and provide students with carefully staged practice of exam-style image description.

The audio model gives students examples of useful language and provides guidance on how best to tackle an exam-style task. There is then another image on the same theme, which they can describe using the model to help them.

Word boxes and tables help students really focus on the speaking topic, heightening their awareness of the common phrases and expressions of English and providing them with an audio model.

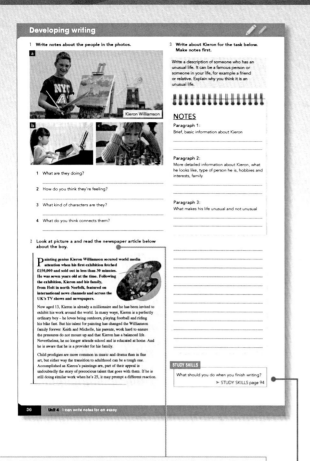

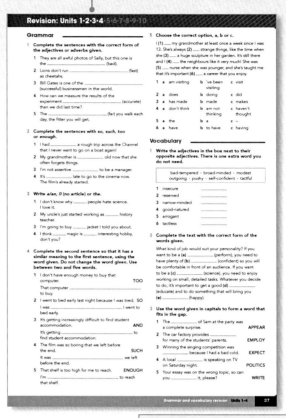

Cumulative revision pages provide essential recycling of language from not only the preceding unit but also earlier units in the book.

Further analysis and highlighting of key language for the same type of writing task as is covered in the Student's Book.

Gateway to exams pages appear every two units, offering Reading, Listening, Use of English and Writing tasks. The topics and tasks reflect what has been covered in the preceding two units, providing students with the opportunity to further develop their exam skills, while recycling key grammar and vocabulary.

Study skills boxes help students to improve their studying habits. Two Study skills boxes appear in every unit, offering guidance on reading, listening, grammar, writing, speaking and vocabulary, with further help at the back of the book.

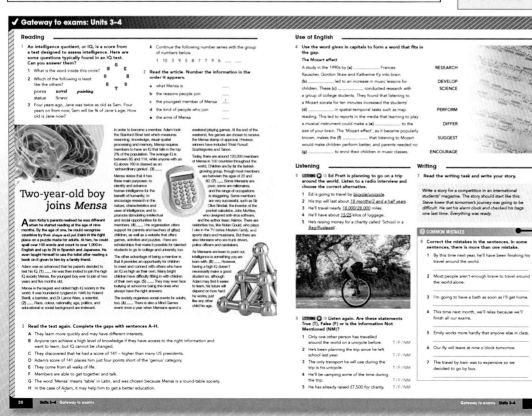

Common mistakes boxes provide error correction practice, with the focus on the language of the preceding two units. They highlight mistakes often made by students at this level, giving them the opportunity to recognise and reflect on any such errors they may be making in their own work.

Course components
Online Workbook

All the printed Workbook content and more in a fully-interactive format for flexible self-study.

Contains:

Interactive
Workbook activities

Complete
Workbook audio

Integrated
video

Automated marking
for instant feedback

Gradebook

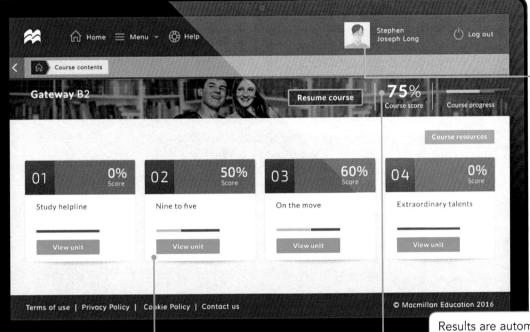

Multiple classes and levels can be managed in a single location, and the content-locking feature gives you control over how you set tasks for your students.

Results are automatically collated in the Gradebook and displayed in an easy-to-read, easy-to-compare way. Learner progress can be monitored at a glance, highlighting areas where students may require additional support or assistance.

Multiple attempts keep students motivated, allowing them to consolidate what they have learned in class in an engaging way. Students can also access the Flipped classroom videos and activities on the Online Workbook, making this an excellent tool for developing independent learning.

The messaging and notification features allow you to correspond with your students, send homework reminders and notify your classes when results are available.

Detailed feedback on activity scores and progress, along with customisable elements such as avatars, all help to create a highly-personalised self-study environment.

Course components
Teacher's and Student's Resource Centres

For teachers and students

The Online Resource Centres contain a wealth of downloadable worksheets, multimedia assets and additional resources to support your *Gateway 2nd Edition* core course content.

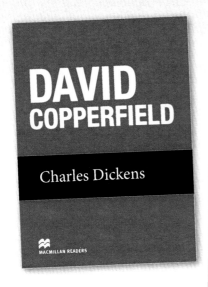

DAVID COPPERFIELD

Charles Dickens

MACMILLAN READERS

Student's Resource Centre

The Student's Resource Centre provides complementary materials to consolidate learning and encourage independent study, including:

- Teen-focused culture worksheets to inspire a broader cultural perspective

- A graded Macmillan Reader, with extra activities and extended reading support

- Study skills materials to encourage students to take control of their learning

- Life skills video worksheets and Flipped classroom video worksheets provide additional support for students to use with the videos.

Teacher's Resource Centre

The Teacher's Resource Centre is your go-to place for resources to deliver dynamic lessons, for homework assignments and to support you in the classroom. The flexible content includes:

- Audio and video files and scripts

- Complete answer keys

- Teacher tips and videos

- Extra grammar worksheets and communication activities

- Everyday English worksheets

- Optional CLIL and literature lessons

- Teacher notes and guides to accompany all material

Sounds: The Pronunication App

This award-winning app helps students practise and play with pronunciation wherever they are. Carefully selected wordlists from the *Gateway 2nd Edition* course are now available to download within the app.

Course components
Testing and assessment materials

For teachers

Extensive resources for assessing your students' progress and preparing them for international and school-leaving examinations.

Test Generator

The Test Generator allows you to create customised tests from an extensive database of exercises.

- Aligned closely to CEFR learning outcomes
- Includes a range of reading, writing, speaking and listening tasks typical of international and school-leaving exams
- Comes with the option to save tests in progress and to preview before printing
- Allows for maximum flexibility in choosing the test content
- Teacher-version of tests complete with answer keys

Printable tests

A comprehensive range of Printable tests are available on the Teacher's Resource Centre in both PDF and editable Word format. Tests matched to the course level can be selected and then customised to meet the specific needs of your school and classes.

- One diagnostic test per level
- Ten Unit tests, three Review tests and one End-of-year test for tracking progress
- Aligned closely to CEFR learning outcomes and international and school-leaving exams
- Complete answer keys, audio and audioscripts for all tests
- Two levels of difficulty for each test

Here are some great teaching tips to help you throughout the year. These tips give you strategies for classroom management, planning and student training that you can use again and again to improve your students' results and get the best out of your teaching.

GAMES IN THE CLASSROOM

Vocabulary games such as *Snowman* are useful for practising and reviewing language. They engage the students, who should remember more as a result. When using games, your instructions need to be clear and precise. As with all instructions, you need to do a comprehension check. For example, after explaining what to do, ask the students to explain the game back to you. Another option is to give a demonstration of the game by playing it yourself with a few of the students while the others watch.

When planning games you need to consider what your aims and objectives are. Games are particularly useful for reviewing work from the previous lesson, checking what students know before teaching a new language item, practising a new language item you have just presented, warming up at the beginning of the lesson or filling in at the end of a lesson.

ORGANISING PAIRWORK ACTIVITIES

Pairwork means more speaking time for students. If 30 students speak in turn in a 60-minute class, students speak an average of two minutes per class. Using pairwork activities, they could speak for 30 minutes. When students are working in pairs, it's a good time to talk to or listen to one student at a time without everyone noticing.

Certain speaking skills are necessary when working with another person so we should explicitly teach phrases which help students interrupt each other (*Yes, I agree, but… / May I say something?* etc.) clarify (*Did you say … ?* etc) and confirm (*So you think …*, question tags etc.).

You could play some quiet music in the background when students are planning a speaking activity to help students feel more relaxed about speaking out in English.

CHECKING ANSWERS

One of the potential difficulties in teaching large classes is getting students to participate. Consider:

- teaching from different points in the classroom to give the students the feeling of being in the middle of the 'action' rather than an observer. Moving around the class makes the room feel smaller and encourages student involvement.
- doing regular feedback and using some of the next class or handouts to clarify points students haven't understood.
- setting up routines (weekly homework assignments of 30 minutes).
- relating what students have learned to the exam (a common goal).
- giving regular short tests and dictations.
- writing an outline on the board about what will be taught in class.
- giving fast finishers something to do or directing them to the workbook.

WRITING TASKS

Although the writing process may vary depending on the task, the basic steps it includes are the same.

- Before beginning to write, students need to consider the purpose of the text and who they are writing to, which will affect the tone (formal or informal).
- The first phase is when students brainstorm ideas (they can make lists, mind maps, or think of the 'six wise men' – Why? What? Where? When? How? Who?). It is important to spend time on this stage as it makes the next steps easier. They then select and order their ideas.
- If students are writing a longer text, they may now need to carry out some research into their chosen topic.
- Next, students write a first draft as quickly as they can, including all the main points from the brainstorming phase.
- The next stage is the revision process when students should take a global look at their text and decide if the text flows in a clear, well-organised way.
- The final stage is the editing process. Students should look closely at spelling, grammar, punctuation and word choice.

✅ REVISING

Students should now have a variety of strategies they can use to revise for exams. It is very useful to share and discuss strategies together in class. Further useful revision tips include:

- Practise writing against the clock using past exam papers.
- Test your knowledge at the end of a study session – you must be able to produce something without notes.
- Make good quality notes and refine them further onto small pieces of card (condense them into lists, diagrams and mind maps, and use colour-coding). Visual memory is strongest in 3D, so spend some time constructing your own mental images of concepts.
- Have a checklist of 10–15 key points for every topic and define key trigger words. Number your points (try to remember how many points there are to jog your memory).
- Prioritise subjects you find most difficult or want to do best in. Identify and improve your performance in non-preferred exam tasks.
- Take notes from your revision material three times.

✅ ORGANISING YOUR TIME IN EXAMS

Make sure students understand the format of each section of the writing exam they are going to take. By doing model or practice tests, students will become familiar with the exam format (how much time they have for each section, how much each section is worth, how many words they have to write, where they should write their text, etc.) and this will help them use their time effectively during the exam.

Each section is worth a certain number of points. Remind students not to spend too much time on one particular section. It is better to answer all the questions than to do an excellent job on some and not have enough time to do the others. If you run out of time, write notes.

Students will have to decide if they have enough time to write a rough draft, and should try to leave some time at the end to check their work. Students should have a mental checklist when they are checking their work.

Checking answers

Using different ways to check answers makes the feedback stage more fun and changes the pace of the lesson. Some ideas include:

- Give the students an answer key or put the answer key on the wall or the board. Students can work in pairs: one student runs to the wall to check the answer and goes back to tell their partner.
- Give half the answers to one student in a pair and half the answers to the other student. They share their information like an information gap activity.
- One student has the answer key and plays the teacher.
- Get students to write their answers on the board.
- Get one student to read out his/her answers - the rest of the class see if they have the same.
- Students nominate each other to say the answer.
- Do it as a competition and award points for correct answers.

🔍 MAXIMISING YOUR MEMORY

It is likely that students will remember words that they have analysed and evaluated in some way. If they have learnt the word in context and they have fully understood the word rather than just learning it based upon a definition, it is more likely to be remembered long-term.

Discuss with students how they learn words best – do they need to hear them, see them written down or write them down themselves? Some students memorise vocabulary by associating new words with ideas or anecdotes. Good learners create mnemonic devices such as short phrases, tunes or poems. In order to internalise vocabulary students should also review vocabulary regularly.

To really improve vocabulary, students need to read. They should only look up words which are important for the story, find their meaning in a good dictionary and make a note in their vocabulary notebook.

✅ BEING SUCCESSFUL IN EXAMS

Being successful in exams means knowing about the format of the exam: *What type of tasks are there? How long do students have for each section? How are the different sections scored?* Encourage students to analyse different exam tasks and reflect on the subskills they need (i.e. skimming and scanning, listening for detailed understanding of numbers and letters, reading quickly for general understanding) and the techniques they need to learn (picking out the important words, ignoring words that aren't important for the question etc.). If students focus on the language, exam techniques and skills they need for the different tasks in their English exam, it will impact on their exam marks.

💬 PERSONALISATION

Students retain language better if it is relevant and meaningful to them. The *What about you?* speaking feature encourages students to apply language to their own situation, but you can also extend other exercises to give students the chance to speak about their own experiences, and people and place they know etc. The Critical thinking questions in the Student's Book give students the chance to think independently and evaluate situations according to their own beliefs and opinions. Therefore it's important to give students time with these activities to think and prepare what they are going to say on their own before discussing in a group. This is particularly important for less-confident students who may find themselves swayed by stronger members of the group.

Dave's top teaching tips

📖 BOOK CLUB

Encouraging teenagers to read outside the classroom can be challenging, but any extra reading students can do in English in their spare time will broaden their vocabulary and increase their fluency of expression. Finding relevant and engaging texts is the first step: look for abridged and adapted versions of texts they may know or that will appeal to their age-group, or start with short stories and articles. Alternatively, nominate a different student each time to recommend something that they think will interest the rest of the group. Give students a fortnight to read a section or all of the text and then hold a 'book club' as part of the lesson, where students discuss their thoughts and opinions on the book or text. Alternatively, you could ask students to find their own books as an optional activity outside class and review them as part of a class blog.

✏️ USING MODEL TEXTS IN CLASS

A model is a text that provides a good example of how texts of a particular kind can be written. Students will notice features such as layout, structure and fixed phrases that they can make use of in their own written text. Model texts can also develop useful exam techniques such as planning and self-correction.

Always read the model text provided and go through the writing tasks in detail so that students are fully aware of why they are writing and who they are writing to.

🏃 REFLECTION

After each Gateway to exams assessment (every other unit), give students time to think how they did and what they need to improve. Encourage students to keep records of specific areas that need work (e.g. types of error) and to refer back to it after each assessment to see whether they are improving. You could do this in the form of a 'SWOT' matrix – strengths (e.g. listening), weaknesses (e.g. collaborative tasks), opportunities (e.g. reading the news in English) and threats (e.g. not finding time to review language after the lesson). After students have had time to analyse their marks and areas for improvement you could spend a lesson or part of a lesson helping students with their specific areas of weakness. One approach could be to put students in groups based on the skill they feel needs improving most and give them 10 minutes to review the Exam success tips for this skill in the Student's Book before asking them to discuss other strategies they could apply to the specific question. Circulate while they do this and help with ideas. If students have problems with accuracy, allow them to correct their mistakes and ask them to reuse the particular word or structure in another context so they have further practice.

Finally, if you have time to do so, you could have students attempt the activity, assessment or part of the assessment again the following lesson or after a week or so and ask them to compare how they did. It's worth reminding students that at this higher level, progress may be slower than previous levels, so not to be disheartened.

Teacher support
Teacher development tips index

There are a number of methodological and practical tips which are strategically placed within the Teacher's notes in the *Gateway 2nd Edition* Teacher's Book to be of most use to the teacher not just during planning, setting up and evaluating activities, but also helping 'on the spot' in certain language or pronunciation areas.

CLASSROOM TIPS AND PLANNING

Pairwork	p30	How to use model texts in class	p41	Promoting class debate	p90
Pyramid discussion	p33	Organising the board	p45	Video clips and questions	p93
Homework	p34	Dictogloss	p52	Checking answers	p94
Communicative activities	p35	Personalised presentations	p53	Using a video camera	p108
Using video in the classroom	p36	Delayed correction	p66	Drilling	p131
Listening tasks	p37	Recording in class	p67	*Find someone who ...*	p135
The flipped classroom	p38	Drilling	p68	Speaking assessment	p166
Error correction	p38	Dubbing a video	p79		

LANGUAGE

State and action verbs	p32	Adjectives and adverbs	p75	Reporting verbs	p120
Present continuous for annoying habits	p32	*less/the least*	p76	Compound adjectives	p121
		Noun suffixes	p77	The passive	p134
do and *make*	p34	*a/an*	p80	*by* + agent	p134
Expressing preferences	p39	Possessive *'s* in shop names	p88	Preposition + gerund	p135
Past simple and past continuous	p48	Modal verbs of speculation and deduction	p95	The passive with *say, know*, etc.	p138
Past simple spelling rules	p49			Giving instructions	p147
Did you use to ...?	p49	Modal verbs of speculation and deduction – past	p95	Relative clauses	p148
Phrasal verbs	p50			Gerunds/Infinitives	p152
Future forms	p63	Conditionals	p105	Future in the past	p160
Prefixes	p64	*play, do, go*	p108	Mixed conditionals	p160
Future tenses	p68	Third conditional	p109	Collocations	p161
Comparatives and superlatives	p75	*I wish/If only*	p110	Question tags	p164

STUDENT TRAINING

Matching activities	p31	Word formation	p77	Listening for the first and second time	p124
Critical thinking	p31, 47, 62	Presentations	p82		
Developing conversation skills	p39	Checking your writing	p83	Discussing and negotiating	p126
CEFR portfolio: speaking	p40	Skimming	p89	Descriptive adjectives	p127
Transactional tasks	p42	Learning phrasal verbs	p91	Writing reviews	p128
Recording vocabulary	p46	Inference in listening	p94	Multiple-choice reading activities	p133
Inference in reading activities	p47	Talking about photos	p97	Listening – True/False/Not Mentioned	p137
Inference in listening	p52	Practising for an oral exam	p97		
Collaborative tasks in oral exams	p55	Writing a letter/email of complaint	p98	Brainstorming	p141
Paragraph organisation	p56	Prediction	p103	Editing	p141
'Can Do' Progress check	p59	Checking information	p104	Writing a report	p155
Missing sentences activities	p62	Sentence transformation	p106	True/False reading activities	p159
Spelling of words with prefixes	p64	Two-part discussion tasks	p111	Multiple-choice listening activities	p163
Before you listen	p67	A for-and-against essay	p112	Giving a presentation	p166
Story writing	p70	Deducing the meaning of new words	p119	Improving writing	p167
Vocabulary records	p73				

PRONUNCIATION

Emphatic stress	p32	*than/as*	p76	Stress in compound nouns	p122
The *-ed* ending	p49	*the/a*	p80	Word stress – the passive voice	p134
used to and *would*	p49	Silent letters	p89	Word stress – nouns and verbs	p146
had/'d	p54	Modal verbs	p90	Intonation	p165
will	p63	*have*	p95		
Future tenses	p68	Word stress	p103		

Teacher support
The CEFR and *Gateway 2nd Edition*

The Common European Framework of Reference (CEFR) is a widely used standard created by the Council of Europe. *Gateway 2nd Edition* is carefully mapped to the CEFR helping teachers identify students' actual progress and helping them to set their learning priorities.

Gateway 2nd Edition offers a wide range of teaching materials in various components which give teachers the opportunity to develop all aspects of their students' language ability. The CEFR can be used to track their progress.

On pages 25–27 are the B1 and the B2 descriptors (description of competences) covered in the B2 level of *Gateway 2nd Edition*. B1 and B2 descriptors are also available in the Gateway B1+ Teacher's Book.

A basic level of confidence with the B2 descriptors is expected as students start using *Gateway 2nd Edition* B2 and, by the end of the course, students should be competent with the B2 level.

In the Teacher's Resource Centre you will also find a list of unit-by-unit CEFR descriptors with suggested targets which can be used for self-assessment. Students can use these at any point to get a detailed picture of their own individual progress.

WHAT IS A EUROPEAN LANGUAGE PORTFOLIO (ELP)?

The European Language Portfolio (ELP) was developed by the Language Policy Unit of the Council of Europe

- to support the development of learner autonomy, plurilingualism and intercultural awareness and competence;
- to allow users to record their language learning achievements and their experience of learning and using languages.

If you are using portfolios as a way of evaluating your students' coursework over the year, you will find a wide variety of opportunities within each *Gateway 2nd Edition* unit to provide material for the dossier.

A portfolio is a means to document a person's achievements. Artists, architects or designers collect samples of their work in portfolios and students are encouraged to do the same. Most of the time, these samples will be texts created by the students, but they could also include photos of classroom scenes, wall displays, audio recordings and videos. All these documents provide evidence of a student's performance, e.g. during a discussion, an oral presentation or a role-play.

Within each unit, there are several opportunities for students to practise speaking and record their conversations for the dossier in their portfolio. Students could record their conversations, date them and include them in their portfolio. They then assess their performance in each speaking activity and give themselves a mark according to the following self-assessment criteria:

CONTENT (1–5)

Did I say what I wanted to say? Was I interesting? Did I speak in English for a long time? Did I hesitate a lot?

VOCABULARY AND GRAMMAR (1–5)

Did I use different words? Did I use words I've learned recently? Were my sentences well constructed? Did I make a lot of errors?

COOPERATION (1–5)

Did I listen to my partner? Did we help each other if we had problems? Did we both speak for approximately the same length of time?

IN ENGLISH! (1–5)

When I didn't know how to say something, did I use English to solve my problem? Did we use English to talk about whose turn it was to speak?

The portfolio consists of three parts: the **Language Passport** with information about a student's proficiency in one or more languages, i.e. qualifications; the **Language Biography** where students reflect on their learning process and progress and say what they can do in their foreign language(s); and the **Dossier**, which is a collection of materials and data put together by students to document and illustrate their learning experiences.

Although it may be a demanding task to set up in the beginning, the overall aim is for students to be involved in planning, collecting and evaluating their own work, thereby taking responsibility for their own learning. This in turn may lead to increased participation and autonomy on the part of the learner.

		1	2	3	4	5	6	7	8	9	10
Listening		page number									
B1	I can generally follow the main points of extended discussion around me, provided speech is clearly articulated in standard dialect.	12	26								
B1	I can understand the main points of radio news bulletins and simpler recorded material on topics of personal interest delivered relatively slowly and clearly.	11 12	18 31	32 38 40	44	64					
B2	I can understand in detail what is said to me in standard spoken language even in a noisy environment.			32		64	75 76				128
B2	I can follow a lecture or talk within my own field, provided the subject matter is familiar and the presentation straightforward and clearly structured.				49 52						130
B2	I can understand most radio documentaries delivered in standard language and can identify the speaker's mood, tone etc. by using contextual clues.	11		37			82			115	135
B2	I can understand TV documentaries, live interviews, talk shows, plays and the majority of films in standard dialect.	11	23	37		63			101	115	127 128
B2	I can understand the main ideas of complex speech on both concrete and abstract topics delivered in a standard dialect, including technical discussions in my field of specialisation.	12	26	38	50	66	70 76 78	90 92	96 101 109	110 116 118	122 127
B2	I can use a variety of strategies to achieve comprehension, including listening for main points; checking comprehension.	12	24	38	50	64	78	90	102	116	128
Reading		page number									
B1	I can guess the meaning of single unknown words from the context thus deducing the meaning of expressions if the topic is familiar.	6									
B1	I can skim short texts (for example news summaries) and find relevant facts and information (for example who has done what and where).	7	19								
B2	I can guess the meaning of unknown words from the context thus deducing the meaning of expressions if the topic is familiar.		19	33	45	59	71	85	97	111	123
B2	I can rapidly grasp the content and the significance of news, articles and reports on topics connected with my interests or my job, and decide if a closer reading is worthwhile.		19 22	33 36	45 48	59 62	71 74	85 88	97 100	111 114 119	122
B2	I can read and understand articles and reports on current problems in which the writers express specific attitudes and points of view.	7	19 22	36	53		71 74 79	85 88	97 105	119	123
B2	I can understand in detail texts within my field of interest or the area of my academic or professional speciality.	10	30	33	48 53		74 79		100 108		126
B2	I can understand specialised articles outside my own field if I can occasionally check with a dictionary.			36	48	59 62	74		100	114	126
B2	I can read reviews dealing with the content and criticism of cultural topics (films, theatre, books, concerts) and summarise the main points.							85 88 93			131
B2	I can read letters on topics within my areas of academic or professional speciality or interest and grasp the most important points.	15				67					
B2	I can understand in a narrative or play the motives for the characters' actions and their consequences for the development of the plot.			41							

The CEFR and *Gateway 2nd Edition*

Speaking: Spoken Interaction

Level	Can-do	1	2	3	4	5	6	7	8	9	10
		page number									
B1	I can start, maintain and close simple face-to-face conversation on topics that are familiar or of personal interest.	6 14	18								
B1	I can give or seek personal views and opinions in an informal discussion with friends.	12 13	24		44 53						
B1	I can agree and disagree politely.	13									
B2	I can initiate, maintain and end discourse naturally with effective turn-taking.	6			52		78			117 118	130
B2	I can exchange considerable quantities of detailed factual information on matters within my fields of interest.		26		49 52			89			127
B2	I can convey degrees of emotion and highlight the personal significance of events and experiences.	12		32					94	116	128
B2	I can engage in extended conversation in a clearly participatory fashion on most general topics.	10 12			49 53 56	59 63	75 76 77 78	85	102	113	122 124 130 131
B2	I can account for and sustain my opinions in discussion by providing relevant explanations, arguments and comments.	10	26 31	40	44 50		79		108 109	116	122 125 127
B2	I can help a discussion along on familiar ground confirming comprehension, inviting others in, etc.			39 40	44		74 76			118	
B2	I can carry out a prepared interview, checking and confirming information, following up interesting replies.	6 7 9	19	32 39		58 61		84	99	117	129

Speaking: Spoken Production

Level	Can-do	1	2	3	4	5	6	7	8	9	10
		page number									
B2	I can give clear, detailed descriptions on a wide range of subjects related to my fields of interest.	14	18 19		52 56 57		71 78 82		104		122
B2	I can understand and summarise orally short extracts from news items, interviews or documentaries containing opinions, argument and discussion.			38			71	85 88	97		126 129
B2	I can construct a chain of reasoned argument, linking my ideas logically.	10	23	37 41	45 52 56 57	59 63 66	82	89	97		130
B2	I can explain a viewpoint on a topical issue giving the advantages and disadvantages of various options.	7 10 14	19 23		52	63 64	71	85		115	127 130
B2	I can speculate about causes, consequences, hypothetical situations.	7 10	23	33 38 39			75		89		123

Speaking: Strategies

Level	Can-do	1	2	3	4	5	6	7	8	9	10
		page number									
B2	I can use standard phrases like 'That's a difficult question to answer' to gain time and keep the turn while formulating what to say.				52 56	66	78	92	109	118	130
B2	I can generally correct slips and errors if I become aware of them or if they have led to misunderstandings.	12 13	20		51	65	83	87 90 91		113 117	

Vocabulary: Language Quality

	page number	1	2	3	4	5	6	7	8	9	10
B1	I can convey simple information of immediate relevance, getting across which point I feel is most important.	9			55						
B1	I have a sufficient vocabulary to express myself with some circumlocutions on most topics pertinent to my everyday life such as family, hobbies and interests, work, travel, and current events.	6	21								
B1	I can express myself reasonably accurately in familiar, predictable situations.	6			55						
B2	I can produce stretches of language with a fairly even tempo; although I can be hesitant as I search for expressions, there are few noticeably long pauses.				55					110	122
B2	I can pass on detailed information reliably.				49 54 55	58			106		
B2	I have sufficient vocabulary to express myself on matters connected to my field and on most general topics.	9 11 16 17	18 28 29	32 35 42 43	44 47 48 49 54 55 56 57	58 61 68 69	70 73 80 81	84 87 94 95	96 99 106 107 109	110 113 120 121	122 125 132 133
B2	I can communicate with reasonable accuracy and can correct mistakes if they have led to misunderstandings.	8 9	21	43	47 54 55	60 61 68 69	72 73 80 81	86 87 94 95	99 106 107	113 120 121	125 132 133

Writing

	page number	1	2	3	4	5	6	7	8	9	10
B1	I can write personal letters to friends or acquaintances asking for or giving them news and narrating events.	15	31								
B1	In a letter I can express feelings such as grief, happiness, interest, regret and sympathy.		31								
B2	I can write clear and detailed texts (compositions, reports or texts of presentations) on various topics related to my field of interest.		27		53		79	93	105	119	131 135
B2	I can write summaries of articles on topics of general interest.				53		83				
B2	I can discuss a topic in a composition or 'letter to the editor', giving reasons for or against a specific point of view.					67			105		131
B2	I can develop an argument systematically in a composition or report, emphasising decisive points and including supporting details.		27		57		79 83	93	109	119	131 135
B2	I can write about events and real or fictional experiences in a detailed and easily readable way.			41	57	67		89	109		
B2	I can write a short review of a film or a book.							93			
B2	I can express in a personal letter different feelings and attitudes and can report the news of the day making clear what – in my opinion – are the important aspects of an event.	15									

KEY LEARNING OUTCOMES

CEF

Students will be able to:

- talk about present situations, routines and actions using the present simple and present continuous
- talk about experiences and recent actions using the present perfect simple and present perfect continuous

- understand written and spoken texts about studying and university
- talk about good time management and revision tips
- express preferences
- reply to informal emails and include relevant information

UNIT OVERVIEW

Vocabulary
Studying at university
Life at university

Reading
Unusual degrees
CRITICAL THINKING Discussing specialised subjects

Grammar in context
Present simple, present continuous and present habits
Present perfect simple and present perfect continuous
PRONUNCIATION Word stress

Developing vocabulary
do and make

Life skills
Organisation: Managing study time

Listening
Revising for exams

Grammar in context
Gerunds and infinitives – 1

Developing speaking
Giving personal information – preferences

Developing writing
An informal email replying to a request for information

Exam success
Reading: Matching activities
Writing: Transactional tasks

DIGITAL OVERVIEW

Presentation Kit

▶ **Flipped classroom video Unit 1:** Gerunds and infinitives – 1
▶ **Life skills video Unit 1:** Managing study time
▶ **Interactive versions of Student's Book activities**
▶ **Integrated audio and answer key for all activities**
▶ **Workbook pages with answer key**

Teacher's Resource Centre

▶ **Flipped classroom video Unit 1:** Gerunds and infinitives – 1
▶ **Life skills video Unit 1:** Managing study time
▶ **Grammar communication activity Unit 1:** True or false?
▶ **Worksheets for this unit, including:**
  – Grammar Practice worksheet Unit 1
  – Flipped classroom video worksheet Unit 1: Gerunds and infinitives – 1
  – Literature worksheet Units 1 and 2
  – Culture worksheet Unit 1
  – Life skills video worksheet Unit 1
  – Everyday English worksheet Unit 1

Student's App
Gateway 2nd Edition wordlist for the award-winning Sounds App (available for download)

✓ TESTING AND ASSESSMENT

Resources for exam preparation and measuring student progress

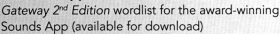

▶ Test Generator Unit 1
▶ Printable test Unit 1
▶ Gateway to exams Units 1 and 2 (end of Unit 2)

Vocabulary p6

Talking about studying and life at university

⟫⟫ FAST TRACK

FAST TRACK

You could ask students to do exercises 1a and 1b at home so that less confident students are prepared for the speaking activity in exercise 1c. They can look up any words they are not sure about in their dictionaries or the Macmillan Online Dictionary and practise saying the names of the subjects.

WARMER

Ask students to look at the unit title *Study helpline* and the photo strip. Elicit a definition of *helpline* (a telephone line, email or Internet forum where people can access information and support). Ask students to provide examples of helplines they know. Elicit what they think the unit is going to be about (information about going to university and guidelines on studying).

Studying at university

1a SPEAKING Divide the class into pairs to look at the subjects in the box and say how many they know. Encourage students to look up any words they are not sure about in their dictionaries, or they can look up the words in the Macmillan Online Dictionary.

✚ EXTRA ACTIVITY

In pairs, students group the words by number of syllables. Drill the pronunciation of each word in open class. Pay attention to the /k/ sound in *architecture,* the short vowel sound /ɪ/ in *business,* and the two different ways of pronouncing *veterinary* /ˈvet(ə)nri/ or /ˈvet(ə)rənəri/.

Answers

1 syllable	O law
2 syllables	Oo business, studies, nursing
3 syllables	Ooo dentistry, medicine, politics, veterinary
4 syllables	Oooo architecture ooOo engineering oOoo geology, philosophy, psychology
5 syllables	Ooooo veterinary ooOoo sociology

1b In pairs, students think of other university subjects. Encourage students to race against each other by setting a three-minute time limit. Ask the pair with the longest list to write their answers on the board. Remind students that we write language subjects with a capital letter.

Example answers

anthropology, archaeology, art, science (biology, chemistry, physics), economics, languages (English, French, Spanish, German, etc.), geography, history

1c In pairs, students discuss which subjects in exercises 1a and 1b interest them and say why. Elicit feedback in open class.

2 SPEAKING In pairs, students read the email paying special attention to the words in red. Ask them to decide if each word is a noun or a verb and what they think the meaning is. Ask different students around the class to say if each word is a noun or a verb.

Answers

(see Answers in exercise 3 below)

3 Encourage students to check the meaning of any words in exercise 2 they are not sure about. Remind students that many English words have more than one meaning and can have more than one form so they should find the correct meaning for their context. Elicit definitions of the words in open class.

Answers

undergraduate (noun) /ˌʌndə(r)ˈgrædʒuət/ – a student who is studying for a first degree at a college or university. (A student who already has a first degree is a graduate.)

graduate (verb) /ˈgrædʒueɪt/ – to complete your studies at a university or college, usually by getting a degree

degree (noun) /dɪˈgriː/ – a course of study at a university, or the qualification that you get after completing the course

master's (noun) /ˈmɑːstə(r)z/ – a university degree that students get if they study for one or two years after their first degree

course (noun) /kɔː(r)s/ – a series of lessons or lectures in an academic subject or a practical skill

lecture (noun) /ˈlektʃə(r)/ – a talk to a group of people about a particular subject, especially at a college or university

tutorial (noun) /tjuːˈtɔːriəl/ – a lesson in which a student or a small group of students discusses a subject with a tutor, especially at university or college

term (noun) /tɜː(r)m/ – one of the periods of time into which the year is divided for students. In the UK, there are usually three terms: the autumn term, the spring term and the summer term

continuous assessment (noun) /kənˈtɪnjʊəs əˈsesmənt/ – a way of judging a student by looking at the work that they do during the year instead of or in addition to looking at their examination results

coursework (noun) /ˈkɔː(r)sˌwɜː(r)k/ – schoolwork that a student must do as part of a course of study, with the mark that they achieve forming part of their exam result

assignment (noun) /əˈsaɪnmənt/ – work that you must do as part of a course of study or as part of your job

tutor (noun) /ˈtjuːtə(r)/ – a teacher in a college or university

grade (noun) /greɪd/ – a letter or number that shows the quality of a student's work

Answers

mark (noun) /mɑː(r)k/ – a school score

notes (noun plural) /nəʊts/ – details from something such as a lecture or a book that you write down so that you can remember them

revise (verb) /rɪˈvaɪz/ – to read and learn information that you have studied in order to prepare for an examination. The American word is *review*.

fail (verb) /feɪl/ – to be unsuccessful in achieving a satisfactory level or standard

resit (verb) /ˌriːˈsɪt/ – to take an examination again after failing it previously

4 LISTENING ▶ 01 Play the track for students to listen to the vocabulary quiz and answer the questions 1–8. Point out to students that the words are from exercises 1 and 2.

Elicit answers from students around the class. See p171 for the audioscript for this exercise.

Answers

1 veterinary medicine **2** lecture **3** mark
4 undergraduate **5** tutor **6** coursework/assignment
7 psychology **8** resit it

Life at university

5 Ask students to complete the sentences with words a–g.

Answers

1 a **2** f **3** e **4** c **5** d **6** b **7** g

6a Ask students to complete the questions with the words a–g in exercise 5. Elicit the answers in open class.

Answers

1 activities **2** facilities **3** friends **4** independent
5 abroad **6** residence **7** loan

6b SPEAKING In pairs, students use the questions in exercise 6a to interview their partner.

TEACHER DEVELOPMENT: CLASSROOM TIPS AND PLANNING

Pairwork

Insist students use English when working in pairs or in groups, even when they are setting up a task. Students could make posters with key expressions for pair- and groupwork and hang them on the classroom walls, e.g. *I'm A and you're B, OK? Are you ready? I think ... How about you?*

In the first few lessons, change students around for pairwork. Students of a similar level can be paired together or you can pair students of different proficiency levels, so that higher-level students can help the lower-level students.

While the students are doing pairwork activities, walk round the classroom and listen to their conversations. Monitoring gives you the opportunity to make notes about pronunciation, vocabulary and grammar points that are causing difficulty. Always carry a notepad and a pen, and write down errors and examples of good language to review at the end of the activity. Offer encouragement and praise where possible.

>>> **FAST FINISHERS**

Students write vocabulary quiz questions, similar to those in exercise 4, for other words from the lesson, e.g. *Which university subject studies the Earth?* (geology). Ask students to read them out for other students to say the word.

HOMEWORK

Assign students page 4 in their Workbook or the relevant sections of the Online Workbook.

Reading p7

Scanning for specific information

>>> **FAST TRACK**

You could ask less confident students to read the text first at home. Tell them they are allowed to look up a maximum of ten words.

WARMER

Put students in groups and ask them to discuss whether any of their hobbies or interests can be studied at university. Do they think any of them would be suitable for formal study?

1 SPEAKING In pairs, students discuss what they can see in pictures 1–5 and say if they think you can study these things at university. Ask them to give reasons why or why not. Elicit opinions from students in open class.

2 READING Ask students to read the comments from an Internet forum and match the comments to the pictures in exercise 1. Set a time limit of two minutes to encourage students not to get stuck on difficult vocabulary at this stage. Let students compare their answers in pairs before checking in open class.

Answers

a 3 **b** 1 **c** 4 **d** 2 **e** 5

>>> **FAST FINISHERS**

Ask students to note down what the exact name of each subject is.

Answers

baking technology management
The Beatles, Popular music and Society
Digital and Social Media
Viking studies
surf science and technology

ⓘ CULTURAL INFORMATION

Every year, over 150,000 students begin degree courses at over 370 institutions around the UK. Nursing, business and design-related studies are some of the most popular courses, but a variety of unusual undergraduate courses on offer has grown considerably in recent years. These more unusual options reflect students' individual interests and career aspirations. Over recent years, there's been some controversy in the press and elsewhere over these degrees. However, in an increasingly competitive jobs market, studying something unusual might help you stand out from the crowd.

According to the US Department of Education, National Center for Education Statistics, statistics – the science of learning from data – is the fastest-growing science, technology, engineering and math (STEM) undergraduate degree in the United States. In order of popularity, students also study business, social sciences and history, health professions, psychology and education.

✔ **EXAM SUCCESS** Students read the Exam Success tip. Then ask them how they approach matching activities for reading texts. Elicit ideas and ask them to read the information on page 144 (Reading: Matching activities).

TEACHER DEVELOPMENT: STUDENT TRAINING

Matching activities

Matching activities are a common type of reading question in both external and school-leaving examinations. Often the main idea and answer are in the title or topic sentence and there are similar words (synonyms) in the paragraphs and paragraph headings to help students match questions or statements with different texts. However, they still need to read the text carefully to check. Remind students that if a match is not immediately obvious, they should move on to the next one. If they are unsure between two answers at first, tell them to note both of them down and eliminate one of the answers when they make a final decision. Remind students to guess when there is no penalty for doing so.

3 Ask students to read the text again and match the people a–e with the questions 1–6. Remind them that the people may be chosen more than once. Elicit answers from different students around the class and ask them to identify key sentences in the text that helped them choose their answers.

Answers

1 d (Undergraduates spend their third year in a Scandinavian university, which I'm looking forward to.)

2 c (Maybe that's why 91% of students who study this course find a job as soon as they graduate.)

3 b (I don't see why they think it's OK to study classical music or literature but not the music and words of a group that changed the modern world.)

4 a (Some people think that all I do is bake bread and cakes.)

5 e (People are usually really jealous when I tell them that I'm studying surf science and technology.)

6 c (But for me the best thing about the course is that it's very hands-on.)

4 CRITICAL THINKING Individually, students read the question and make notes before comparing their ideas with the rest of the class.

Example answers

I think these subjects aren't too specialised. It's a good idea to study something unusual because you are more likely to be interested and study more. Also they often give you very specific skills that are more useful in the workplace. Furthermore, an unusual degree could make your CV stand out in a competitive marketplace.

In my opinion, these subjects are too specialised and they are a bad thing because your employment options are very narrow when you finish your degree. You can't transfer your skills easily to another subject area. Also, they are often not very academically rigorous so they don't show what you are intellectually capable of.

TEACHER DEVELOPMENT: STUDENT TRAINING

Critical thinking

Critical thinking is an essential skill for study at university and is increasingly identified as a key skill for leadership in the workplace. The most effective way to foster critical-thinking skills is to ask as many questions as we can that encourage evaluation and synthesis of facts and concepts. Higher-level thinking questions should start or end with words or phrases such as, 'Explain ...' 'Compare ...' 'Why ...' 'Which is a solution to the problem ...,' 'What is the best and why ...' and 'Do you agree or disagree with this statement?'

We can encourage students at every opportunity to formulate questions, gather and interpret evidence, and draw conclusions. Key critical-thinking skills include analysing similarities and differences, explaining how they solve a problem, creating categories and ranking items appropriately and learning how to identify relevant information, distinguish fact from opinion and construct arguments and test out ideas.

5 Encourage students to guess the meaning of the underlined words in the text. Allow them to use a dictionary to check their answers.

Answers

uni = short form of 'university'

drives me mad = makes someone feel extremely angry or upset

in great depth = in a very detailed way and giving a lot of information

implications = possible results or effects

hands-on = hands-on experience or training involves you doing something rather than just reading about it or watching other people do it

specialise = to be an expert in a particular part of a subject or profession

6 SPEAKING **What about *you*?** Ask students to think about their answers to the questions, and then to discuss them with a partner. Elicit some answers from different students.

HOMEWORK

Assign students page 5 in their Workbook or the relevant sections of the Online Workbook.

Grammar in context pp8–9

Talking about present situations, habits, routines and actions using the present simple, present continuous, present perfect simple and present perfect continuous

⟫ FAST TRACK

You could ask students to do exercises 1 and 2 at home. Then they could do exercise 3 at the beginning of the lesson.

Test before you teach

Do this exercise to find out how much students remember about the present simple/present continuous and present perfect simple/present perfect continuous tenses.

Tell students to write three true sentences and one false sentence about themselves or other people using the four tenses. In pairs, students read their sentences to each other for their partner to guess which is the false sentence. If they seem to be familiar with the use and form of these tenses, move through the Grammar guide exercises quickly in open class.

Present simple, present continuous and present habits

1a Ask students to look at the verbs in the sentences and name the tenses.

Answers

1 present simple **2** present continuous **3** present simple **4** present continuous **5** present simple

1b Ask students to read the explanations and match them with the sentences in exercise 1a. Check answers in open class.

Answers

a 1 **b** 3 **c** 5 **d** 2 **e** 4

2 Ask students to choose the correct alternative. Have students compare in pairs before you check their answers.

Answers

1 understand **2** goes **3** is coming **4** are getting **5** usually walks, is going **6** Do you wear **7** don't agree **8** sounds

TEACHER DEVELOPMENT: LANGUAGE

State and action verbs

State verbs generally fall into four groups:

Verbs of feeling – *love, like, hate, want, prefer, need*

Verbs of thinking – *know, understand, believe, remember, mean*

Verbs of the senses – *sound, look, hear, see, taste, smell, feel, seem*

Verbs of possession – *have, own, belong*

When a verb describes a state and not an action, we do not use the continuous tense. Remind students that some words can be both state verbs and action verbs, and in each case the meaning of these verbs is different. For example:

I **have** a car. (state verb showing possession)

I'm **having** a bath. (action verb which, in this case, means *taking*)

I **think** you are cool. (state verb meaning *in my opinion*)

I'm **thinking** about buying a motorbike. (action verb meaning *considering*)

3a PRONUNCIATION ▶ 02 Play the track for students to listen to the sentences and mark the word which the speaker stresses most. Check their answers.

Answers

1 constantly **2** always **3** forever **4** continually

TEACHER DEVELOPMENT: LANGUAGE

Present continuous for annoying habits

The present continuous with *always, constantly, continually* and *forever* is used here not to signify an action that is happening now, but an action that happens with regularity. However, the speaker chooses to use the present continuous and not the present simple to show annoyance and irritation at the action (we can also use this tense to talk about habits which are in some way unusual). Write this sentence on the board: *She's always complaining.* Ask a few concept-checking questions: *Does she complain all the time? (Yes); Is she complaining right now? (Not necessarily); Is the speaker annoyed that she complains a lot? (Yes)*. To highlight our annoyance, we shift the stress to the adverb in this type of sentence.

3b In pairs, students practise saying the sentences with the stress on the correct words.

TEACHER DEVELOPMENT: PRONUNCIATION

Emphatic stress

Some words carry more 'volume' (stress) than others. In any given sentence in English, there will be words that carry stress and others that don't. This is not a random pattern. Stressed words carry the meaning or the sense behind the sentence.

4a Ask students to complete the dialogues with the correct form of the verbs in the box. Remind them to use the present simple for general routines and habits or the present continuous with *always, constantly, continually* or *forever* for annoying habits. Let students compare their answers in pairs before checking in open class.

Suggested answers

1 's forever playing   **2** studies   **3** 're always leaving
4 's constantly saying   **5** coach

4b SPEAKING In pairs, students practise saying the dialogues. Remind them to stress some of the words when necessary.

✚ EXTRA ACTIVITY

In pairs, students invent a dialogue similar to the ones in exercise 4a using the present continuous with *always, constantly, continually* or *forever*. They then read out their dialogues for the rest of the class stressing some of the words when necessary.

5 SPEAKING In pairs or small groups, students talk about things people do that annoy them. In a less confident class, brainstorm a few ideas and write them on the board, e.g. *biting their nails, whistling, eating with their mouth open, speaking too loudly.* Walk round, monitoring students and helping them if necessary. Ask some students around the class to tell the rest of the class about the things that annoy them.

TEACHER DEVELOPMENT: CLASSROOM TIPS AND PLANNING

Pyramid discussion

You could organise a pyramid discussion for this speaking activity. Students start in small groups and agree on the top three things people do to annoy them. They can then join up with another group, share their ideas and discuss until the whole group agrees on their top three things. They then join up with another group, and so on, until you have finally a full-class discussion to agree on the top three annoying things people do.

Present perfect simple and present perfect continuous

6a Ask students to match sentences 1–4 with the explanations of their uses a–d.

Answers

1 a   **2** b   **3** d   **4** c

6b Ask students to look at the sentences and say which is present perfect simple and which is present perfect continuous. Elicit how we form these two tenses.

Answers

1 present perfect continuous   **2** present perfect simple
Present perfect simple: subject + *has/have* + past participle
Present perfect continuous: subject + *has/have* + *been* + verb + *-ing*

6c Students match the tenses to the correct usage.

Answers

1 present perfect simple   **2** present perfect continuous
3 present perfect simple   **4** present perfect continuous

7 SPEAKING In pairs, students talk about why and how we use the words that often go with the present perfect simple and present perfect continuous. You may wish to discuss the first one in open class as an example. Elicit answers from different students around the class and ask students to write example sentences on the board.

Answers

1 *for* goes with periods of time, like *three hours, ten minutes, a long time.* It goes just before the time period.
2 *since* goes with points in time, like *1990, Christmas, last week.* It goes just before the time period.
3 *ever* means 'sometime before now'. It is used in questions, e.g. *Have you ever/Haven't you ever …?,* and in negative statements, e.g. *Nobody has ever travelled there before.* It goes between *have* + subject pronoun and the past participle.
4 *never* means 'at no time before' and it is used in negative statements, e.g. *I've never been to New York before.* It goes between *have* and the past participle.
5 *just* means 'not so long ago'. It comes between *have* and the past participle, e.g. *They have just gone out.*
6 *already* shows an action has been completed. It comes between *have* and the past participle, e.g. *I have already heard that song.*
7 *yet* means 'up to a specified time' and is used only in the negative and question forms of the present perfect tense. It is normally placed at the end of a sentence, e.g. *I haven't been to the supermarket yet.*

8 Ask students to rewrite the sentences using the correct tense and the words in exercise 7, if necessary.

Answers

1 She's failed   **2** since 2012   **3** We went   **4** I've been doing   **5** has just had   **6** has painted   **7** for five hours   **8** I've lost   **9** I haven't done   **10** I've been waiting

9a Ask students to complete the questions with the present perfect simple or present perfect continuous.

Example answers

1 How long have you lived here?
2 How long have you been watching TV?
3 Have you ever done a bungee jump?
4 How many times have you eaten sushi?
5 What have you been doing all day?
6 Have you just had your lunch?

9b SPEAKING In pairs, students take it in turns to interview their partner using their completed questions. Round up the activity by asking students to tell the class one interesting thing they found out about their partner.

Students think of things that they have done more of or have been doing for longer than their partner (i.e. things where the number in their answer is bigger than their partner's). Individually, they note down questions using the present perfect simple or present perfect continuous tense. In pairs, students take turns asking and answering questions, e.g. *How long have you been wearing the shoes you have on now? How many countries have you visited? How long have you been studying in this class?*

TEACHER DEVELOPMENT: CLASSROOM TIPS AND PLANNING

Homework

Try to vary the length of homework assignments between those that last 30 minutes to an hour and quick ten-minute activities. Set homework in every class and make sure you write it on the board before the end of the class. (Students might miss the homework because they are rushing out of class.) Take some time to go over the exercise to make sure the students know what is expected.

Go over homework in the next class and correct it together. Students can check their own work or that of another student. Keep a note of who does their homework and who doesn't and note grades as part of your ongoing assessment of students' progress.

Refer students to the Grammar reference on page 16 if necessary.

HOMEWORK

Assign students page 6 in their Workbook or the relevant sections of the Online Workbook.

Developing vocabulary p9

Using do and make appropriately

>>> FAST TRACK

If students are familiar with the target vocabulary, you could do exercise 1 as a class activity by inviting individual students to read out the words and the rest of the class to call out *do* or *make*.

do and make

1 Ask students to match the words with the verb they usually go with (*do* or *make*) and write two lists.

Answers

do – a course, an assignment, an exam, chores, homework, the shopping, the washing, well
make – a cake, a decision, a noise, friends, the dinner

TEACHER DEVELOPMENT: LANGUAGE

do and make

Collocations with the verbs *do* and *make* are very often confused by students. These verb + noun combinations just sound 'right' to native English speakers, who use them all the time. In the next exercise, students learn some general usage guidelines. However, there are many exceptions and students must regularly revise and memorise words which collocate with *make* and *do* to avoid making mistakes.

2 Ask students to complete the rules with *do* and *make*.

Answers

1 do **2** do **3** make **4** do **5** make **6** do

3 Students complete the text with the correct form of *do* or *make*. Elicit answers from different students around the class.

Answers

a made **b** made **c** do **d** is doing **e** is making
f do **g** do **h** are making **i** do **j** do **k** make
l make **m** do **n** do

4a Students choose three expressions with *do* and three expressions with *make* and write questions to ask other people in the class. Draw students' attention to the example questions.

4b SPEAKING Students use their questions to interview as many people as possible. Round up the activity by asking them to tell the class something interesting they found out about the other students.

TEACHER DEVELOPMENT: CLASSROOM TIPS AND PLANNING

Communicative activities

In monolingual classrooms, it can be difficult to get students to talk in English during pair and groupwork. Point out to your class that in a one-hour lesson with 25 learners, each learner will speak for just 60 seconds if the teacher speaks for half the lesson. However, they can increase that percentage substantially if they try to use English in group activities.

You could put some quiet music on while students 'mingle' (move around) asking each other their *do* and *make* questions. If you have enough space, you could organise an 'onion ring'. Half the class forms a small circle in the middle, with their backs to the centre, and the other half stands facing one person in the circle, so forming an outer ring. The students ask and answer with their partner for a couple of minutes. The students in the outer circle then move one person to the left to change partners.

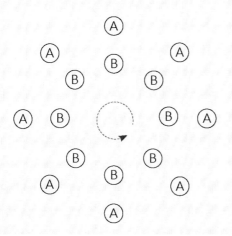

HOMEWORK

Assign students page 7 in their Workbook or the relevant sections of the Online Workbook.

Gateway to life skills pp10–11

Managing study time

To think about how you manage your study time, to learn some tips for saving time when you're studying and to plan your study time for the next few weeks

⟫⟫ FAST TRACK

Students could do the quiz in exercise 1a at home and discuss the results in exercise 1b in class as a first activity.

ℹ BACKGROUND INFORMATION

As teenagers become more independent and have to balance different demands on their time, they need time-management skills so they can plan ahead in order to fulfil their responsibilities. People are not born with good time-management skills. Like any skills, they have to be practised. Encourage students to buy a planner or a mobile phone app to write lists and schedules that can be checked at a later time.

This lesson helps students assess how good their time-management skills are, and offers strategies and solutions to help them plan, prioritise and deal with distractions.

WARMER

Bring some balloons to class. Elicit different things that students dedicate their time to during the day, e.g. school, family life, homework, etc. Ask a volunteer to come to the front of the class and toss him/her a balloon to keep it in the air. This balloon represents school. Toss in additional balloons, one by one, which could represent homework, family life, assignments, extracurricular activities, etc. Keep going until the balloons start falling to the ground. Tell students that the lesson is going to be about how they manage time. Ask students to look at Key concepts on page 10 to see if they are familiar with these words.

1a Individually, students read the statements in the quiz and decide how true each one is for them – very true (VT), quite true (QT) or not true (NT).

1b SPEAKING In pairs, students discuss if their answers are similar. Refer them to the key and ask them to read it and then discuss the questions.

2 SPEAKING In pairs, ask students to look at the headings from a study guide about effective time management and say what advice each section will give. Elicit some ideas in open class.

3 READING Ask students to read the text and match each heading in exercise 2 with the correct section. Check their answers and ask students to read out the key sentences that helped them decide on their answers.

Answers

1 D (The only way you can remember all that is by having it written down somewhere.)
2 A (Decide on a specific time to start and finish ...)
3 B (Break a big task into smaller pieces.)
4 F (Don't let yourself get distracted ...)
5 G (... have a plan B ...)
6 E (When you know the deadline for handing in a piece of work ...)
7 C (... have more time to relax!)

4 Ask students to read the text again and answer the questions. Give students a minute to compare in pairs before you check their answers in open class.

Answers

1 Students are busy people.

2 The sooner you start, the earlier you finish.

3 It can encourage you to continue.

4 Your phone, social media networks, friends' posts, videos, your family.

5 No, you have to be prepared for potential problems.

6 Start at the date you need to finish and calculate how long you need to do each step, and you will find the date you need to start.

✚ EXTRA ACTIVITY

In pairs, ask students to discuss how they think the advice can save them time with their studies. Elicit opinions from different students around the class.

🔍 VOCABULARY FOCUS

The video contains some useful words and phrases about managing study time that students may not be familiar with. You could pre-teach the following vocabulary with the class before watching:

leisure [n]: time for relaxation (i.e. not spent working or studying)

study buddy/buddies [n]: study companion

concept [n]: an idea of something that exists

Go for it! [v]: exclamation of encouragement

5 **LISTENING** ▶ 03 Tell students they are going to watch a video or listen to four students talking about their time management. Play the video or audio track and ask students to note down the issues they ask for advice about. Check their answers. See the Teacher's Resource Centre for the audioscript/videoscript for this exercise.

Suggested answers

Sam: He wants advice on managing free time and study time.

Vanessa: She wants to know more about study buddies and if they help.

Bea: She wants to know how to schedule her time in a more balanced way.

Chris: He wants advice on any tools or resources to help with time management.

6 ▶ 03 Play the video or audio track again for students to make notes about the tips Deana gives to the four students. Nominate different students around the class to read out the tips.

Answers

Sam: prioritise your tasks, have a timetable

Vanessa: study buddies help you focus, and help you to understand difficult concepts and your position

Bea: prioritise your work, set yourself a timer

Chris: talk to your teacher, use websites and books, use a timer and set yourself half-hour working time and five-minute breaks

TEACHER DEVELOPMENT: CLASSROOM TIPS AND PLANNING

Using video in the classroom

On-topic videos help students engage with the material on a deeper level. Teachers who use video in the classroom say that their students retain more information, understand concepts more rapidly and are more enthusiastic about what they are learning.

Videos that offer a real-world context and are relevant to the lesson are motivational and provide a valuable platform for sparking discussions in class.

Students have the chance to listen to topics and teenagers from other cultures and value their opinions and ideas. With video as one component in a thoughtful lesson plan, students often make new connections between curriculum topics, and discover links between these topics and the world outside the classroom. By exploiting the power of video to deliver lasting images, teachers can engage students in problem-solving and investigative activities, help students practise media literacy and critical-viewing skills and provide stimulation for discussion in the classroom.

7 **SPEAKING** In pairs, students discuss which of the ideas in the video/listening they do already or think are a good idea to try out. Encourage students to share their ideas in open class.

LIFE TASK

Tell students they are going to work on a task to manage their time better. Ask them to follow the plan:

■ *Step 1*
Ask students to work individually and read the instructions. Students start by making a list of all the schoolwork they have to do in the next few weeks, plus the deadline for each piece of work.

■ *Step 2*
Then ask students to work backwards from the deadline dates and decide when they should start each piece of work.

■ *Step 3*
Students write a plan for the next few weeks and mark any work which is most urgent in one colour and any work that can wait in another colour.

■ *Step 4*
Finally, ask students to make signs with the five most useful tips for them to manage their study time better. Draw students' attention to the example. Encourage them to keep the signs with them or in their room and to try and follow the advice.

Listening p12

Listening for specific information

WARMER

Write the words *continuous assessment* on the board. In small teams, students use these letters to make as many words as they can in three minutes. The team with the most correctly spelt words wins.

Suggested answers

aim, assess, contain, continue, count, meat, mess, minute, mountain, mouse, neat, nine, nose, seat, section, see, seen, steam, team, tease, ten, tent, time, etc.

TEACHER DEVELOPMENT: CLASSROOM TIPS AND PLANNING

Listening tasks

At the end of a listening task, try to develop a class discussion on how students can listen more effectively. Remind students that they must always read the instructions and questions before the first listening. This will help them know what they are listening for and predict content (from key words in the questions or visual clues, etc.). Students need to learn how to take good notes during the listening to help them choose the right answer.

Ask students to evaluate how well they did and if they thought it was a difficult task and why. For the CEFR dossier, students could record the listening activities they have done in class on a self-evaluation sheet. They can write the subject and date and evaluate their progress:

I understood the first time I listened.   1 2 3 4 5
I understood when we had finished listening.   1 2 3 4 5
I understood after listening with the audioscript. 1 2 3 4 5

1   SPEAKING In pairs, students read the statements made by students about revising for exams and decide which ones are good ideas. Elicit opinions from different students around the class.

Suggested answers

Useful ideas are 1, 2 (as long as all the students are focused on revising), 3, 4, 6, 8 (breaks should be short and involve drinking water and taking some exercise), 9.

2   LISTENING ▶ 04   Play the track for students to listen to two teenagers talking about revision and ask them to decide which three ideas in exercise 1 the boy mentions. Ask students if the boy has prepared well for the exam. See p171 for the audioscript for this exercise.

Answers

The boy mentions ideas 7, 5 and 10.
He hasn't prepared well for the exam.

3   ▶ 04   Play the track again for students to choose the best answer. Elicit from students which key phrases helped them decide on their answers for each question.

Answers

1 b (… didn't go to sleep until half three.)
2 a (We've known about it for a month!)
3 b (I've got basketball practice … on Mondays, Wednesdays and Fridays.)
4 c (… I haven't got any notes for some of them.)
5 a (… in this exam you have to answer everything.)

4   SPEAKING **What about you?** In pairs or small groups, students discuss the questions about preparing for exams.

✚ EXTRA ACTIVITY

Students develop a list of top five revision tips. Elicit ideas from students around the class and agree on a list that students can copy into their notebooks and add new ideas to during the unit.

HOMEWORK

Assign students page 7 in their Workbook or the relevant sections of the Online Workbook.

Grammar in context pp12–13

Using gerunds and infinitives

≫ FAST TRACK

You could do exercise 1 as a class activity by inviting different students to read out the sentences in Listening exercise 1 and nominating another student to say the answer.

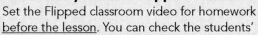
Test before you teach: Flipped classroom
Set the Flipped classroom video for homework <u>before the lesson</u>. You can check the students' Flipped classroom video answers on the Flipped classroom worksheet which you can give them to complete while watching the video or in the Online Workbook. This will allow you to assess the needs of the students before the class. Students can then move on to the relevant grammar practice activities.

Talk to students about this change in the classroom model. Go over the guidelines for watching the videos and discuss the procedure in class. After the students have completed several Flipped classroom lessons, encourage them to evaluate if they think the learning video has been effective and helpful.

The Flipped classroom

Flipped classroom videos 'flip' the traditional teaching methods for presenting grammar by moving parts of a lesson outside the classroom. The teacher has more class time to help students develop their communication skills and give feedback and assistance. In this way, students have more talk time in English during class using the target language.

The Flipped classroom videos enable students to take an active role in their learning and give them confidence in their capacity for autonomous study. Flipped classroom videos cater for different learning styles as students have more control over the pace of their learning. Students can come to class prepared with any questions and they can identify which areas they are confident in or the areas they might need to practise more. You can have more time to work with students individually rather than whole-class teaching. Remind students that they can refer to the videos at any time for homework help.

Gerunds and infinitives – 1

1 Students match statements 1–10 from Listening exercise 1 with the rules. Point out that they can use one rule twice.

Answers

2 g **3** f **4** c **5** d **6** b **7** e **8** i **9** h **10** e

2a Start by setting a time limit of 20 seconds and asking students to read and identify the two unusual techniques in the text. Then ask students to read the text and choose the correct alternative for a–o.

Answers

a to think **b** revising **c** to use **d** keeping **e** doing
f Leaving **g** to check **h** to get **i** to have **j** singing
k singing **l** cycling **m** to help **n** to keep
o listening

2b SPEAKING In pairs, students discuss if they would use either of the techniques and say why or why not. Elicit any unusual revision techniques students know or use.

3 Individually, students decide if the gerund or infinitive is used correctly in each sentence. Ask them to rewrite the incorrect sentences. Students compare their answers in pairs before you check in open class.

Answers

1 to pass **2** studying **3** correct **4** to find
5 to pass **6** correct **7** failing **8** studying

4 Ask students to complete the exam advice with the gerund or infinitive form of the verbs given. Check answers in open class.

Answers

1 to finish **2** Starting **3** taking **4** creating
5 leaving, to check **6** to complete **7** to answer

5a In pairs, students complete the questions with the gerund or infinitive form of an appropriate verb.

Example answers

1 Do you enjoy *going out* in the evening?
2 When you sleep, do you ever dream of *falling*?
3 Have you ever thought of *being famous*?
4 Do you find it difficult *to study*?
5 Have you ever considered *changing schools*?
6 Do you think that you are brave enough *to jump out of a plane*?
7 Would you like to be the first person *to live on Mars*?
8 Are you interested in *studying surf science and technology*?
9 At the weekend, do you ever go *mountain biking*?
10 Next year do you want *to study another language*?

5b SPEAKING Students interview others using their questions and make notes of any funny or interesting answers. You could ask a more confident pair to model this activity first. Monitor students and note down errors and good use of language to go over in a feedback session at the end of the class. Finally, ask students to tell the class some of the things they have discovered.

TEACHER DEVELOPMENT: CLASSROOM TIPS AND PLANNING

Error correction

It is important not to over-correct in more fluency-based activities as this can make students lose confidence. Not correcting, however, leads to students developing bad habits and decreases their communicative ability.

A key skill to develop is the ability to distinguish between 'errors' and 'mistakes'. A mistake is a slip; you know the correct thing to say, but you said the wrong thing by accident. Mistakes are not critical to correct unless they are repeated too often. Errors are when the student does not know the correct form, term or usage.

It is then important to decide whether it is better to correct errors on the spot or at the end of the activity or later, and decide on an appropriate correction technique. If you correct on the spot, it must be quick: you can ask students to repeat the sentence again, echo the sentence up to the error for students to finish, write the word on the whiteboard and underline it, etc. As much as possible, encourage self-correction. Alternatively, you can do the error correction later (error correction makes a nice transition between parts of the lesson). Write the errors on the board in an anonymous way (change some of the words if necessary) and elicit correct answers from the class.

✚ EXTRA ACTIVITY

Students write answers to their own questions in exercise 5a.

Refer students to the Grammar reference on page 16 if necessary.

HOMEWORK

Assign students page 8 in their Workbook or the relevant sections of the Online Workbook.

Developing speaking p14

Expressing preferences using a variety of structures

⟫⟫ FAST TRACK

You could ask students to complete exercise 1 at home in preparation for the listening activity. They can then compare their answers in pairs before you check their answers.

WARMER

Students think of typical questions connected with personal information that are usually in the first part of an oral exam, e.g. *What's your first name? What's your surname? How do you spell that? How old are you? Where are you from? What's your favourite school subject?*

1 Ask students to read questions 1–6 and match each one with one of the categories a–d.

Answers

1 a **2** d **3** c **4** b **5** b **6** c

2 LISTENING ▶ 05 Tell students they are going to listen to six students answering the questions in exercise 1. Play the track for them to match each student to one of the questions. As you check answers, elicit the key sentences that helped students decide. See p171 for the audioscript for this exercise.

Answers

Student A: question 2 (I think I'd like to study languages at university.)
Student B: question 4 (We go to the cinema if there's a good film on ...)
Student C: question 5 (Yes, I like reading.)
Student D: question 3 (I prefer revising alone ...)
Student E: question 6 (I prefer doing mental work.)
Student F: question 1 (... I like being able to walk everywhere ...)

3 ▶ 05 Play the track again for students to listen and decide if each student gives a reason or any personal details to support their answer. Encourage students to discuss if it is a good idea to give reasons and/or personal details and say why or why not.

Answers

All the students answer the questions well except Student C who does not give reasons or personal details to support their answer.
It's a good idea to give reasons and personal details because it helps promote further conversation. A short response can indicate that you are annoyed, uninterested or very shy.

TEACHER DEVELOPMENT: STUDENT TRAINING

Developing conversation skills

To keep a conversation going, students need to contribute something positive or interesting. Basic rules for engagement in a conversation include giving examples, making related comments, expanding on what others are saying and advancing your own opinion clearly and politely. Most students will really know conversation rules from their first language, but it is helpful to point out that by not giving reasons or personal details in a reply, students can appear to be impolite. Knowing these strategies will help students avoid confusion and gain experience in different types of conversations.

4 SPEAKING In pairs, students take it in turns to ask and answer the questions in exercise 1. Remind them to give reasons and personal details. In a less confident class, give students time to make notes before they do this as a speaking activity.

5 Ask students to look at the different ways of expressing preferences in the Speaking bank before they do exercise 6.

TEACHER DEVELOPMENT: LANGUAGE

Expressing preferences

We often use words like *prefer, would prefer, would rather* to talk or ask about preferences. We tend to use *prefer* to talk generally about likes, dislikes and what we want.
The expressions *would prefer* and *would rather* are used when we want to be a little more specific, e.g. *I would prefer to be a translator (not a musician).*
Draw students' attention to the differences in form:
I prefer living in a city. (followed by the gerund)
I would prefer not to study music. (followed by the infinitive with *to*)
Would you rather stay at a hotel? (followed by the base form of the verb without *to*)
Would rather is very common in spoken English and is usually abbreviated to *'d rather*. *Would rather* is also followed by a past tense when we want to involve other people in the action, even though it has a present or future meaning, e.g. *They'd rather I studied music.*

6 Ask students to put the verbs in the correct form. Check answers in open class.

Answers

1 playing, doing **2** go, walk **3** not to stay
4 writing **5** write, do **6** to go, (to) fly

PRACTICE MAKES PERFECT

7a **SPEAKING** In pairs, ask students to take it in turns to ask and answer the questions. Remind them to give reasons and personal details and to use the expressions from the Speaking bank. Walk around checking students are on task and speaking English to each other. Note down errors and good use of language you can talk about when you give feedback on this activity.

For students who are less confident, photocopy the model dialogue below, and either read it aloud yourself, or alternate the roles with you and a strong student. Then instruct students to read aloud in pairs, alternating between roles A and B. Then ask them to read it again, changing the underlined information so that it is true for them.

Model dialogue

A: Which subjects do you prefer studying?

B: <u>I prefer studying literature and languages. I spend hours reading books and I love finding out about different cultures and speaking other languages.</u>

A: Would you rather study at home or in a library?

B: <u>I would rather study at home because I have a desk in my bedroom and it is quiet and I can concentrate better when I am on my own. When I go to the library, I usually meet my friends and we don't do as much work.</u>

A: Would you like to have an end-of-year school trip this year or would you prefer to go somewhere with your family?

B: <u>I'd prefer to have an end-of-year school trip because I think it's nice to finish the academic year with your schoolmates.</u>

B: Would you prefer to study in your country or abroad?

A: <u>I'd prefer to study abroad because I can learn another language better and enjoy living in another culture.</u>

B: Do you prefer studying with books or using a computer?

A: <u>I prefer using a computer because it's more fun and you can store and change the information you find.</u>

B: Would you rather have a school uniform or wear what you like?

A: <u>I'd rather wear what I like. I prefer wearing my own clothes and being individual to wearing the same clothes as other people.</u>

7b Ask students to change partners and repeat the activity. You can change pairs easily by taking a chair and putting it at the end of the row of students. The student from the other end of the row then moves to that chair, and all the other students turn to their other side to work with someone new.

HOMEWORK

Assign students page 9 in their Workbook or the relevant sections of the Online Workbook.

Developing writing p15

Replying to informal emails with relevant information

⟫⟫ FAST TRACK

You could ask students to do exercise 1 at home and check their answers at the start of the lesson. Alternatively, you could set the writing task in exercise 6 as homework.

WARMER

Write these three statements on the board and ask students to discuss if they are true or false:

1 *We start an informal email with the words 'Dear Sir or Madam'.* (false)

2 *We end an informal email with words like 'I look forward to hearing from you soon'.* (false)

3 *When we finish an informal email, we usually only write our first name.* (true)

1 Ask students to read the email from a British girl called

Amy to a friend who lives in Italy. Encourage them to underline the four pieces of information that Amy asks for. Check their answers in open class.

Answers

What have you been doing recently?
Which month do you think is better, July or August?
What do you think is the best way for me to do that?
Please let me know what type of things you'd like to do here.

2 Ask students to look at the style of the email in exercise 1 and say what things in it are typical of informal emails. Elicit answers from different students around the class.

Answers

informal words
Hi! as a greeting,
simple sentences
contractions (*I've, I'd,* etc.)
Best wishes at the end

3 Ask students to look at the Writing bank and to match the topics with the groups of expressions. Elicit more expressions to add to each group.

Answers

a 3 (Hello …, Hey …)
b 4 (Great to hear from you. Thanks for telling me all your news. I just wanted to get in touch about …)
c 5 (What have you been up to? What have you been doing recently/lately? How have you been?)
d 1 (On another note …, That reminds me …)
e 2 (I'll be in touch soon. See you!)

4 In pairs, students imagine they have received Amy's email. Ask them to make notes about the information she wants. Draw their attention to the example.

5 Tell students they are going to write a reply to Amy. Ask them to make a paragraph plan and decide what information to include in each paragraph. Draw their attention to the example.

Answers

Paragraph 2: Describe the best time to visit my country/ the best way to learn my language
Paragraph 3: Describe things I'd like to do in England
Paragraph 4: Say goodbye

PRACTICE MAKES PERFECT

6 Ask students to write a reply to Amy using their notes and paragraph plan to help them. Remind them to check they have included all the information she needs. Tell them to write between 120 and 150 words. They can also follow the advice in the Writing bank on page 150. For students who are less confident, photocopy the model text below for extra support during the writing task.

Model text

Hi Amy

Thanks for your email. Sorry I haven't written for a long time, but we've had lots of exams recently at school. I hope I've passed everything! How are you? What have you been doing recently?

The best time of the year to visit my country is in summer. It's warm, but it's not too hot in July and all the flowers and trees are in bloom. August is usually much hotter. If you want to start learning Italian while you're here, the best idea is to do a language course in the morning. I can find a good school that is close to my home if you want. In the afternoon, we can speak in Italian and I can take you to see some exciting places in Pisa.

I'd really like to come back with you and visit your family in England. I've always wanted to visit London, so we could spend a day there. I know you like science so maybe we could visit the Science Museum. I would also like to do some shopping because I love British fashion and music!

Anyway, I've got to go and revise for my last exam!

Bye for now,
Sonia

TEACHER DEVELOPMENT: CLASSROOM TIPS AND PLANNING

How to use model texts in class

A model is a text that provides a good example of how texts of a particular kind can be written. As students become familiar with the structures of different text types, they will feel more comfortable in approaching written exam tasks. The overall aim is to provide the students with a solid framework from which they can notice features (such as layout, structure and fixed phrases) that they can make use of in their own written text. Always read the model text provided and go through the writing tasks in detail so that students are fully aware of why they are writing and who they are writing to.

✓ EXAM SUCCESS Students discuss the importance of using the correct style and including the correct information in their written texts. Tell students to turn to page 144 (Writing: Transactional tasks) to compare their ideas.

TEACHER DEVELOPMENT: STUDENT TRAINING

Transactional tasks

A 'transactional' letter is one that is written for the purpose of getting something done in the real world, as opposed to a 'non-transactional' letter, which might be just to share feelings, opinions or experiences with someone else.

In order to successfully complete transactional writing tasks in exams, students must analyse the instructions carefully and identify the key information they must include:

- Who is writing – students may be asked to assume a role, e.g. Amy's friend
- Who you are writing to, e.g. a friend
- The purpose for writing the text, e.g. to reply to Amy's request for information, as well as the reader's purpose for reading it, e.g. to find out information
- The format (informal email) and number of words required (120–150 words)

This information guides the students' choice of style, content and tone. Remind students that marks are awarded for appropriate response to the task and if all the necessary information is included.

HOMEWORK

Assign students page 10 in their Workbook or the relevant sections of the Online Workbook.

Language checkpoint: Unit 1

>>> FAST TRACK

The extra support provided in the Grammar and Vocabulary reference sections makes the Grammar and Vocabulary revision sections ideal for setting as homework. You could get students to complete the whole revision page or just certain exercises for homework.

Grammar revision p17

Present simple, present continuous and present habits

1 Ask students to complete the sentences with an appropriate word. Point out that, in some questions, there may be more than one option.

Answers

1 don't 2 are 3 start 4 always/constantly/forever
5 always/constantly/continually/forever 6 asking

Present perfect simple and continuous

2 Ask students to choose the correct alternative.

Answers

1 switched 2 for 3 been standing 4 seen 5 been staying 6 been reading 7 finished

Gerunds and infinitives

3 Ask students to read the first sentence, and then complete the second sentence so that it has a similar meaning to the first. Point out that they must use between two and five words including the word given. Remind students that they mustn't change the word given.

Answers

1 risk failing 2 go cycling 3 can't stand getting up
4 consider joining 5 having a valid passport
6 the first to finish 7 'd love to see

Vocabulary revision p17

STUDYING AT UNIVERSITY

1 Ask students to complete the sentences with the words. Remind them there are two extra words.

Answers

1 resit 2 grades 3 notes 4 tutor 5 degree
6 undergraduate 7 lecture

LIFE AT UNIVERSITY

2 Ask students to write words to complete the sentences.

Answers

1 abroad 2 loan 3 facilities 4 independent
5 hall 6 Extracurricular

DO AND MAKE

3 Ask students to choose the correct alternative.

Answers

1 do 2 make 3 do 4 make 5 make 6 make
7 do

HOMEWORK

Assign students page 11 in their Workbook or the relevant sections of the Online Workbook.

2 Nine to five

KEY LEARNING OUTCOMES

Students will be able to:

- talk about past events, situations and habits using a wide variety of tenses and structures
- discuss and evaluate different factors related to jobs
- understand written and spoken texts related to the world of work

- negotiate and collaborate in conversations
- write texts expressing their opinion on topics related to school and work

UNIT OVERVIEW

Vocabulary	Work conditions and responsibilities Working life
Reading	Working life CRITICAL THINKING Discussing dream jobs
Grammar in context	Past simple and past continuous Past habits PRONUNCIATION Past simple -ed ending
Developing vocabulary	Phrasal verbs connected with work
Life skills	The world of work: Evaluating jobs
Listening	A gap year
Grammar in context	Past perfect simple and past perfect continuous
Developing speaking	Negotiating and collaborating – 1
Developing writing	An opinion essay – 1
Exam success	Listening: Matching people and statements Speaking: Negotiating and collaborating

DIGITAL OVERVIEW

Presentation Kit

- ▶ **Flipped classroom video Unit 2:** Past habits
- ▶ **Life skills video Unit 2:** Evaluating jobs
- ▶ **Interactive versions of Student's Book activities**
- ▶ **Integrated audio and answer key for all activities**
- ▶ **Workbook pages with answer key**

Teacher's Resource Centre

- ▶ **Flipped classroom video Unit 2:** Past habits
- ▶ **Life skills video Unit 2:** Evaluating jobs
- ▶ **Grammar communication activity Unit 2:** A week in the life
- ▶ **Worksheets for this unit, including:**
  - Grammar Practice worksheet Unit 2
  - Flipped classroom worksheet Unit 2: Past habits
  - Literature worksheet Units 1 and 2
  - Culture worksheet Unit 2
  - Life skills video worksheet Unit 2
  - Everyday English worksheet Unit 2

Student's App
Gateway 2nd Edition wordlist for the award-winning Sounds App (available for download)

✓ TESTING AND ASSESSMENT

Resources for exam preparation and measuring student progress

- ▶ Test Generator Units 1–2
- ▶ Printable test Unit 2
- ▶ Gateway to exams Units 1 and 2 (end of Unit 2)

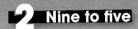

Vocabulary p18

Talking about issues related to the world of work

>>> **FAST TRACK**

You could ask students to do exercises 2 and 3 at home. They can look up any words they are not sure about in their dictionaries or the Macmillan Online Dictionary.

WARMER

Ask students to look at the unit title *Nine to five* and discuss what they think it refers to (typical working hours in many European countries). Elicit what they think the unit is going to be about (issues related to the world of work). Write these questions on the board for students to discuss in pairs: *What are the typical working hours in your country? How many hours a week do most people work? At what age do people usually start work in your country? At what age do people usually retire (stop work) in your country?*

TEACHER DEVELOPMENT: CLASSROOM TIPS AND PLANNING

Organising the board

Clarity of board work = clarity of lesson! At the end of a class, look at your board work and ask: *Does it make sense? Is it organised? Could the information be laid out in a clearer way? Is my writing big enough, clear enough and visible to everyone?* Check it from the back of the room. In some classrooms, students will not be able to see the bottom one-third of the board from the back of the room.

Many teachers divide the board into different sections, e.g. class objectives and homework, grammar and vocabulary section, notepad. The most important material should go in the middle section. You can use different colours, e.g. one colour for highlighting vocabulary/grammar, another for pronunciation. Remember not to stand with your back to the class when you are writing on the board and ask students if you are going to erase something from the board, e.g. *Is it OK if I erase this?*

Work conditions and responsibilities

1 **SPEAKING** In pairs, students try to think of one job for each letter of the alphabet.

Example answers

A – architect, B – builder, C – chef, D – doctor, E – engineer, F – farmer, G – grocer, H – historian, I – investigator, J – judge, K – karate instructor, L – lawyer, M – mechanic, N – novelist, O – ophthalmologist, P – photographer, Q – quantum physicist, R – receptionist, S – shop assistant, T – teacher, U – umpire, V – violinist, W – waiter, X – X-ray technician, Y – yachtsman, Z – zoo-keeper

2 Students read the job descriptions and name the jobs.

Answers

a taxi driver   **b** police officer

3 Students look at the expressions in red in the texts in exercise 2 and check that they understand what they mean. Provide dictionaries if necessary. Elicit definitions from students around the class.

Answers

qualifications /ˌkwɒlɪfɪˈkeɪʃ(ə)nz/ – something such as a degree or a diploma that you get when you successfully finish a course of study

deal with /diːl wɪð/ – to take action to do something, especially to solve a problem

be responsible for /biː rɪˈspɒnsəb(ə)l fə(r)/ – someone who is responsible for someone or something is in charge of them and must make sure that what they do or what happens to them is right or satisfactory

stressful /ˈstresf(ə)l/ – involving or causing a lot of pressure or worry

outdoors /ˌaʊtˈdɔː(r)z/ – not in a building

good conditions /ɡʊd kənˈdɪʃ(ə)nz/ – favourable work situation or environment

self-employed /ˌself ɪmˈplɔɪd/ – working for yourself instead of for an employer and paid directly by the people who you provide a product or service to

employee /ɪmˈplɔɪiː/ – someone who is paid regularly to work for a person or an organisation

earn /ɜː(r)n/ – to receive money for work that you do

salary /ˈsæləri/ – a fixed amount of money that you earn each month or year

dangerous conditions /ˈdeɪndʒərəs kənˈdɪʃ(ə)nz/ – situation or environment that is likely to harm or kill someone, or to damage or destroy something

indoors /ɪnˈdɔː(r)z/ – in a building

do paperwork /duː ˈpeɪpə(r)ˌwɜː(r)k/ – do the part of a job that involves producing reports, keeping records and writing letters

manual work /ˈmænjʊəl wɜː(r)k/ – a job which involves physical work using your hands

well paid /ˌwel ˈpeɪd/ – a well-paid person receives a good amount of money for work

skilled /skɪld/ – having the ability and experience to do something well

training /ˈtreɪnɪŋ/ – the process of training people or of being trained for a profession or activity

experience /ɪkˈspɪəriəns/ – knowledge and skill that is gained through time spent doing a job or activity

✚ EXTRA ACTIVITY

Ask students to underline the stressed syllables (see Answers in exercise 3 above) and mark the schwa /ə/ sound – the most frequent sound in the English language. Drill the pronunciation of the words.

4 **LISTENING** ▶ 06 Play the track for students to listen to four people describing their jobs. Ask students to match each person to one of the jobs. Elicit the key words that helped students decide on their answer. See page 171 for the audioscript for this exercise.

Answers

1 school caretaker (key words: indoors, manual work, fixing things, school building)

2 software engineer (key words: designing special computer systems, work for banks or big offices, big companies)

3 personal assistant (PA) (key words: employee, arranging meetings, taking calls, writing letters, deal with … paperwork)

4 physiotherapist (key words: injuries, moving again using special physical exercises, walk or run again)

5 **SPEAKING** In pairs, students take turns to describe a job using the expressions in red in exercise 2 for their partner to guess. In a less confident class, ask students to note down some key words to use in their description before this speaking activity.

Working life

6 Students match the expressions on the right with the definitions 1–5. Point out that there are two extra expressions and check that students understand what these extra expressions mean.

Answers

1 e **2** b **3** g **4** a **5** f

work full-time – work the number of hours that people normally work in a complete week

work from nine to five – work 'normal' working hours (from 9 am to 5 pm)

7 **SPEAKING** In pairs, students discuss in which jobs or situations they think it is common to work in each way.

Suggested answers

1 in a normal office job

2 people with a lot of responsibility and who are well paid often work long hours, e.g. managers, directors

3 in a stressful job when there is a lot of work to do; when you can earn extra money; when there is a chance of promotion

8a Ask students to put the different events in a logical order.

8b **LISTENING** ▶ 07 Play the track for students to listen and check their answers. See p171 for the audioscript for this exercise.

Answers

2 apply for a job **3** be offered a job **4** sign a contract **5** get a promotion

9 Students match the expressions 1–5 with meanings a–e. They can look up any words they are not sure about in their dictionaries or the Macmillan Online Dictionary.

Answers

1 a **2** e **3** d **4** c **5** b

10 **SPEAKING** In pairs, students talk about their work plans. Draw their attention to the example. In a less confident class, give students time to prepare their ideas in written form before doing this as a speaking activity. Elicit comments and ideas from different students around the class.

✚ EXTRA ACTIVITY

Students order the jobs in exercise 4 from most to least well paid. They then compare their list in pairs to see if they have got the same order and discuss any differences.

TEACHER DEVELOPMENT: STUDENT TRAINING

Recording vocabulary

A mind map is a useful way to record vocabulary and can provide a very effective revision tool at exam time. They appeal to visual learners and help to show how words connect and relate to each other. For the topic of work, students write 'WORK' in the centre of a blank page in their notebooks and record the words related to this theme as they move through the unit. Students draw branches from the centre and choose appropriate sub-headings for each group of vocabulary. Remind students to use different colours and illustrations to make their mind maps more memorable.

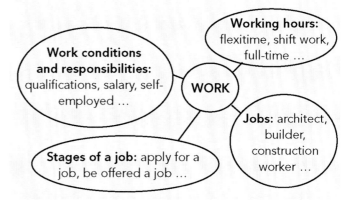

HOMEWORK

Assign students page 12 in their Workbook or the relevant sections of the Online Workbook.

Reading p19

Predicting content and reading for detail

>>> FAST TRACK

You could ask students to think about the questions in exercise 4 at home and make some notes in preparation for a class discussion.

WARMER

Play *Noughts and crosses* with words from the previous lesson. Draw a 3 x 3 grid on the board. Choose a word and draw a short line on the board to represent each letter. Write small numbers 1–9 in each square on the grid so it is easy for students to name the square. Divide the class into two teams and toss a coin to see who goes first. Assign noughts (0) to one group and crosses (X) to the other. The first group chooses a square from the grid and says a letter. If the letter is in the word, write it on the corresponding short line. That group can then continue guessing letters. If they say a letter which is not in the word, play passes to the other team. If they guess the word correctly, their symbol (0 or X) goes in the space they nominated. The other team can then choose a square and try to guess a new word. The first team to get three noughts or crosses in a row (horizontal, vertical or diagonal) is the winner.

1 **SPEAKING** In pairs, students look at the photos of two people with unusual jobs. Ask them to discuss where they think the people work. Elicit ideas from students in open class.

TEACHER DEVELOPMENT: STUDENT TRAINING

Inference in reading activities

Making inferences means using what you know to make a guess about what you don't know. It requires abstract thinking and it is therefore a higher-level skill. Poor readers often start reading a text word by word, without first predicting what a text will be about.

Good readers use a variety of strategies to assist comprehension before they start reading. Predictions can encourage active reading and keep students interested, whether or not the predictions are correct. Students can look at text titles and visual information such as pictures, photos, maps and diagrams along with their own experiences to make predictions and tap into prior knowledge they have about the subject. On first reading, students are then checking and revising their predictions.

2 Ask students to read the articles and check their answer in exercise 1. Set a time limit of three minutes to encourage students not to get stuck on difficult vocabulary at this stage.

3 Ask students to read the articles again and decide if the statements are True (T), False (F) or the information is Not Mentioned (NM). Elicit from students where they found their answer when the answer is true or false.

Answers

1 T (While 22-year-old student Sebastian Smith was doing his final university assignment, he heard an advert on the radio ...)
2 F (Sebastian felt that the job was a dream come true.)
3 NM
4 T (And Sebastian was also responsible for evaluating other factors, such as safety.)
5 T (He hid the structure in his gold-painted suit and learnt to sit back with just one foot on the ground and make it look as if he was defying gravity.)
6 T (These statues have to put up with children and adults coming up to them and touching them to see if they are real.)
7 F (And standing still for hours can bring serious health problems.)
8 NM

ⓘ CULTURAL INFORMATION

Living statues

Living statues are street performers who pose immobile for hours in places where lots of tourists pass. They only move an arm or a leg or smile to get a funny or shocked reaction out of the passers-by. Living statues' clothes, make-up and poses can look realistic; some living statues paint their entire bodies and clothes silver or gold to mimic a proper statue. The more realistic they are, the more successful they are. In the UK, professionals can earn over £200 a day, but it is much harder than it looks. Most living statues perform for only an hour and a half per set at a time because their blood stops circulating properly.

4 **CRITICAL THINKING** Individually, students read the questions and make notes before comparing their ideas with the rest of the class.

Example answers

I think dream jobs do exist because there are people who love their jobs and get paid well for them.

In my opinion, a dream job is something you do that is really your hobby and you love it. It is also well paid and gives you lots of free time to do other things as well.

TEACHER DEVELOPMENT: STUDENT TRAINING

Critical thinking

Critical thinking is required to navigate the ever-complex environment in which we live. Critical thinking comprises a number of different skills that help us learn to make decisions. To think critically about an issue or a problem means to be open-minded and consider alternative ways of looking at solutions. Teenagers know how to access and locate, interpret, and apply information, but if they don't invest time in evaluating the information they use, their efforts often result in a low-quality product. Key critical thinking skills are **reasoning**: teenagers are able to explore the implications of information, explain what they think and give reasons for their opinions, and **flexibility**: teenagers can take what they learn in one situation and transfer it to another situation.

5 Encourage students to guess the meaning of the underlined words in the texts. Allow them to use a dictionary to check their answers.

Answers

resort = a place where many people go for a holiday

trials = the process of testing a product, plan or person over a period of time

all-inclusive = including everyone or everything, especially all the costs, charges and services that make up the total price of something

drawback = a feature of something that makes it worse than it could be

defying = to happen in a way that is different from what usually happens or what you expect

put up with = to accept someone or something unpleasant in a patient way

still = without movement

at a time = continuously for this period of time

spot = the particular place where someone or something is

6 SPEAKING **What about *you*?** Ask students to consider their own answer to the question, and then discuss it with a partner. Ask some students to share their thoughts with the class. Elicit some answers from different pairs.

┌───┐
✚ EXTRA ACTIVITY

Write these questions on the board for students to discuss in pairs: *What are some common occupations in your country? What do some of your friends and family do? What is your dream job?* Ask them to write about their dream job for homework.
└───┘

┌───┐
HOMEWORK

Assign students page 13 in their Workbook or the relevant sections of the Online Workbook.
└───┘

Grammar in context pp20–21

Talking about past events, situations and habits using a variety of tenses and structures

⟫⟫ FAST TRACK

You could ask students to do exercises 1 and 2a at home. Then they could do exercise 2b at the beginning of the lesson.

Test before you teach

Tell students a short personalised story using both the past simple and past continuous tenses (see example below). Tell the story twice – the first time students just listen and the second time they note down key points. Ask them to retell the story in pairs. Elicit the story from students around the class and check how familiar they are with these tenses.

Example story

Last week I was trying to think of a good present to buy for my friend Aisha's birthday, but I couldn't think of anything. On Friday, I walked into town and as I was standing outside a shop, I saw Aisha inside. What a coincidence! I saw that she was looking at a scarf and she obviously liked it, but then her phone rang, she answered it, and she rushed out of the shop. When I next saw her, she was waving to someone who was waiting for her over the road. I went into the shop and bought the scarf.

Last night we had a dinner to celebrate Aisha's birthday. I gave her the scarf and she was very happy, and amazed!

If they seem to be familiar with their use, move through the Grammar guide exercises quickly in open class.

Past simple and past continuous

1a Ask students to look at the sentences and say which verbs are past simple and which are past continuous. Check their answers.

Answers

1 past simple   **2** past continuous   **3** past simple   **4** past continuous, past simple   **5** past continuous, past simple

1b Ask students to look at the rules and decide if each rule is for the past simple (PS) or the past continuous (PC). Check their answers. Remind students that the spelling rules for adding *-ing* to make the past continuous tense are the same as for the present continuous tense.

Answers

1 PS   **2** PC   **3** PC   **4** PS   **5** PC

1c Elicit from students if it is more common to use *while* and *as* with the past simple or the past continuous.

Answer

past continuous

TEACHER DEVELOPMENT: LANGUAGE

Past simple and past continuous

The most common use of the past continuous tense is to talk about something that was happening around a particular time in the past. We often use the past continuous and the past simple tenses together. When this happens, the past continuous describes a longer, 'background' action or situation and the past simple describes the action or events. Often, the action described by the past simple tense interrupts the situation described by the past continuous tense.

2a Ask students how we spell the *-ed* form of the verbs.

Answers

cried, developed, happened, hated, mentioned, occurred, planned, preferred, stepped, stopped, studied, travelled, tried, visited

TEACHER DEVELOPMENT: LANGUAGE

Past simple spelling rules

If the accent falls on the last syllable, the consonant is doubled to form the past tense, e.g. *occurred.* When the word ends in a short vowel + consonant, the final consonant is not usually doubled to form the past tense, e.g. *developed.* However, verbs that end in 'l', are exceptions to this rule in British English, e.g. *travelled.* Verbs that end in 'y' often change to 'i' before *-ed.*

2b PRONUNCIATION 08 Elicit from students how we pronounce the *-ed* form of the verbs in exercise 2a: /d/, /t/ or /ɪd/. Play the track for students to listen and check their answers. See p171 for the audioscript for this exercise.

Answers

/d/: cried, happened, mentioned, occurred, planned, preferred, studied, travelled, tried
/t/: developed, stepped, stopped
/ɪd/: hated, visited

TEACHER DEVELOPMENT: PRONUNCIATION

The *-ed* ending

Teaching the regular past simple verb forms offers an opportunity to teach students the difference between voiced and unvoiced sounds. Voiced consonants use the voice. Ask students to test this by putting their finger on their throat as they say the letters *b, g, l, m,* etc. If they feel a vibration, the consonant is voiced. Unvoiced consonants do not use the voice. They are hard sounds and there is no vibration in your throat, just a short explosion of air as you pronounce. Knowing the difference between these sounds helps us to know how the *-ed* ending is pronounced.

Verbs ending with a voiced vowel sound or a consonant: *-b, -g, -l, -m, -n, -v* or *-z,* we say /d/.

Verbs ending with an unvoiced sound: *-f, -k, -p, -s, -sh, -ch, -x, -h,* we say /t/.

Verbs ending in *-d* or *-t,* we say /ɪd/.

The /ɪd/ is the most important thing to pronounce correctly since this is the most noticeable sound.

3 Ask students to decide if the underlined verbs are in the correct tense and rewrite them if they are not correct. Check their answers.

Answers

1 made **2** correct **3** correct, was raining
4 spent **5** correct, was doing, correct **6** was walking
7 was crying

4a Ask students to write the correct questions for the answers. Let students compare their answers in pairs before checking in open class.

Answers

1 What did you do when you got home after school yesterday?
2 Were you watching TV at 9 o'clock last night?
3 What were your parents doing yesterday at 10 am?
4 Where did you go last summer?
5 Were you listening to music while you were doing your homework yesterday?
6 What did you do last Saturday?
7 What were you doing at 6 o'clock this morning?

4b SPEAKING In pairs, students interview their partner using the questions in exercise 4a.

> **Test before you teach: Flipped classroom**
> Set the Flipped classroom video and tasks for homework <u>before the lesson</u>. This will allow you to assess the needs of the students before the class. Students can then move on to the relevant grammar practice activities.

Past habits

5a Ask students to read the sentences and answer the questions below.

Answers

1 a, b, c **2** d

TEACHER DEVELOPMENT: LANGUAGE

Did you use to ...?

Remind students that when writing questions with *used to,* we remove the 'd' in the same way as with regular verbs, e.g. *Did you use to live in this house?*

5b Ask students to read rules 1–5 and complete 1–3 with *used to, would* or *the past simple.*

Answers

1 used to, would **2** the past simple **3** would

TEACHER DEVELOPMENT: PRONUNCIATION

used to and *would*

The past of the verb *to use* is *used.* This is spelt the same as *used to,* but the pronunciation is very different. *Used* is pronounced with a /z/ sound, whereas *used to* is pronounced with an /s/ sound:
He used a computer. /juːzd/
He used to work here. /juːst/
Remind students that the contracted form of *would* is 'd and that *would* is also used in the conditional tense.

6 Ask students to choose the best alternative. Point out that if they think both alternatives are correct, they should choose both.

Answers

1 used to **2** lived **3** didn't use to **4** both **5** met
6 both **7** used to

7 Ask students to complete the text with *used to, would* or the past simple form of the verbs given. Remind them that sometimes there is more than one possible answer. When both *used to* and *would* are possible, ask them to use *would*. Check their answers and ask them if Ben's job would be their idea of a dream job.

Answers

a lived **b** didn't have **c** used to work **d** would do **e** would write **f** used to love **g** jumped **h** died **i** saved

ⓘ CULTURAL INFORMATION

Ben Southall studied Automotive Systems Engineering at a university in England. After a series of badly paid jobs, he went to Africa to work for a company who ran 4×4 tours for travellers. While he was there he planned Afritrex, his African adventure (five marathons, five mountains, one year, 65,000 km in a Land Rover), to raise money for charity and to fulfil a lifetime's goal. He then saw the advert for the 'Best Job in the World' and campaigned successfully to win the job.

≫ FAST FINISHERS

Write these definitions on the board and ask students to find the words that match them in the text.

large meetings (conferences)

when something (plant or animal) penetrates into your skin and hurts you (sting)

attract people's attention to something (promote)

a soft round, transparent sea animal (jellyfish)

expensive and of very good quality (luxurious)

8a Individually, students complete the sentences and make some of them true and some false.

8b SPEAKING In pairs, students read out their sentences for their partner to say which ones are true and which are false. Walk round, monitoring students and helping them if necessary. Round up the activity by asking students to tell the class one interesting thing they found out about their partner.

Refer students to the Grammar reference on page 28 if necessary.

HOMEWORK

Assign students page 14 in their Workbook or the relevant sections of the Online Workbook.

Developing vocabulary p21

Using phrasal verbs connected with work

≫≫ FAST TRACK

If students are familiar with the target vocabulary, you could do exercise 1 as a class activity by inviting individual students to read out the phrasal verbs and the rest of the class to call out the meanings.

Phrasal verbs connected with work

1 Ask students to match the phrasal verbs in red in sentences 1–8 with their meanings a–h.

Answers

1 d **2** g **3** h **4** b **5** c **6** a **7** f **8** e

TEACHER DEVELOPMENT: LANGUAGE

Phrasal verbs

Phrasal verbs consist of a verb and one or two particles (prepositions and adverbs). The meaning of a phrasal verb is not always easy to guess from the verb or particle. Encourage students to use a dictionary carefully when they look up phrasal verbs as the same phrasal verb can have different meanings.

Phrasal verbs are often found in informal texts and spoken language. Remind students that it is not usually appropriate to use phrasal verbs in formal situations (like a letter of complaint).

There are five types of phrasal verb:

- Intransitive (with no object), e.g. *You're driving too fast – can you* **slow down***?*
- Transitive verbs whose object is either after the verb or after the particle, e.g. *I think I'll* **put** *my jacket* **on***./I think I'll* **put on** *my jacket.* If the object is a pronoun, the object must come between the verb and the particle, e.g. *I think I'll* **put** *it* **on***.* (NOT *I think I'll put on it.*)
- Transitive verbs whose object must always come between the verb and the particle, e.g. *Its high-quality designs* **sets** *the company* **apart** *from its rivals.*
- Transitive verbs whose object must come after the particle, e.g. *The baby* **takes after** *his mother. Why do you* **put up with** *the way he treats you?*
- Verbs with two objects – one after the verb, the other after the particle, e.g. *They* **put** *their success* **down** *to good planning.*

2 Ask students to complete the sentences with the correct form of the phrasal verbs in exercise 1. Check their answers.

Answers

1 Keep at **2** get ahead **3** fill in **4** turned, down **5** set up **6** keep up with **7** work on **8** took, over

3a Ask students to complete the questions with the correct preposition or adverb. Elicit answers from different students around the class.

Answers

1 on **2** up with **3** ahead **4** up

3b SPEAKING In pairs, students take it in turns to ask and answer the questions in exercise 3a. Round up the activity by asking them to tell the class anything interesting they found out about their partner.

HOMEWORK

Assign students page 15 in their Workbook or the relevant sections of the Online Workbook.

Gateway to life skills pp22–23

Evaluating jobs

To think about what you want from work, to decide what factors in a job you value the most, and to consider what different jobs can offer and decide if they are attractive to you

▶▶▶ FAST TRACK

Students could read the careers advice leaflet in exercise 2 in preparation for the class activity.

ℹ BACKGROUND INFORMATION

Unemployment among young people in many countries is high and even higher among young people without educational qualifications. They sometimes get stuck in badly paid service-sector jobs with few employee benefits and unstable hours. Teenagers may lack realistic knowledge about their preferred careers.

The first stage of career choice is self-awareness. In this lesson, students examine their values, interests and expectations when choosing a job and reflect on the skills necessary to meet their future adult career needs. This is important both in choosing the right career and also for success in applications and interviews where students will find many questions which test whether they have been through this process.

WARMER

Play *20 questions*. Ask students to think of a job without telling anybody what it is. In small groups, students take it in turns to ask questions to discover the job. The group can ask up to 20 questions to each student and the student can only answer *yes* or *no*. Then ask students to look at Key concepts on page 22. Elicit from students if they can apply these words to the jobs they thought of.

1 SPEAKING In pairs, students make a list of important factors when choosing a job. Draw students' attention to the examples given.

2 READING Ask students to read the careers advice leaflet to see if it mentions any of their ideas in exercise 1. Elicit some ideas in open class.

3 Ask students to read the text again and find the key factor in each speech bubble (1–9). Draw students' attention to the example given.

Suggested answers

2 salary, well paid
3 enjoy, salary isn't … important
4 in-service training, chance to keep on learning, interesting, new opportunities
5 working with others, team, deal with people
6 long holidays, flexibility to work from home, fewer hours
7 outdoor, connected with the environment or nature
8 travel, different countries, see the world
9 prospects, getting ahead, more responsibility, getting a promotion, challenging

4a Individually, students give each factor (1–9) a mark from 0 (you completely disagree) to 5 (you completely agree).

4b Ask students to use their marks in exercise 4a to create a 'factors diamond'. Remind them to put the most important factor at the top of the diamond and the least important factor at the bottom of the diamond. Draw their attention to the example and elicit what the person thinks is most and least important in a job.

Answer

The example shows most important = in-service training, least important = outdoors

4c SPEAKING In pairs, ask students to compare diamonds and justify their answers. Elicit from students if their diamonds are similar or different.

🅐 VOCABULARY FOCUS

The video contains some useful colloquial language about the world of work that students may not be familiar with. You could pre-teach the following with the class before watching:
passionate [adj]: feeling strongly about something
handle the workload [phr]: be able to manage the amount of work
adulthood [n]: the state of being an adult
worthy [adj]: to deserve respect or admiration
first and foremost [phr]: before everything, and above all
knowledgeable [adj]: knowing a lot of things
carpenter [n]: a person who works with wood
copywriter [n]: a person who writes the words for ads

5 LISTENING ▶ 09 Tell students they are going to watch or listen to three people talking about their jobs. Play the video or audio track and ask students to note who works with young people. See the Teacher's Resource Centre for the audioscript/videoscript for this exercise.

Answers

Deana: Yes
James: No
Tope: Yes

6 ▶ 09 Play the video or audio track again for students to decide which speaker or speakers say the prompts 1–8. Nominate different students around the class to say the answers.

Answers

1 D **2** T **3** D **4** J **5** D, J **6** D, T **7** J **8** J

✚ EXTRA ACTIVITY

Books closed. Play a few sentences of the audio or video track and do a *Dictogloss* activity:

Ask students to listen intensively and write down as many words as they can. Then, in pairs, students try to combine their versions to get the version as close to the original as possible. Play the section one more time. Then give students two minutes to write their final version. Ask pairs to combine to make groups of four to work together on the final version. Groups swap texts to peer-correct any mistakes they see (misspelled words, bad punctuation, etc.) and count them. The team with the fewest mistakes is the winner.

TEACHER DEVELOPMENT: CLASSROOM TIPS AND PLANNING

Dictogloss

Dictogloss is a dictation activity where learners listen to a short text and then reconstruct it. It is a multiple skills activity where students practise listening, writing and speaking (when they are comparing in groups). In this activity, students get a chance to work intensively on the key features of spoken discourse, e.g. contractions, intonation, fillers such as *you know, the thing is …,* as well as words such as *this, that, here, there* which refer backwards or forwards and are very much a context-dependent feature of talk.

LIFE TASK

Tell students they are going to try and find the right job for themselves. Ask them to follow the plan:

- *Step 1*
  Individually, students choose a job that they think they might possibly be interested in doing in the future. Ask them to research the job and find out which factors from the leaflet in exercise 2 it involves.

- *Step 2*
  Ask students to write up a fact file about the job. Encourage them to use their chosen job in the title, e.g. *So you want to be a (software engineer)?* and then write a list based on their research: *This job is good for people who …*

- *Step 3*
  Ask students to share job fact files with other members of the class. Finally, elicit from students which jobs they can find that fit with their 'factors diamond' in exercise 4b.

Listening p24

Listening for general and specific information and inferring

WARMER

Play the game *First to five.* Divide the class into groups of three or four. Explain that you are going to give them a category. The first group to write down five words from that category and shout *Stop!* gets a point for their team if they are all correct. Repeat with five or six categories: *work conditions, stages in a job, professions, phrasal verbs connected with work, important factors when choosing a job,* etc.

1 **SPEAKING** In pairs, students read the definition of a gap year and decide if it sounds interesting. Elicit answers from students and ask them to justify their answers.

Example answers

I think a gap year sounds good because you can have a break from studying before you go to university.

I think a gap year is a bad thing because many people don't do anything useful or interesting, and they get out of the habit of studying.

ℹ CULTURAL INFORMATION

In the UK, almost a quarter of students take a gap year. Reasons for doing a gap year could be to see the world, earn money, have a break from studying, learn to be more independent and to get work experience. Most young people fund their gap year through a variety of sources: paid work, savings and sponsorship, as well as parental support. Popular choices are travelling, humanitarian work or volunteer work and staying in a country to learn the language. Universities see well organised gap years as positive because students can become more mature and independent.

✔ **EXAM SUCCESS** Ask students how they prepare for listening tasks. Ask them to read the advice in the Exam success box and then turn to page 144 for more information on how to do this type of activity (Listening: Matching people and statements).

TEACHER DEVELOPMENT: STUDENT TRAINING

Inference in listening

Drawing inference is a key strategy for listening. Good listeners use their prior knowledge about a topic and the key words in the questions to make predictions about what the text is going to be about. One of the most important strategies in listening is to listen for the main ideas – simply understanding the words is not enough. Students should make sure that their inferences are based on the text rather than their own feelings or experience. Always ask students to check to see if they can actually identify the parts of the text that led them to their conclusion to check their comprehension.

2 **LISTENING** 10 Tell students they are going to listen to five young people talking about their gap year experiences. Play the track for students to match each statement (A–F) with the correct speaker (1–5). Remind students that they can use the letters only once and that there is one extra letter. See p172 for the audioscript for this exercise.

Answers

Speaker 1: C   Speaker 2: B   Speaker 3: F
Speaker 4: E   Speaker 5: A

+ EXTRA ACTIVITY

Write these comprehension questions on the board or dictate them to students. Play the track again and ask students to match each statement with the correct speaker (1–5).
Which student(s) ...
1 *planned their gap year for a long time?*
2 *didn't make any plans?*
3 *worked first and then travelled?*
4 *enjoyed being with or seeing unusual animals?*
5 *say the gap year has helped them to be more positive when things go wrong?*

Answers
1 Speaker 5   **2** Speakers 1, 2   **3** Speakers 1, 2, 4
4 Speakers 4, 5   **5** Speaker 3

---

3 **SPEAKING** **What about you?** Ask students to consider and discuss their own opinions of the different students' gap years and then to describe their ideal gap year.

+ EXTRA ACTIVITY

Students research their perfect gap year and write an advertisement with details about the cost, accommodation, activities and benefits. Students could swap adverts and decide which gap year looks the most interesting.

HOMEWORK

Assign students page 15 in their Workbook or the relevant sections of the Online Workbook.

Grammar in context pp24–25 Ⓖ

Talking about past events and situations using the past perfect simple and the past perfect continuous

---

≫≫ FAST TRACK

You could ask students to do exercises 1 and 2 at home. Check their answers and start the next lesson on exercise 3.

Test before you teach

Tell students a short personalised story using the past perfect simple (see example below). Tell the story twice – the first time students just listen and the second time they note down key points. Ask them to retell the story in pairs. Elicit the story from students around the class and check how familiar they are with these tenses.

Example story
I went to the theatre last night. I had bought tickets months ago because I had read some very good reviews. I had arranged to meet my friend in the café in front of the theatre before the show, but she didn't arrive. By the time I left the café, I had already drunk five coffees and had waited for over an hour. When I walked out the café, I saw my friend standing on the other side of the street. She had already picked up the tickets and was angry because she had waited for a long time. She hadn't got my message about meeting in the café.

Monitor to see how comfortable students are with using the past perfect simple. If they seem to be familiar with its use, move through the Grammar guide exercises quickly in open class.

TEACHER DEVELOPMENT: CLASSROOM TIPS AND PLANNING

Personalised presentations

Personalised presentations by the teacher provide a model of good, natural language for the students and can be highly memorable. Listening to the teacher talking about real events and issues can be more motivating than listening or reading about people, places or events in which they have no personal interest. Remember that it need not be a monologue – you can tell students to interrupt and ask questions as you go.

Past perfect simple

1a Ask students to look at the sentence and decide which action happened first.

Answer
a I finished school.

1b Ask students to choose the correct alternative.

Answer
before

1c Elicit from students how we form the past perfect simple. Check students are also familiar with the negative and question form. Elicit some examples from around the class.

Answer
subject + *had/hadn't* + past participle

had/'d

Point out to students the contracted form of *had* (*'d*) and practise the pronunciation by drilling the sentence from exercise 1a and further examples using the contracted form of *had*. It is difficult for students to hear short forms and they must listen carefully for *'d/hadn't* and pay attention to the context to be sure of the tense being used.

2 Ask students to complete the sentences with the past simple or past perfect simple form of the verbs given.

Answers

1 had written **2** had started **3** stepped **4** hadn't spoken **5** blew **6** had seen **7** had eaten

3 Ask students to complete the sentences in a logical way using a verb in the past perfect simple and the words in bold. Students compare their answers in pairs before you elicit possible sentence endings in open class.

Suggested answers

1 someone had locked it.
2 she had answered the questions well.
3 I hadn't done my homework.
4 she had missed the bus.
5 he had dropped his ice cream.
6 someone had seen a shark.
7 he had eaten too much pizza.
8 they hadn't taken an umbrella with them.

Past perfect continuous

4a Ask students to look at the sentences and say if they contain verbs in the past perfect simple or the past perfect continuous. Check their answers.

Answers

1 past perfect continuous **2** past perfect simple
3 past perfect continuous **4** past perfect simple

4b Ask students to decide which sentences give more importance to the duration of the action and which give more importance to the completion of the action.

Answers

Sentences 1 and 3 with the past perfect continuous give more importance to duration. Sentences 2 and 4 with the past perfect simple give more importance to the completion of the action.

4c Elicit from students how we form the past perfect continuous.

Answer

had + been + verb -ing

5 Ask students to choose the best alternative in each sentence.

Answers

1 been waiting **2** had **3** eaten **4** written **5** lost
6 been crying **7** been talking

6 Ask students to write sentences in the past perfect simple or past perfect continuous to explain the situations. Draw students' attention to the example sentence. Check their answers.

Answers

2 He hadn't studied hard enough.
3 She'd been working all morning in the garden.
4 She'd been studying for hours.
5 He'd read it twice before.
6 He hadn't paid attention to his teacher all year.

7a Students read the story of Yu Youzhen to find out what she did and why. Ask students to ignore the gaps for the moment and read to get a gist of the text. Nominate a student to say the answer.

Answer

She kept working even though she was a millionaire; to set a good example to her children.

7b Ask students to read the text again and think of the word that best fits each gap. Remind students to use only one word in each gap.

Answers

a been **b** had **c** for **d** up **e** didn't **f** made
g were **h** doing **i** earned **j** have

7c SPEAKING In pairs, students discuss what they think of the story of Yu Youzhen. Elicit opinions from different students around the class.

Refer students to the Grammar reference on page 28 if necessary.

HOMEWORK

Assign students page 16 in their Workbook or the relevant sections of the Online Workbook.

Developing speaking p26

Negotiating and collaborating in conversations

⟫⟫ FAST TRACK

You could ask students to note down ideas for exercise 1 at home in preparation for the speaking activity. Students can then compare their ideas in pairs at the beginning of the class.

WARMER

Play the game *First to five*. Divide the class into groups of three or four. Explain that you are going to give them a category. The first group to write down five words from that category and shout *Stop!* gets a point for their team if they are all correct. Repeat with five or six categories, e.g. *verbs that go with 'do', verbs that go with 'make', university subjects, words related to studying or life at university, words related to work*, etc.

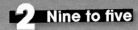

1 SPEAKING In pairs, students look at the jobs in the diagram and discuss if they would like to do any of these jobs. Ask them to give reasons why or why not. Elicit answers from different students around the class.

TEACHER DEVELOPMENT: STUDENT TRAINING

Collaborative tasks in oral exams

In many official speaking examinations, there is a collaborative task where the examiner gives the students material to discuss with another candidate and make a decision. Students may be given a group of pictures and asked to do two related but different tasks – first to discuss the material and then decide which one or two pictures they would choose for some particular purpose. In collaborative tasks, it is typical for the examiner to take no active part in the discussion.

They may have only three minutes to work on both tasks in this part of the exam, so students need a lot of practice in responding well within a time limit. Students should discuss as many of the pictures as they can before moving onto the second part of the task and remember to leave at least one minute for the second part of the task, where they should work towards a conclusion. Remind students that they will achieve points for working well together. You will need to focus on students in your class who talk too much or too little as this will cause them to lose points in the collaborative task.

2 LISTENING ▶ 11 Tell students they are going to listen to two students doing a speaking task. Give them time to read the questions and then play the track. See p172 for the audioscript for this exercise.

Answers

1 how dangerous the different jobs are
2 decide which of the jobs you think is the most dangerous
3 firefighter
4 Students' own answers

3 ▶ 11 Play the track again for students to listen and answer the questions. Elicit answers from different students around the class.

Answers

1 yes **2** yes **3** no **4** yes **5** no

✔ EXAM SUCCESS Ask students to turn to page 144 for more information on how to do this type of activity (Speaking: Negotiating and collaborating).

4 Ask students to look at the expressions in the Speaking bank and write titles for the three different categories.

Suggested answers

1 Asking your partner's opinion **2** Agreeing
3 Disagreeing

5 SPEAKING In pairs, ask students to practise doing the task in exercise 2 giving their own opinions. Note down errors and good use of language you can talk about when you give feedback.

✛✛ EXTRA ACTIVITY

Ask students to change partners and repeat the activity. Tell students the person who 'wins' the task is the one who makes their partner talk the most. Divide the class into groups of three where one student is the secretary who monitors turn-taking language and equal speaking time. Tell secretaries to stop the pairs after three minutes and give feedback.

PRACTICE MAKES PERFECT

6 SPEAKING Read out the instructions. In pairs, students do the task. Remind them to use expressions from the Speaking bank. After two minutes ask them to move towards an agreement. Stop them at the end of three minutes and say *What did you decide?* Ask for feedback.

For students who are less confident, photocopy the model dialogue below, and either read it aloud yourself, or with a strong student. Then instruct students to read aloud in pairs, alternating between roles A and B. Then ask them to read it again, changing the underlined information so that it is true for them.

✂

Model dialogue

A: OK. How do you think being <u>an architect</u> improves society?

B: Well, I think <u>they can improve society quite a lot. Architects create the environment we live in. Many architects are involved in sustainable designs that help the environment.</u>

A: Maybe, but <u>I don't think they improve society as much as journalists, for example. I think journalists improve society by telling us news that is vital to the public. They have to be honest and courageous.</u>

B: I see what you mean, but <u>a lot of journalists are not exactly neutral</u>. What about <u>scientists</u>, then. How do you think they improve society?

A: Well, they <u>certainly improve our quality of life.</u>

B: <u>Yes, I agree. Think of all the things scientists have invented and discovered.</u>

A: And what about <u>software engineers? I think they do a lot to improve how we communicate with each other.</u> Do you agree?

B: Yes, I see what you mean. What about <u>artists</u>, though? <u>They help us reflect on where we are and where we are going.</u>

Teacher: Now you have a minute to decide which job you think helps society the most.

A: I think <u>scientists</u> help society the most. <u>They research and innovate to improve society.</u>

B: I agree up to a point, but I think <u>technology improves society more than science so I think software engineers help society the most.</u>

A: That's true. <u>And software engineers can create new technology that can change our world.</u>

B: OK, so why don't we choose the <u>software engineer</u>?

A: <u>OK, let's do that.</u>

HOMEWORK

Assign students page 17 in their Workbook or the relevant sections of the Online Workbook.

Developing writing p27

Writing an opinion essay

>>> **FAST TRACK**

You could ask students to do exercise 1 at home in preparation for the writing activity.

WARMER

Write two true sentences and one false one about part-time jobs you had when you were a teenager on the board, e.g. *I picked cherries when I was a teenager. I used to deliver newspapers on Saturday mornings. I worked in a sweet shop at the weekends.* Ask students to guess which one is the false sentence by asking you questions about the jobs.

1 **SPEAKING** In pairs, students read the writing task and discuss whether they agree or disagree with the statement and explain why. Tell students to write notes about their ideas.

2 In pairs, students complete the paragraph plan with their ideas.

TEACHER DEVELOPMENT: STUDENT TRAINING

Paragraph organisation

Writing well-constructed paragraphs is the key to getting good marks in writing exams. Students need help to develop strategies for combining various ideas into well-formed sentences which then combine to make concise paragraphs. A well-constructed paragraph has a topic sentence, supporting details and a concluding sentence and includes only relevant information.

3 Students read the essay, ignoring the gaps, and decide if it follows the paragraph plan in exercise 2. Elicit from them if the writer's opinion is similar to theirs.

Answer

Yes, it follows the paragraph plan in exercise 2.

4 Students complete the essay with the phrases given and check answers in pairs before checking in open class.

Answers

a As far as I'm concerned **b** To begin with
c Furthermore **d** On the other hand
e I agree with this **f** To sum up

5 Students write the words and expressions from exercise 4 in the correct place in the Writing bank.

Answers

Expressing opinions

As far as I'm concerned   I agree with this

Adding opinions

To begin with   Furthermore

Contrasting opinions

On the other hand

Concluding

To sum up

PRACTICE MAKES PERFECT

6a In pairs, students look at the task and write notes about their ideas. Ask them to complete a paragraph plan like the one in exercise 2 for this topic.

6b Students use their plan from exercise 6a as well as words and expressions from the Writing bank to write their essay. Remind them to follow the advice in the Writing bank on page 151. For students who are less confident, photocopy the model text below for extra support during the writing task.

✂ -

Model text

The world of work is constantly changing due to new technology and the global economy. Personally, I think school does prepare you for the future job market, although there could be some improvements.

Firstly, school teaches you how to read and write, and about science and maths. These are essential skills that everyone needs for the future. Secondly, school teaches you English and ICT, invaluable skills that can help you get a well-paid job. Furthermore, school also teaches you to communicate, work in a team and solve problems. All these skills are important in the world of work.

On the other hand, I think there should be a stronger connection between school subjects and the job market. Teachers should make it clear how the things we learn in class relate to the world of work. What is more, we need to learn to have initiative and be adaptable.

In conclusion, I believe school prepares us for the world of work if we take advantage of all the opportunities that are offered. Nevertheless, I think we should make the connection between school and work much stronger and study more about how to find and keep a job.

- -

HOMEWORK

Assign students page 18 in their Workbook or the relevant sections of the Online Workbook.

Language checkpoint: Unit 2

>>> FAST TRACK

The extra support provided in the Grammar and Vocabulary reference sections makes the Grammar and Vocabulary revision sections ideal for setting as homework. You could get students to complete the whole revision page or just certain exercises for homework.

Grammar revision p29

Past simple and past continuous

1 Students put the verbs in the correct form of the past simple or past continuous.

Answers

a got b looked c was shining d was looking
e saw f were playing

Past habits

2 Students choose the correct alternative. Ask students to say in which sentence both alternatives are correct.

Answers

1 used to 2 studied 3 usually 4 had 5 use
6 both correct 7 didn't use to

Past perfect simple and past perfect continuous

3 Students decide if the underlined part of the sentence is correct and if not, rewrite it.

Answers

1 had been waiting 2 had been painting
3 had written 4 correct 5 had eaten
6 correct 7 had finished

Vocabulary revision p29

WORK CONDITIONS AND RESPONSIBILITIES

1 Students complete the sentences with the words in the box.

Answers

1 for 2 dealing 3 employee 4 earn 5 skilled
6 shift 7 overtime 8 qualifications

PHRASAL VERBS CONNECTED WITH WORK

2 Students match the two parts of the phrasal verbs and then their definitions.

Answers

1 set up = start a new business, office, etc.
2 get ahead = progress faster than other people
3 turn down = not accept an offer, request or application
4 work on = spend time working or improving something
5 fill in = add information on a document
6 take over = take control of something

WORKING LIFE

3 Students complete the text with the correct words.

Answers

a look b applied c redundant d unemployed
e fired/sacked/dismissed f offered

HOMEWORK

Assign students page 19 in their Workbook or the relevant sections of the Online Workbook.

Reading p30

> ➤ **TIP FOR READING EXAMS**
>
> Ask students to read the tip on doing matching activities in exams. Elicit other things students should remember to do and ask them to turn to Exam success on page 144 for more ideas.

1 Ask students to read the first paragraph of the text and discuss what the Erasmus programme is and the advantages of doing an Erasmus exchange.

Example answers

On an Erasmus exchange, students spend at least three months studying in a university in one of the 30 countries involved in the programme.

Some of the advantages of this exchange could include: it looks good on your CV, you learn life skills, you make an international network of friends and have fun, you discover a different culture, and you learn another language.

2 Students read the text and answer the questions.

Answers

1 Students' own answers
2 Nelly Samuels – modern history, John Vaughan – business, Teresa Lopez – media studies, Keith Johnson – politics

3 Ask students to decide which person (A–D) matches each situation (1–8). Remind students that the people may be chosen more than once. Elicit reasons and sentences which helped students decide on their answers.

Answers

1 B (It was so frustrating at first … spoke the language worse than a five year old … after a month or two I'd made sufficient progress …)
2 C (I have invitations from people in about 20 different countries round the world to go and visit …)
3 A (Before, I found it difficult to make new friends …)
4 C (That was something that I'd always wanted to do …)
5 D (… only on the condition that I can do at least part of it abroad.)
6 A (… I immediately fell in love with the style of the lessons we received.)
7 D (The one thing that affected me … was realising … I didn't consider myself British. I was now European.)
8 C (In terms of studying, it took me a bit longer to get used to a different style of teaching … But in the end I came to prefer UK style education!)

4 SPEAKING **What about *you*?** In pairs, students discuss if they would like to study in another country and say why or why not. Ask different students to share their ideas with the class.

Writing p31

> ➤ **TIP FOR WRITING EXAMS**
>
> Students read the tip for doing transactional tasks. Ask them to turn to Exam success on page 144 for more ideas.

5 Ask students to read the email from a friend and underline the information that they should include in their reply to the email.

Answers

Students should answer these questions in their reply:
How are you?
What do you think (about the welcome home party)?
Could you come and give me a hand getting things ready on Thursday afternoon?
Apart from food, is there anything that you can think of that would make the party really special?

6 Students make a plan of their reply to the email. Ask them to decide how many paragraphs to use and what to include in each one.

Suggested answer

Paragraph 1: greeting, say how I am, mention pizza place
Paragraph 2: the party is a good idea; yes, I can help
Paragraph 3: ideas for party
Paragraph 4: suggest a time to meet on Thursday; say goodbye

7 Ask students to write their reply and include all the necessary information. They should write 120–150 words. For students who are less confident, photocopy the model text below for extra support during the writing task.

✂ -

Model text

Hi JT!

I'm fine. How are you? I enjoyed the pizza place, too. We should definitely go again soon.

Yes, I remember that Rachel has been away on a German exchange. That's great that she's coming back on Wednesday. A special welcome home party for her would be great and I'd love to come over and give you a hand.

I think it would be really special for Rachel if we invited Jamie and Gillian. They are really good friends of Rachel and it'd be a big surprise for her. Do you want me to contact them? I've got their email addresses. We could also make her a cake. Does she like chocolate cake?

I can come over at 3 pm on Thursday to help you with the food and the decorations. Does that sound OK?

See you soon
Celia

- -

Listening p31

8 SPEAKING In pairs, students read the extract from a newspaper article and decide if they think 'helicopter' parents or 'lawnmower' parents are a good or bad thing and say why. Elicit opinions from different students around the class.

Example answers

'Helicopter' parents and 'lawnmower' parents are good because they support their children.

I think 'helicopter' and especially 'lawnmower' parents are a bad thing because children don't learn to become independent and take care of themselves.

9 LISTENING 12 Play the track for students to listen to five people talking about helicopter and lawnmower parents. Students decide which opinion (A–F) each speaker expresses. Remind students that they must only use each letter once and that there is one extra letter. Elicit from students the section of each text which helped them decide on their answers. See pp 172–173 for the audioscript for this exercise.

Answers

Speaker 1: C (It's true, it isn't always easy being an adult, but I need to try doing things my own way, even when it's the wrong way.)

Speaker 2: F (Parents have started doing everything for their children and now children aren't doing anything for themselves. It didn't use to be like that.)

Speaker 3: B (I like to make life easy for my kids. That's only natural, isn't it?)

Speaker 4: A (To do this job, you need to be independent, responsible and want to get ahead. Having your mum with you at a job interview doesn't really show that you have those qualities. And that was it, I said goodbye to them and closed the door!)

Speaker 5: D (I've never really tried influencing our daughter's decisions … I think everyone needs to live their own life and make their own mistakes.)

10 SPEAKING **What about *you*?** In pairs or small groups, students discuss the ways they show their parents that they are responsible and ready for independence.

Speaking p31

11 Ask students to look at the task and diagram on page 158 and think about what they are going to say.

12 SPEAKING In pairs, students do the task. For students who are less confident, photocopy the model dialogue below for extra support during the speaking task.

Model dialogue

1

A: OK. What do you think the advantages and disadvantages of doing manual work are?

B: Well, I think there are more disadvantages than advantages. It can make you strong and it's not very stressful, but often manual work is very repetitive and that can be bad for your body.

A: Yes, I agree. It's not very well paid.

B: What about working outdoors? You can get a lot of fresh air and it's healthier than sitting in an office.

A: True. But you have to be outside in the winter when it's cold. If you do skilled work, you are better paid and you usually have good work conditions.

B: I can see what you mean. So what's better – working alone or working in a team?

A: In my opinion, working in a team has a lot of advantages. You can exchange ideas and learn from other people.

B: And it's more fun.

A: Yes, but working alone has advantages, too. You can concentrate more when you are on your own.

2

A: I think being outdoors is important to me. I wouldn't like to be inside. I love nature.

B: I agree up to a point, but I think doing a skilled job is more important to me. I would like to have a well-paid job working as an engineer or an architect.

A: You have to remember that money isn't everything. It's more important to me to have a job I enjoy and I don't want any stress.

B: Well, I think if I worked in a team, it would be fun and I would like my job.

A: OK, so we agree on some things that are important for choosing a job, but we don't want the same job!

HOMEWORK

Assign students pages 20–21 in their Workbook or the relevant sections of the Online Workbook.

---

1 Ask students to mark from 1–4 how well they feel they can do each thing in English.

2 Ask students to look at their marks and decide what they need to do to improve. Elicit ideas from students around the class.

TEACHER DEVELOPMENT: STUDENT TRAINING

'*Can Do*' Progress check

Each unit objective has a corresponding descriptor, which describes what the student can do in English. The descriptors are useful in helping students decide if they have or have not achieved the unit's objectives and in helping teachers to plan instruction.

3 On the move

KEY LEARNING OUTCOMES

CEF

Students will be able to:

- talk about the future using different tenses including the future continuous, future perfect simple and future perfect continuous
- talk about transport and travel
- use prefixes to change the meaning of words
- compare and contrast photos
- write stories using a variety of tenses, structures and linkers

UNIT OVERVIEW

Vocabulary
Words connected with transport and travel
journey, travel, trip, voyage

Reading
A journey into the future
CRITICAL THINKING Evaluating future transport projects

Grammar in context
Future forms

Developing vocabulary
Prefixes
PRONUNCIATION Word stress

Life skills
The world around you: Investigating food miles

Listening
The future of drones

Grammar in context
Future continuous, future perfect simple and future perfect continuous

Developing speaking
Talking about photos – 1

Developing writing
A story

Exam success
Reading: Missing sentences activities
Writing: Stories

DIGITAL OVERVIEW

Presentation Kit

- ► **Flipped classroom video Unit 3:** Future continuous, future perfect simple and future perfect continuous
- ► **Life skills video Unit 3:** Investigating food miles
- ► **Interactive versions of Student's Book activities**
- ► **Integrated audio and answer key for all activities**
- ► **Workbook pages with answer key**

Teacher's Resource Centre

- ► **Flipped classroom video Unit 3:** Future continuous, future perfect simple and future perfect continuous
- ► **Life skills video Unit 3:** Investigating food miles
- ► **Grammar communication activity Unit 3:** In the future
- ► **Worksheets for this unit, including:**
  - Grammar Practice worksheet Unit 3
  - Flipped classroom video worksheet Unit 3: Future continuous, future perfect simple and future perfect continuous
  - Literature worksheet Units 3 and 4
  - Culture worksheet Unit 3
  - Life skills video worksheet Unit 3
  - Everyday English worksheet Unit 3

Student's App
Gateway 2nd Edition wordlist for the award-winning Sounds App (available for download)

✓ TESTING AND ASSESSMENT

Resources for exam preparation and measuring student progress

- ► Test Generator Units 1–3
- ► Printable tests Unit 3/Review
- ► Gateway to exams Units 3 and 4 (end of Unit 4)

Vocabulary p32

Talking about transport and travel

>>> FAST TRACK

You could ask students to do exercises 2 and 4 at home in preparation for the speaking activities. They can look up any words they are not sure about in their dictionaries or the Macmillan Online Dictionary.

WARMER

Discuss the meaning of the unit title *On the move* (an adjective or adverb to describe something mobile or while moving, e.g. *My smartphone helps keep me informed while I'm on the move./He was constantly on the move.*). Elicit from students what it means to have a job where you are always on the move (you travel a lot). Ask students what they think the unit is going to be about (transport and travel).

Write four types of transport on the board – three that have something in common and an 'odd one out'. Ask students to say which word they think is the odd one out and why, e.g.

train, underground, bus, car (car – because the others are all forms of public transport)

bus, coach, lorry, tram (tram – it goes by rail not road)

plane, helicopter, jet, rocket (rocket – it's the only one that travels in space)

journey, get in, board, take off (journey – all the others are verbs)

Brainstorm more words connected to transport and travel. Ask students to open their books on page 32 to see if they have thought of similar words.

Words connected with transport and travel

1 SPEAKING In pairs, students look at and discuss the photos using as many of the words in the box as they can, e.g. *rocket: spacecraft, take off; high-speed train: get on/off, passenger, platform; traffic jam: motorway.* Elicit some ideas from students around the class.

2 Ask students to match words in exercise 1 with the definitions. Check their answers.

Answers

1 crew **2** traffic jam **3** the Underground/subway/tube **4** spacecraft **5** take off **6** land **7** gate

>>> FAST FINISHERS

Ask students to categorise the words in exercise 1 into vocabulary connected with space, road vehicles and trains. Students can use the same word more than once if necessary.

3 LISTENING ▶ 13 Play the track for students to listen to six short travel announcements. Ask students to choose the correct alternative.

Elicit answers from students around the class. See p173 for the audioscript for this exercise.

Answers

1 stand away from the edge of the platform **2** shouldn't **3** shouldn't **4** a, West **5** need **6** bags

journey, travel, trip, voyage

4 Ask students to choose the correct alternative in each sentence, using the dictionary entries to help them.

Answers

1 trip **2** voyage **3** Travel **4** journey **5** trips **6** voyages **7** travel **8** trip

5 SPEAKING In pairs, students take it in turns to ask and answer the questions. In a less confident class, students can make notes on their answers before doing this as a speaking activity. Elicit answers from students around the class.

✚ EXTRA ACTIVITY

Play *Just a minute*. In pairs, students take turns to talk about one of the photos for one minute without any repetition, deviation or hesitation. If a student repeats a word, goes off the topic or hesitates, they are challenged by their partner. It is, of course, very difficult to do this, but adding a fun, challenging element to this speaking activity can be motivating for students and can help them feel more confident in speaking exams.

HOMEWORK

Assign students page 22 in their Workbook or the relevant sections of the Online Workbook.

Reading p33

Reading for general information and inferring

>>> FAST TRACK

You could ask students to read the text and do exercise 2 at home in preparation for in-class activities.

WARMER

Students write two true and two false sentences about themselves using these words from the previous lesson: *trip, travel, voyage, journey*, e.g. *I have recently been on a trip to London. I travel to Paris monthly. I have never been on a voyage around the world. The journey to my grandparents' house takes more than five hours.* In pairs, students take it in turns to read their sentences to each other. Their partner must guess which sentences are true and which are false.

1 SPEAKING In pairs, students discuss what they think the photo in the article shows. Elicit ideas from students in open class.

2 Ask students to read the article quickly and answer the questions. Set a time limit of three minutes and remind students that it is not necessary for them to understand everything at this stage, they just need to answer the questions.

Answers

1 Hyperloop

2 electric car, sports car, high-speed train, planes, supersonic air travel, self-driving car, flying cars, drones, elevator

3 Ask students to read the text more carefully and complete the gaps with sentences a–f. Elicit from students the key sentences, before or after the gap, which helped them decide on their answers.

Answers

1 c (Our world is on the move.)

2 b (With his Tesla Motors company he has managed ...)

3 f (per capsule ... With no friction ...)

4 a (In the last 50 years, there has been a sharp increase in the number ...)

5 e (flying cars in our skies ... Soon, when you look up, you'll see hundreds ...)

6 d (Maybe that's one of the reasons why Japanese engineers … using a massive elevator …)

✓ EXAM SUCCESS Ask students to read about missing sentences activities in Exam success. Tell them to turn to page 144 for more tips on how to do this kind of activity (Reading: Missing sentences activities).

TEACHER DEVELOPMENT: STUDENT TRAINING

Missing sentences activities

Completing the gaps in a reading text with missing sentences is a common type of reading question in official examinations. This type of task, where students insert missing sentences into a reading text, tests students' understanding of the whole text and their ability to infer information. One of the most important strategies in reading is drawing inference – really getting at the meaning of things, how significant some information is and how one event influences another. Completing this type of activity requires critical-thinking skills and allows teachers to gauge how well students are able to use semantic and syntax cues to construct meaning from the text, as well as their knowledge of vocabulary and grammar. After students have completed the activity, spend time discussing specific context clues that are found around the gap that helped them choose a particular response.

ⓘ BACKGROUND INFORMATION

The Hyperloop

The entrepreneur, Elon Musk, has described the Hyperloop as a 'cross between a Concorde and a railgun (projectile launcher) and an air hockey table'. Some critics of the Hyperloop have said that it could be an unpleasant and frightening experience. Passengers would ride in a narrow, windowless capsule, inside a sealed steel tunnel and be subjected to significant acceleration forces, high noise levels and vibration. Moreover, the technological and economic feasibility of the Hyperloop is unproven and a subject of significant debate.

4 **CRITICAL THINKING** Individually, students note down ideas on how useful they think the future transport projects mentioned in the text are before comparing their ideas with the rest of the class.

Example answers

I think the Hyperloop is very useful as it is much faster than ordinary transport and more ecological.

I think the self-driving car is useful because while you are on the move you can do anything you want.

I think drones are very useful because they can do dangerous work more cheaply and safely than humans can.

I think the lunar space elevator is a fascinating idea, but it's not very useful.

TEACHER DEVELOPMENT: STUDENT TRAINING

Critical thinking

Bloom's Taxonomy offers a wide variety of questions that teachers can use in the classroom to promote critical thinking. We can encourage students to reflect more deeply and develop and strengthen their critical thinking skills if we use not just *What? Where?* and *When?* questions but also *Why? How? How do you know?* and *What if ...?*

Bloom's Taxonomy is named after Benjamin Bloom who in 1956 developed the classification of questions according to six levels of higher-order thinking. Bloom's Taxonomy was revised in 2001. A key teaching skill is being able to ask questions that generate more questions. Below are some forms that good questions take:

- Questions that focus attention: *Do you notice?* or *Have you seen?*, etc.

- Questions that invite assessment: *How many? How often?*, etc.

- Questions that ask for clarification: *Can you give me an example? What do you mean by?*, etc.

- Questions that invite inquiry: *What do we need to know? How can we find out? What would happen if?*

- Questions that ask for reasons: *How did you know? Why do you say that?*

5 Encourage students to guess the meaning of the underlined words in the text. Allow them to use a dictionary to check their answers.

Answers

boldest = riskiest

capsule = the part of a space vehicle in which people travel

currently = at the present time

sharp increase = sudden rise

self-driving = an autonomous or driverless vehicle

norm = something that is normal or expected

drawing up = to prepare or write something

6 SPEAKING What about *you*? In pairs or small groups, students take it in turns to ask and answer the questions and share their thoughts. Elicit some answers from different pairs/groups.

✚ EXTRA ACTIVITY

Divide the class into small groups. Ask students to choose one of the types of future transport and research more information about it to present in class.

HOMEWORK

Assign students page 23 in their Workbook or the relevant sections of the Online Workbook.

Grammar in context pp34–35

Talking about the future using a variety of tenses

⨠⨠⨠ FAST TRACK

You could ask students to do exercise 1 at home. Then they start the next class with the speaking activity in exercise 2.

Test before you teach

Write these sentences on the board and ask students to choose the correct alternative:

1 *That's the phone!* **I'll / I'm going to** *answer it!*
2 *Look at those clouds. It* **will / is going to** *rain.*
3 *What are your plans? What* **are you doing / will you do** *this Friday?*
4 *I think that the world* **will be / is going to be** *more dangerous in the future.*

Monitor to see how comfortable students are with these future forms. If they seem to be familiar with their use, move through the Grammar guide exercises quickly in open class.

1a Ask students to decide what tense the verb in blue is in each sentence.

Answers

a *be going to*   **b** present continuous   **c** *be going to*
d *will*   **e** present simple

1b Ask students to complete the rules with *will*, *be going to*, *the present simple* or *the present continuous*.

Answers

1 *be going to*   **2** *be going to*   **3** *will*   **4** the present continuous   **5** the present simple

1c Ask students to look at sentences a–c and complete the rules 1–3 with *will* or *the present simple*.

Answers

1 *will*   **2** *will*   **3** the present simple

TEACHER DEVELOPMENT: LANGUAGE

Future forms

The present simple is used to talk about a future event that is part of a timetable or routine, e.g. *My class starts in five minutes.* This is because a timetable is true in the future, but it is also true in the present. These sentences usually contain future words or the future is understood from the context. There are only a few verbs that are used in this way, e.g. *be, open, close, begin, start, end, finish, arrive, come, leave, return.*

The present continuous is used to talk about future arrangements or plans that have been confirmed, e.g. *I'm meeting Sarah at 10 pm.* Since these constructions can imply present as well as future meaning, a time adverbial is usually employed to help specify the meaning. English teachers often call the present continuous future form the 'diary form' because you can use it for anything written in your diary or agenda. Fixed arrangements can also use *be going to*, but the present continuous is more common.

Be going to is generally found in informal spoken English, e.g. *We're going to eat lunch now.* These constructions indicate the future as a fulfilment of the present. The implication is that the factor leading to the future event is already present. *Be going to* constructions often imply an intention and thus an expectation that the intention will be carried out.

Will is generally used for predictions about the future, e.g. *It will be dark when we get there.* A less common alternative to *will* is *shall* (negative form: *shan't*). *Will* can be used with subjects of all three persons, whereas *shall* is only used with first person pronouns.

TEACHER DEVELOPMENT: PRONUNCIATION

will

Remind students that we usually use the contracted form *'ll* in spoken English. *'ll* is pronounced with the 'dark' /l/ sound, i.e. it sounds like the *ull* in *full* rather than the *l* in *light*. Drill the contracted form of *will* with this sentence: *I'll close the window now.*

2 SPEAKING In pairs, students look at the sentences and explain why *will* is used in each sentence. Elicit answers from different students around the class.

Answers

1 future fact   **2** sudden decision   **3** prediction based on opinion   **4** prediction based on expectations   **5** future fact   **6** sudden decision

3 Ask students to decide if the underlined part of the sentence is correct. If it is not correct, they rewrite it. Check their answers.

Answers

1 starts **2** 'll **3** 's going to rain **4** correct
5 's taking **6** are going **7** are, doing **8** 'm going to
eat **9** correct **10** 's going to drop

4a Ask students to complete the sentences with an
appropriate future form of the verbs given.

Answers

1 will land, am **2** will be/is **3** are meeting
4 are, going to do **5** will snow **6** 's going to
have **7** 'll open **8** get, 'll switch **9** 'm seeing
10 's going to rain

4b **SPEAKING** In pairs, ask students to compare their answers in
exercise 4a and be ready to explain their choices. Draw
attention to the mini-dialogue and remind students that
you expect them to discuss this in English. Elicit answers
from different students around the class.

5 Ask students to read the text and choose the correct
alternative. In pairs, students compare their answers
before you check in open class.

Answers

a have **b** are going to become **c** are
d will be **e** off **f** will be **g** won't **h** are talking

6a Ask students to complete the *Yes/No* questions about
the future with their own ideas. Draw students' attention
to the example sentence.

6b Students try to predict their partner's answers to each of
their questions, and write down their predictions.

6c **SPEAKING** Ask students to take it in turns to ask their
partner their questions. Ask them to tell each other how
many predictions they got right.

Refer students to the Grammar reference on page 42 if
necessary.

HOMEWORK

Assign students page 24 in their Workbook or the
relevant sections of the Online Workbook.

Developing vocabulary p35

Using prefixes

>>> FAST TRACK

You could ask students to do exercise 1 at home and
then check the answers in open class at the beginning of
the lesson.

Prefixes

1 In pairs, students find the prefix in each word and think
about what meaning the prefix gives to the word. Ask
them to match the prefixes with the meanings 1–10.

Answers

1 mis **2** post **3** under **4** over **5** inter **6** dis
7 re **8** co **9** sub **10** super

TEACHER DEVELOPMENT: LANGUAGE

Prefixes

Prefixes and suffixes are generally known as affixes.
Affixes create new words, usually by modifying
or changing the meaning of a root word. A good
knowledge of affixes will help students develop
vocabulary without the need to always check in their
dictionary. By memorising the meaning of prefixes,
suffixes and root words, students can unlock the meaning
of difficult vocabulary when reading texts.

TEACHER DEVELOPMENT: STUDENT TRAINING

Spelling of words with prefixes

The spelling of words with prefixes can sometimes be
difficult for students, and it is advisable that they check
them in their dictionary. Some prefixes such as *non-*
and *ex-* are usually separated from the following noun,
adjective or verb by a hyphen, e.g. *Cooperation between
the woman and her ex-husband was a non-starter.*
Remind students to keep a special section in their
vocabulary notebook for this information.

2 Ask students to complete each sentence by adding one
of the given prefixes to one of the words in the box.
Check their answers in open class and make sure they
have spelt the words correctly.

Answers

1 disappeared **2** underpaid **3** misunderstood
4 sub-zero **5** rewrite **6** overbooked **7** superhuman

3a Ask students to make the negative form of the words
using the prefixes *dis-, il-, im-, in-, ir-* or *un-*. Provide
dictionaries if necessary.

3b ▶ 14 Students listen and check their answers. See p173
for the audioscript for this exercise.

Answers

disad<u>van</u>tage, disa<u>gree</u>, unbe<u>lie</u>vable, in<u>ca</u>pable,
incom<u>plete</u>, unex<u>pec</u>ted, un<u>like</u>ly, il<u>logi</u>cal, un<u>ne</u>cessary,
diso<u>bey</u>, im<u>pa</u>tient, im<u>poss</u>ible, ir<u>regu</u>lar, irre<u>spon</u>sible,
unsu<u>cess</u>ful, in<u>vi</u>sible

3c **PRONUNCIATION** ▶ 14 Ask students to underline the stress in
the negative form of the words in exercise 3a. Then play
the track again for them to check and repeat the words
(see Answers in exercise 3b above).

>>> FAST FINISHERS

Ask students to find patterns in exercise 3 that can
be used as rules of thumb. For example, *im-* is used
before some words beginning with *p* or *m, il-* is used
before some words beginning with *l*. It is a good idea
to emphasise that there are exceptions.

4a Ask students to write three sentences using a negative
word from exercise 3a in each sentence. Draw students'
attention to the example. Encourage them to use three
different prefixes.

4b SPEAKING Ask students to read out their sentences without saying the negative word for their partner to guess the missing word. At the end of the activity, ask different students to read out their sentences for the rest of the class to guess.

Gateway to life skills pp36–37

Investigating food miles

To learn about food miles and their impact on the environment, to think about what we can do to reduce the impact of food miles and to investigate and evaluate our own food buying habits

⋙ FAST TRACK

Divide the class into A and B pairs. Ask Student A to read Text A and Student B to read Text B in preparation for the lesson.

ⓘ BACKGROUND INFORMATION

The impact we have on the environment today is the subject of alarming and catastrophic news reports in the media. Today's teenagers increasingly need to make informed environmental decisions and to take responsible actions.

Teenagers usually learn about helping the environment and the importance of going green at school. However, they can sometimes find it difficult to believe that they can make a difference. In this lesson, students learn about food miles and the impact they have on the environment and how they can incorporate practical steps to reduce this impact every time they buy food.

WARMER

Play *Snowman* with the word ENVIRONMENT. Draw 11 short lines on the board and ask students to choose letters from the alphabet to try and complete the word. If they guess correctly, fill in the blank with that letter(s) in the right place(s). If the word does not contain the suggested letter, draw one element of a snowman figure. The objective is to guess the word before the snowman is complete. You could give students a tip at the end of the game. Elicit the meaning and drill the pronunciation: /ɪnˈvaɪrənmənt/. Ask students to work in pairs and brainstorm as many causes, problems and solutions connected to this topic as they can. Ask students to turn to Key concepts on page 36 to check the meaning of other key words related to this lesson.

1a SPEAKING In pairs, students look at the food label of a product sold in the US. Ask them to estimate how far it travelled before getting to the US. Point out the spelling of *fiber* in American English as the label is from the US. In British English the correct spelling is *fibre*.

Answer

It travelled from Turkey to Thailand, and then eventually to the US – approximately 22,000 km/14,000 miles.

1b Ask students to look at the title of the article *Food miles: The great debate* and discuss what they think 'food miles' are. Elicit some ideas in open class.

Answer

The distance food travels from where it is produced to our table.

2 READING Ask students to read the introduction to the article to check if their ideas in exercise 1 were correct. Discuss in open class how serious a problem students think food miles are and ask them to give reasons for their answers.

3 READING Divide the class into A and B pairs. Ask Student A to read Text A and Student B to read Text B and answer the corresponding questions. Tell students to make a note of their answers. Go round and monitor or assist students as they work. Weaker students could compare their answers with another student who read the same text before moving on to exercise 4.

Answers

Text A

1 They weren't in season then.
2 They produce 25% of all CO_2 emissions.
3 They are responsible for 11% of all carbon emissions.
4 They are an example of unnecessary food travel.
5 We need to produce more food locally and buy locally produced food.

Text B

1 We need to keep them cool for a year or buy them from another country.
2 Buying them from another country as the energy used in keeping them fresh for ten months is worse for the environment.
3 Because they have conditions to grow tomatoes all year and if they are produced in the UK, you need energy to heat the greenhouses.
4 The workers and economy of these countries depend on selling fruit, etc. to other markets.
5 Food miles are not good, but sometimes they are better than the alternative.

4 SPEAKING In pairs, ask Student A to explain why food miles are a serious problem and Student B to explain why the alternative to food miles can be worse. Remind students to use their notes in exercise 3 to help them. Walk round, monitoring and noting down good use of language and errors to go over in a feedback session at the end of this exercise.

TEACHER DEVELOPMENT: CLASSROOM TIPS AND PLANNING

Delayed correction

In freer fluency-based activities, where students are engaged in extended talking, error correction will stop the flow of the conversation. Set up speaking activities in such a way that you can easily move between the different groups of students. You can monitor students and note down pronunciation errors, mistakes in the target language or errors which make it difficult for you to understand what the student is saying, as well as good use of language.

You can use your notes in a feedback session at a different stage of the lesson. This ensures students can use the language uninterrupted and naturally. You can give delayed correction by writing the sentences on the board and inviting your students (as a class or in smaller groups) to decide together which sentences need to be changed and how to change them.

5 In pairs, ask students to talk about how serious they think the question of food miles is and what they think is good advice when they go to buy food. Remind students to use the information in texts A and B to help them. Elicit ideas from different students around the class.

>>> FAST FINISHERS

Write two lists of definitions on the board and ask students to find the words in the text that match the definitions. (Alternatively, students could do this activity while you check the other group's comprehension of their text.)

<u>Student A</u>

something that is likely to have a sudden and bad effect on a situation in the future (time bomb)

put in a packet (packaged)

a particular distance in all directions from a central point (radius)

in the area where you live or that you are talking about (locally)

<u>Student B</u>

something that shocks you because it seems unfair or wrong (scandalous)

a building made of glass used for growing plants (greenhouse)

to make something exist again (recreate)

to consider something when you are trying to make a decision (take into account)

VOCABULARY FOCUS

The video contains some useful words and phrases about food miles and sourcing produce that students may not be familiar with. You could pre-teach the following with the class before watching:

source [v]: research and find something particular from its place of origin

found [v]: start a company, institution, etc

field to fork [phr]: the process from (food) producer to the consumer

accessible [adj]: easy to use or obtain

harvest [v]: to collect a growing crop (food, plants, etc.)

sums (of money) [n]: mathematical calculations

shipping out [phr v]: sending goods from one country to another (usually by sea)

agribusiness [n]: business/farm that produces as much food for profit as possible

deceptive [adj]: appearing to be something different from what it is

make an assumption [phr v]: to decide without evidence, based on your feelings rather than information

decipher (information) [v]: to succeed in understanding something difficult (usually writing)

6a **LISTENING** ▶ 15 Tell students they are going to watch or listen to a man named Ben talking about his job. Play the video or audio track for students to listen and find out if he mentions any of their ideas in exercises 4 and 5. See the Teacher's Resource Centre for the audioscript/videoscript for this exercise.

6b ▶ 15 Ask students to complete the sentences with one or two words. Play the video or audio track again for students to watch or listen again and check their answers. Nominate different students around the class to say the answers.

Answers

1 running 2 to fork 3 cold storage 4 seasonally
5 food miles 6 market

6c In pairs, students discuss the three topics Ben talks about, and exchange examples of each. Monitor students and note down errors and good use of language for feedback at the end of the class. Finally, elicit ideas from different pairs around the class.

⁺⁺ EXTRA ACTIVITY

In groups of three, ask students to perform an improvised interview between a host and two guests on a fictional radio show, talking about food miles. The main task of the host is to conduct the interview, keep the time and to be in control. The main task of the guests is to answer the questions and defend their argument (one student should defend the ideas in Text A, the other student defends the ideas in Text B). Encourage them to use information from the texts and the sentences in exercise 6. Give students time to prepare their interview and, if possible, record them for review and feedback.

TEACHER DEVELOPMENT: CLASSROOM TIPS AND PLANNING

Recording in class

Recording in class, either video or audio-only, can be time-consuming, but it has lots of benefits. You can record in one lesson and review in a later one. In this later lesson, you could ask your students to write notes about their own performance, focusing on what they thought went well and what they could change or work on next. You should make your own notes as well, for subsequent whole-class discussion. Audio-only recordings might be less threatening for shyer students, and, of course, you always need to get permission from your class before you start recording them. Students and teachers can also include the recordings in their portfolios to monitor progress.

21ST CENTURY TASK

Tell students they are going to find out more about food miles in their area. Divide the class into small groups and ask them to follow the plan:

- *Step 1*

  Ask students to collect food labels or packaging and bring them to class.

- *Step 2*

  Ask students to create a display to show each item and where it came from and/or where it was packaged on a world map.

- *Step 3*

  Ask students to investigate which of the products could be produced or packaged closer to where they live. Encourage students to investigate if there are any benefits in buying the food from where it originally came from.

- *Step 4*

  Ask students to present their findings and their conclusions to the class.

Listening p38

Predicting content and listening for general and specific information

WARMER

Elicit all the prefixes students can remember from the Developing vocabulary lesson and write them on the board. Students then play *Word tennis* in pairs or teams. Student A says a prefix and Student B must immediately say a word using that prefix. Then Student B says a prefix, and so on. Students win a point for each correct word they say. The student or team with the most points wins the game.

1 SPEAKING In pairs, ask students to look at the photo of a drone and make a list of ways a drone could be used. Draw students' attention to the example. Elicit ideas from students around the class.

TEACHER DEVELOPMENT: STUDENT TRAINING

Before you listen

Students who predict the content of the track before they listen can improve their performance and reduce their anxiety. By reading the questions first, they can detect important words, predict the answer and clarify exactly what information they are listening for. Key vocabulary may be illustrated and can give clues to the content of a listening.

ℹ CULTURAL INFORMATION

Drones are mostly known for their use in military operations, but that is likely to change as they are increasingly adopted into the commercial market. As accessibility, cost and safety improve, drones are expected to generate more than \$82.1 billion in annual revenue by 2025. The emerging drone market is expected to create nearly 104,000 manufacturing, IT and technical jobs over the next decade.

2 LISTENING 16 Tell students they are going to listen to a radio programme about drones. Play the track for students to tick any of the ideas in their list they mention. See p173 for the audioscript for this exercise.

3 ▶ 16 Play the track again for students to listen and choose the correct alternative.

Answers

1 Aerial   **2** negative   **3** stop   **4** aerial images
5 offers us new reporting possibilities   **6** quite possible
7 thinks

4 Ask students to note down positive points of UAVs according to Scott and Kim. Elicit answers from students and ask them if they mention any possible negative points and if so, what.

Answers

Positive points: patrolling parks/protecting wild animals; examining sites of natural disasters; taking medicine, water or food to victims; making movies; filming sports events

Negative points: privacy – spying on ordinary people; create laws on why/how/when/who can use them

5 SPEAKING **What about you?** In pairs or small groups, students say if they think UAVs will change the world in a good or bad way. Ask them to justify their opinions.

Example answers

I think drones will change the world in a good way. They can save lives and do dangerous jobs. Moreover, drones will generate a lot of money and jobs.

I think drones will change the world in a bad way. It's possible for terrorists to take control of drones and use them against us.

HOMEWORK

Assign students page 25 in their Workbook or the relevant sections of the Online Workbook.

Grammar in context pp38–39

Talking about the future using the future continuous, future perfect simple and future perfect continuous

⟫⟫ FAST TRACK

Students could do exercises 1 and 2 at home. Check their answers at the beginning of the class and go on to exercise 3a.

Test before you teach: Flipped classroom

Set the Flipped classroom video and tasks for homework <u>before the lesson</u>. This will allow you to assess the needs of the students before the class. Students can then move on to the relevant grammar practice activities.

Future continuous, future perfect simple and future perfect continuous

1a Students look at the sentences and decide what tense the verbs in blue are. Elicit how we form the tenses.

Answers

1 future continuous   **2** future continuous   **3** future perfect simple   **4** future perfect simple   **5** future perfect continuous
Future continuous: *will/won't + be + verb-ing*
Future perfect simple: *will/won't + have + past participle*
Future perfect continuous: *will/won't + have + been + verb-ing*

TEACHER DEVELOPMENT: LANGUAGE

Future tenses

Point out to students that *will* and *be going to* can be used interchangeably in these future tenses, e.g. *Maybe by the time I'm 40 I'm going to be directing my own company. By that time, she's going to have found a new boyfriend. Next January, we're going to have been living here for ten years.*

1b Students complete the rules with *future continuous, future perfect simple* or *future perfect continuous*. Check the answers in open class.

Answers

1 future perfect simple   **2** future continuous   **3** future perfect continuous   **4** future perfect simple, future perfect continuous

TEACHER DEVELOPMENT: PRONUNCIATION

Future tenses

It is often difficult for students to get the word order and pronunciation right in these tenses because they feature long strings of words. Point out to students that the conjugation is simple because only the subject changes. Pay special attention to the contracted forms of *will* and *have*, as well as the <u>stressed</u> words in each sentence:
for <u>ten years</u>. [repeat]
we'll 've been <u>living here</u> [repeat]
we'll 've been <u>living here</u> for <u>ten years</u>. [repeat]
<u>Next January</u> [repeat]
<u>Next January, we'll</u> 've been <u>living here</u> for <u>ten years</u>. [repeat]

TEACHER DEVELOPMENT: CLASSROOM TIPS AND PLANNING

Drilling

Drilling plays an important role in the classroom and is mainly used for modelling target language. In choral drills, where the whole class repeats a word or sentence in unison, the goal is accuracy and the standard is high. The teacher says a word or sentence out loud and students try to repeat it verbatim with correct pronunciation, stress and intonation. You could mark the utterance on the board with phonetic script, stressed syllables and rising or falling intonation or tap out the rhythm of the stressed syllables while enunciating.

2   Ask students to explain the difference between the sentences in each pair. Elicit answers from different students around the class.

Answers

1a At 7 o'clock, the activity is in progress.
1b At 7 o'clock, the activity has finished.
2a In half an hour the activity will start.
2b In half an hour, the activity will be finished.
3a This action will happen sometime before 2050.
3b This action will happen in 2050.
4a I have a plan to have lunch at 1 pm tomorrow.
4b At 1 pm tomorrow, lunch will be in progress.

3a Ask students to read Sarah's schedule for tomorrow and complete the sentences with the future continuous, future perfect simple or future perfect continuous form of the verbs given.

Answers

1 will be having   **2** will have eaten   **3** will have arrived   **4** will have been going   **5** will be having   **6** will have seen   **7** will be watching   **8** will have been watching

3b Ask students to write four questions about the schedule, two using the future continuous and two using the future perfect. Draw attention to the example.

3c SPEAKING Ask students to take it in turns to ask and answer their questions.

4   Ask students to put the verbs in the correct form of the future continuous or future perfect simple.

Answers

a will, be doing **b** will, be working **c** will have finished **d** will have left **e** won't be living **f** will have learnt **g** will have bought **h** will be saving

5a Individually, students write predictions about themselves in the year 2040. Remind them to use the future continuous, future perfect simple or future perfect continuous. Draw attention to the example sentences. Go round and assist students while they work.

5b SPEAKING In small groups, students compare their sentences from exercise 5a and ask questions to find out what their partners have written. Students discuss if there are any particularly common answers. In a less confident class, elicit the question form for each phrase in exercise 5a before starting this activity, e.g. *live with my parents → Will you be living with your parents?* Draw students' attention to the examples.

5c Encourage students to share any common answers with the class. Draw students' attention to the example sentence. You could put up these prompts on the board to help students in a less confident class:
All of us … Most of us … Some of us …
A few of us … None of us …

✚ EXTRA ACTIVITY

Students write a short text predicting their lives in 2040 based on their answers from the speaking activity.

Refer students to the Grammar reference on page 42 if necessary.

HOMEWORK

Assign students page 26 in their Workbook or the relevant sections of the Online Workbook.

Developing speaking p40

Comparing and contrasting photos

⟫⟫ FAST TRACK

You could ask students to note down ideas for exercise 1 at home in preparation for the speaking activity. Students can then compare their ideas in pairs at the beginning of the class.

WARMER

Play *Hot seat*. One volunteer from each team sits with their back to the board. Write a word from the unit on the board so that only the teams can see the word. Teams give clues to their volunteer so that he/she guesses the word and gets a point for their team. The first one to guess the word gets a point for their team.

1 SPEAKING In pairs, students look at the photos and write down the similarities and differences between the two photos in a simple two-column table. Elicit ideas.

2 LISTENING ▶ 17 Tell students they are going to listen to a student doing a speaking task. Ask them to read the task and then play the track for them to listen and answer the questions. Check their answers. See pp173–174 for the audioscript for this exercise.

Answers

1 Students' own answers **2** yes **3** yes

3 ▶ 17 Ask students to complete what the student said with phrases from the Speaking bank. Play the track again if necessary. Elicit answers from different students.

Answers

a Both photos show **b** In the first photo **c** whereas **d** One big difference between the photos is that **e** while **f** Compared with **g** Another important difference **h** One similarity

4 SPEAKING In pairs, students use the phrases in the Speaking bank to talk about the similarities and differences between the photos in exercise 1.

PRACTICE MAKES PERFECT

5a SPEAKING Divide the class into A and B pairs. Ask Student A to look at the photos on the page. Ask Student B to look at the photos on page 158. Ask them to think about the similarities and differences between their two photos.

5b Ask Student A to do the task and Student B to listen.

5c Ask students to swap roles. Tell Student B to look at their task on page 158 and Student A to listen to their partner. For students who are less confident, photocopy the model text below.

Model text

<u>Both photos show</u> people using different types of transport. <u>In the first photo,</u> I can see an astronaut walking in space, <u>whereas</u> in the second photo there is a family at an airport. <u>In both photos,</u> the people look prepared for their journey. The astronaut is probably feeling a bit nervous, but he's enjoying the sensation of being in space. In the second photo, the family is probably feeling excited about going on holiday, but they may also be feeling nervous about flying. <u>One big difference between the photos</u> is that the astronaut is doing something as part of his or her job, while the family are going to enjoy free time together on holiday. <u>Another important difference</u> is that travelling into space is very dangerous and travelling by plane is not. <u>Compared with</u> other forms of transport, travelling by plane is a very safe form of transport.

✚ EXTRA ACTIVITY

Ask students to change partners and photos, and repeat the activity. Tell students the person who 'wins' the task is the one who uses all the expressions in the Speaking bank. The student who listens should time them for a minute and note down all the expressions their partner uses.

Assign students page 27 in their Workbook or the relevant sections of the Online Workbook.

Developing writing p41

Writing a story using a variety of tenses, structures and linkers

≫ FAST TRACK

You could ask students to do exercise 1 at home in preparation for the writing activity.

WARMER

In pairs, students describe the picture in exercise 2 on page 41.

Suggested answer

The photo shows a person looking through a telescope to observe the stars.

1 SPEAKING In pairs, students read the writing task and note down some ideas for a story. In a less confident class, elicit ideas from different students around the class and write key vocabulary on the board.

2 Students read the story and decide if there are any similarities with their ideas.

3 Ask students if this type of trip would interest them and elicit reasons why or why not.

4 Ask students to put the events of the story in order. Check their answers.

Answers
1 f **2** d **3** a **4** g **5** c **6** e **7** b

5 Ask students to look at the advice in the Writing bank and find examples in the story in exercise 2 for each one. Draw students' attention to the example and ask them to find examples of other tenses that the writer uses.

Answers

Variety of past tenses: past continuous: *… We were soon preparing for landing*; past simple *… I learnt that …*, past perfect simple: *… I had flown …*, past perfect continuous: *… I had been waiting …*, past with 'would': *… we would observe …*, future with 'will': *I'll never forget*

Participle clauses: *Having collected my luggage, I immediately saw …*

Linkers of time and sequence: *Four months ago, Luckily*

Adjectives and adverbs: *excited and nervous, brilliant, immediately, amazing*

✔ EXAM SUCCESS Ask students to read the exam tips about writing a narrative. Then tell them to turn to Exam success on page 145 for more ideas (Writing: Stories).

TEACHER DEVELOPMENT: STUDENT TRAINING

Story writing

In narrative writing, it is important to develop plot, character and setting using specific detail, and to order events clearly using chronological order. Students need a rich language base to effectively write a narrative writing task in order to 'fill up' the narrative structure with engaging language.

In a less confident class, brainstorm possible events and characters for students' stories and place the words or phrases they suggest under the following headings on the board: *Characters, Setting, Situation, Feelings, Vocabulary.*

Monitor as students work on their plans and help individual students if necessary. Students could swap and comment on each other's plans before they write the story for homework or in class.

PRACTICE MAKES PERFECT

6a Ask students to look at the task in exercise 1 again and plan their own story. Ask them to think about the main events, the background and any important scenes.

6b Ask students to write their own story. Remind them to follow the advice in the Writing bank and Exam success. They can also follow the advice in the Writing bank on page 152. For students who are less confident, photocopy the model text below for extra support during the writing task.

Model text

I was both excited and nervous as I stood there waiting at the airport. It was the first time I had flown alone and I didn't know what to expect when I arrived. Five months ago, I had applied to a voluntary agency to teach English in a foreign country in my gap year. It was a brilliant surprise when I found out I had got a place working in a rural school in Cambodia. Now the moment had arrived and I was going on my way – and on my own!

It was a long flight and I had to stop over in three places. Having collected my luggage, I was happy to see a young woman with a sign with my name on it. A small group of people were waiting with her and I soon realised that they were other volunteers on the same programme.

Teaching English to children in Cambodia was an amazing experience. My fellow teachers were from all over the world and I made fantastic friends. I learnt a lot about their culture and I met some incredible people. At first, it was quite difficult because the classes were very large and there were no books. In the end, I discovered a lot of ways to keep my students happy and learning. Apart from learning more about teaching English, it was a trip I'll never forget.

Assign students page 28 in their Workbook or the relevant sections of the Online Workbook.

Language checkpoint: Unit 3

>>> FAST TRACK

The extra support provided in the Grammar and Vocabulary reference sections makes the Grammar and Vocabulary revision sections ideal for setting as homework. You could get students to complete the whole revision page or just certain exercises for homework.

Grammar revision p43

Future forms

1 Students write the correct future form of the verbs given, using *will*, *be going to*, the present simple or the present continuous.

Answers

1 comes **2** 'll help **3** 'm going to do
4 are getting **5** will take **6** leaves

2 Students match the sentences in exercise 1 to the correct use of each future form.

Answers

a 4 **b** 5 **c** 6 **d** 3 **e** 2 **f** 1

Future continuous, future perfect simple, future perfect continuous

3 Students tick the correct sentences and rewrite the incorrect ones.

Answers

1 I can't go out at 7 o'clock because **I'll be doing** my homework then.
2 ✔
3 ✔
4 I can write a summary of the book tomorrow because **I'll have read** it by then.
5 At 5 o'clock next Saturday **I'll be playing** basketball.
6 I can't give you my assignment tomorrow because **I won't have finished** it.
7 ✔
8 ✔

Vocabulary revision p43

WORDS CONNECTED WITH TRAVEL AND TRANSPORT

1 Students complete the sentences with the correct word.

Answers

1 platform **2** crew **3** landed **4** traffic jam **5** gate
6 high-speed **7** space station **8** launch

JOURNEY, TRAVEL, TRIP, VOYAGE

2 Students complete the sentences with *journey*, *travel*, *trip* or *voyage*.

Answers

1 trip **2** travel **3** voyage **4** journey **5** trip

PREFIXES

3 Students complete the sentences with prefixes added to the words in capitals.

Answers

1 misunderstand **2** unexpected **3** incapable
4 overbooked **5** unnecessary **6** disobey
7 postgraduate

HOMEWORK

Assign students page 29 in their Workbook or the relevant sections of the Online Workbook.

4 Extraordinary talents

KEY LEARNING OUTCOMES

Students will be able to:

- make comparisons using a variety of structures, including comparative and superlative adverbs
- form nouns by using suffixes
- understand and talk about different kinds of intelligences and special talents
- give structured presentations on different topics
- write articles giving detailed personal descriptions

UNIT OVERVIEW

Vocabulary

Personality adjectives

Reading

The incredible rise of Dynamo
CRITICAL THINKING Discussing the reasons behind a person's success

Grammar in context

Comparative and superlative adjectives and adverbs
Other ways of making comparisons

Developing vocabulary

Noun suffixes

Life skills

Learning to learn: Learning about intelligence

Listening

Hidden talent

Grammar in context

Articles
so, such, too, enough

Developing speaking

Presentations – 1

Developing writing

An article – 1

Exam success

Use of English: Word formation cloze activities
Speaking: Giving presentations

DIGITAL OVERVIEW

Presentation Kit

- ▶ **Flipped classroom video Unit 4:** Other ways of making comparisons
- ▶ **Life skills video Unit 4:** Learning about intelligence
- ▶ **Interactive versions of Student's Book activities**
- ▶ **Integrated audio and answer key for all activities**
- ▶ **Workbook pages with answer key**

Teacher's Resource Centre

- ▶ **Flipped classroom video Unit 4:** Other ways of making comparisons
- ▶ **Life skills video Unit 4:** Learning about intelligence
- ▶ **Grammar communication activity Unit 4:** Animal articles
- ▶ **Worksheets for this unit, including:**
  - – Grammar Practice worksheet Unit 4
  - – Flipped classroom video worksheet Unit 4: Other ways of making comparisons
  - – Literature worksheet Units 3 and 4
  - – Culture worksheet Unit 4
  - – Life skills video worksheet Unit 4
  - – Everyday English worksheet Unit 4

Student's App

Gateway 2nd Edition wordlist for the award-winning Sounds App (available for download)

✓ TESTING AND ASSESSMENT

Resources for exam preparation and measuring student progress

- ▶ Test Generator Units 1–4
- ▶ Printable test Unit 4
- ▶ Gateway to exams Units 3 and 4 (end of Unit 4)

Vocabulary p44

Talking about someone's personality

>>> **FAST TRACK**

You could ask students to do exercises 1, 2 and 3 at home in preparation for the speaking activity. They can look up any words they are not sure about in their dictionaries or the Macmillan Online Dictionary.

WARMER

Discuss the meaning of the unit title *Extraordinary talents* (people with very unusual or surprising abilities). Elicit from students any people they know who have extraordinary talent. Ask students what they think the unit is going to be about (talented people and what makes people talented).

Personality adjectives

1 **SPEAKING** In pairs, students think of the possible opposites and synonyms of the words in the box. Elicit answers from students around the class. Draw students' attention to the example.

Suggested answers

friendly – unfriendly, kind/outgoing
hard-working – lazy, diligent
patient – impatient, considerate
polite – impolite/rude, courteous
quiet – noisy, reserved
reliable – unreliable, dependable
serious – fun-loving, solemn
tidy – untidy/messy, neat

2 Ask students to read the description of a teenager called Luke and say if they think they would like him. Elicit reasons why or why not from different students around the class.

3 Ask students to match the words in red in the text with their opposites in the box. Ask students which two words in the text do not have an opposite in the box and elicit what they mean.

Answers

big-headed – modest, down-to-earth
good-natured/easygoing – bad-tempered
immature – mature
narrow-minded – broad-minded
outgoing – shy, reserved
self-confident – insecure
tactless – sensitive, tactful
gifted = with an impressive natural ability
talented = someone who is talented is very good at something

4 From each pair of adjectives in exercise 3, students choose the adjective that describes them best. Remind them that they can qualify their answers with *very, quite* or *a little bit*.

5 **SPEAKING** In pairs, students discuss the adjectives they chose in exercise 4 and say why they chose them.

6 Ask students to decide which adjective in each pair has a positive (+) meaning and which has a negative (–) meaning. Provide dictionaries if necessary.

Answers

1 ambitious +/pushy –
2 self-confident +/arrogant –
3 bossy –/assertive +
4 frank +/brusque –
5 stubborn –/determined +

TEACHER DEVELOPMENT: STUDENT TRAINING

Vocabulary records

Encourage your students to keep good personal vocabulary records. A good range of vocabulary allows students to communicate clearly and enriches both their spoken and written language. Vocabulary is also important in exam situations.

When you write a new word on the board, always consider what extra useful information you could include, e.g. a short example to show meaning and usage, other related words (derivatives, words with similar meaning, opposites, collocations or an idiom based on the word), phonemic script. This approach helps students record and learn new words and expand their awareness of language systems. Recycle vocabulary on a continuous basis and ask students to use new words in their own writing.

7 **LISTENING** ▶ 18 Play the track for students to listen to descriptions of three people. Ask students to write down two adjectives from the page to describe each one. Elicit answers from students around the class. See p174 for the audioscript for this exercise.

Answers

1 bossy/self-confident **2** tactless/big-headed
3 stubborn/slow

8a **SPEAKING** In pairs, students decide what type of personality is necessary in order to do the jobs and give reasons for their answers.

Example answers

1 A professional musician needs to be gifted and play at least one instrument extremely well. To be a professional musician, you have to be very ambitious as it is very difficult to succeed as a musician.

2 The director of an international bank needs to be clever, because you need to understand complex numerical operations. You need to be self-confident, serious, reliable and assertive because you are the leader.

3 To be the President, you need to be very self-confident and determined because you receive a lot of criticism. You need to be hard-working and serious because there are many difficult situations that you have to face.

4 A Formula 1 driver has to be hard-working and talented. You also need to be self-confident as drivers deal with the media a lot. They work in teams so it helps to be outgoing and friendly.

5 A TV presenter needs to be outgoing and friendly. It usually involves many hours in the studio so you need to be hard-working, patient and ambitious to succeed in this job. Because you are in the public eye, you need to be self-confident.

8b Invite students to discuss their ideas in open class.

✚ EXTRA ACTIVITY

Students think of a job and write a brief description of the kind of personality you need in order to do it, without mentioning the job. In pairs, students take turns to read out their texts for their partner to guess which job is being described.

HOMEWORK

Assign students page 30 in their Workbook or the relevant sections of the Online Workbook.

Reading p45

Scanning and reading for general and specific information

≫ FAST TRACK

You could ask students to read the text in exercise 2 at home in preparation for in-class activities.

WARMER

Write the names of these people on the board: *Matt Groening, Judit Polgár, Pau Gasol, Lionel Messi, Pablo Picasso*. Ask students if they know what any of them are famous for. Ask students to work in pairs to match the people with these occupations: *NBA basketball player, chess grandmaster, creator of* The Simpsons*, artist, football player*. Ask students if they know the names of any famous illusionists.

Answers

Matt Groening – creator of *The Simpsons*
Judit Polgár – chess grandmaster
Pau Gasol – NBA basketball player
Lionel Messi – football player
Pablo Picasso – artist

---

1 SPEAKING In pairs, students describe what they can see in the photos.

Suggested answer

In one photo, I can see Dynamo walking on water. In the other photo, he is holding a pack of cards.

2 Ask students to read the article quickly to find out if Dynamo had an easy childhood and note down why or why not. Set a time limit of three minutes to encourage students not to focus on difficult vocabulary at this stage.

Answer

No, he didn't have an easy childhood. He had a serious stomach illness and was bullied for being weak and shy.

3 Ask students to read the text again and choose the best answers. Elicit from students the key sentences which helped them decide on their answers.

Answers

1 b (… we all want to feel young again … tricks and illusions can give us that feeling.)
2 a (… he wasn't as strong as his classmates. Weak and shy …)
3 c (… nobody wanted to be near him. So he spent his time in his bedroom practising …)
4 c (He started doing tricks in the street.)
5 c (… if I started explaining it all … you'd be begging me to stop after a minute.)

ⓘ CULTURAL INFORMATION

Unlike traditional illusionists, Steven 'Dynamo' Frayne (born 17 December 1982), performs without stage props or glamorous assistants. By delivering close-up tricks to young people on the street, he brought a new style to the world of illusionists. He is best known for his documentary show, *Dynamo: Magician Impossible* in which he amazed his audience by swallowing jewellery, then pulling it out of his stomach, transforming snow into diamonds, walking on water across the Thames and bench-pressing 155 kg in the gym.

4 CRITICAL THINKING Individually, students think about the reasons for Dynamo's success. Then ask students to say what they think and justify their opinion. For less confident classes, you could write some ideas on the board to start students off, e.g. *talent, hard work, getting/taking opportunities, resilience or creativity*.

Example answer

I think Dynamo is successful because he works hard. He spent thousands of hours practising tricks when he was younger.

5 Encourage students to guess what the underlined words in the text mean and then check in their dictionaries. If students have access to computers, they can look up the words in the Macmillan Online Dictionary.

Answers

pack of cards = a box containing cards for playing games
talked his way = to persuade someone to let you do something
surface = the top layer or outside part of something
begging = asking for something in a way that shows you want it very much
distraction = something that gets your attention and prevents you from concentrating on anything else

6 SPEAKING **What about *you*?** In pairs or small groups, students discuss the questions. Elicit some answers from different pairs/groups.

In pairs, students tell each other about a skill they could become really good at if they practised for 10,000 hours. Ask them to calculate how many hours they have spent practising this skill up to now and work out at what age they could be really talented at this skill.

HOMEWORK

Assign students page 31 in their Workbook or the relevant sections of the Online Workbook.

Grammar in context pp46–47

Making comparisons using a variety of structures, including comparative and superlative adjectives and adverbs

⟩⟩⟩ FAST TRACK

You could ask students to do exercise 1 at home. Then they start the next class with the speaking activity in exercise 2.

Test before you teach

Ask the class to name eight countries and write them on the board. Divide the class into four to six teams and give them five minutes to write comparative and superlative sentences about the countries, e.g. *Canada is colder than Japan. Russia is the biggest country.* At the end of the five minutes, the teams win a point for each correct sentence. The team with the most points is the winner. If students seem familiar with comparative and superlative forms, move through the Grammar guide exercises quickly in open class.

Comparative and superlative adjectives and adverbs

1a Ask students to look at the sentences and decide which contain comparative forms and which contain superlative forms.

Answers
Comparative: 1, 3, 4, 7
Superlative: 2, 5, 6

TEACHER DEVELOPMENT: LANGUAGE

Comparatives and superlatives

We use the comparative and superlative form to compare and contrast different things. We use the comparative form to show the difference between two things and the superlative form when speaking about three or more things to show which object is 'the most' of something. A few two-syllable adjectives can take either *-er/-est* or *more/most*.

The usual comparative and superlative forms of the adjective *old* are *older* and *oldest*. However, the alternative forms *elder* and *eldest* are sometimes used. *Elder* and *eldest* are generally restricted to talking about the age of people.

1b Ask students to look at the sentences again and decide which contain adjectives and which contain adverbs.

Answers
Adjectives: 2, 4, 7
Adverbs: 1, 3, 5, 6

TEACHER DEVELOPMENT: LANGUAGE

Adjectives and adverbs

Adjectives are used to modify nouns, e.g. *The dog is friendly. What is the dog like? Friendly.*

Adverbs are used to modify verbs, adjectives or other adverbs, e.g. *The dog barks loudly. How does the dog bark? Loudly.*

2 **SPEAKING** In pairs, students complete the table and then explain the rules for the different groups of adjectives. Draw students' attention to the examples. Elicit and check their answers in open class.

Answers

Adjective	Comparative	Superlative
long	longer	the longest
slow	slower	the slowest
big	bigger	the biggest
thin	thinner	the thinnest
friendly	friendlier	the friendliest
tidy	tidier	the tidiest
ambitious	more ambitious	the most ambitious
hard-working	more hard-working	the most hard-working
good	better	the best
bad	worse	the worst
far	farther/further	the farthest/furthest
little (determiner)	less	the least

Rules:

For one-syllable adjectives, add *-er* to make the comparative and *-est* to make the superlative. (If an adjective ends in *-e*, this is removed before adding *-er/-est*, e.g. *wide, wider, widest*.)

If a one-syllable adjective ends in a single vowel letter followed by a single consonant letter, the consonant letter is doubled before adding *-er/-est*, e.g. *big, bigger, biggest*.

If an adjective ends in a consonant followed by *-y*, *-y* is replaced by *-i* when adding *-er/-est*, e.g. *friendly, friendlier, friendliest*.

For many two-syllable and all three-syllable adjectives, form the comparative with *more* and the superlative with *most*. (For some two syllable adjectives, both *-er* and *more* forms are possible.)

less/the least

Comparative and superlative forms with -er/-est and more/the most are always used to talk about a quality which is greater in amount relative to others. If we want to talk about a quality which is smaller in amount relative to others, we use the forms *less* (the opposite of comparative *more*), and *the least* (the opposite of superlative *the most*). *Less* is used to indicate that something or someone does not have as much of a particular quality as someone or something else, e.g. *This sofa is less comfortable than that one.* The least is used to indicate that something or someone has less of a quality than any other person or thing of its kind, e.g. *It's the least expensive way to travel.*

3a Ask students to match the rules for comparative and superlative adverbs 1–3 with the examples a–c.

Answers

1 b **2** c **3** a

3b Ask students to make the comparative form of the adverbs in exercise 3a (a–c).

Answers

a better, worse, less
b more carefully, more quietly, more easily, more beautifully, more often
c faster, harder, earlier, later, longer, sooner, nearer

4 Ask students to rewrite the sentences using the correct comparative and superlative forms.

Answers

1 In my opinion, Caleb is the friendliest person in this class.
2 I think Emma is slightly taller than Claire.
3 That is definitely the silliest thing I've heard today!
4 You can write much more quickly on a computer than by hand.
5 Sorry I couldn't come sooner.
6 Is it much further to your house?
7 You need to try harder if you want to be a professional illusionist.
8 Houdini was one of the most famous illusionists in the world.
9 That film was terrible! It's the least interesting film I've ever seen.
10 She did better than me in the test.

5a SPEAKING In pairs, students discuss and decide who in the class matches the descriptions.

5b As a class, students take turns to say one of the names they chose in exercise 5a for their classmates to guess the description.

Other ways of making comparisons

 Test before you teach: Flipped classroom
Set the Flipped classroom video and tasks for homework <u>before the lesson</u>. This will allow you to assess the needs of the students before the class. Students can then move on to the relevant grammar practice activities.

6 Ask students to look at the sentences and answer questions a–c.

Answers

a We use *as … as* to say two things are the same.
b We use *not as … as, not so … as* or *less … than* to say that the second person or thing is more … than the first one.
c Students' own answers

7 Ask students to complete the second sentence so that it has a similar meaning to the first sentence, using the word given. Remind students that they cannot change the word given and they must use between two and five words including the word given.

Answers

1 is as enjoyable as playing **2** is less healthy than
3 faster you walk, the **4** is not as good as **5** as quickly as **6** much less difficult to write **7** taller you are, the easier **8** better and better

than/as

Remind students that *than* (/ðən/) and *as* (/əz/) are usually unstressed when we speak. Practise these sounds by choral drilling the sentences in exercise 7.

8 SPEAKING In pairs, students match the halves of the common expressions. Check that they understand what they mean and ask them to think of a situation when they might use them. Draw students' attention to the example.

Answers

2 c (You use this to say it's better to do something late than not to do it at all.)
3 a (You use this to say that something will be difficult to achieve in practice.)
4 g (You use this to say that you should behave cautiously, even if it seems difficult or unnecessary, in order to avoid problems later.)
5 e (You use this to say you will be happy if more people come or take part in what you are doing.)
6 b (You use this to say a bad situation is deteriorating/ getting worse.)
7 d (You use this to say that more powerful people/ organisations have more to lose.)

>>> FAST FINISHERS

In pairs, students invent dialogues using the expressions in exercise 8. For example:
A: *I'm having a party on Saturday.*
B: *Who have you invited?*
A: *Oh, loads of people!*
B: *Aren't you worried there will be too many?*
A: *No, the more the merrier.*
Ask different pairs to act out their dialogues for the class.

Refer students to the Grammar reference on page 54 if necessary.

HOMEWORK

Assign students page 32 in their Workbook or the relevant sections of the Online Workbook.

Developing vocabulary p47

Forming nouns by using suffixes

>>> FAST TRACK

Students could do exercises 1 and 2 at home using a dictionary to help them check the spelling. Check the answers in open class and practise the pronunciation.

Noun suffixes

1 Ask students to look at the words with noun suffixes and decide which of the nouns are for a person.

Answer

actor, artist, politician, writer

2 Ask students to change the words into nouns or a different type of noun using the suffixes in exercise 1. Remind them that they may need to change the spelling and that sometimes they can make more than one noun from each word. Let them compare their answers in pairs before you check them in open class. Drill the pronunciation of any difficult words.

Answers

actor, action
appearance
confidence
creator, creation
difference
education, educator
electricity, electrician
employment, employer
happiness
improvement, improver
invention, inventor
investigation, investigator
madness
musician, musicality
relevance
scientist

TEACHER DEVELOPMENT: LANGUAGE

Noun suffixes

Suffixes come at the end of the word. Just as prefixes (e.g. *im-*, *re-*) change the <u>meaning</u> of a word, suffixes change the <u>type</u> of word. They show whether a word is a verb, noun, adjective or adverb. If students learn these suffixes, they will be able to recognise different parts of speech more easily.

✓ EXAM SUCCESS
Ask students to read the tip for completing word-formation exercises and then turn to page 145 (Use of English: Word formation cloze activities) for more ideas.

3 Ask students to complete the text with the correct form of the words given. Students compare in pairs before you check their answers.

Answers

a scientists **b** importance **c** electricity **d** creation
e inventor **f** improvements **g** disappearance
h ability **i** difference

TEACHER DEVELOPMENT: STUDENT TRAINING

Word formation

Word formation is one of the keys to success for students at this level. English exams such as the TOEFL, Cambridge ESOL First Certificate, CAE and Proficiency use word formation as a key testing element. Encourage students to record vocabulary in word groups, e.g. with the concept noun, the personal noun, adjective, verb form.

>>> FAST FINISHERS

Students write a word formation exercise to test their partner using one of the words from exercise 2, e.g. *There was lots of _____ in the film so it was very exciting. ACT*

HOMEWORK

Assign students page 33 in their Workbook or the relevant sections of the Online Workbook.

Gateway to life skills pp48–49

Learning about intelligence

To find out about Gardner's Theory of Multiple Intelligences, to learn some study tips and think about the type of learner they can help and to find out which type of learner you are

>>> FAST TRACK

Students could do the *Multiple Intelligence Test* on page 159 at home in preparation for the Academic task at the end of the lesson.

ℹ️ BACKGROUND INFORMATION

Howard Gardner's Theory of Multiple Intelligences

With today's increasing diversity among students, it has become even more important to find strategies that meet a wide range of needs. Howard Gardner's Theory of Multiple Intelligences (MI) has introduced a better appreciation of the various ways in which we can express our different talents, abilities and preferences and has made us question the way we perceive intelligence. Not only can MI increase students' confidence and enthusiasm for learning, it can also improve their academic achievement and change our perceptions of students' learning abilities.

In this lesson, students learn that there are multiple ways to learn and that they possess multiple types of intellectual strengths and life skills. At the end of the lesson, students complete a questionnaire and identify their areas of strength in the context of MI and reflect on which intelligences would enhance their performance. Self-assessment is a way to assist the development of intrapersonal intelligence. This can be valuable to understanding one's own weakness and strengths, and develop awareness that others think and learn differently. Intrapersonal intelligence is valuable in many practical endeavours, including career planning.

WARMER

Encourage students to reflect on the lessons they have had so far and look back over the first units of their Student's Book. Individually, ask students to copy this diagram into their books and make notes on the four areas. Tell students to refer to Key concepts if they are unsure of the meaning of *grasp* or *strength*. In pairs, students then compare their notes and discuss any similarities or differences.

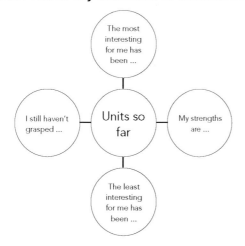

1 **SPEAKING** In pairs, ask students to discuss what we mean when we call somebody 'intelligent'. Encourage them to think of people they think are, or were, intelligent. Elicit examples from different students around the class.

Suggested answers

Garry Kasparov, Marie Curie, William Shakespeare, Galileo Galilei, Nicolaus Copernicus, Leonardo da Vinci, Albert Einstein

2a Ask students to choose the best alternative in each sentence and think about why.

2b **SPEAKING** Ask students to compare with a partner to see if they have similar answers. Elicit answers from students around the class and ask them to explain their choices. Do not confirm any answers at this point.

3 **READING** Ask students to read a text about one theory of human intelligence and say which of the alternatives in exercise 2a the writer agrees with. Elicit the arguments the writer gives to justify the answers.

Answers

1 doesn't mean   **2** isn't   **3** can't   **4** doesn't stay
5 affect

4 Ask students to read the text again and answer the questions. Check their answers.

Answers

1 That some people believe this is what shows you are clever, but this is only one type of intelligence.
2 Because people are good at different things.
3 It is difficult to measure intelligence because it depends on what type of intelligence you are talking about.
4 Children who have access to musical instruments can become great musicians if they start early; bilingual or multilingual children.

5 Ask students to look at the list of Gardner's Multiple Intelligences and say where they think the activities and concepts should go. Give students a minute to compare in pairs before you check their answers in open class.

Answers

a 5   **b** 4   **c** 1   **d** 3   **e** 7   **f** 2   **g** 6

🔍 VOCABULARY FOCUS

The video contains some useful words about different learning styles that students may not be familiar with. You might want to pre-teach these words and phrases with students before watching:

spatial [adj]: related to space, size or position of things
kinaesthetic [adj]: the use
interpersonal [adj]: about relationships between people
clarify [v]: make clear and comprehensible
intrapersonal [adj]: happening or existing within the mind

6 **SPEAKING** In pairs, ask students to discuss what they think of Gardner's Theory of Multiple Intelligences and if they agree with it. Ask them to give reasons why or why not.

7 **LISTENING** ▶ 19 Tell students they are going to watch or listen to someone named Deana talking about study tips. Play the video or audio track for students to make notes about her study tips for each of the seven intelligences. Check their answers. See the Teacher's Resource Centre for the audioscript/videoscript for this exercise.

Answers

Intelligence 1: use flashcards for difficult concepts, extensive notes

Intelligence 2: organise notes in alphabetical/numerical order

Intelligence 3: use graphs or mind maps

Intelligence 4: use music to remember concepts and words

Intelligence 5: use real-life examples to relate to concepts

Intelligence 6: set up a study group, talk to a classmate

Intelligence 7: keep a journal, study in a quiet area

8 SPEAKING 19 Play the video or audio track again. In pairs, students talk about each tip and say which of these things they already do and which they would like to try. Ask them to give reasons for their choices. Encourage students to share their ideas in open class.

EXTRA ACTIVITY

Ask students to dub the video. Prepare copies of a section or all of the audioscript and divide the class into pairs. Students take it in turns to read sections of the video and try to synchronise their speaking with the video. Play the video with the sound down.

TEACHER DEVELOPMENT: CLASSROOM TIPS AND PLANNING

Dubbing a video

Dubbing a video means that the students try to synchronise their words as much as possible to the face on the screen. Dubbing a video makes students focus on the rhythm and the pace of the person's voice and how important word stress is in English. Students can record themselves using an audio-recording editor which they can download for free from the Internet.

ACADEMIC TASK

Tell students they are going to work on a task to find out what type of learner they are. Ask them to follow the plan:

- **Step 1**

  Individually, students do the Multiple Intelligence Test on page 159.

- **Step 2**

  In pairs, students discuss their results in the test and decide if they agree with the results. Ask students to discuss how the results might help them in their studies.

- **Step 3**

  Ask students to do some research to find a study tip or activity that can help learners with their natural strengths. When they are ready, divide the class into groups and ask students to share their tips and activities.

Listening p50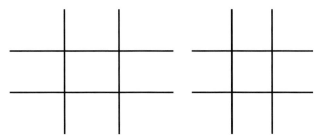

Listening for gist and specific information

WARMER

Play *Noughts and crosses* to recycle vocabulary from the unit so far.

- Split the class into two teams: Xs and 0s.
- Draw two tic-tac-toe grids on the board, side by side. One grid for reference and one for actually drawing Xs and 0s.

- Write these responses to questions in each square: *He's shy; Immature and big-headed; There are eight types; Scientific thinking; Howard Gardner; To beat bullies; Bradford, England; Albert Einstein; The theory of relativity.*
- Each team must think of a grammatically correct question for the response to win a square, e.g. *What's he like? How would you describe him? How many types of Multiple Intelligences are there? Can you name one type of MI? Who invented MI? Why did Dynamo learn to do tricks? Where was he born? Can you name a very intelligent person? What did Einstein invent?*

1 SPEAKING In pairs, ask students to look at the photo and answer the questions. Elicit ideas from students around the class.

Example answers

1 I would like to try rock climbing, but I think it looks very risky.
2 People who like doing extreme sports.
3 I think you have to train a lot to do this and be very fit.

CULTURAL INFORMATION

Rock climbing is a physically and mentally demanding sport. It tests climbers' strength, endurance, agility and balance and requires great concentration and courage. It can also be a dangerous activity and climbers have to be familiar with different techniques and have specialised equipment to do this sport safely.

2 LISTENING 20 Tell students they are going to listen to two people talking about a new TV series. Play the track for students to decide if the statements are True (T), False (F) or the information is Not Mentioned (NM). See p174 for the audioscript for this exercise.

Answers

1 T **2** T **3** F **4** NM **5** T **6** F **7** NM **8** T

3 ▶ 20 Play the track again for students to listen and answer the questions.

Answers

1 900
2 nine
3 She's a grandmother and very busy.
4 60 metres
5 it is surrounded by water; bad weather
6 one in 400
7 how to watch body language and to notice typical things we say when we're nervous
8 It's a pity to spend our lives not realising we have a special talent.

4 SPEAKING **What about *you*?** In pairs or small groups, students discuss the questions and justify their opinions.

Example answers

1 I think I would like to watch this TV series because it is different from ordinary talent shows. I love watching other people be good at things.
2 I would love to do tests to see if I have a hidden talent because it could change my life.

✚ EXTRA ACTIVITY

Have a *Balloon debate*. Divide the class into groups of about four or five. Ask each person to imagine they have a hidden talent that is very special. Explain to the groups that they are all in a hot-air balloon, floating in the sky, when it gets into trouble and starts to sink. If it continues to sink, they will all die so someone must be thrown out of the balloon. Ask students to decide on their hidden talent. Each person has one minute to say why they should not be thrown out of the balloon (i.e. explain why what they do is interesting or important). When everyone has spoken, the group votes for the person they think should be thrown out.

HOMEWORK

Assign students page 33 in their Workbook or the relevant sections of the Online Workbook.

Grammar in context pp50–51

Using articles and so, such, too and enough

>>> FAST TRACK

Students could do exercises 1, 2 and 3 at home. Check their answers and start the class on exercise 4.

Test before you teach

Write these sentences on the board for students to complete with articles (where necessary):

_____ *Chinese is a difficult language to learn.*
_____ *teenagers talked about what happened yesterday.*
I like to play _____ *music.*
_____ *dress she is wearing is blue.*
The chimp is _____ *really intelligent animal.*

Elicit when we use the definite and indefinite article, and when articles can be omitted. If students seem familiar with the use of articles, then move through the Grammar guide exercises quickly in open class.

Articles

1 Ask students to read the sentences, focusing on the articles in blue.

2 Ask students to match the sentence halves to make rules. Then ask them to look back at exercise 1 and find an example of each rule.

Answers

1 a, a programme   **2** b, the programme, the series
3 d, the world   **4** e, the best diver, the first
5 c, nurses, patients, emergencies

TEACHER DEVELOPMENT: LANGUAGE

a/an

Remind students that we use *an* before a vowel sound, not a vowel. For example, *university* starts with the same sound as *yacht* (/j/), and so takes the same article *a*.

TEACHER DEVELOPMENT: PRONUNCIATION

the/a

The is pronounced with the schwa sound /ə/ before words beginning with consonants: /ðə/. *The* has the vowel sound /i/ before words beginning with vowels and with proper nouns in the stressed form: /ðiː/.

When the article *a* is stressed, students should say the letter of the alphabet – a long vowel sound /eɪ/. Point out that the mouth is wide and open and the jaw and the back of the tongue are down when we make this sound. However, when the article *a* is unstressed it is pronounced /ə/.

3 Ask students to choose the correct alternative. Elicit answers from different students.

Answers

1 –, – **2** a, a, a **3** the, – **4** – **5** The, the **6** a, –, –
7 an, the, a **8** –, the

4 Ask students to complete the text with *a, an, the* or – (no article).

Answers

a a **b** an **c** an **d** – **e** a **f** the **g** the **h** a
i the **j** the

5 Ask students to read the text and correct seven mistakes in the use of articles. Give them time to compare answers in pairs before checking them.

Answers

One of the most interesting episodes of *Hidden Talent* was about a boy called James Whinnery. He was only 19. They discovered that the boy had a special talent for (1) ~~the~~ languages. He learnt (2) ~~the~~ Arabic in just 19 weeks. He did a test working in (3) <u>a</u> Turkish restaurant for a day, talking to the waiters in Arabic. Then, for his training, they say he learnt (4) ~~the~~ new words – one hundred words each day! At the end of the episode, he travelled to Jordan and they interviewed him in Arabic on a special programme. Of course, nobody can really learn (5) <u>a</u> new language in just 19 weeks. But James learnt a lot of things in that time. It seems that sometimes (6) ~~the~~ TV programmes can have (7) <u>a</u> positive effect on people and their lives.

so, such, too, enough

6 Ask students to look at the sentences a–f and complete the rules 1–6 with *so, such, too* or *enough*.

Answers

1 too **2** enough **3** such **4** so **5** too, enough
6 so, such

7 Ask students to complete the sentences with the words in the box. Remind students that they can use a word more than once if necessary. If no word is necessary, tell students to put – .

Answers

1 too **2** a **3** enough **4** to **5** – **6** so **7** enough
8 such **9** so

8 Ask students to complete the second sentence so that it has a similar meaning to the first sentence, using the word given. Remind students that they must not change the word given and they should use between two and five words including the word given.

Answers

1 are so good that everyone **2** too cold to **3** are good enough to **4** such a cold day that **5** isn't self-confident enough to **6** sing well enough

9a Encourage students to use their imagination to complete the sentences.

Example answers

1 they could go all day without seeing each other!
2 she built herself a golden palace.
3 he ended up without any friends.
4 get up in the morning and spent every day in bed.
5 climb that mountain.
6 I'll pass all my exams first time.
7 he can do university-level maths.

9b SPEAKING In small groups, students compare their sentences in exercise 9a and choose the best ones. Students then read out the best sentences to the class.

Refer students to the Grammar reference on page 54 if necessary.

> HOMEWORK
>
> **Assign students page 34 in their Workbook or the relevant sections of the Online Workbook.**

Developing speaking p52

Giving structured presentations on different topics

> **≫ FAST TRACK**
>
> You could ask students to note down ideas for exercise 8 at home in preparation for the speaking activity.

> WARMER
>
> Write these words on the board: *HUMAN INTELLIGENCE*. In pairs, students race to make as many words as they can from these letters in three minutes. The students with the most correctly spelt words are the winners (and have the highest 'linguistic intelligence'!).
>
> **Suggested answers**
>
> man, main, tell, huge, night, light, tight, let, melt, nice, team, meat, tan, the, time, game, neat, hate, gate, mate, gene, lime, tin, name, nail, etc.

1 SPEAKING In pairs, students talk about the people in the photos and say who they are and why they are famous. Elicit ideas from students around the class.

Answers

A Martin Luther King Junior – US civil rights campaigner
B Marie Curie – scientist famous for work on radioactivity
C Cristiano Ronaldo – international football player
D Emma Watson – actor (in Harry Potter films); UN Ambassador

2 SPEAKING Ask students to say how they would define a 'hero'. Elicit from students if they would call any of the people in exercise 1 heroes and ask them to give reasons why or why not.

3 SPEAKING In pairs, ask students to look at the presentation topic 'There are no heroes in today's world, just celebrities.' and discuss if they agree or disagree with the statement. Give them a few minutes to make notes of their ideas and think of arguments to justify and explain their opinions. Point out that both students should make notes as these notes will be used later to prepare a presentation. Elicit ideas from students around the class.

4 LISTENING ▶ 21 Play the track for students to listen to a student giving a presentation on the topic in exercise 3. Ask students to say what the speaker's opinion is and if the speaker mentions any of their ideas in exercise 3. See pp174–175 for the audioscript for this exercise.

Answer

The student disagrees with the statement and believes there are celebrities who can be called heroes.

5 ▶ 21 Draw students' attention to the expressions in the Speaking bank. Then play the track again for students to listen and tick the expressions that they hear.

Answers

I'd like to begin by saying, First of all, Furthermore, What's more, It's also true that, To sum up, In short

6 Ask students to work individually to organise their notes from exercise 3 in a logical order, with an introduction and a conclusion.

7 SPEAKING Ask students to read the advice in Exam success. In pairs, students then take it in turns to give a presentation with their opinion. Remind them to use expressions from the Speaking bank. When they finish, ask students to discuss how well they did their presentations.

✔ **EXAM SUCCESS** **Students read some tips on how to give an interesting presentation. Elicit other 'do and don'ts' from students (do take your time, do be enthusiastic, do remember to breathe, don't fidget, don't put your hands in your pockets, etc.). Then ask students to turn to page 145 (Speaking: Giving presentations) for more ideas.**

PRACTICE MAKES PERFECT

8a SPEAKING Ask students to prepare a presentation about somebody that they admire. Point out that it can be a famous person or someone in their life, for example a friend or relative, and remind them to give reasons why they admire them.

8b Students give their presentation to the class, or to a group of classmates if time is short. For students who are less confident, photocopy the model presentation below, and either read it aloud yourself, or ask a strong student to do so. Tell students to use this as a basis for their own presentation.

Model presentation

I'm going to talk about someone I admire very much, my cousin Laurence. He's six years older than me and he lives in Canada. He's extremely fit because he's a dancer. Firstly, I'd like to talk about when he was at school. Secondly, I want to talk about how he is now. At school, he was often bullied because he liked classical ballet while his classmates preferred hip hop and street dance. He was insecure and he didn't have many friends. Nowadays, he's very friendly and confident. This is because he had a fantastic teacher who changed his life and believed in him.

It's important to remember that dancing is a very difficult profession because it's so competitive. He doesn't have a lot of free time, but he teaches dance to young children who have difficult times at home. What's more, his groups have won prizes in different competitions.

In conclusion, I think Laurence is a very hard-working and gifted person and I admire him very much.

TEACHER DEVELOPMENT: STUDENT TRAINING

Presentations

Students may have to deliver oral presentations in English for an exam or at university. Planning and structuring an oral presentation is similar to the process of writing, except it should sound like natural speech. The main steps in oral presentations are planning, structuring, preparing and presenting.

1 Planning: Students brainstorm ideas.

2 Structuring: Students organise their thoughts in a logical order: introduction, body and conclusion. Students include as many phrases as possible from the Speaking bank. These are 'signposts' to guide their listeners.

3 Preparing: Students rehearse their presentations, paying attention to time limits, using notes without reading them, body language and use of voice.

4 Presenting: Students give their oral presentation and welcome questions at the end.

Ask students to evaluate each other using the simple form below. This will encourage students to listen to each other's presentations and provide positive feedback at the end:

Content	1	2	3	4	5
Organisation	1	2	3	4	5
Delivery	1	2	3	4	5

✚ **EXTRA ACTIVITY**

Develop the ideas from the presentations into a class debate to close the activity.

HOMEWORK

Assign students page 35 in their Workbook or the relevant sections of the Online Workbook.

Developing writing p53

Writing an article giving detailed personal descriptions

>>> FAST TRACK

You could ask students to make the list in exercise 2 at home in preparation for the writing activity.

WARMER

In pairs, students study each other for one minute before turning to sit back-to-back. Students describe their partner, remembering as many details as they can about their appearance today.

1 SPEAKING In pairs, students read the announcement and talk about people they could write about and talents they have.

2 Ask students to read an article written about the singer Ed Sheeran. Ask students to make a list of the talents the writer of the article says that Ed Sheeran has.

Answers

He writes great songs and performs concerts on his own. He's modest, funny and friendly. He plays and sings in lots of different styles. He can write lyrics. He makes brilliant videos. He's a talented dancer.

3 Ask students to match the paragraphs A–D to the topics.

Answers

D, A, C, B

4 Ask students to read the Writing bank and underline any examples of this language in the article in exercise 2.

Suggested answers

doesn't look very special, he tends to wear …, incredibly special, what I love about him …, most important talents, great talents, he shows that, great singer, most exciting thing

5 SPEAKING Ask students to use the expressions in the Writing bank to talk about the people they chose in exercise 1. Draw students' attention to the example.

PRACTICE MAKES PERFECT

6a Ask students to choose one person and write an article. Remind them to follow the paragraph plan in exercise 3 and use expressions from the Writing bank. They can also follow the advice in the Writing bank on p153. For students who are less confident, photocopy the model text below for extra support during the writing task.

Model text

Aung San Suu Kyi is a Burmese politician. She was born in 1945 in Rangoon, Burma (Myanmar). Her father, a national hero who helped Burma to gain its independence from Britain, was assassinated when Aung San Suu Kyi was only two years old. She left Burma, studied at Oxford University and worked for the United Nations in Japan and Bhutan. When she returned to Burma in 1988, Aung San Suu Kyi became involved in political protests against the government. A few months later, without charge and without trial, Aung San Suu Kyi was placed under house arrest. She spent more than ten years under house arrest.

She is older now, and she is very beautiful. She is quite small and thin, but she has got a strong and determined look. She has a kind face and bright brown eyes. She often wears flowers in her hair. She is extremely patient and kind, but she is a very intelligent and brave person. She also seems to be a very modest person.

Aung San Suu Kyi is a very talented politician. She has had many difficult moments but she is an expert negotiator and peacemaker. In 1991 she won the Nobel Prize for Peace. She is a Buddhist and I think this helps her be such a calm person.

In conclusion, I think Aung San Suu Kyi is one of the most talented people in the world. What I like most about her is her strength. She fights for democracy without using violence and her courage is a lesson to us all.

6b When students finish writing their articles, remind them to check them carefully. Ask them to check that they have included all the relevant information and that it is easy to understand the ideas and information. Students should also check for grammar or spelling mistakes.

TEACHER DEVELOPMENT: STUDENT TRAINING

Checking your writing

Encourage students to use this checklist to check their work before they hand it in to you:

Have I answered the question?

Does the text answer the task?

Is the writing style appropriate for the task?

Is the text logically ordered with good paragraph organisation?

Is it the right length?

Is the grammar, punctuation and spelling acceptable?

Is there a wide variety of vocabulary and structures?

Is it neat and legibly written?

HOMEWORK

Assign students page 36 in their Workbook or the relevant sections of the Online Workbook.

Language checkpoint: Unit 4

⟫⟫ FAST TRACK

The extra support provided in the Grammar and Vocabulary reference sections makes the Grammar and Vocabulary revision sections ideal for setting as homework. You could get students to complete the whole revision page or just certain exercises for homework.

Grammar revision p55

Making comparisons

1 Students choose the correct alternative.

Answers

1 hard 2 than 3 the hotter it gets 4 faster 5 as
6 most 7 earlier 8 carefully

Articles

2 Students add seven articles in the correct places in the sentences.

Answers

1 I met **a** friend yesterday in **the** city centre.
2 **The** most important thing in life are good friends.
3 Experts say **the** government is having problems.
4 When I'm bored I pick up **a** book and read.
5 I like listening to actors and **the** things they say about life in Hollywood.
6 **The** programmes I watch are all on late at night.

so, such, too, enough

3 Students match the sentence halves and complete the sentences with *so, such, too* or *enough*.

Answers

1 h (too) 2 f (so) 3 e (enough) 4 a (too) 5 b (such)
6 d (enough) 7 g (so) 8 c (such)

Vocabulary revision p55

PERSONALITY

1 Students complete the sentences with adjectives of personality.

Answers

1 tactless 2 down-to-earth 3 broad-minded
4 insecure 5 pushy 6 stubborn 7 immature
8 gifted 9 frank/honest

NOUN SUFFIXES

2 Students complete the sentences with the correct noun form of the words given.

Answers

1 musician 2 improvement 3 confidence
4 education 5 darkness 6 creator 7 electrician
8 appearance

HOMEWORK

Assign students page 37 in their Workbook or the relevant sections of the Online Workbook.

Reading p56

> **TIP FOR READING EXAMS**

Ask students to read the tip about missing sentence activities and look at Exam success on page 144 for more ideas.

1 Tell students they are going to read a text called 'What makes a genius?' Discuss the questions in open class before they read the article.

2 READING Ask students to read the text and ask them to formulate one sentence that summarises the text's main message. Encourage students to compare in pairs before you elicit sentences from students around the class.

Suggested answer

To become a genius you have to work hard and have opportunities.

3 Ask students to read the text again and complete the gaps with sentences A–H. Elicit the key sentences that helped students decide on their answers.

Answers

1 G (… same age – around five. In those first few years … Six hours a week by age nine …)

2 D (… totalled 10,000 hours of practice … And the third group just 4,000 hours.)

3 F (It's 10,000 hours. … this number comes up again and again.)

4 C (People generally agree that Mozart didn't write his first masterwork …)

5 A (… an enormous amount of time … You need parents who are encouraging and supportive. You can't be poor …)

6 E (One year the school spent $3,000 on a computer terminal.)

7 H (… 1,575 hours of computer time … So, he had spent a lot more than 10,000 hours on computers.)

8 B (Who was in the best position to take advantage of it? You don't want to be too young.)

4 SPEAKING **What about you?** In pairs, students discuss if they agree with what the text suggests – that to be a genius you need to work hard and have opportunities. Ask them to debate how important natural talent is.

Use of English p57

> **TIP FOR USE OF ENGLISH**

Students read the tip on how to do word formation cloze activities. Discuss other tips for completing this type of exercise and tell students to turn to Exam success on page 145 to compare their ideas.

5 In pairs, students make a list of things that they think they know about Albert Einstein. Then ask them to read the short text and see if it mentions any of the things on their list.

6 Ask students to read the text again and complete the gaps with the correct form of the words at the end of the lines.

Answers

a importance **b** scientific **c** unusually **d** scientist
e underestimate **f** ability **g** physicist
h mathematician **i** connection **j** unsuccessfully

Speaking p57

> **TIP FOR SPEAKING EXAMS**

Ask students to read the tip about what not to do in presentations. Elicit other tips students can remember and ask them to turn to Exam success on page 145 to check their ideas.

7 Individually, students prepare a presentation on the topic by making notes. Remind students not to write complete sentences.

8 SPEAKING In pairs, students brainstorm any expressions they know for the different stages of a presentation. Tell them to refer to the Speaking bank on page 52 to check their answers.

9 SPEAKING In groups, students take it in turns to give their presentations, using the expressions they thought of in exercise 8.

For students who are less confident, photocopy the model presentation below, and either read it aloud yourself or ask a strong student to do so. Then instruct students to build their own presentation using this structure as a guide.

Model presentation

I'm going to talk about three famous people I'd like to go on an excursion with. First of all, I'd like to go with Rafael Nadal. He is one of the greatest tennis players of all time. What's more, he is a very special person.

Secondly, I'd like to go on an excursion with Usain Bolt, the Jamaican sprinter and a World and Olympic gold medallist in the 100 metres, the 200 metres and the 4x100 metres relay. He is very funny and I think we would laugh a lot. Furthermore, he's the coolest sportsman in the world.

The third person I'd like to go on an excursion with is Lionel Messi, who plays for Spanish football club FC Barcelona and the Argentina national team. He is one of the best footballers in the world.

In conclusion, you can see that my excursion is going to be very interesting. I think we will probably do a lot of sport and it will be a very active excursion!

Model text

Jack didn't usually enjoy travelling, but today was different. He had won a competition that he had entered on the Internet called Cricket Australia. The prize was a ticket to Australia's one-day international match against India at the Sydney Cricket Ground (SCG). It was a long flight, something he didn't like, but he was going to Sydney!

Jack found out he had won the competition around two weeks before the game. He had to say in fewer than 25 words who was his favourite player and why. He didn't believe it when he got the email saying he'd won.

He had been watching cricket on TV since he was little, and he was keen to meet all the famous cricket stars, but he wasn't sure if that would be possible. Luckily, after the match, the competition winners were taken to the press conference room. There were some of the most famous cricket stars answering questions. When the press conference finished, he had the chance to meet Shane Watson and Mitchell Johnson, the famous Australian cricket all-rounder and bowler. Jack asked them to sign his T-shirt and they took a selfie together. They also went to the indoor cricket centre at the SCG and bumped into more Australian players. Meeting these stars was the highlight of the experience for him.

Writing p57

➤ TIP FOR WRITING EXAMS

Ask students to read the tip about writing stories. Elicit other things students should remember to do and ask them to turn to Exam success page 145 to remind them of important tips and strategies.

10 In pairs, students read the task and plan their story. Remind them to think about the main events, the background and any important scenes.

11 Individually, students write their story, following advice in the Writing bank on page 152. For students who are less confident, photocopy the model text below for extra support during the writing task.

HOMEWORK

Assign students pages 38–39 in their Workbook or the relevant sections of the Online Workbook.

1 Ask students to mark from 1–4 how well they feel they can do each thing in English.

2 Ask students to look at their marks and decide what they need to do to improve. Elicit ideas from students around the class.

5 Money matters

KEY LEARNING OUTCOMES

Students will be able to:

- talk about obligation, prohibition and advice in the present and past
- make speculations and deductions about the past, present and future
- understand written and spoken texts on topics related to money
- discuss ways to avoid getting into debt
- make present and past speculations about photos
- write a formal letter of complaint

UNIT OVERVIEW

Vocabulary
Buying and selling
Money and banking
PRONUNCIATION Silent letters

Reading
Money: A brief history
CRITICAL THINKING Discussing how money will evolve over time

Grammar in context
Modal verbs of obligation, prohibition and advice – present
Modal verbs of obligation, prohibition and advice – past

Developing vocabulary
Phrasal verbs connected with money and shopping

Life skills
Money and finance: Avoiding debt

Listening
Bitcoins

Grammar in context
Modal verbs of speculation and deduction – past, present and future

Developing speaking
Talking about photos – 2

Developing writing
A formal letter/email of complaint

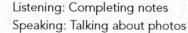

Exam success
Listening: Completing notes
Speaking: Talking about photos

DIGITAL OVERVIEW

Presentation Kit
- ▶ **Flipped classroom video Unit 5:** Modal verbs of obligation, prohibition and advice – past
- ▶ **Life skills video Unit 5:** Avoiding debt
- ▶ **Interactive versions of Student's Book activities**
- ▶ **Integrated audio and answer key for all activities**
- ▶ **Workbook pages with answer key**

Teacher's Resource Centre
- ▶ **Flipped classroom video Unit 5:** Modal verbs of obligation, prohibition and advice – past
- ▶ **Life skills video Unit 5:** Avoiding debt
- ▶ **Grammar communication activity Unit 5:** On the money
- ▶ **Worksheets for this unit, including:**
  - – Grammar Practice worksheet Unit 5
  - – Flipped classroom video worksheet Unit 5: Modal verbs of obligation, prohibition and advice – past
  - – Literature worksheet Units 5 and 6
  - – Culture worksheet Unit 5
  - – Life skills video worksheet Unit 5
  - – Everyday English worksheet Unit 5

Student's App
Gateway 2nd Edition wordlist for the award-winning Sounds App (available for download)

✔ TESTING AND ASSESSMENT

Resources for exam preparation and measuring student progress

- ▶ Test Generator Units 1–5
- ▶ Printable test Unit 5
- ▶ Gateway to exams Units 5 and 6 (end of Unit 6)

Vocabulary p58

Talking about issues related to buying and selling and to money and banking

⋙ FAST TRACK

You could ask students to do exercises 2 and 4 at home. They can look up any words they are not sure about in their dictionaries or the Macmillan Online Dictionary.

WARMER

In pairs, students discuss the meaning of the unit title *Money matters* and what they think the unit is going to be about (different aspects of finance and how students can make the most of their money). Elicit other words and expressions students know that are related to the theme, e.g. *to make/earn/win money; money makes the world go round; time is money; money talks*. Drill the pronunciation of the word *money*: /ˈmʌni/.

▌Answer

Money matters is a play on words. The word *matters* means <u>the subject</u> (things related to money) but it can also mean <u>to be of importance</u> (money is important).

Buying and selling

1 **SPEAKING** In pairs, students write down as many different names for shops as they can in two minutes. Elicit answers from the class and encourage students to add any that they missed to their list.

Example answers

baker's, bank, bookshop, butcher's, charity shop, clothes shop, DIY/hardware shop, department store, electrical goods store, greengrocer's, jeweller's, music shop, newsagent's, post office, shoe shop, sports shop, stationery shop, supermarket, travel agent's

⋙ FAST FINISHERS

Students say things that they can buy in a shop on their list for their partner to name the shop.

TEACHER DEVELOPMENT: LANGUAGE

Possessive 's in shop names

The possessive *'s* is often used when talking about shops, restaurants, hospitals, schools and colleges, following the name or job title of the owner or patron, e.g. *the grocer's, the jeweller's, King's college.*

2 Ask students to complete the text with the words. Provide dictionaries if necessary.

Answers

a a<u>ff</u>ord /əˈfɔː(r)d/   **b** sale /seɪl/   **c** dis<u>c</u>ount /ˈdɪsˌkaʊnt/
d <u>bargain</u> /ˈbɑː(r)gɪn/   **e** <u>value</u> for <u>money</u> /ˈvæljuː fə(r) ˈmʌni/
f cash /kæʃ/   **g** change /tʃeɪndʒ/   **h** re<u>ceipt</u> /rɪˈsiːt/
i waste /weɪst/   **j** <u>refund</u> /ˈriːfʌnd/

⋙ FAST FINISHERS

Students mark the stressed syllables and practise the pronunciation of the words (see Answers in exercise 2 above).

3 **SPEAKING** In pairs, students take it in turns to ask and answer the questions. Elicit answers from different students around the class.

Example answers

1 Yes, I have a few coins and a couple of notes. It's useful for simple, everyday transactions.
2 They usually pay by credit card.
3 We often go to the sales to buy coats and shoes.
4 I always keep the receipt in case I need to exchange my purchase or get a refund.
5 My dad asked for a refund on a fridge that didn't work.
6 Students get special discounts on public transport and at many leisure centres.
7 I wasted my money on some fake designer trainers. They were really bad quality.
8 I bought some boots in a second-hand shop last year and they were a real bargain and great value for money.

Money and banking

4 Ask students to match the words and phrases with the definitions. Provide dictionaries if necessary.

Answers

1 overdraft   **2** savings account   **3** lend money/give somebody a loan   **4** bank charges/fees
5 current account   **6** withdraw money   **7** interest
8 bill   **9** ATM/cashpoint   **10** get into debt

5 **LISTENING** ⏵ 22 Play the track for students to listen and answer the eight questions. Point out that they will hear each question twice. Check their answers. See p175 for the audioscript for this exercise.

Answers

1 £45   **2** £7   **3** no   **4** yes   **5** yes   **6** £4   **7** yes
8 no

6a **PRONUNCIATION** Elicit from students how we say the words in the box and what they all have in common.

Answer

All the words have a silent letter.

6b ⏵ 23 Play the track for students to listen to the words and correct their pronunciation if necessary.

✚ EXTRA ACTIVITY

Students write down the words in their notebooks and put a line through the silent letters.

Answers

answ̶er /ˈɑːnsə(r)/   busi̶ness /ˈbɪznəs/   clim̶b /klaɪm/
deb̶t /det/   doub̶t /daʊt/   eig̶ht /eɪt/   hal̶f /hɑːf/
h̶onest /ˈɒnɪst/   k̶nowledge /ˈnɒlɪdʒ/   lis̶ten /ˈlɪs(ə)n/
litre /ˈliːtə(r)/   psychological /ˌsaɪkəˈlɒdʒɪk(ə)l/
receipt /rɪˈsiːt/   tal̶k /tɔːk/   throug̶h /θruː/   wr̶itten /ˈrɪt(ə)n/

TEACHER DEVELOPMENT: PRONUNCIATION

Silent letters

One of the noted difficulties of English spelling is a high number of silent letters. Silent letters are letters that you can't hear when you say the word, but that are there when you write the word. There are no rules; you just have to learn them.

The reason is often historic and shows how the word was pronounced in the past, although sometimes it is phonological and helps us to understand how to pronounce a vowel sound.

HOMEWORK

Assign students page 40 in their Workbook or the relevant sections of the Online Workbook.

Reading p59

Skimming and scanning for global and specific information

⟫⟫ FAST TRACK

You could ask students to read the article in exercise 2 at home in preparation for in-class activities.

WARMER

Divide the class into two teams: A and B. Choose a word from the unit so far and say it to Team A for them to spell out, letter by letter. If they spell the whole word correctly, they score one point. However, if at any point they say an incorrect letter, the 'part-word' is handed over to Team B to complete (and back again if they make an error). This continues until one team finishes off the word and wins a point. The team with the most points wins the game.

1 **SPEAKING** In pairs, students look at the photos and answer the questions.

2 **READING** Ask students to skim-read the article and check their answers in exercise 1. Set a time limit of three minutes to encourage students not to focus on difficult vocabulary at this stage.

Answers

1 The objects were all used as money over the years.
2 Not now, because their value changes.

TEACHER DEVELOPMENT: STUDENT TRAINING

Skimming

Skimming is a reading technique that you can use when you want to read quickly to get an overall understanding, perhaps to decide if the text is interesting and if you should read it in more detail. We use this technique to extract the main ideas from a text. Explain that students should not read every word when they skim a text. They should read the first and last line of each paragraph and train their eyes to skim over the surface of the text to look out for key words. They should also use any clues available, e.g. pictures, photos, vocabulary from the question or title to give them background information.

3 Ask students to read the text again and answer the questions with information from the text. Elicit answers from different students around the class.

Answers

1 We exchange items for services.
2 You have to find the right person to barter with.
3 You don't have to find 'the right person'.
4 Their uses gave them a basic value.
5 They last for such a short time.
6 They maintained their value over time, can be easily translated into prices and were widely accepted.
7 They were heavy to carry around.
8 The first paper money was a type of receipt or note.
9 The cash we carry around with us.
10 It leads to higher prices and money loses its value.

4 **CRITICAL THINKING** Individually, students think about how money will evolve over time and then compare their ideas with the rest of the class. Ask students to justify their opinions.

Example answer

I think society will become more collaborative and we will share our things. The more you share, the more points you will get.

ℹ CULTURAL INFORMATION

The digital money revolution has already started but it will take a few years to develop. The *digital wallet* is a software platform designed to run on our smartphones that supports a variety of money and ID oriented apps. The digital wallet will emerge as the standard for accessing money, as well as financial and identity information. Near Field Communications (NFC) enable mobile devices to be used for contactless payments in shops and on public transport. Smartphones use fingerprint and retinal recognition for transactions that require a higher measure of security. There are new kinds of banking relationships and all sorts of innovative apps to help spread and transform *m-business*.

5 Encourage students to guess the meaning of the underlined words in the text. Allow them to use a dictionary to check their answers.

Answers

barter = to exchange goods or services for other goods or services instead of using money
medium = a way of communicating information and ideas, especially to a lot of people
standardising = keeping something the same
widely = by a lot of people, or in a lot of places
worthless = not having any value, or not useful

6 **SPEAKING What about you?** In pairs or small groups, students discuss whether society gives too much importance to having money. Ask students to say why or why not. In a less confident class, ask students to write down their ideas first before doing this as a speaking activity.

Example answers

I think many people are thinking about giving up money. Money is the cause of unemployment, wars, crime, terrorism, pollution, etc. A lot of people are beginning to share resources and build a better world for everyone.

I think people in general are motivated by money and profits. We have been doing this for so long that it seems like a very important part of our lives.

✚ EXTRA ACTIVITY

Divide the class into teams and hold a class debate on the topic.

TEACHER DEVELOPMENT: CLASSROOM TIPS AND PLANNING

Promoting class debate

Divide the class into two sides by flipping a coin to see who can choose their 'side' in the argument. The other side has to take the opposite view. After students have rehearsed their arguments in pairs, open it up to a whole-class debate. Ask students to vote (by raising their hands) at the end of the debate to see which side of the argument won the debate.

Elicit key phrases for agreeing and disagreeing and write them on the board for students to refer to during the speaking activity.

Agreeing: *I think you're right; I agree with you …*
Agreeing in part: *I agree with you up to a point, but …*
Disagreeing: *I'm not sure I agree with you. (I'm afraid) I don't agree. (I'm afraid) I disagree. I strongly disagree.*

HOMEWORK

Assign students page 41 in their Workbook or the relevant sections of the Online Workbook.

Grammar in context pp60–61

Using modal verbs of obligation, prohibition and advice to talk about the present and past

Test before you teach

In pairs, students think of a board game that other students will know well, e.g. *Monopoly*. Write these sentence stems on the board and ask students to complete them with the rules of the game: *You ought to …, You should …, You have to …, You don't have to …, You must …, You mustn't …, You'd better …, You aren't allowed to …, You need to …, You don't need to …, You can't …*

If students seem to be familiar with these modals, move through the Grammar guide exercises quickly in open class.

Modal verbs of obligation, prohibition and advice – present

1a Ask students to look at the sentences and answer questions 1–4.

Answers

1 have to/must/need to   **2** don't have to/doesn't need to/needn't   **3** mustn't/aren't allowed to/can't   **4** ought to/should/'d better

1b Students answer the questions.

Answers

1 *to + infinitive:* ought, have/don't have, allowed, need/don't need

the infinitive without *to:* should, must/mustn't, 'd better, needn't, can't

2 Do we all **have to** use money?

3 It **shouldn't** be something that maintains its value.
You**'d better not** keep your money in your pocket.

4 You **need to** carry it all with you.

5 had

TEACHER DEVELOPMENT: PRONUNCIATION

Modal verbs

When pronounced in the contracted form, *would* and *had* sound the same (*'d*), so the listener must rely on the context of the sentence to determine which word the speaker is using. Write these sentences on the board and elicit if the contraction *'d* is for *would* or *had*. Then drill the pronunciation:

I'd say it was more expensive than the other one. (would)
It'd be better if we left now. (would)
You'd better go now. (had)
I'd already left when she arrived. (had)

Draw attention to the silent letter *l* in *should* and the silent *t* in *mustn't*. Drill the pronunciation of these two forms.

Have to is usually pronounced /hæv tuː/.
Has to is usually pronounced /hæz tuː/.
Drill the pronunciation of *ought:* /ɔːt/.

2 Ask students to correct the sentences. Give them time to compare their answers in pairs before checking them in open class.

Answers

1 You mustn't   **2** Do you have to   **3** You needn't open   **4** She'd/had better   **5** We ought to   **6** don't need to have

3 Ask students to complete the sentences with the words in the box. Point out that there are four extra words.

Answers

1 had   **2** has   **3** ought   **4** aren't   **5** needn't
6 mustn't

⟫⟫⟫ FAST FINISHERS

Students write a sentence for each of the four extra words in the box in exercise 3.

4 **SPEAKING** In pairs, students use the words and expressions in the box to write sentences with useful information for a British student who is coming to study at their school for one month. In a less confident class, brainstorm some ideas first in open class. Elicit answers and ask students to decide on the five most useful pieces of information.

Suggested answers

You can't use your mobile phone at school.

You don't have to wear a school uniform.

You had better not talk in Mrs Williams' class – she's very strict.

You must start learning our language because most of our lessons aren't in English.

You mustn't chew gum in the class.

You needn't buy textbooks – the school will lend them to you.

You ought to buy a big rucksack to carry your books.

 Test before you teach: Flipped classroom
Set the Flipped classroom video and tasks for homework <u>before the lesson</u>. This will allow you to assess the needs of the students before the class. Students can then move on to the relevant grammar practice activities.

Modal verbs of obligation, prohibition and advice – past

5a Ask students to look at the sentences and answer the questions.

Answers

1 had to/needed to **2** needn't have **3** didn't have to/didn't need to **4** weren't allowed to/couldn't **5** should have/ought to have/shouldn't have

5b Ask students to complete the structure.

Answer

have + past participle

6 Ask students to write the sentences in the past.

Answers

1 You should have asked them for advice.

2 She had to arrive on time every morning.

3 Did you have to go to the meeting?

4 We couldn't wear jeans and T-shirts.

5 I needn't have got up early (but I did).

6 She didn't need to wear a uniform (so she didn't).

7 We ought to/should have worked as a team.

7 Ask students to rewrite the sentences. Remind them they should use each of the expressions once.

Answers

1 I had to do the exercises last night.

2 We needn't have taken food to the party, but we did.

3 She ought to have revised for the exam.

4 They weren't allowed to go into the office.

5 The plane needed to land.

6 I didn't have to show my receipt to the shop assistant.

7 I shouldn't have got angry with you yesterday.

8a Encourage students to think about when they were at primary school and write sentences about things that were obligatory, not obligatory, prohibited and that they should or shouldn't have done. Remind students to use the structures in exercise 5a. Draw attention to the example sentence.

Example answers

I didn't have to wear a tie, but I had to wear short trousers.

I couldn't run in the corridors.

I had to arrive on time.

I needed to go to the school doctor a couple of times.

I needn't have worried about secondary school, but I did.

I ought to have studied more.

I shouldn't have talked so much in class.

I wasn't allowed to leave before three o'clock.

8b SPEAKING Have students compare their sentences in small groups and find out if their experiences were similar.

Refer students to the Grammar reference on page 68 if necessary.

HOMEWORK

Assign students page 42 in their Workbook or the relevant sections of the Online Workbook.

Developing vocabulary p61

Using phrasal verbs connected with money and shopping

>>> FAST TRACK

Students could do exercise 1 at home and check answers before doing exercise 2 in class.

Phrasal verbs connected with money and shopping

1 Ask students to match the phrasal verbs used in sentences 1–8 with the definitions a–h.

Answers

1 b **2** c **3** a **4** g **5** f **6** d **7** h **8** e

TEACHER DEVELOPMENT: STUDENT TRAINING

Learning phrasal verbs

Point out to students that most dictionaries tell them when phrasal verbs are separable. For example, if a dictionary says *give (something) away*, students know that the phrasal verb *give away* is separable. Remind them that it is a good idea to include *something/somebody* when they write a new phrasal verb in their notebooks to tell them if the verb needs a direct object (and where to put it).

2 Students rewrite the sentences using the correct form of one of the phrasal verbs in exercise 1.

Answers

1 Can you **pick up** some milk on the way home?
2 That coat is expensive, but I'm going to **splash out** on it.
3 We need to **cut back** on luxury items.
4 We haven't got much money, but we **get by**.
5 I can't go to the concert because I need to **set** money **aside** for the summer holidays.
6 You should buy the game now because they're **selling out** fast.
7 I'll **pay back** the money you lent me tomorrow.
8 The book was £10 and the magazine was £2.50 so the total **came to** £12.50.

3 Ask students to choose the correct alternative. Check their answers.

Answers

1 aside **2** back **3** out **4** out **5** by **6** up

4 SPEAKING Students take it in turns to ask and answer the questions in exercise 3. Remind students that if their partner answers yes, they should ask questions to find out more information. In a less confident class, give students time to make some notes on their answers before they do this as a speaking activity.

EXTRA ACTIVITY

Students write a short text using all the phrasal verbs in exercise 1. They then write out the text with the phrasal verbs missing and give it to another student for him/her to complete.

HOMEWORK

Assign students page 43 in their Workbook or the relevant sections of the Online Workbook.

Gateway to life skills pp62–63

Avoiding debt

To learn about student debt and its different causes, to learn some tips to avoid getting into debt and to practise planning a simple budget

>>> FAST TRACK

You could ask students to do exercises 1 and 2 at home and then elicit their ideas in a brief class discussion at the beginning of the next class.

BACKGROUND INFORMATION

Knowing the basic concepts involved with earning, spending, saving, and investing can help young people establish good financial-management habits and avoid making costly mistakes.

One of the life skills most critical to success is knowing how to manage money.

Surveys suggest that the average student at a British university could find themselves in up to £50,000 worth of debt when they graduate. Student debt is now so high compared to average salaries that many graduates in reasonably good jobs will be unable to repay their fees even by the end of the 30-year repayment period. Students are expected to start repaying their student loans once they earn a salary of £21,000.

WARMER

In pairs, students imagine that they are going to open a bank account and make a list of questions they would like to ask before they open the account. Elicit ideas from students around the class and pre-teach some of the vocabulary for the lesson. Ask students to open their books on page 62 to check they know the vocabulary in Key concepts.
Suggested questions:
Do they give you a debit/credit card?
Are there any charges for using the account?
What happens if I run out of money?
What happens if I go into the red?
What information do I need to give to open an account?
How much money do I need to deposit in the account?
How much money can I withdraw each day?

1 In pairs, ask students to match the expressions with their definitions. Provide dictionaries if necessary. Elicit answers from different students around the class.

Answers

1 b **2** a **3** d **4** c

2 Ask students to discuss in pairs or small groups how they think the things in exercise 1 could encourage young people to spend too much money. Elicit ideas from students in open class.

3 READING Ask students to read the article called 'The dangers of debt' quickly and decide what the numbers refer to. Elicit ideas from students around the class.

Answers

1 £750 a month for accommodation
2 Average credit card debt £3,657
3 38% splash out more often than they should
4 Average overdraft £1,509

4 Ask students to read the article again and decide if the statements are True (T) or False (F). Check answers and ask students to identify the sentences that helped them decide.

Answers

1 T (38% admit that they splash out more often than they should)

2 F (… may need as much as £750 a month … leave … just £400 to live on each month.)

3 T (… into the red on their overdrafts … help with credit card debt … payday-loan debt …)

4 T (… so many financial companies are throwing credit at students …)

5 T (There is not enough financial education at school or in the home …)

6 F (Most universities and colleges now offer some form of face-to-face debt advice service …)

7 T (Limiting yourself to cash really helps you to control your spending.)

8 F (… avoid accounts that offer large overdrafts …)

5 SPEAKING In pairs, ask students to answer the questions.

Answers

1 Both – students are often influenced to spend more than they have; banks throw credit at students

2 payday loans, store cards, not enough financial education at school or at home

3 Students' own answers

4 withdraw cash and only spend that; resist temptation to use debit card; avoid accounts with large overdraft facilities; check bank account regularly; discuss money with friends; use discount card

5 Students' own answers

VOCABULARY FOCUS

The video contains some useful colloquial language about managing finances and debt that students may not be familiar with. You might want to pre-teach these words and phrases with students before watching:

cut through [phr v]: go through an area instead of around it

cashpoint [n]: also called ATM, where we withdraw money from a bank

likely [adj]: probably going to happen

workshop(s) [n]: where people meet to learn about (or discuss and study) a subject

specifically [adv]: for one particular thing or type of thing

keep a log [phr]: keep a record of things that happen

keep a lockdown [phr, coll.]: take total control of something

contactless payment [n]: using a credit card to pay through a device that recognises information without typing in numbers

6 LISTENING 24 Tell students they are going to watch or listen to Tope explaining how to manage your money. Play the video or audio track and ask students to answer the questions 1–5. Check their answers. See the Teacher's Resource Centre for the audioscript/videoscript for this exercise.

Answers

1 developing budgeting skills as a teenager will help you in the future

2 before you buy anything, ask if it is an essential purchase; only take out the cash you need from the cashpoint

3 look at your income; look at how much you're spending; look how much money you have left

4 to trace where your money is going in order to better plan your money

5 contactless payment means that sometimes we spend more money than we want to

7 24 Play the video or audio track again, then encourage students to discuss in pairs how many of the things Tope suggests they do. Elicit students' opinions in open class.

✚ EXTRA ACTIVITY

Ask students to write three questions about the video. In pairs, students give their partner their questions and have them write the answers.

> Question 1: ....
> Answer: ....
> Question 2: ....
> Answer: ....
> Question 3: ....
> Answer: ....

TEACHER DEVELOPMENT: CLASSROOM TIPS AND PLANNING

Video clips and questions

A good way to use short video clips to generate critical thinking involves students watching a short video clip and then writing questions about the clip. Students divide into pairs, exchange their papers, and answer their partner's questions. Students can then exchange papers again to read and mark their partner's answers. The fact that students are writing questions for a real audience motivates them to write better questions. Students may also take more time answering the questions because they know their partner will be 'marking' them.

LIFE TASK

Tell students they are going to work on a task to plan a simple budget. Ask them to follow the plan:

■ *Step 1*

Ask students to read the information about a student called Samara on page 159.

■ *Step 2*

Encourage students to use the information to plan a monthly budget for Samara following their answers in exercise 6.

■ *Step 3*

Ask students to work in a small group and compare their budgets to see if they are similar or not. Encourage students to discuss if they agree about what is essential and non-essential.

Listening p64

Predicting and listening for specific information

WARMER

Play *Who wants to be a millionaire?* with the class. Each student (or pair) writes a question on a subject area of their choice on a piece of paper. Remind them to include four answer options (A, B, C and D). Divide the class into two teams and collect the questions in from each team. Write the sequence for 'cash prizes' on the board from bottom to top: *£100, £200, £300, £500, £1,000, £2,000, £4,000, £8,000, £16,000, £32,000, £64,000, £125,000, £250,000, £500,000, £1,000,000*. Ask each team a question written by someone on the other team. If they get the answer right, they move up the board to the next 'cash prize'. If they get the answer wrong, they move down to the previous amount. The team in the highest position when all the questions have been asked, or the first team to reach £1,000,000, is the winner.

1 **SPEAKING** In pairs, students look at the photo and discuss what they think it represents.

Suggested answer

Someone is touching a screen. There is a logo or financial symbol above the words 'touch to begin'.

2 Ask students to read through the text ignoring the gaps and say if they think Bitcoins are good or bad. Elicit answers from students around the class and ask them to say why or why not.

ℹ CULTURAL INFORMATION

Bitcoins are an electronic money system which is not controlled by any single bank or country. They are usable across the Internet and are starting to enter the mainstream economy. Bitcoins are used by people as an investment tool. Currently there are over 12 million Bitcoins in circulation, with an approximate creation rate of 25 every ten minutes. The total supply is limited to 21 million and every four years the creation rate is halved. Many banks regard Bitcoins as unregulated.

3 **SPEAKING** In pairs, students predict what words or types of word could go in each gap.

✔ EXAM SUCCESS Ask students to read the tip on completing notes in listening activities. Ask them to turn to Exam success on page 145 for more ideas (Listening: Completing notes).

TEACHER DEVELOPMENT: STUDENT TRAINING

Inference in listening

Listening is a process of matching speech (bottom-up processing) with what listeners already know about the subject (top-down processing). Students need to be trained in techniques to improve their top-down approach to predict content before they move to the bottom-up approach to check their understanding. When listeners know the context of a text, the process is facilitated considerably because listeners can activate prior knowledge and make the appropriate inferences essential to comprehending the message. We need to help students organise their thoughts, to activate appropriate background knowledge for understanding and to make predictions and to prepare for listening. This helps reduce anxiety and improves students' performance.

4 **LISTENING** ▶ 25 Play the track for students to listen to an interview with an expert on Bitcoins and complete the text in exercise 2 with one word or number in each gap. Check their answers. See p175 for the audioscript for this exercise.

Answers

a digital **b** files **c** real **d** mining **e** difficult
f governments **g** dramatically **h** criminals
i California **j** 64 **k** identity **l** billion

TEACHER DEVELOPMENT: CLASSROOM TIPS

Checking answers

We need to check students' answers to check if they have understood the language point in question. However, checking answers can be boring and slow. Keep the students on their toes by eliciting the answers to the questions randomly, e.g. 5, 2, 6, 7. In this way, they cannot anticipate which question they are likely to get. You can let the students decide which questions to answer. This is good for less confident students because it allows them to answer questions they think they have answered correctly. By not letting them know what to expect, your students will be attentive and engaged.

5 **SPEAKING** What about *you*? In pairs or small groups, students discuss if they would buy or use Bitcoins and give reasons why or why not. Elicit opinions from students in open class.

Example answers

I wouldn't like to buy or use Bitcoins because I think it is a sort of pyramid operation run by cybercriminals.
I would like to buy or use Bitcoins because it is going to be very popular. Just like gold, the more people want it, the higher the price goes.

✚ EXTRA ACTIVITY

Students research a currency and find out about its history and any interesting facts. Students could present the results from their investigation at the beginning of the next class.

Grammar in context pp64–65

Making speculations and deductions about the past, present and future

>>> FAST TRACK

Students could do exercises 1, 2 and 3 at home. Check their answers and start the class on exercise 4.

Test before you teach

To test the use of modals in the present/future and the past, write this mystery riddle on the board: *Tim and Tom are in the living room dead on the floor. They are surrounded by glass and water. How did they die?*
Write *can't, may, might, could, must* on the board and ask students to use these words to speculate about what happened to Tim and Tom, e.g. *It could be a crime. They might have cut themselves with the glass.* If students seem familiar with modal verbs of deduction, move through the Grammar guide exercises quickly in open class.

Answer

Tim and Tom are goldfish. A cat came through the window and the bowl smashed on the floor.

Modal verbs of speculation and deduction – present and future

1 Ask students to look at the sentences and complete the rules with the verbs in blue.

Answers

1 We use *might, may* and *could* when there is a 50% possibility that something is or will be true. The negative forms are *may not* and *might not.* We cannot use the negative form of *could* when there is a 50% possibility that something isn't true.
2 We use *must* when we are 90% certain that something is true.
3 We use *can't* when we are 90% certain that something isn't true.
4 When we are speculating and making deductions, the opposite of *must* is *can't.*

TEACHER DEVELOPMENT: LANGUAGE

Modal verbs of speculation and deduction

Modal verbs of speculation and deduction with the infinitive (without *to*) are used to express our degree of certainty about the past, present or future. Remind students that modal verbs do not take *s* in the third person present tense, e.g. *He/She must be at school.*

2 Ask students to look at the things and speculate about what they may, must or can't be. Ask students to give reasons for their answers.

Answers

A a dollar bill/bank note   **B** a calculator   **C** a wallet
D a credit or debit card   **E** a receipt

3 Ask students to complete the sentences with *must, can't, may* or *might (not).* Elicit answers from different students around the class.

Answers

1 can't   **2** must   **3** might not/may not   **4** may/might   **5** must   **6** can't   **7** must   **8** may/might, may not/might not

Modal verbs of speculation and deduction – past

4 Ask students to look at sentences a–d and complete rules 1–3 with the verbs in blue. Check their answers.

Answers

1 We use *may have, might have* and *could have* when there is a 50% possibility that something was true, but we cannot use *could have* + past participle in the negative form with this meaning.
2 We use *must have* when we are 90% certain that something was true.
3 We use *can't have* when we are 90% certain that something wasn't true.

TEACHER DEVELOPMENT: LANGUAGE

Modal verbs of speculation and deduction – past

Modal verbs of speculation and deduction + *have* + past participle are used to express a degree of certainty about a past action or situation.
If we are guessing about a situation/state in the past, we use: modal verb + *have* + past participle, e.g. *She might have resigned from her job.*
If we are guessing about an ongoing action in the past, we use: modal verb + *have* + *been* + *-ing*, e.g. *She must have been working all night because her bedroom light is still on.*

TEACHER DEVELOPMENT: PRONUNCIATION

have

Drill the strong and weak forms of *have* in these sentences:
You have to go now. (strong form of *have*: /hæv/)
You must have known. (weak form of *have*: /əv/, /v/)

5 Ask students to correct the mistakes in the sentences.

Answers

1 It's only lunchtime and you look terrible. You **must have had** a bad morning.

2 Somebody's unlocked the door. It **can't have been** Mike because he hasn't got a key.

3 I think Josh **might have sent** me an email last night.

4 Emma hasn't replied to my email. She **might not have received** it.

5 William isn't here. He **must have gone** already.

6 Let's not buy her that DVD. I'm not sure, but I think she **might have bought** it already.

7 You **can't have read** that book already! It's 600 pages long and you only started yesterday!

8 It **can't have rained** last night because all the streets are dry.

6 Ask students to complete the text with past modal verbs of speculation and the verbs given.

Answers

a must have been   **b** can't have left   **c** must have had   **d** may/might (not) have been   **e** may/might have worked   **f** must have moved   **g** may/might have had

7a SPEAKING In pairs, students look at the situations and write at least two sentences with *must have*, *might have* and *can't have* to explain them.

Suggested answers

1 He must have won the lottery. He might have been successful in his business.

2 She might have been tired. She can't have studied enough.

3 He must have done something wrong. He might have missed school.

4 He can't have been concentrating on driving. He must have been tired.

5 She must have been playing a better player. She might have been ill that day.

6 They must have lost the game. The team might have played really badly.

7 She must have gone on a fitness programme. She might have started a new sport.

8 She might have gone to an English-speaking country. She must have practised a lot.

7b Ask students to compare their ideas with the rest of the class.

✚ EXTRA ACTIVITY

Brainstorm problematic situations and write them on the board, e.g. *I can't find my textbook. I haven't got enough money. The lights have gone out. No students came to school today.* The students respond with an explanation using *must have/could have/ might have.*

Refer students to the Grammar reference on page 68 if necessary.

HOMEWORK

Assign students page 44 in their Workbook or the relevant sections of the Online Workbook.

Developing speaking p66

Making present and past speculations about photos

≫ FAST TRACK

You could ask students to do exercise 4 at home in preparation for the speaking activity.

WARMER

Play *Noughts and crosses* with words from previous lessons. Draw a 3 x 3 grid on the board. Choose a word and draw a short line on the board to represent each letter. Write small numbers 1 to 9 in each square on the grid so it is easy for students to name the square. Divide the class into two teams and toss a coin to see who goes first. Assign noughts (0) to one group and crosses (X) to the other. The first group chooses a square from the grid and says a letter. If the letter is in the word, write it on the corresponding short line. That group can then continue guessing letters. If they say a letter which is not in the word, play passes to the other team. If they guess the word correctly, their symbol (0 or X) goes in the space they nominated. The other team can then choose a square and try to guess a new word. The first team to get three noughts or crosses in a row (horizontal, vertical or diagonal) is the winner.

1 SPEAKING In pairs, students make a list of words and expressions they can use to talk about similarities and differences between photos. Draw their attention to the expressions given as examples. Allow them to look back at page 40 to remind themselves if necessary.

Suggested answers

In both photos, …

In the first photo …, but in the second photo …

One similarity/big difference is …

Another important difference is …

Compared with …

2 Ask students to use the words and expressions in exercise 1 to talk about the two photos. Walk round, monitoring and noting down good use of language and errors to go over in a feedback session at the end of the activity.

3 LISTENING 🔊 26 Play the track for students to listen to a student talking about the photos and answer the questions. Check their answers. See pp175–176 for the audioscript for this exercise.

Answers

1 Students' own answers
2 No, just briefly and then she moves on to compare them.
3 Which kind of shopping is more successful? or What kind of shopping do you enjoy more?

✔ **EXAM SUCCESS** Ask students to read about the importance of following instructions in a speaking exam and how to carry out a 'compare and contrast' task. Tell students to turn to page 145 (Speaking: Talking about photos) for more ideas.

TEACHER DEVELOPMENT: STUDENT TRAINING

Talking about photos

In many exams there is an oral examination, in which students are often asked to compare and contrast photos. Students can easily panic and they need to have a lot of practice to reduce their anxiety. These simple tips can help them:

1 Brief description of each photo: You do not have to describe them in detail. If you are not sure what the picture is, use your imagination and say what you think it is. It doesn't matter if you are wrong.

2 Compare and contrast: Talk about the first photo in one sentence. Talk about the other photo in one sentence. Compare and contrast them.

3 Give personal feelings: Use phrases such as *I think, In my opinion, If you ask me, It looks like*, etc.

Students also need to know the vocabulary for referring to the different parts of a photo or a picture: *at the top, at the bottom, in the left-hand corner, in the background, at the front, behind, next to, on the right, on the left, in the middle*, etc.

4 Ask students to look at the lists of words and expressions in the Speaking bank and match a title to each list. Elicit when each list of expressions is useful in a speaking exam.

Answers

Speculating (when you are not exactly sure what is happening in the photo)
Comparing (to compare and contrast two photographs)
Using fillers (when you are trying to find a word or need time to think)
Describing (to give a general and then more specific description of the photo(s) at the beginning of the speaking exam)
Giving opinions (to respond to a task which asks you to state your opinion or preference)

5 SPEAKING In pairs, students use each expression in exercise 4 to talk about the photos in exercise 2.

TEACHER DEVELOPMENT: STUDENT TRAINING

Practising for an oral exam

Remind students that the best way to practise for an oral examination is with another student. If they already know the student who will be taking the speaking test with them, they should try to practise with him/her as often as possible.

PRACTICE MAKES PERFECT

6a SPEAKING Divide the class into A and B pairs. Student A looks at the photos and does the task; Student B listens to their partner. Set a time limit of one minute.

6b Ask students to change roles and tell Student B to look at their task on page 158.

For students who are less confident, photocopy the model description below, and either read it aloud yourself, or ask a strong student to do so. Tell students to use this as a basis for the speaking activity, using the underlined phrases as a frame.

✂- -

Model description (Task A)

<u>Both photos show</u> groups of teenagers enjoying their free time. <u>In this photo there is</u> a group of teenagers eating out, sitting round a table. <u>They may be having</u> coffee or <u>they might be eating</u> some food. <u>In the other photo there is</u> a group of teenagers together in a park. <u>One big difference is</u> that the first photo is taken inside and the second photo is taken outside. <u>In the background, we can see</u> several bikes, <u>so it looks like</u> they might have cycled to the park. <u>It seems like</u> a sunny day. <u>In my opinion</u>, I think people enjoy meeting in these ways because it is fun and relaxing. <u>Personally</u>, I prefer meeting my friends in the park because I like being in the fresh air.

✚ **EXTRA ACTIVITY**

Give students practice at saying things in another way, so they get used to describing things if they can't remember the exact word. Words and expressions such as *It's a kind of, It's sort of, It's a thing that you use when, It's something that you do when* help students explain a word they can't remember.

In pairs, students look at the vocabulary list for the unit in the Student's Book on page 68. Students choose two words and rephrase them for their partner to guess. Each acceptable rephrasing is worth one point. The student with the most points wins.

HOMEWORK

Assign students page 45 in their Workbook or the relevant sections of the Online Workbook.

Developing writing p67

Writing a formal letter/email of complaint

>>> FAST TRACK

You could ask students to do exercise 1 at home in preparation for the speaking activity in exercise 2.

WARMER

Students take turns to describe the photo on page 67. Elicit what they think the formal letter/email is going to be about.

1 Ask students to look at the instructions about how to use a cashpoint to withdraw money and put the steps in the correct order.

Answers

1 d **2** e **3** a **4** b **5** f **6** c

2 **SPEAKING** In pairs, students explain the different steps in exercise 1 using *must*, *shouldn't*, etc. Elicit answers from different students.

3 Ask students to read the email and answer the questions. Check their answers.

Answers

1 He is writing to complain to the bank about bad customer service after the cash machine took his card.
2 He wants a new card urgently, without paying bank fees for the issue of this card.
3 If there is no solution, he will consider moving his current account to another bank.

4 Ask students to find the formal equivalents of the words and expressions in the letter. Check their answers.

Answers

2 caused me a great deal of inconvenience **3** selected
4 wished **5** sufficient **6** informed **7** I shall be forced to

5 **SPEAKING** In pairs, ask students to read the information in the Writing bank and find examples of the characteristics in the email in exercise 3.

Answers

- Dear Sir or Madam; Yours faithfully, Jonathan Squire
- I am writing; I am disappointed; I have received; The incident has left; I would also like
- has caused me a great deal of inconvenience; through no fault of my own; I shall be forced to
- insert (put in); withdraw (take out); contact (call up)
- The incident has left me without my debit card and has caused me a great deal of inconvenience.
- Anderson Street; Sunday 21st December
- I am writing to complain about; I look forward to hearing from you very soon.

PRACTICE MAKES PERFECT

6a Ask students to look at the task and write notes and add their own details.

TEACHER DEVELOPMENT: STUDENT TRAINING

Writing a letter/email of complaint

Writing a letter/email of complaint is a popular task in many exams. It is formal and this affects students' choice of grammar and vocabulary. Learning formulaic expressions by heart will help students score higher marks in an exam. Remind students that writing a paragraph plan makes a text more logical and coherent. Students should divide their writing plan into three or four paragraphs with three or four sentences per paragraph. The most common format includes an introduction (reason for writing); paragraph 2 (describing the incident); paragraph 3 (consequence of this incident); and a concluding paragraph (summary of key points and an action plan).

6b Ask students to write their letter using their notes and the information in the Writing bank. Remind them that they can also follow the advice in the Writing bank on page 154. For students who are less confident, photocopy the model text below for extra support during the writing task.

Model text

Dear Sir or Madam,

I am writing to complain about an incident that took place last week at Reading Station. The incident has caused a great deal of inconvenience and no solution has been provided.

On the evening of Friday 21st September I inserted the correct amount of money into your vending machine selling books – £12.50. I wanted a book to read on the train because it was a very long journey. I selected the book I wished to read – Ken Follett's *Fall of Giants* – but the machine didn't give me the book or any change. I tried to cancel the operation, but the machine had already swallowed my money.

I contacted your company the next day and they informed me that they could not give me my money back because I had no proof of purchase. I asked for a complaint form to be sent by post, but they told me there was no form available.

I am very disappointed with the treatment I have received from your company. I now have no book and I have paid you £12.50, through no fault of my own. I demand an apology and I expect you to send me the book urgently or a full refund of my money. I would also like assurance that you will not charge me for postage for sending me the book. If I do not hear from you in the next fourteen days, I shall be forced to consider contacting the Consumer Advice Bureau.

I look forward to hearing from you very soon.

Yours faithfully,
Hattie Jacks

✚ EXTRA ACTIVITY

Students make a mind map of the words they have learnt so far in this unit related to the theme of *money*.

Expressions: 'Money matters'

Buying and selling: afford, sale, discount, bargain ...

MONEY

Money management: payday loans, store card, credit card, debt advice ...

Phrasal verbs: splash out, get by, sell out, be in/go into the red

Planning a budget: expenses, income, budget

HOMEWORK

Assign students page 46 in their Workbook or the relevant sections of the Online Workbook.

Language checkpoint: Unit 5

>>> FAST TRACK

The extra support provided in the Grammar and Vocabulary reference sections makes the Grammar and Vocabulary revision sections ideal for setting as homework. You could get students to complete the whole revision page or just certain exercises for homework.

Grammar revision p69

Modal verbs of obligation, prohibition and advice – present

1 Students choose the correct alternative. Point out that in two sentences, both alternatives are correct.

Answers

1 needn't   2 both correct   3 don't have to   4 both correct   5 Should   6 mustn't

Modals of obligation, prohibition and advice

2 Students write sentences with the correct form of the modal verbs and verbs given.

Answers

1 had to talk   2 needn't have worried   3 mustn't write   4 ought to have read   5 shouldn't have lied   6 didn't need to get   7 don't have to write

Modals of speculation and deduction

3 Students match the pairs of sentences.

Answers

1 b   2 c   3 a   4 g   5 e   6 d   7 f

Vocabulary revision p69

BUYING AND SELLING

1 Students match the words with the definitions.

Answers

1 refund   2 receipt   3 change   4 value for money   5 sale   6 bargain   7 afford

MONEY AND BANKING

2 Students match the words or parts of a word.

Answers

1 g   2 f   3 e   4 a   5 b   6 d   7 c

PHRASAL VERBS: MONEY AND SHOPPING

3 Students rewrite the sentences without the phrasal verb, expressing the same meaning with different words.

Suggested answers

1 Last week we spent a lot of money on lunch in a restaurant.
2 They only spend £500 a month.
3 People are spending less money on holidays abroad this year.
4 The bill reaches a total of £24.
5 I couldn't get that new game because there weren't any left.
6 I need to buy something for dinner tonight.

HOMEWORK

Assign students page 47 in their Workbook or the relevant sections of the Online Workbook.

6 Healthy living

KEY LEARNING OUTCOMES

Students will be able to:

- talk about possible, imaginary and impossible situations and their consequences using different types of conditional structures
- talk about wishes for the present, past and future
- talk about the body and health using a range of vocabulary and idioms
- collaborate with a partner using different expressions to agree, disagree and make choices
- express opinions, contrasts and consequences in for-and-against essays

UNIT OVERVIEW

Vocabulary
Parts of the body
Words connected with health
PRONUNCIATION Word stress

Reading
Health news
CRITICAL THINKING Evaluating the quality of information in health articles

Grammar in context
Zero, first and second conditionals
unless, as long as, provided/ providing (that), in case

Developing vocabulary
Idioms connected with health and illness

Life skills
Physical well-being: Understanding nutrition

Listening
Teenagers and sport

Grammar in context
Third conditional
I wish/If only

Developing speaking
Negotiating and collaborating – 2

Developing writing
A for-and-against essay

Exam success
Use of English: Sentence transformation activities
Writing: For-and-against and opinion essays

DIGITAL OVERVIEW

Presentation Kit
- ▶ Flipped classroom video Unit 6: *I wish/If only*
- ▶ Life skills video Unit 6: Understanding nutrition
- ▶ Interactive versions of Student's Book activities
- ▶ Integrated audio and answer key for all activities
- ▶ Workbook pages with answer key

Teacher's Resource Centre
- ▶ Flipped classroom video Unit 6: *I wish/If only*
- ▶ Life skills video Unit 6: Understanding nutrition
- ▶ Grammar communication activity Unit 6: On one condition
- ▶ Worksheets for this unit, including:
  - – Grammar Practice worksheet Unit 6
  - – Flipped classroom video worksheet Unit 6: *I wish/If only*
  - – Literature worksheet Units 5 and 6
  - – Culture worksheet Unit 6
  - – Life skills video worksheet Unit 6
  - – Everyday English worksheet Unit 6

Student's App
Gateway 2nd Edition wordlist for the award-winning Sounds App (available for download)

✓ TESTING AND ASSESSMENT

Resources for exam preparation and measuring student progress

- ▶ Test Generator Units 1–6
- ▶ Printable tests Unit 6/Review
- ▶ Gateway to exams Units 5 and 6 (end of Unit 6)

Vocabulary p70

Talking about the body and health using a range of vocabulary

>>> FAST TRACK

You could ask students to do exercise 1 at home by drawing a simple diagram of the human body and labelling the parts of the body in the box. They can look up any words they are not sure about in their dictionaries or the Macmillan Online Dictionary.

WARMER

In pairs, students discuss the meaning of the unit title *Healthy living* and what they think the unit is going to be about (*healthy living* means living in healthy ways). Elicit suggestions for complete physical and social well-being. Drill the pronunciation of the title: /ˈhelθi ˈlɪvɪŋ/.

Suggested answers

Physical: good nutrition, appropriate weight, drinking water, regular exercise, adequate rest and proper stress management …

Social: positive thoughts, laugh a lot, strong relationships with others …

Parts of the body

1 **SPEAKING** In pairs, students check that they understand the words. Provide dictionaries if necessary. If possible, use a diagram to check answers.

Answers

ankle /ˈæŋk(ə)l/ – the part at the bottom of your leg where your foot joins your leg

bone /bəʊn/ – one of the hard parts that form a frame inside the body of a human or animal

brain /breɪn/ – the organ inside your head that allows you to think and feel, and controls your body

chest /tʃest/ – the upper front part of your body between your neck and your stomach

chin /tʃɪn/ – the centre of the bottom part of your face, below your mouth and above your neck

forehead /ˈfɒrɪd/ or /ˈfɔː(r)ˌhed/ – the upper part of your face between your eyes and your hair

heart /hɑː(r)t/ – the organ in your chest that makes blood flow around your body

heel /hiːl/ – the back part of your foot, below your ankle

hip /hɪp/ – one of the two parts at either side of your body between your waist and the top of your legs

kidney /ˈkɪdni/ – one of the two organs in your body that clean your blood and remove waste

liver /ˈlɪvə(r)/ – the organ in your body that cleans your blood and produces bile (= a liquid that helps your body process fat)

lungs /lʌŋz/ – one of the two organs in your chest that fill with air when you breathe

skin /skɪn/ – the outer layer of a person's or animal's body

thigh /θaɪ/ – the top part of your leg, above your knee

throat /θrəʊt/ – the area at the back of your mouth and inside your neck

toe /təʊ/ – one of the five individual parts at the end of your foot. Your big toe is the largest and your little toe is the smallest

tongue /tʌŋ/ – the long soft piece of flesh fixed to the bottom of your mouth that you use for tasting, speaking, etc.

veins and arteries /ˈveɪnz n ˈɑː(r)təriz/ – a tube that returns blood to your heart is called a vein. A tube that carries blood away from your heart is called an artery

wrist /rɪst/ – the part of your body between your hand and your arm

Words connected with health

2 **SPEAKING** In pairs, students take it in turns to talk about the photos. Elicit descriptions from different students around the class.

Suggested answers

1 Someone with a bandaged hand and wrist in a sling

2 A healthy meal/salad

3 An unhealthy meal/junk food

4 A woman with a headache/temperature

3 Ask students to read the texts, ignoring the gaps for the moment, and match each one to the correct photo.

Answers

1 D   **2** A   **3** B   **4** C

4a Ask students to complete the texts in exercise 3 with the words in the box. Provide dictionaries if necessary. Do not check the answers yet.

Answers

a balanced   **b** allergic   **c** putting on   **d** addicted
e infection   **f** prescription   **g** dislocated   **h** painful

4b **LISTENING** 🔊 27 Play the track for students to listen and check their answers in exercise 4a (see Answers in exercise 4a above). Students then look at the words in red in the texts and check they understand what they mean. Tell students to use a dictionary if necessary. See p176 for the audioscript for this exercise.

Answers

work out – to do physical exercise as a way of keeping fit

check-up – a medical examination, especially one taken at regular intervals to verify a normal state of health or discover a disease in its early stages

blood pressure – the pressure at which blood flows from your heart around your body. Blood pressure that is either very high or very low can be dangerous to your health

injection – a drug or another substance that is injected into your body

relieves – makes pain or another bad physical feeling less unpleasant

symptoms – the unpleasant effects of an illness

fatty food – food that contains fat

processed food – food that has had chemicals or other substances added to it to keep it fresh for a long time

high in – have a large amount of

in danger of – at risk of

obese – too fat, in a way that is dangerous for your health

increasing the risk of heart disease – multiplying the possibilities of developing a serious medical condition in your heart

a temperature – the feeling of being hot because you are ill

dizzy – feeling as if you or the things around you are spinning, especially when you think you are going to fall

shivering – shaking slightly, for example, because you are cold or frightened

treated – cured

got over – recovered from

injured myself – did damage to myself/hurt myself

twisted – injured a part of your body by bending it in the wrong direction

sprained – injured a joint such as your wrist by suddenly stretching or turning it too much

fracture – to crack a bone (but not completely break it)

break – to crack or separate into two pieces

operation – surgical intervention

5a PRONUNCIATION Ask students to mark where the stress goes in the words in exercise 4a.

Answers

ad<u>dict</u>ed /ə'dɪktɪd/

al<u>ler</u>gic /ə'lɜː(r)dʒɪk/

<u>bal</u>anced /'bælənst/

<u>dis</u>located /'dɪsləkeɪtɪd/

in<u>fec</u>tion /ɪn'fekʃ(ə)n/

<u>pain</u>ful /'peɪnf(ə)l/

pre<u>scrip</u>tion /prɪ'skrɪpʃ(ə)n/

<u>put</u>ting on /'pʊtɪŋ ɒn/

TEACHER DEVELOPMENT: PRONUNCIATION

Word stress

All words of more than one syllable have what is called 'word stress'. This means that at least one of the syllables is longer and louder than the other syllables. Use this opportunity to review how to use a dictionary to learn pronunciation. Ask students if they know how to use the phonological information in a dictionary. Remind them that each word is spelt phonetically and an accent mark (') shows which syllable is spoken louder than the rest of the word. Long words have a primary accent and a secondary accent because two of the syllables receive more stress than the other syllables. Primary accent marks mean that this syllable is stressed the most.

5b LISTENING ▶ 28 Play the track for students to listen and check their answers (see Answers in exercise 5a above). In pairs, students practise saying the words with the correct stress.

6 SPEAKING In pairs, students take it in turns to ask and answer the questions and give details.

Example answers

1 I go to a local gym three times a week. It makes me feel good and I enjoy seeing the changes in my body.

2 I am allergic to peaches. I have to have an injection at the hospital if I eat one accidentally.

3 I injured myself when I was playing hockey. I broke my arm.

4 I'm not afraid of injections, but I don't like them very much!

5 I don't feel dizzy when I see blood, but I know a lot of people who do.

✚ EXTRA ACTIVITY

In pairs, students role-play a visit to a doctor. Each student thinks of a complaint and explains it to their doctor (their partner). The doctor then gives advice on how to relieve the symptoms. In a less confident class, students could prepare a written dialogue before doing this as a speaking activity.

HOMEWORK

Assign students page 48 in their Workbook or the relevant sections of the Online Workbook.

Reading p71

Reading for general and specific information

≫ FAST TRACK

You could ask students to read the articles in exercise 2 at home in preparation for in-class activities.

WARMER

In pairs, students take it in turns to say a part of the body. If they repeat a word, say an incorrect word or can't think of a word, they lose the game.

1 SPEAKING In pairs, students discuss if they think the things are good or bad for us and say why.

TEACHER DEVELOPMENT: STUDENT TRAINING

Prediction

Prior knowledge is one of the most important components in the reading process and activation of this knowledge must be included in the comprehension process. Strategies to activate prior knowledge include asking questions, brainstorming, making word maps and using visual clues. Students should ask themselves *What do I know?* and *What do I want to learn?* before they approach a text.

2 Students read the four articles from a health website to check their answers in exercise 1. Elicit from students what the basic message of each text is.

Answers

A says that 'drinking eight glasses of water is good' is a myth. Our bodies adjust, and drinks don't have to be water.

B says action films make you eat more (junk food).

C says feeling pain is better than not feeling pain.

D says brain freeze is painful but disappears fast.

3 Ask students to read the articles again and decide if the sentences are True (T) or False (F). Ask students to point out the part of the text where they found their answer.

Answers

1 F (It's also true that the water we need each day can be contained in other drinks such as coffee, tea or juice, or even in food. It certainly does not have to be mineral water.)

2 F (… some 'scientific' articles … are sponsored by mineral water manufacturers.)

3 T (The volunteers watching the action film with sound ate 98% more than those watching the talk show. Even those watching the action film without sound ate 36% more!)

4 T (It seems that faster programmes make you eat faster and pay less attention to how much food you're eating.)

5 T (Pain prevents us from injuring a body part even more …)

6 T (You can also put your tongue up to the roof of your mouth or drink something neither hot nor cold to normalise the temperature in your mouth.)

4 CRITICAL THINKING Encourage students to think about the information they read and to say how much they believe this kind of article. Encourage them to explain their answers. Ask students to discuss how they can check any information they read.

Example answers

I don't believe everything I read because a lot of what people say is marketing not science.

I always check the website to find out what kind of domain it is (.edu, .gov, .org, .net, .com), as well as finding out who the author is and when the article was published. I check who the organisation is, who is paying for the article and what they want to sell. I try to crosscheck information using at least three independent resources if I have a doubt. I ask myself about authority, objectivity and reliability.

>>> FAST FINISHERS

Ask students to discuss if they think they should change their lifestyle after reading the articles, e.g. *I think I will stop drinking two litres of water a day and calculate my total liquid intake instead./I think I will prepare healthy food to eat when I'm watching action films.*

TEACHER DEVELOPMENT: STUDENT TRAINING

Checking information

Students need to learn to evaluate the quality of information they find on the web as well as other information resources such as books, magazines and television. Ask students to be sceptical of everything they find. Encourage them to compare and contrast different information resources and consider the following ideas:

Authority
Who created this information and why?
Are they stating fact or opinion?
What else has this author written?

Objectivity
Is the information objective or subjective?
Is it full of fact or opinion?

Authenticity
Where does the information originate?
Is the information from an established organisation?
Is this a primary source or secondary source of information?
Are original sources clear and documented?
Is there a bibliography that provides a list of the sources used?

Reliability
Who is sponsoring this publication?
What's the purpose of the information resource: to inform, instruct, persuade, sell? Does this matter?
How current are the resources or links?

5 Ask students to work out the meaning of the underlined words in the text by looking at the context and guessing before they check in their dictionaries.

Answers

adjusts = to change something slightly in order to make it better

sponsored = paid for as a way to advertise products or services

marketing = the ways in which a company encourages people to buy its products

lack = a situation in which you do not have any, or enough, of something that you need or want

disorder = an illness or medical condition

prevents us from = to stop us from doing something

roof (of mouth) = the hard top part of the inside of your mouth

6 SPEAKING **What about *you*?** In pairs or small groups, students discuss which information from the articles could make a difference to them and their health. Elicit answers from different students around the class.

✚ EXTRA ACTIVITY

In pairs, students choose a word from the reading and say it to their partner for them to spell out, letter by letter. If they spell the whole word correctly, they score one point. The one with the most points wins the game.

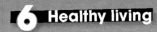

Grammar in context pp72–73

Using the zero, first and second conditionals and unless, as long as, provided/providing (that) and in case

>>> FAST TRACK

You could ask students to do exercises 1, 2, 3 and 4 at home. Then they start the next class with the speaking activity in exercise 5a.

Test before you teach

Write these prompts on the board and ask students to make full sentences: *If you don't eat, _____. If I study hard for the exams, _____. If I found a bag of money, _____.*
Monitor closely and ask students to read out their sentences to the class. If students seem to be familiar with these conditionals, move through the Grammar guide exercises quickly, eliciting answers from students in open class.

Zero, first and second conditionals

1a Students decide which type of conditional each sentence uses.

Answers
1 zero conditional 2 second conditional
3 first conditional

1b Ask students to read the rules and decide which type of conditional each rule applies to.

Answers
zero conditional: 3, 5
first conditional: 2, 4
second conditional: 1, 6

TEACHER DEVELOPMENT: LANGUAGE

Conditionals

Remind students that when the *if* clause comes first, a comma is usually used and that clauses are interchangeable with no difference in meaning, e.g. *If she wanted to see you, she would have come to the party./She would have come to the party if she wanted to see you.*
Students should also note that they can use *was/were* with *If I/he/she*, e.g. *If I were you, I would call your dad now.*

2 Ask students to complete each sentence to make a general statement using the zero conditional.

Suggested answers
1 If you drink too much coffee, your heart beats fast.
2 If you never do any exercise, you are unfit.
3 If you only sleep a few hours a night, you get sick.
4 If you eat a lot of junk food, you risk your health.
5 If you sit in front of a computer all day, you get bad eyesight.

3 Ask students to decide if the sentences are correct and rewrite the incorrect sentences.

Answers
1 If I **were/was** the Prime Minister, I would ban junk food.
2 We'll go to the concert if the tickets **aren't** too expensive./We**'d** go to the concert if the tickets weren't too expensive.
3 correct
4 What **will** you do if it rains all day tomorrow?
5 If I had a million pounds, I**'d travel** around the world.
6 If you mix blue and yellow, you **get** green.
7 correct
8 What will you do if you **lose** the match?/What **would** you do if you lost the match?

4 Ask students to complete the questions with the correct form of the verbs given.

Answers
1 would, live **2** had **3** go **4** would, meet

5a SPEAKING In pairs, students take it in turns to ask and answer the questions in exercise 4.

5b Encourage students to tell the class something interesting they discovered about their partner.

unless, as long as, provided/providing (that), in case

6 Ask students to look at the sentences and match the words in blue with the expressions a–c.

Answers
a unless **b** Provided/Providing (that), As long as
c in case

7 Ask students to choose the correct alternative.

Answers
1 in case **2** as long as **3** unless **4** as long as
5 providing **6** in case **7** as long as

✔ EXAM SUCCESS Ask students to read the tip for doing sentence transformation exercises. Elicit other strategies and techniques students may have for doing these exercises and tell them to turn to page 146 (Use of English: Sentence transformation activities) for more ideas.

Sentence transformation

Many students consider this to be the hardest section of any exam and need a lot of practice in this area. A good technique is to underline the parts that are repeated in both sentences (even if they are somewhat paraphrased). In this way, students can concentrate better on the section they have to transform using a key word. Students should then try to locate the position of the key word in the missing part. Remind students to 'fight for each point' – in some examinations two marks are awarded for each correct answer, so partially correct constructions may obtain points. Structures that are usually tested in this way are: modal and semi-modal verbs, phrasal/multi-word verbs, the active to the passive voice, gerunds and infinitives, the third conditional, direct to reported speech and – as in this exercise – linking words, as well as idiomatic expressions.

8 Ask students to complete the second sentence so that it has a similar meaning to the first sentence, using the word given. Remind students that they must not change the word given and they should use between two and five words including the word given.

Answers

1 unless you want to lose   **2** provided (that) you bring   **3** if I were/was tall   **4** if you don't switch it   **5** as long as you promise   **6** unless I meant   **7** would go if I were/was   **8** in case it

9 Ask students to complete the sentences in a logical way. Then invite them to read one of their sentences to the class.

Suggested answers

1 your computer breaks down.
2 she finishes all her homework.
3 he hears you.
4 you are over 18.
5 I am sensible.
6 the TV is switched off.

>>> FAST FINISHERS

In pairs, students compare their sentences from exercise 9.

Refer students to the Grammar reference on page 80 if necessary.

HOMEWORK

Assign students page 50 in their Workbook or the relevant sections of the Online Workbook.

Developing vocabulary p73

Using idioms connected with health and illness

>>> FAST TRACK

Students could do exercises 1a and 1b at home.

Idioms connected with health and illness

1a Ask students to match the pictures to two of the idioms in red.

Answers

a 2   **b** 4

1b Ask students to match the idioms in exercise 1a with the explanations a–g.

Answers

1 c   **2** g   **3** b   **4** e   **5** a   **6** f   **7** d

2 Ask students to correct the mistakes in the sentences. Give them time to compare their answers in pairs before you check them in open class.

Answers

1 back on your feet   **2** keeps in shape   **3** pull through   **4** black out   **5** under the weather

3 SPEAKING Ask students to complete the questions with the correct word and then interview their partner. Encourage students to share their answers in open class.

Answers

1 keep   **2** out   **3** down   **4** under

4 Ask students to draw a cartoon to represent one of the idioms from exercise 1. In pairs or small groups, students swap cartoons for the others to guess the idiom.

HOMEWORK

Assign students page 51 in their Workbook or the relevant sections of the Online Workbook.

Gateway to life skills pp74–75

Understanding nutrition

To study the nutritional needs of teenagers, to look at the role of schools in promoting healthy eating and to plan a healthy eating campaign at school

>>> FAST TRACK

Students could read the text in exercise 2 in preparation for the in-class activities.

ⓘ BACKGROUND INFORMATION

Knowing the importance of good nutrition is a key life skill that is important for brain development and growth, maintaining a healthy weight and preventing chronic diseases as adolescents develop.

Many of the official changes in school food mentioned in exercise 6 came after a TV series made by the famous TV chef Jamie Oliver. In the TV series, called *Jamie's School Dinners*, he tried to improve the quality of school lunches by taking away processed foods and introducing fresh vegetables – changes that were not always popular with students (or parents).

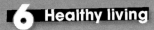

In pairs or small groups, students race to think of the names of food and drink items for each letter of the alphabet. Tell them they don't need to find words for letters *U, X* or *Z*. Set a time limit of five minutes. The winner is the first pair or group to complete their list, or the pair/group with the longest list of correct words at the end of the time. Ask students to read through the Key concepts and check any vocabulary they don't understand.

Example answers

apple, bread, cheese, dates, egg, fish, grapes, honey, ice cream, juice, kiwi, lemon, mango, nuts, orange, pizza, quiche, raisin, spinach, tomato, veggie burger, watermelon, yoghurt

1 SPEAKING In pairs, students discuss the questions. Elicit some answers from different students around the class.

2 READING Ask students to read the summary of the results of a survey about British teenagers and nutrition and complete the table with information they find in the text. Remind students that they can refer to Key concepts for definitions of words they are not sure about. Elicit answers from students around the class.

Answers

Short-term benefits of healthy eating: appearance (hair, skin), energy

Long-term benefits of healthy eating: prevent chronic diseases

British teenagers eat too much/many ...: saturated fat, added sugars

British teenagers eat too little/few ...: dietary fibre, iron, vitamin A, riboflavin, calcium, magnesium, etc.

3 Ask students to read the text again and answer the questions. Check and ask students to identify the sentences that helped them decide on their answers.

Answers

1 slightly better
2 teenage girls
3 children from families with higher incomes
4 none
5 No, it is highest in socially deprived children.
6 Schools need to highlight the importance of good nutrition and provide healthy food and drink in schools.
7 Quite positive – there have been improvements, but there is still room for improvement.

4 SPEAKING In pairs, ask students to discuss the questions and make a list of the things that schools can do to help. Encourage students to share some of their ideas with the class.

The video contains some useful colloquial language about healthy eating that students may not be familiar with. You might want to pre-teach these words and phrases with students before watching:

tempting [adj]: making you want it

orientated towards [adj]: positioned in the direction of something

aimed at [phr]: having the goal of achieving a particular thing

conflicted agenda [phr]: having different, often contrasting priorities

to deal with consequences [phr v]: to accept the outcome of something

tactics [n]: methods to follow

on display [adj]: arranged attractively so that people can choose something

stalls [n]: temporary shops (usually in markets)

readily available [adj]: easy to find

on the move [phr]: while walking or travelling

patronising [adj]: with an attitude of looking down at someone

in-your-face [adj]: bold or aggressive (especially for advertising)

5 LISTENING ▶ 29 Tell students they are going to watch or listen to four students in the UK talking about how their university and the government helps to encourage good nutrition. Play the video or audio track for students to tick any of the ideas on their list in exercise 4 that they mention. See the Teacher's Resource Centre for the audioscript/videoscript for this exercise.

6 ▶ 29 Play the video or audio track again for students to complete the table with notes about what each student said. Point out they should write between one and five words. Ask them to check in pairs before checking answers as a class.

Answers

Sam: (healthy options at uni) fruit and vegetables at cafés, no posters or campaigns; (UK government) campaigns for younger children; (encourage healthy eating) change school menu, water more available

Vanessa: (healthy options at uni) salad bar in Students' Union but next to fast-food place; (UK government) schools and canteens more healthy options, students – limited budget, unhealthy foods; (encourage healthy eating) try something new, exotic fruits

Bea: (healthy options at uni) fresh produce, salads; (UK government) sugar tax, dentists, supermarkets, conflicted agenda; (encourage healthy eating) change general attitude, good relationship with food

Chris: (healthy options at uni) fast-food chains; (UK government) individual's own choice; (encourage healthy eating) knowledge about what's in food

Write these questions on the board:
What do you usually eat for lunch at school?
What do you usually eat for lunch at the weekend?
What changes do you think you should make?
Divide the class into A and B pairs. Students role-play an interview with each other. Student A chooses healthy food options and Student B chooses unhealthy options. Ask students to plan their answers and practise their interview. Students could act out their interviews in front of the class. You could record students and play the interviews back for discussion.

TEACHER DEVELOPMENT: CLASSROOM TIPS AND PLANNING

Using a video camera

Students learn a lot by watching themselves on video. Most cameras can be connected directly to a television for instant playback, analysis and discussion. You can record the students, give the camera to your students or let them produce a video with their own devices. Playback is a time for positive critical analysis and positive encouragement. Suggest or elicit alternative ways to say something and helpful tips on body language, but don't correct them on every preposition! You could consider making copies for students to take away with them.

7 **SPEAKING** In pairs, students discuss what the speakers say about healthy eating in the UK and how it compares with the situation in their country. Ask them to think of similarities and differences. Elicit answers in open class.

LIFE TASK

Tell students that their school wants to promote healthy eating for teenagers. Ask them to think of ideas that could help teenagers to eat well, in and outside school, and a way to present those ideas to other students. Ask them to follow the plan:

- *Step 1*

  Ask students to discuss the ideas on the two pages that they think would be useful.

- *Step 2*

  Ask students to think of other ideas that could work, e.g. making people pay extra for fizzy drinks.

- *Step 3*

  Ask students to plan and prepare a healthy eating campaign for their school. Ask students how they are going to present their campaign – a poster, a video, a presentation and/or an information leaflet – and make sure they have all the resources they need.

- *Step 4*

  Ask students to present their campaign ideas to the rest of the class. Encourage them to compare the different ideas and come up with the best selection to make a school campaign.

Listening p76

Listening for general and specific information

Give students three minutes to think of as many sports as they can. Elicit the names of these sports from students and write them on the board. Then tell students to write the correct verb – *play, do* or *go* – next to each sport, e.g. *play basketball, do gymnastics, go swimming.*

TEACHER DEVELOPMENT: LANGUAGE

play, do, go
Play is used with ball sports or competitive games where we play against another person, e.g. *play football.*
Do is used for a recreational activity or a non-team sport that does not use a ball, e.g. *do yoga.*
Go is used with activities that end *-ing.* We go somewhere to do something, e.g. *go dancing.*

1 **SPEAKING** In pairs, students look at pictures a–c and discuss what sports they show, and if they have tried them or if they would like to. Remind them to say why or why not. Elicit any interesting experiences.

Answers

a scuba diving   **b** surfing   **c** pilates/gym

2 **LISTENING** 30 Play the track for students to listen to five people talking about sport. Ask students to note down which sport each person does. See p176 for the audioscript for this exercise.

Answers

Speaker 1: swimming
Speaker 2: basketball
Speaker 3: water sports
Speaker 4: pilates
Speaker 5: diving

3 30 Ask students to read the statements and then play the track again for them to match the statements A–F with each speaker. Remind students that there is one extra statement.

Answers

Speaker 1: D
Speaker 2: F
Speaker 3: C
Speaker 4: E
Speaker 5: A

4 **SPEAKING** **What about *you*?** In pairs, students discuss the questions. Ask them to ask as many follow-up questions as they can and develop a conversation.

Assign students page 51 in their Workbook or the relevant sections of the Online Workbook.

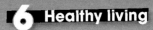
Grammar in context pp76–77

Using the third conditional and I wish/If only

⟫⟫ FAST TRACK

You could ask students to do exercises 1, 2 and 3 at home. Check their answers and then start the class on exercise 4.

Test before you teach

Write these situations and prompts on the board:

1 I can't go to university because my grades aren't good enough. (work harder/get better grades)

2 I didn't have time to see him and now it's too late. (have time/see him)

3 We arrived late. (catch an earlier train/arrive on time)

Ask students to use the prompts to write sentences in the third conditional. If students seem familiar with the use and form of the third conditional, move quickly through the Grammar guide exercises quickly in open class.

> **Answers**
>
> 1 If I'd worked harder at school, I would have got better grades.
> 2 If I'd had time, I would have seen him.
> 3 If we'd caught an earlier train, we would have arrived on time.

Third conditional

1 Students look at sentences a–b and answer questions 1–3.

> **Answers**
>
> 1 past perfect   2 would (not) have + past participle
> 3 the past

TEACHER DEVELOPMENT: LANGUAGE

Third conditional

The past cannot be changed. We use the third conditional to speculate about the past and what could have happened if things had been different. The third conditional gives the imaginary result or consequence of an unreal past.

The third conditional is formed by an *if* clause and a main clause, namely the condition and the consequence. The order of these two elements can be inverted. In this case, we do not usually separate the clauses with a comma, e.g. *I would have got to work on time if my alarm clock had gone off.* The main clause in a third conditional sentence can contain any of the modal verbs *would, could* or *might* according to the meaning we wish to convey.

It is common to use contractions with the third conditional, e.g. *If **I'd** studied harder, **I'd** have passed the exam.*

2 Ask students to complete the sentences with the correct form of the verb given.

Answers

1 'd practised   2 would have become
3 'd been   4 would have got   5 hadn't explained
6 wouldn't have learnt   7 'd injured

3 Ask students to write sentences about the past situations using the third conditional.

Answers

1 She wouldn't have caught a cold if she hadn't gone running in the rain.
2 If I had known how to play tennis properly, I wouldn't have injured myself last week.
3 The stadium would have been full if the match had been important.
4 She would have won the race if she hadn't twisted her ankle.
5 If we had drunk water before the race, we wouldn't have been so thirsty.
6 If the sun had shone, we would have swum in the sea.
7 If he had needed extra vitamins, he would have taken them.

4 Ask students to look at the situations and write third conditional sentences. Draw students' attention to the example sentence.

Answers

2 If he'd had enough time yesterday, he would have done sport./He would have done sport yesterday if he'd had enough time.
3 If she hadn't got up late, she wouldn't have missed the bus./She wouldn't have missed the bus if she hadn't got up late.
4 If the water hadn't been cold, I would have swum./I would have swum if the water hadn't been cold.
5 If we'd had rackets, we would have played./We would have played if we'd had rackets.
6 If I'd had some sun cream, I would have sunbathed./I would have sunbathed if I'd had some sun cream.
7 If he hadn't been afraid of water, he would have learnt to surf./He would have learnt to surf if he hadn't been afraid of water.
8 If her knee hadn't hurt, she would have gone for a run./She would have gone for a run if her knee hadn't hurt.

I wish/If only

 Test before you teach: Flipped classroom

Set the Flipped classroom video and tasks for homework <u>before the lesson</u>. This will allow you to assess the needs of the students before the class. Students can then move on to the relevant grammar practice activities.

5 Ask students to look at sentences a–c and answer the questions 1–6.

Answers

1 the past perfect
2 a past situation
3 the past simple
4 a present situation
5 *would* + infinitive
6 habitual behaviour that we want to change

I wish/If only

There are three distinct types of *I wish/If only* sentences:
1 regret with the past perfect
2 wanting change for the present or future with the simple past
3 complaints with *would* + infinitive

Remind students that when we use the verb *to be*, we often use *were* in the first and third person, e.g. *I wish I were a millionaire! He wishes he were richer.*

If only is used as a means of stressing the importance of the wish or hypothetical situation. This form is often used with an exclamation mark.

6 Ask students to complete the sentences with the correct form of the verb given.

Answers

1 had gone **2** would listen **3** knew
4 would make **5** had seen **6** had

7 Ask students to complete the text with one word in each space. Elicit answers from different students around the class.

Answers

a only **b** hadn't **c** wouldn't **d** Unless **e** didn't
f long **g** wouldn't **h** take

8 Ask students to rewrite the incorrect sentences. Ask them to compare in pairs before you check their answers.

Answers

1 I wish I **was/were** on a beach right now.
2 I wish you **wouldn't** interrupt me when I'm talking.
3 If only I **had** studied more last night.
4 correct
5 correct
6 If only I **could** pass my exams without studying.

9a Ask students to write three true sentences with *I wish* using each of the tenses and situations in exercise 5.

9b SPEAKING In small groups, students compare their sentences. Encourage students to ask follow-up questions to find out more information. Draw students' attention to the model dialogue.

Students think about five things they wish were different about their lives and make a *Wish list* poster. They should write complete sentences using *I wish/If only* and illustrate their wishes. Remind them that their wishes don't have to all be materialistic!

Refer students to the Grammar reference on page 80 if necessary.

Assign students page 52 in their Workbook or the relevant sections of the Online Workbook.

Developing speaking p78

Negotiating and collaborating with a partner using different expressions to agree, disagree and make choices

You could ask students to do exercise 1 and remind themselves of the Exam success for Unit 2 (Speaking: Negotiating and collaborating) on page 144 in preparation for the speaking activity.

Play *Hot seat* to start the class. Divide the class into two teams: Team A and Team B. A volunteer from Team A sits with their back to the board. Select vocabulary from the unit and write the words on the board one by one. Team A defines as many words as they can in one minute for the volunteer student to guess. Repeat with Team B. The student who correctly guesses the most words in one minute wins the round for their team.

1 SPEAKING In pairs, students look at both parts of the task and make a list of advice on how to do this type of task. Remind students that they can look at Exam success for Unit 2 (Speaking: Negotiating and collaborating) on page 144 if necessary. Elicit ideas from students around the class.

Answers

See Exam success (Speaking: Negotiating and collaborating) on page 144.

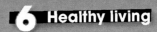

2 SPEAKING Ask students to do both parts of the task with their partner. Walk round, monitoring to get an idea of how well students are performing the task at this stage.

3 LISTENING 🔘 31 Play the track for students to listen to two students doing the task. Elicit from students if they think the speakers do the task well and ask them to give reasons why or why not. Ask pairs to discuss how well they think they did in comparison and elicit opinions from students round the class. See pp176–177 for the audioscript for this exercise.

TEACHER DEVELOPMENT: STUDENT TRAINING

Two-part discussion tasks

Two-part discussion tasks are typical in oral examinations and test students' ability to discuss, interpret, agree/disagree, negotiate, collaborate, rank or classify. Ask students to notice that there are two instructions. The first asks them to discuss ideas that could encourage students to live healthier lives, and the second task asks them to decide which two ideas they think are best.

Remind students that this means that they must not only talk about ideas, but also show their ability to negotiate and collaborate with their partner. Remind them that they don't have to reach an agreement in the examination, but they should work towards this. Students should use appropriate body language by facing each other and maintaining eye contact. They should show each other they are listening by nodding and making short comments, e.g. *Really? Uh huh. I see. That's interesting.* They should also encourage their partner to continue talking by using more direct prompts/questions, e.g. *What do you think about this photo, then?*

4a Ask students to complete the expressions in section 4 of the Speaking bank with the words in the box.

Answers

a choice   **b** choose   **c** best   **d** better   **e** Let's

4b In pairs, students make a list of expressions for sections 1–3 of the Speaking bank. Ask them to compare their answers with the Speaking bank on page 26.

Answers

See Speaking bank on page 26.

PRACTICE MAKES PERFECT

5 SPEAKING In pairs, students do the task together. Remind them to use expressions from the Speaking bank.

For students who are less confident, photocopy the model dialogue below, and either read it aloud yourself, or alternate the roles with you and a strong student. Then instruct students to read aloud in pairs, alternating between roles A and B.

Model dialogue

Part One

A: OK. So what do you think about yoga classes? They can help you beat stress.

B: Yes, I agree. I think regular yoga classes are a really good way to help you relax and calm your mind, but I think it may be a bit boring.

A: I see what you mean, but I don't think yoga is boring. There are lots of different types of yoga. Maybe we could suggest a faster, more active type of yoga. What's your opinion on relaxation rooms with sofas?

B: It's a really good idea because it gives you somewhere to rest and helps calm your nerves. I think it's a good idea to have a special place to relax in.

A: Yes, you're right. We could suggest some relaxing music in the background.

B: That's true. Classical music and chill-out music are best for stress, I think. The idea of playing table tennis is good too; it's good exercise and it's good for your brain. What about you? What do you think about table tennis?

A: I agree with you. I think it's a good way to beat stress and make friends.

B: What about starting school later? I think that's one of the best ways to beat stress.

A: I suppose so, but I like getting up early. What's your view on outdoor pianos?

B: I'm not sure. It's a good idea but only for some people. Not everyone plays the piano.

A: I agree.

Part Two

A: OK, so which two ideas are the best ways to beat stress?

B: I like the idea of table tennis tables around the school. It's a sport everyone can play.

A: I'm not sure. I think we should choose yoga. That way everyone will have a class. I think table tennis and outdoor pianos are good solutions, but they won't help everyone. Good yoga classes help beat stress and teach us how to be relaxed.

B: You have a point. What about the relaxation rooms with sofas? They do the same thing, don't they?

A: Yes, they are similar, but you're not learning about how to deal with stress. I prefer yoga.

B: What about yoga and table tennis tables, then?

A: OK. I think they're the best ideas, too.

➕ EXTRA ACTIVITY

Play *Just a minute*. Have a list of subjects to talk about, e.g. football, cooking. Tell students they have one minute and choose one person to start talking about the subject. If the person repeats a word, hesitates or makes a grammatical error, another person in the class can take over by saying *repetition*, *hesitation* or *error*. Pause the clock and decide if the interruption is valid. If so, tell the person who interrupted to continue talking about the same subject and start the clock again. The winner is the person talking at the end of the minute.

Developing writing p79

Writing a for-and-against essay

▶▶▶ FAST TRACK

You could ask students to research ideas for the essay task in exercise 6.

WARMER

Play *Snowman* to start the class with the phrase *unhealthy lifestyle*. Draw short lines for each letter of the phrase. Students take turns to say a letter. If that letter is in the word, then write the letter on the correct lines. If the letter isn't in the word, draw part of the snowman. The students continue guessing letters until they can either say the phrase (they win) or you have completed the snowman drawing (they lose). Elicit examples of the activities which might form part of an unhealthy lifestyle.

1 **SPEAKING** In pairs, students describe what they can see in the photo and discuss what it says about modern life.

Example answers

The photo shows a stressed-out woman eating fast food, speaking on the phone, and driving, all at the same time. It shows the stress of modern life and how people need to do too many things.

2 In pairs, students read the essay title 'Life today is unhealthier than 50 years ago.' and make notes with ideas for and against the statement.

3 Ask students to read the essay to see if any of their ideas from exercise 2 appear in it. Ask students to decide if they agree with the writer and their conclusion, and say why or why not. Elicit answers from different students around the class.

4 Ask students to look at the essay again and answer the questions.

Answers

1 **Paragraph 1:** Introduce the topic
Paragraph 2: Arguments for
Paragraph 3: Arguments against
Paragraph 4: Conclusion
2 In for-and-against essays, the arguments are objective and equally balanced. An opinion essay is subjective as you only give your side of the argument.

5 Ask students to put the underlined words in the essay in the correct place in the Writing bank.

Answers

Introducing and sequencing arguments
Firstly,
Adding arguments
What is more,
Furthermore,
In addition,
Making contrasts
On the other hand,
despite …
However,
Expressing consequences
As a result,
Expressing opinions
I think that
Concluding
All in all,

6 In pairs, students read the essay task and make a paragraph plan with notes of ideas for each paragraph.

✔ EXAM SUCCESS Students read about writing for-and-against essays in exams. Then tell them to turn to page 146 (Writing: For-and-against and opinion essays) for more ideas.

TEACHER DEVELOPMENT: STUDENT TRAINING

A for-and-against essay

A for-and-against essay is a formal piece of writing in which a topic is considered from opposing points of view. Students should not use an informal style (e.g. short forms, colloquial language, etc.) or strong language to express their opinion. Point out to students that this type of essay presents both sides in a fair way by discussing them objectively and in equal detail.

This kind of essay is structured into paragraphs to distinguish the arguments for a reader. Information is grouped logically and students should use adverbs and conjunctions to establish cohesion within paragraphs.

PRACTICE MAKES PERFECT

7 Individually, students write their essays. Remind them to use their notes and the expressions in the Writing bank. They can also follow the advice in the Writing bank on page 155. For students who are less confident, photocopy the model text below for extra support during the writing task.

Model text

The use of animals for the testing of medical products is a topic that a lot of people feel very strongly about, and there are different points of view. It is clear that we would not have the same range of medicines today if scientists had not tested their products on animals, but what about the future?

Many people nowadays believe that testing new medical products on animals is wrong. Firstly, many people protest against the torture that these animals suffer during medical testing, and believe that it is wrong to take the life of an innocent animal just because humans are stronger. Animal rights activists argue that we must fight for laws to stop this cruelty and injustice. Furthermore, people blame the greed of medical and pharmaceutical companies who do all these tests just to make money.

On the other hand, many people argue that testing new medical products on animals is necessary and has been very important throughout our history. Louis Pasteur experimented on rabbits and dogs and his results have saved millions of humans. Most deadly diseases have been cured because of this type of medical research, which has not only improved people's lives but has increased life expectancy greatly.

In conclusion, in spite of all the arguments in favour of animal experimentation, personally I am against it. Most people will continue to support experimentation on animals when it is absolutely necessary, but I wish they would put themselves in an animal's position. Imagine that you are made to suffer for the benefit of humans. I have pets and I'm against animal testing. Many research and scientific experiments are impractical and immoral, and I think we should fight for better laws to prevent testing on animals.

✚ EXTRA ACTIVITY

Students review their texts from exercise 7 (or their partner's text) giving a grade from 1–5 according to these criteria:

- My ideas are structured clearly, with sentences organised into appropriate paragraphs.
- I think carefully about the way I develop ideas in the texts I write (e.g. closings refer back to openings; I develop ideas in different ways).
- Within paragraphs/sections, I use linking words to support cohesion (e.g. pronouns, connectors).
- I make clear links between paragraphs and make sure that these support the overall direction of the text.

HOMEWORK

Assign students page 54 in their Workbook or the relevant sections of the Online Workbook.

Language checkpoint: Unit 6

>>> **FAST TRACK**

The extra support provided in the Grammar and Vocabulary reference sections makes the Grammar and Vocabulary revision sections ideal for setting as homework. You could get students to complete the whole revision page or just certain exercises for homework.

Grammar revision p81

Conditionals

1 Students complete the sentences with the correct form of the verb given. Ask them to say which type of conditional each sentence is.

Answers

1 wouldn't eat (second conditional)
2 had known (third conditional)
3 would have called (third conditional)
4 is (zero conditional)
5 Will, give (first conditional)
6 had gone (third conditional)
7 will, tell (first conditional)
8 would get (second conditional)

unless, as long as, provided/providing (that), in case

2 Students rewrite the sentences using the words given.

Suggested answers

1 They'll let you in providing that you have your ID card.
2 Take your mobile phone in case you need to call me.
3 We will win the match provided we do our best.
4 They won't need Danny in the team unless someone is ill.
5 We'll be able to make sandwiches as long as Kate remembers to bring the bread.
6 You won't finish in time unless you hurry.

I wish/If only

3 Students write sentences with *I wish* or *If only* for the situations.

Suggested answers

1 I wish I was/were fit.
2 I wish my sister would take less time in the bathroom.
3 If only I'd bought the concert tickets yesterday.
4 If only my parents would let me have parties at home.
5 I wish I hadn't eaten such a big lunch.
6 I wish I wasn't/weren't allergic to cats.

Vocabulary revision p81

PARTS OF THE BODY

1 Students reorder the letters to make parts of the body.

Answers

1 hip   2 lungs   3 thigh   4 kidney   5 brain
6 forehead   7 tongue

WORDS CONNECTED WITH HEALTH

2 Students complete the sentences with words connected with health.

Answers

1 dizzy   2 allergic   3 prescription   4 pressure
5 fractured   6 over   7 relieve

IDIOMS: HEALTH AND ILLNESS

3 Students complete the idioms with the correct word.

Answers

1 pulled   2 weather   3 shape   4 top   5 down
6 feet

HOMEWORK

Assign students page 55 in their Workbook or the relevant sections of the Online Workbook.

Speaking p82

➤ **TIP FOR SPEAKING EXAMS**

Ask students to read the tip on talking about photos in exams. Elicit other things students should remember to do and ask them to turn to Exam success on page 145 to remind them of important tips and strategies.

1 SPEAKING In pairs, students look at the words and expressions in the box and decide when they would use each one. Elicit from students what other words and expressions they know for the same uses.

Answers

To describe: at the top, in the background
To compare and contrast: in both photos, whereas
To speculate: can't be, might have
To give personal opinion: personally

2 Ask Student A to look at photos 1a and 1b and Student B to look at photos 2a and 2b. Encourage them to make notes about the similarities and differences between their two photos and what they could say about them.

3 SPEAKING Ask Student A to read the task and talk about their photos.

4 SPEAKING Ask Student B to read the task and talk about their photos. For students who are less confident, photocopy the model texts below, and either read them aloud yourself or ask a strong student to do so.

Model text (1a/1b)

Both photos show people outdoors. In the first photo, there are some young people on a beach. It looks like a sunny day. They are having a picnic. I can see lots of nice things to eat and drink. In the second photo, there is a small group of people on a trek and they're in the middle of crossing a field. They are walking in the countryside, whereas in the first photograph they are on the coast. One big difference between the photos is that the people in the second photo might be having some kind of walking holiday because they are carrying big rucksacks, while the people on the beach are probably having a picnic just for the afternoon.

In both pictures, I would say that the people have chosen these activities because they enjoy doing outdoor activities, and spending quality time with their friends.

Model text (2a/2b)

Both photos show people doing activities which help them relax and in both photos the people are having fun. In the first photo, I can see a young man windsurfing. In the second photo, however, there are some young people doing yoga. In both pictures the people look like they are enjoying the activities, but one big difference between the photos is that the person in the first photo is doing a very exciting physical activity outside, while the second photo shows people inside doing a more relaxed type of exercise.

I think that in both photos, the people are enjoying doing the activity because it makes them feel alive and it also helps to keep them in shape. The first photo makes me feel like I want it to be summer again. If I had the opportunity to learn how to windsurf, I would certainly do it. I wouldn't be as interested in trying yoga. To be honest, it looks like it might be quite boring for me.

5 SPEAKING What about *you*? Ask students to say which activities in the photos they like or would like to try.

Example answers

Personally, I like the second photo more than the first. I prefer going away for the weekend for long walks or climbs more than just being lazy on a beach.

I love water sports and the sea and I'd love to learn how to windsurf. I think yoga makes you feel calm and peaceful, but I would prefer to do windsurfing.

Listening p82

➤ **TIP FOR LISTENING EXAMS**

Students read the tip about how to successfully carry out listening activities where they have to complete notes. Students discuss techniques and ideas and look at Exam success on page 145 for more ideas.

6 SPEAKING In pairs, students discuss the questions. Encourage them to share some of their ideas with the class.

7 Ask students to read the text and predict what word or type of word could fill each gap.

8 LISTENING ▶ 32 Play the track for students to listen to a radio programme about energy drinks and complete the text in exercise 7. Remind students to write no more than one word or a number for each space. See p177 for the audioscript for this exercise.

Answers

a minerals **b** might **c** ten **d** dehydrates
e basketball **f** drivers **g** teaspoons **h** Taurine
i waste **j** diet

Writing p83

Students read the tip for writing for-and-against and opinion essays and turn to Exam success on page 146 for more ideas.

9a SPEAKING In pairs, students look at the essay title and decide if the ideas are for or against the statement.

Answers

1 for **2** against **3** for **4** against

9b In pairs, students make notes with other ideas for and against the statement.

10 Elicit from students how many paragraphs they think they should write and what the content of each paragraph should be.

Suggested answers

Paragraph 1: State the topic of the essay using general statements

Paragraph 2: Make points for (or against)

Paragraph 3: Make points against (or for)

Paragraph 4: Conclusion – restate the most important arguments and give your own opinion

11 Ask students to write their essay. Remind them to use linkers to introduce and sequence arguments and to make contrasts. For students who are less confident, photocopy the model text below for extra support during the writing task.

✂ -

Model text

A tax on cigarettes and alcohol pays for the extra health care people who smoke or drink need. It would therefore seem logical that there was a tax on fast food. Fast food causes obesity and is bad for you. People usually eat fast food because it is cheap, so if it were more expensive, people would choose healthier foods. However, if it is not implemented properly, it could end up as another way of raising money for the state and not a method of making people's eating habits more healthy.

Firstly, a new tax on foods like burgers, chips, fizzy drinks and other fast foods with high sugar and fat levels would help to cut rising obesity rates. In some countries, more than a third of the population is obese and many of these cases are children. People need to be re-educated on how to eat and a food tax would make people think twice before they buy fast food.

However, not only do people need to be re-educated about food, they also need to be able to buy healthy foods at good prices. Putting up the costs of fast food while not cutting the costs of healthy food would make the situation worse. In addition, many fast-food restaurants offer low-carbohydrate, low-fat options nowadays. People should have the right to choose and we should be careful about introducing legislation which restricts our freedom.

To sum up, people need to be educated about healthy eating, but implementing a fast-food tax is only one step towards solving the problem. In order to be effective, a comprehensive nutritional health education scheme should be implemented. In my opinion, although a fast-food tax would help people see what a big problem fast food is, it is better to focus on education first.

Use of English p83

Students read the tip on how to do sentence transformation activities. Discuss other tips for completing this type of exercise and tell students to turn to Exam success on page 146 to compare their ideas.

12 Students complete the second sentence so that it has a similar meaning to the first sentence, using the word given. Remind students that they should not change the word given and they must use between three and five words including the word given.

Answers

1 unless I really needed **2** wish I'd drunk **3** provided (that) you eat **4** 'd better not go **5** were allowed to drink **6** picked up some orange juice **7** look under the weather **8** as long as you come

HOMEWORK

Assign students pages 56–57 in their Workbook or the relevant sections of the Online Workbook.

1 Ask students to mark from 1–4 how well they feel they can do each thing in English.

2 Ask students to look at their marks and decide what they need to do to improve. Elicit ideas from students around the class.

7 Creative arts

KEY LEARNING OUTCOMES

CEF

Students will be able to:

- report what other people have said or asked using different reporting verbs and structures
- talk about music, film and media habits
- join words to make compound nouns and adjectives
- present solid arguments in discussions
- write reviews using a wide variety of adjectives

UNIT OVERVIEW

Vocabulary
Music and film
Media habits

Reading
Aloe Blacc: If songwriters can't afford to make music then who will?

CRITICAL THINKING Discussing arguments for and against music streaming

Grammar in context
Reported speech – statements
Reported speech – questions

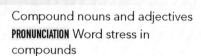

Developing vocabulary
Compound nouns and adjectives
PRONUNCIATION Word stress in compounds

Life skills
Autonomy and enterprise: Bringing ideas to life

Listening
Superfans

Grammar in context
Reported speech – other reporting verbs
Reported speech – other reporting structures

Developing speaking
Discussions – 1

Developing writing
A review

Exam success
Speaking: Discussions
Writing: Reviews

DIGITAL OVERVIEW

Presentation Kit
- ▶ **Flipped classroom video Unit 7:** Reported speech – other reporting structures
- ▶ **Life skills video Unit 7:** Bringing ideas to life
- ▶ **Interactive versions of Student's Book activities**
- ▶ **Integrated audio and answer key for all activities**
- ▶ **Workbook pages with answer key**

Teacher's Resource Centre
- ▶ **Flipped classroom video Unit 7:** Reported speech – other reporting structures
- ▶ **Life skills video Unit 7:** Bringing ideas to life
- ▶ **Grammar communication activity Unit 7:** Party plans
- ▶ **Worksheets for this unit, including:**
  - – Grammar Practice worksheet Unit 7
  - – Flipped classroom video worksheet Unit 7: Reported speech – other reporting structures
  - – Literature worksheet Units 7 and 8
  - – Culture worksheet Unit 7
  - – Life skills video worksheet Unit 7
  - – Everyday English worksheet Unit 7

Student's App
Gateway 2nd Edition wordlist for the award-winning Sounds App (available for download)

✓ TESTING AND ASSESSMENT

Resources for exam preparation and measuring student progress

- ▶ Test Generator Units 1–7
- ▶ Printable test Unit 7
- ▶ Gateway to exams Units 7 and 8 (end of Unit 8)

Vocabulary p84

Talking about music, film and media habits

FAST TRACK

You could ask students to do exercise 2 at home. They can look up any words they are not sure about in their dictionaries or the Macmillan Online Dictionary.

WARMER

In open class, discuss the meaning of the unit title *Creative arts* and what they think the unit is going to be about (creative arts include drama or theatre, music, film, creative writing, graphic design, photography and visual arts. Creative arts are studied at various levels in education). Elicit areas of the creative arts and design sector that students can work in (advertising; animation; architecture; arts heritage and conservation; craft; design; fashion; film; literature; music; performing arts; photography). Drill the pronunciation of *creative* /kri'eɪtɪv/ and brainstorm words in the same word family (*creativity, creativeness, creatively, uncreative, create, creator*).

Music and film

1 **SPEAKING** Individually, students brainstorm different types of music. In pairs, students compare their answers and score one point for a correct word and two points for any word their partner does not have. Students total their points to see who has the most. Elicit types of music from different students around the class. Then students repeat the same procedure with different types of film.

Example answers

Music: alternative, blues, classical, country, dance, folk, funk, heavy metal, hip hop, house, indie, jazz, pop, punk, rap, rock, ska, soul, techno, world
Film: action, adventure, animated, biographical, comedy, crime, documentary, drama, fantasy, historical, horror, martial arts, musical, mystery, romance, science fiction, sports, spy, thriller, war, western

2 Ask students to complete the blog texts with the words. Provide them with dictionaries if necessary.

Answers

a gig **b** live **c** stage **d** crowd **e** recorded
f tracks **g** lighting **h** lyrics **i** starred **j** role
k performance **l** acting **m** plot **n** scene
o soundtrack

3 **LISTENING** 33 Play the track for students to listen to the definitions of eight words and write the correct form of the words in exercise 2 that match them. See p177 for the audioscript for this exercise.

Answers

1 gig **2** lyrics **3** live **4** crowd **5** tracks **6** scene
7 record **8** soundtrack

EXTRA ACTIVITY

Students write a definition for another word from the box in exercise 2 to test their partner.

Media habits

4 Ask students to match words or expressions in red in the questionnaire to the definitions.

Answers

1 download **2** stream **3** live streams **4** mobile device **5** purchase **6** file-sharing sites
7 peer-to-peer **8** transfer

5 **SPEAKING** In pairs, students take it in turns to ask and answer the questions in the questionnaire. Elicit answers from students around the class.

EXTRA ACTIVITY

Students write a short text about their partner's media habits.

HOMEWORK

Assign students page 58 in their Workbook or the relevant sections of the Online Workbook.

Reading p85

Reading for gist and specific information

FAST TRACK

You could ask students to read the article in exercise 2 at home in preparation for in-class activities.

WARMER

Play *Noughts and crosses* with words from the previous lesson. Draw a 3 x 3 grid on the board. Choose a word and draw a short line on the board to represent each letter. Write small numbers 1–9 in each square on the grid so it is easy for students to name the square. Divide the class into two teams and toss a coin to see who goes first. Assign noughts (0) to one group and crosses (X) to the other. The first group chooses a square from the grid and says a letter. If the letter is in the word, write it on the corresponding short line. That group can then continue guessing letters. If they say a letter which is not in the word, play passes to the other team. If they guess the word correctly, their symbol (0 or X) goes in the space they nominated. The other team can then choose a square and try to guess a new word. The first team to get three noughts or crosses in a row (horizontal, vertical or diagonal) is the winner.

1 **SPEAKING** In pairs, students discuss if they like using streaming music services. Elicit opinions from different students around the class.

2 Elicit from students what they know about the singer and songwriter Aloe Blacc. Ask them to read the article and decide what he is complaining about and why. Check the answer.

Answer

legal streaming of songs because songwriters aren't paid fairly for their songs which are streamed

ℹ CULTURAL INFORMATION

Blacc is from Orange County, California, and his parents are Panamanian. His last name is pronounced like the colour black. Aloe Blacc chose his name for its smoothness: the first name references the plant associated with lotion and he exchanged the K in 'Black' for another C because he considers K a harsher consonant. He is married to Australian rapper Maya Jupiter, and they had their first baby, a daughter named Mandela, in 2013. *Lift Your Spirit* is his third solo album, the first having been released in 2006. Blacc is actively involved in Malaria No More – a charity whose mission is to end malaria deaths and deliver education to families across Africa.

3 Ask students to read the article again and answer the questions.

Suggested answers

1 Power to capture people's emotions and imaginations, to transcend traditional barriers of age, language and culture, and to generate positive social change.
2 She wants to be fairly paid for her work.
3 They have more control over their work.
4 It was the most streamed song on Spotify and 13th most played song on Pandora.
5 Streaming services make big profits, but songwriters don't.
6 Buy albums and encourage streaming services to respect the value of song writing.

4 CRITICAL THINKING Encourage students to discuss if they agree with the arguments Aloe Blacc gives in his article and say why or why not.

Example answers

I don't agree with Aloe Blacc's arguments. Artists and musicians make enough money as it is, and downloading a few songs won't hurt them much. True fans will still buy their albums or support them in other ways. People already download music for free, so let's just leave it as it is.

I agree with Aloe Blacc. Music isn't going to be around much longer. I wouldn't like to work and not get paid. When we download music for free we are essentially doing this to the musician. We are, in effect, stealing their music.

5 Ask students to work out the meaning of the underlined words in the text by looking at the context and guessing before they check in their dictionaries.

Answers

master his craft = become good at the skill needed for his profession
high-end = more expensive and more advanced
devalued = reduce the value
spins = in radio broadcasting, a spin is a single play of a song
royalties = a payment that someone such as a writer or musician gets each time their work is sold or performed
is it any wonder that = an expression that means that something isn't surprising or that the following conclusion is obvious. You can replace it with 'I think it's obvious why …'
given way to = to be replaced by something, especially something newer or better
imbalanced = unevenly or unfairly arranged

TEACHER DEVELOPMENT: STUDENT TRAINING

Deducing the meaning of new words

Students who guess the meaning of words by looking at the context read better and quicker. This strategy involves four steps: 1 determining the part of speech of the word; 2 looking at the immediate grammar; 3 studying the wider context (usually the conjunction relationships); 4 guessing the word and checking the guess.

6 SPEAKING **What about *you*?** In pairs or small groups, students discuss where and how they prefer to listen to music. Elicit answers from different students around the class and try to develop a class discussion.

✚ EXTRA ACTIVITY

Ask students to write a for-and-against essay with the arguments Aloe Blacc gives and their ideas in exercise 4.

HOMEWORK

Assign students page 59 in their Workbook or the relevant sections of the Online Workbook.

Grammar in context pp86–87

Reporting what other people have said or asked using a variety of reporting verbs and structures

>>> **FAST TRACK**

You could ask students to do exercises 1, 2 and 3 at home.

Test before you teach

Write these direct statements on the board:

Jill: I love chocolate.

Kate: I went to the beach.

Sam: Do you like rock music?

Paul: Where are you going tomorrow?

Ask students to rewrite the statements and questions using reported speech, i.e. *Jill/Kate said/asked …* Monitor carefully. If students seem to be familiar with reported speech, move through the Grammar guide exercises quickly in open class.

Answers

Jill said (that) she loved chocolate.

Kate said (that) she had gone to the beach.

Sam asked if I liked rock music.

Paul asked where I was going the next day.

Reported speech – statements

1 Ask students to read the sentences and answer questions 1–5.

Answers

1 The tense of the verbs usually goes one tense 'back' in reported speech. Some tenses cannot go any further back and stay the same.

2 If the reporting verb is in the present simple or present perfect (i.e. *He says/He has said*), the tense does not change.

3 *I* changes to *he* in the reported speech.

4 When we use *say*, we do not need a personal object to say who you are saying something to. With *tell*, we must use a personal object to say who we are saying something to.

5 No, we do not always need to use *that* after *say* and *tell*.

TEACHER DEVELOPMENT: LANGUAGE

Reporting verbs

The most common verbs used to report statements are *say*, *tell* and *ask*. When *tell* is used in reported speech, it is always followed by a noun or a pronoun indicating the person spoken to, e.g. *Jane told **us** (that) we were going to the cinema on Saturday.*

When we report another person's words, we can consider replacing the more common *say*, *tell* or *ask* with a more accurate reporting verb. Accurate selection of the correct reporting verb is often expected in examinations at B2 level.

✚ **EXTRA ACTIVITY**

Say some simple sentences and ask students to report them back to you, e.g. *I like English.* → *She said she liked English. He's going to the bank.* → *He said he was going to the bank.*

2 Ask students to complete the table showing how the tenses change when we use reported speech. Draw students' attention to the example. Elicit if all tenses change.

Answers

Most tenses move one tense back, but some tenses (i.e. past perfect/*would*) can't go any further back and stay the same.

1 past continuous 2 past perfect 3 past perfect continuous 4 past perfect 5 past perfect
6 *would* 7 *would* 8 *could* 9 *might* 10 *had to*

3 Ask students to complete the table to show how the words change when they go into reported speech. Draw students' attention to the example.

Answers

1 there 2 that day 3 the day before 4 the next/following day 5 that night 6 the following (week/month/year) 7 the previous (week/month/year)
8 a (week/month/year) before

4 Ask students to complete the sentences with *said* or *told*.

Answers

1 said 2 said 3 told 4 told 5 said 6 said

5 Ask students to put the sentences in direct speech into reported speech.

Answers

1 Steve says (that) he never buys DVDs.

2 Sam told us (that) we had to leave if we wanted to get to the cinema on time.

3 Emma said (that) those books were hers.

4 Alicia said (that) she was going to record a new album.

5 Juliet said (that) the crowd had been screaming throughout the concert.

6 Dave told Simon (that) he would see him the next day.

Reported speech – questions

6 Ask students to read the sentences and answer questions 1–5.

Answers

1 Yes, they do.

2 No, we don't.

3 Yes, the subject goes before the verb in reported questions (i.e. normal word order).

4 No, reported questions are not real questions and therefore do not need question marks.

5 Questions that do not begin with a question word are reported by using *ask + if/whether*.

7 Ask students to report the conversation using *said, told, asked* and *wanted to know.*

Suggested answer

Olivia wanted to know if Tom had ever been to a music festival.

Tom said he had and that he had been to one the previous year.

Olivia asked who had been the best band.

Tom told her that he had really enjoyed the Foo Fighters and that he was going to see them again later that year.

Olivia said she might go if it wasn't too expensive. She asked him when they were playing.

Tom said he thought the concert would be in July and asked her if she was going to be there in July.

Olivia said she thought so. She told him that she had been saving up money to go to the US, but she still hadn't got enough.

Tom wanted to know when Olivia thought she would be able to go. Olivia said she was probably going to go the following year and that she would love to go to a festival there.

8a Students write five questions to ask people in the class about music.

8b SPEAKING Students ask as many people as possible their questions and make notes about the answers.

8c Ask students to write a report about some of the questions they asked and the answers people gave. Draw their attention to the example report.

>>> FAST FINISHERS

In small groups, students compare their reports and choose the most interesting information. Ask students to report this information to the rest of the class using reported speech.

Refer students to the Grammar reference on page 94 if necessary.

HOMEWORK

Assign students page 60 in their Workbook or the relevant sections of the Online Workbook.

Developing vocabulary p87

Using compound nouns and adjectives

>>> FAST TRACK

You could ask students to do exercise 3 before class and compare answers in pairs in preparation for exercise 4.

Compound nouns and adjectives

1 Students look at the compounds and decide which are compound nouns and which are compound adjectives.

Answers

Nouns: download, file-sharing, marketplace, songwriter, soundtrack

Adjectives: brand new, fast-moving, thought-provoking

TEACHER DEVELOPMENT: LANGUAGE

Compound adjectives

A compound adjective is formed with two words or sometimes three. The second part is often a present participle, e.g. *-provoking*, or a past participle, e.g. *-fashioned.* Many compound adjectives describe a person's character, appearance or situation.

Most compound adjectives are hyphenated when they modify nouns. This is to clarify meaning, e.g. *The short legged man ran for the door.* (You are saying that the man is short and had legs!) *The short-legged man ran for the door.* (Now you are saying that the man's legs are short.)

In the following circumstances, compound adjectives are *always* hyphenated when they are not written as one word:

■ An adjective preceding a noun to which *-d* or *-ed* has been added as a past-participle construction, used before a noun, e.g. *old-fashioned.*

■ A noun, adjective or adverb preceding a present participle, e.g. *thought-provoking.*

■ Numbers, either spelt out or not, e.g. *a nine-year-old boy / a 20-year-old man.*

■ Colours in compounds, e.g. *a dark-blue sweater, a reddish-orange dress.*

2 PRONUNCIATION ▶ 34 Play the track for students to listen to the words. They decide where the stress is in the compound nouns – on the first word, the last word or both and then say if this is the same with compound adjectives.

Answers

In compound nouns, the stress usually falls on the first word. For compound adjectives, we usually pronounce both parts with equal stress.

<u>down</u>load, <u>file</u>-sharing, <u>market</u>place, <u>song</u>writer, <u>sound</u>track

brand <u>new</u>, fast-<u>moving</u>, thought-<u>provoking</u>

Stress in compound nouns

There are three forms of compound nouns: separated (board rubber), hyphenated (twenty-one) and combined (textbook). Compound nouns tend to have more stress on the first word; we consider *board rubber* to be a single noun and so it has a single main stress – on the first word. Stress is important in compound nouns and can help avoid confusion, e.g. a <u>green</u> <u>house</u> is a house that has been painted green, whereas a <u>green</u>house is a glass building for growing plants.

3 Students match the compound nouns 1–8 with the definitions a–h.

Answers
1 c **2** b **3** g **4** h **5** f **6** e **7** d **8** a

4 Students complete the sentences with the compound nouns in exercise 3. Give them time to compare their answers in pairs.

Answers
1 blockbuster **2** outcome **3** page-turner
4 drawback **5** feedback **6** box office **7** turnout
8 screenplay

Write these words in columns on the board for students to match and make compound adjectives:

world	humoured
good	famous
middle	skinned
thick	handed
left	aged

Ask them to write a sentence using each compound adjective, e.g. *Rihanna is a world-famous pop star.*

Answers
world-famous   good-humoured   middle-aged
thick-skinned   left-handed

Assign students page 61 in their Workbook or the relevant sections of the Online Workbook.

Gateway to life skills pp88–89 🏃

Bringing ideas to life

To learn about crowdfunding, to look at how to make a crowdfunding video and to create a crowdfunding campaign for a project

Students could do exercises 2 and 3 at home.

The increasing number and popularity of crowdfunding websites provides many options for youth in need of financial resources to support community service projects and other social, human or environmental causes. Crowdfunding has been used to fund many different types of projects, such as projects that help artists and film-makers, animal welfare organisations, and health and environmental causes.

Some examples of successful teenage crowdfunding campaigns include Guillaume Rolland, an 18-year-old French entrepreneur, who invented SensorWake, a new innovation in alarm clock technology. It's an alarm clock that wakes you up to the smell of coffee. Lily Born, from Chicago, designed unbreakable, unspillable kitchenware to help people with Parkinson's disease. She raised over $60,000 in a Kickstarter crowdfunding campaign to develop the product.

In pairs or small groups, students race to think of as many music festivals as they can. Set a time limit of two minutes and find out which pair/group has the longest list. Ask students to read through the Key concepts and check any vocabulary they don't understand.

1 SPEAKING In pairs, students imagine that they play in a band and they want to record an album. Ask them to brainstorm ways they can do this. Draw students' attention to the example. Elicit some answers from different students around the class.

2 READING Elicit what the abbreviation *FAQs* stands for (*Frequently Asked Questions*) and ask students to read the answers to the FAQs on a website about crowdfunding. In open class, discuss how this could help them make their album. Remind students that they can refer to Key concepts for definitions of words they are not sure about. Elicit answers from students around the class.

3 Ask students to read the text again and match the questions to answers 1–8 in the text. Students can compare their answers in pairs. Check answers in open class by asking one partner to read the correct question and the other to read out the corresponding answer. This way it becomes evident that they are a natural match.

Answers
1 f **2** c **3** a **4** d **5** g **6** h **7** b **8** e

4 SPEAKING Ask students to work in pairs and take turns to answer the questions in exercise 3 in their own words. Ask them to try and answer without looking at the text. Draw students' attention to the example.

Suggested answers

b Some examples of successful projects include a video game and a digital music player.

c Crowdfunding can work well for albums, books, films, video games, new technology, or even charities.

d The artist or creator can make the item as they want to make it without commercial pressures, for example.

e You have to decide what you want to achieve and offer in return, and then you can make a video explaining the project and the rewards.

f A way to raise money for a project from a large number of people, usually via the Internet.

g They usually get rewards, and they feel part of the project.

h It's very successful – in 2013 it was worth over $5.1 billion.

5 SPEAKING In pairs, students discuss what they think of the idea of crowdfunding and justify their opinions. Elicit answers from different students around the class.

6 SPEAKING Remind students that for crowdfunding, it's a good idea to make a video to attract backers. In pairs, students discuss how important they think the points 1–5 are for a successful video. Elicit opinions from students around the class.

🔍 VOCABULARY FOCUS

The video about crowdfunding contains some useful words and phrases that students may not be familiar with. You might want to pre-teach these words and phrases with students before watching:

platform (hosting) [n]: the type of computer system that you have and the programs that you can use with it

hosting capabilities [n]: in computing, the functions that a platform has

backer/s [n]: people who give you money to allow you to do something (sponsors)

hiring [v]: giving people work

streamline [v]: make things work as easily and smoothly as possible

target [v]: to aim something at a particular person or people

underestimate [v]: to expect less than someone or something is capable of

to have creative control (over) [phr]: to be responsible for the development of something

7 **LISTENING** ▶ 35 Tell students they are going to watch or listen to James talking about his experience of crowdfunding. Play the video or audio track for students to note down what he used crowdfunding for and how many people were involved in funding his project. See the Teacher's Resource Centre for the audioscript/videoscript for this exercise.

Answers

He used crowdfunding to fund making a short film that he had written.

Eighty people (backers) were involved in funding his project.

8 ▶ 35 Play the video or audio track again. Students then work in pairs to ask and answer questions 1–6. Check answers in open class.

Answers

1 He chose the host for his campaign because it was the biggest and most well-known host, and it offered international backers.

2 The money was mainly used for hiring equipment and locations, and actors.

3 James's crowdfunding video was a simple and personal video of James talking directly to the camera.

4 It was a very effective video because James reached his target of £3,500.

5 If he did it again, he would have allowed more time for getting all the information ready before beginning the crowdfunding campaign.

6 Yes, he does. Because you get to keep creative control of the project and there aren't many other ways to get the funding.

➕ EXTRA ACTIVITY

Ask students to work in pairs and make a list of all the projects they can think of that could benefit from crowdfunding. Students compare their list with another pair.

21ˢᵀ CENTURY TASK

Tell students they want to create a crowdfunding campaign. Ask them to work in groups of three to five students and follow the plan:

- **Step 1**

  Ask students to decide on a project that they would like to bring to life, e.g. a movie, video game, new technology, work of art or an item of fashion.

- **Step 2**

  Ask students to outline the crowdfunding campaign for their project. Ask them to think about what they will create to publicise their project and attract backers (it could be a video, a poster, a presentation, etc.). Encourage them to think about what rewards they could offer.

- **Step 3**

  Ask students to create the publicity for their crowdfunding campaign. Encourage them to make it as informative and attractive as possible. Refer them to the ideas from exercise 6.

- **Step 4**

  Ask students to present their crowdfunding campaign to the other groups. Give time for each group to agree on which project to back (they cannot back their own!). Ask students to raise their hands to vote for the project they would like to back. Count hands to see which project got the most backers.

Listening p90

Listening for general and specific information

WARMER

Play *Hot seat.* Divide the students into two or three groups. One volunteer from each group sits in a chair with their back to the board, facing their group. Write a word from the unit on the board so that the volunteers can't see the word. Their group must give hints to their volunteer so that their volunteer guesses the word first. The first one to guess the word gets a point for their team.

1 **SPEAKING** In pairs, students describe who and what they can see in the photo. Elicit answers and ask students what they think a 'superfan' is.

Suggested answers

The photo shows a group of fans holding out paper and pens for a celebrity to sign their autograph.
Students' own answers

2 **LISTENING** ▶ 36 Play the track for students to listen to a radio programme about superfans and answer the questions. See p178 for the audioscript for this exercise.

Answers

1 Superfans are people who devote most of their time to their passion.
2 Very important – they would be nothing without the passion of their fans.
3 Sarah M is the world's most famous superfan.

TEACHER DEVELOPMENT: STUDENT TRAINING

Listening for the first and second time

Remind students that it is more effective to listen for the general idea in the first listening and then in more detail in the second. Remind students to look at the task and questions and make predictions about what type of information they are going to listen for, before the first listening. In the first listening, students should not expect to understand everything. They are listening for main ideas and a general understanding of the text (listening for gist). Remind them to listen to the stressed words and make an image in their mind of what the listening is about. In the second listening, students move from global to more detailed listening and focus on listening for the information they need to answer the questions.

3 ▶ 36 Play the track again for students to decide if the statements are True (T), False (F) or the information is Not Mentioned (NM).

Answers

1 F **2** T **3** F **4** T **5** NM **6** T **7** NM **8** F **9** T
10 NM

4 **SPEAKING** What about *you?* Ask students to discuss what or who they are a fan of and if they think they could ever become a superfan. Encourage students to give reasons to justify their answers.

HOMEWORK

Assign students page 61 in their Workbook or the relevant sections of the Online Workbook.

Grammar in context pp90–91

Reporting speech with a variety of reporting verbs and structures

⟫⟫ FAST TRACK

Students could do exercises 1 and 2a at home. Check their answers and start the class on exercise 2b.

Test before you teach

Write these sentences on the board:
1 She _____ me that we needed to buy milk.
2 My mum _____ me not to talk to strangers.
3 The teacher _____ that the tense usually changes in reported speech.
4 My brother _____ that he would come and watch me play football.
Ask students to complete the sentences with one of these verbs: *promise, warn, remind, explain.* Monitor and check if students seem familiar with these other reporting verbs. If so, move through the Grammar guide exercises quickly in open class.

Answers

1 reminded **2** warned **3** explained **4** promised

Reported speech – other reporting verbs

1a Students look at the sentences and decide which reporting verbs have a person (like *told*) and which don't (like *said*).

Answers

Reporting verbs that have a person: warn, remind
Reporting verbs that don't have a person: explain, claim

1b Elicit the meaning of the reporting verbs in the sentences in exercise 1a.

Answers

explain – to tell someone something in a way that helps them understand it better

warn – to make someone conscious of a possible problem or danger so that they will not be hurt

remind – to help someone to remember something that they have forgotten or not considered

claim – to say that something is true, even though there is no definite proof

2a Ask students to choose the best alternative.

Answers

a announced **b** claimed **c** agreed **d** admitted
e added **f** complained **g** warned **h** promised

2b Ask students to rewrite the sentences in exercise 2a in direct speech. Draw their attention to the example. Elicit answers from different students around the class.

Answers

b 'Critics have destroyed my career.'
c 'I deserve criticism for my last film.'
d 'I didn't put much effort into the role.'
e 'And it was made too quickly.'
f 'Critics have been making personal insults about me in their reviews.'
g 'I will do something if they continue.'
h 'I will take legal action against them.'

3 Ask students to rewrite the sentences in reported speech using the verbs in the box. Ask them to compare their answers in pairs before you check them.

Answers

1 Tom complained that the film was too short.
2 Andy admitted that he wasn't very good at remembering film titles.
3 Danny promised that he would remember to give me my DVD back.
4 The Prime Minister announced that the government was going to spend more money on the arts.
5 Jack claimed that he hadn't known it was illegal to download the film.
6 Kate warned Josh that it was dangerous to sit too close to the screen.
7 Jamie reminded Dave that the match started at 7 pm.

Reported speech – other reporting structures

 Test before you teach: Flipped classroom
Set the Flipped classroom video and tasks for homework <u>before the lesson</u>. This will allow you to assess the needs of the students before the class. Students can then move on to the relevant grammar practice activities.

4a Check students understand the reporting verbs in a–e. Then ask them to look at the structure in each sentence and write each verb in the correct list in 1–5.

Answers

1 refuse **2** ask **3** suggest **4** apologise for
5 criticise somebody for

4b Check that students understand the other reporting verbs in lists 1–5 in exercise 4a. Tell students to use their dictionaries if necessary.

>>> **FAST FINISHERS**

Ask students to choose a verb from each list and write an example sentence.

5 Ask students to choose the correct alternative.

Answers

1 seeing **2** arriving **3** for watching **4** to go
5 not to tell **6** liking **7** to buy **8** knowing

6 Ask students to rewrite the sentences using reported speech.

Answers

1 Connor apologised to Emma for not waiting for her.
2 She warned Ashley not to come that way because it was dangerous.
3 She accused Ella of taking the book from the library.
4 Elizabeth promised to tell her mum exactly what had happened.
5 Taylor denied taking the CD.
6 William's dad told him not to go out with his friends that weekend.
7 Cathy and Lucas agreed to help Lara with her homework the next day.
8 The actor refused to let them take his photo.

7 Ask students to complete the sentences with information about themselves. Remind students that they must use a verb in the correct form.

Example answers

1 Once somebody accused me of taking something in a shop.
2 I once refused to go to school.
3 When I was small, my parents insisted on visiting my relatives every week.
4 Once I promised to cook dinner for my mum.
5 If you want to take up a new hobby, I suggest you join the sports club.
6 Somebody once congratulated me on scoring a goal in a football match.
7 My parents have always warned me not to walk home alone at night.
8 At school, they always tell you to work harder.

8 SPEAKING In pairs, students compare their sentences to find out if any are similar or the same. Elicit sentences from different students around the class.

Refer students to the Grammar reference on page 94 if necessary.

HOMEWORK

Assign students page 62 in their Workbook or the relevant sections of the Online Workbook.

Developing speaking p92

Presenting solid arguments in discussions

>>> FAST TRACK

You could ask students to read the website article in exercise 2 at home in preparation for the speaking activity.

WARMER

Give students some strips of paper with famous lines from films or songs, e.g. *I'll be back. (Terminator)*. Each student reads out their sentence in reported speech, e.g. *He said he would be back.* The others try to guess who said it/which film it is from and transform the sentence back into direct speech. More ideas for sentences include: *I see dead people. (Sixth Sense)*, *Luke, I'm your father. (Darth Vader in Star Wars)*, *It's a thin line between love and hate. (Aloe Blacc)*, *I'll think about that tomorrow. (Gone with the Wind)*, etc.

1 SPEAKING In pairs, students look at the posters and think of other films they know where the star is female. Elicit names of films from different pairs around the class.

2 Students read the website article. In pairs, students discuss if the information surprises them and say why or why not.

3 LISTENING ▶ 37 Play the track for students to listen to two teenagers discussing the website article and answer the questions. Check their answers. See p178 for the audioscript for this exercise.

Answers

Girl: films don't give enough importance to women; the movie business needs more female writers and directors; female stars can be just as successful as male stars; examples are Sandra Bullock in *Gravity* and Anne Hathaway in *Interstellar*.

Boy: agrees that there are not enough female heroes in films, but he thinks the situation is changing e.g. *The Hunger Games*. They should use the test to evaluate a new film when writing the screenplay.

4 ▶ 37 Ask students to read through the expressions in the Speaking bank. Then play the track again for students to listen and tick the expressions they hear. Check their answers.

Answers

Giving emphasis

Don't forget that …
There's no doubt in my mind that …
I really do think that …
I'm totally convinced that …
You can't deny that …

Giving examples

For instance,
Take …, for example
What about the case of …?
Look at …
You only have to think of …
… such as …

5 SPEAKING Divide students into groups of three. Ask them to discuss their own opinions about the article in exercise 2 and give examples. Walk round, monitoring students and noting down good use of language and errors to go over in a short feedback session at the end of the activity.

✓ EXAM SUCCESS Students read about how important it is to listen carefully to what other people are saying and react to it. Tell students to turn to page 146 (Speaking: Discussions) for more ideas.

TEACHER DEVELOPMENT: STUDENT TRAINING

Discussing and negotiating

In some examinations, the final part of the oral test is a discussion on a topic where candidates are expected to express and justify their opinion and agree and disagree with their partner(s). In order to have an effective discussion, students must listen carefully to their partners, react to what they have said and ask follow-up questions to keep the discussion going. Successful candidates initiate conversation and encourage others to contribute their ideas, as well as dealing tactfully with more controversial ideas and attitudes.

PRACTICE MAKES PERFECT

6a SPEAKING Individually, students look at the discussion topics and decide what their opinion is for each one. Ask them to make a note of their arguments and some examples.

6b In groups of three, students discuss the different topics in exercise 6a. Remind them to use expressions from the Speaking bank.

For students who are less confident, photocopy the model dialogue below, and either read it aloud yourself, or alternate the roles with you and two strong students. Then instruct students to read aloud in threes, alternating between roles A, B and C. Then ask them to conduct their own discussion using the model dialogue as a guide.

Model dialogue (topic 2)

A: Anna, what do you think about the topic 'Violent films and video games create violent teenagers'?

B: I'm totally convinced that it's true. You only have to think of the shootings in schools in recent years. One of those was related to the video game *Doom*.

C: Yes, but you have to remember that millions of people play those video games and watch violent films and only a small number are violent in real life. Maybe they would be violent people anyway – with or without the video games and films.

A: There's no doubt in my mind that violent films and video games have a negative effect on teenagers, but there is no evidence to say they make people do violent things.

6c Ask groups to share their ideas with the whole class and find out if they have similar opinions or not. Try to develop a class discussion.

✚ EXTRA ACTIVITY

Students write a brief report about their discussion. Remind them to use the reporting verbs and structures they have seen in this unit. Students swap their reports with other groups for them to read and correct.

HOMEWORK

Assign students page 63 in their Workbook or the relevant sections of the Online Workbook.

Developing writing p93

Writing a review

⟫ FAST TRACK

You could ask students to read the review of a book in exercise 2 and prepare their opinion for discussion in class.

WARMER

In groups, students discuss which books are most popular with teenagers, and the names of popular authors and books that they have read recently.

1 **SPEAKING** In pairs, students look at the notice on a website and decide which book(s) they would recommend and say why.

2 Ask students to read the review of a book for teenagers and decide if they would like to read the book after reading the review. Elicit opinions from different students around the class.

3 Ask students to read the review again and decide what the purpose of each paragraph is.

Answers

Paragraph 1: introduction; facts about the book and overview

Paragraph 2: plot

Paragraph 3: opinion

Paragraph 4: summary and recommendation

4 Ask students what they think of the use of adjectives in the book review. Ask them to justify their opinions.

Suggested answer

The use of the adjective *good* is limited and repetitive.

TEACHER DEVELOPMENT: STUDENT TRAINING

Descriptive adjectives

To communicate more powerfully in English, students need to avoid weak, boring and overly used words such as *good* and *bad*. Encourage them to choose more specific, descriptive adjectives that convey greater meaning in order to get better marks in official examinations.

5a In pairs, students look at the adjectives in the Writing bank and say which ones they know. Provide dictionaries if necessary for students to check the meaning of any words they don't know.

5b Ask students which adjectives they think are positive and which are negative. Check their answers.

Answers

Most are positive. The negative adjectives are: *awful, clichéd, predictable, scary* (could be positive), *stupid, terrible, unconvincing, uninspiring*

6 Ask students to use adjectives from the Writing bank to replace the adjective *good* in the review in exercise 2.

Suggested answer

Legend is a really <u>amazing</u> book for teenagers written by an American writer called Marie Lu.

The plot of the story is <u>gripping</u> because you're never really sure what is going to happen next.

One <u>clever</u> thing about the book is both June and Day are narrators, so you know exactly what each of them thinks. There are some <u>convincing</u> scenes where June and Day's feelings for each other change and the plot takes lots of <u>spectacular</u> turns that you don't expect.

In my opinion, this book is really <u>appealing</u> for teenagers because there is action and romance, but it also makes <u>perceptive</u> points about loyalty to family, friends and your country. I also like the <u>brilliant</u> descriptions of how our world might be in the future.

If you're a fan of stories that combine action, <u>realistic</u> characters and <u>vivid</u> descriptions, you'll love *Legend*.

✔ EXAM SUCCESS **Students read about how to make reviews interesting for the reader. Tell students to turn to page 146 (Writing: Reviews) for more ideas.**

Writing reviews

In the first paragraph, students identify the book by author, title, the type of book, e.g. fiction, non-fiction, biography, autobiography, and the book's theme. Students can skim the first few pages to find the date the book was published.

In the second paragraph, students should briefly describe the content or the storyline: what happens, the main events and who is in the book. Students could also describe their favourite part of the book: a particular piece of action, description or character's speech that they enjoyed.

In the third paragraph, students provide their reactions to the book: was it interesting, memorable, entertaining? Why? They can also talk about any weak parts in the book: unrealistic characters or chapters which were slow-moving, etc.

In the last paragraph, students summarise their ideas and close with a direct comment on the book. Students briefly restate their main points and offer advice for potential readers.

PRACTICE MAKES PERFECT

7a Ask students to make notes about one of the books they thought about in exercise 1. Remind them to organise their notes into paragraphs and follow the paragraph plan in exercise 3. They can also follow the advice in the Writing bank on page 156.

7b Ask students to write their review.

7c Encourage students to exchange their reviews with other students and decide which of the books they want to read. For students who are less confident, photocopy the model text below for extra support during the writing task.

Model text

The Name of the Wind is a brilliant fantasy novel by novelist Patrick Rothfuss. It was written in 2007 and is 900 pages long. It's hot at the moment because everyone is waiting for the second book to come out (it's a trilogy).

The plot of the story is incredible, rich and realistic. It is the chronicle of a young boy called Kvothe, from his happy beginnings with his family as a troupe of travelling entertainers to his life on the streets, and then to his time at university where he starts on the road to becoming a powerful wizard. There is a thrilling scene when Ben, an old man who has special powers, tells Kvothe of the powers and great things he can learn at the university.

In my opinion, this book is gripping. The story starts rather typically and you feel you are reading a familiar and comfortable story, until Rothfuss changes gears in the most intriguing way. One of the things that I liked most about the novel is the power of story. From the stories Kvothe remembers his father telling, to the stories and plays his family performed, the book has many stories within stories. There are, however, some predictable parts, like when Kvothe says goodbye to Denna.

All things considered, if you are a fan of fantasy fiction that combines thought-provoking characters, fascinating landscapes and a fast-moving story, this is the book for you!

HOMEWORK

Assign students page 64 in their Workbook or the relevant sections of the Online Workbook.

Language checkpoint: Unit 7

>>> **FAST TRACK**

The extra support provided in the Grammar and Vocabulary reference sections makes the Grammar and Vocabulary revision sections ideal for setting as homework. You could get students to complete the whole revision page or just certain exercises for homework.

Grammar revision p95

Reported speech – statements

1 Students complete each second sentence so that it has a similar meaning to the first. Remind students to use between two and five words including the word given.

Answers

1 he wasn't able to **2** me I had to **3** was on TV that night **4** that he had not passed **5** was sure those were their **6** maybe they had made

Reported speech – questions

2 Students complete the sentences using reported speech.

Answers

1 Charlie asked Holly where she had just been.
2 He asked Jo if she wanted to go out that night.
3 Lucy asked the boy if he could speak English.
4 Dave wondered if it would rain the following week.
5 Sophie wanted to know how they had done that stunt.
6 Grace asked Jack if he was going to buy a car.
7 Mum asked us what we had been doing that morning.

Reported speech – other reporting structures

3 Students complete the text with the correct form of the verbs given, adding prepositions if necessary.

Answers

a promised to do **b** accused one man of making
c refused to answer **d** admitted doing **e** confessed to copying **f** apologised for causing **g** told him not to do

Vocabulary revision p95

MUSIC AND FILM

1 Students complete the sentences with the correct words.

Answers

1 live **2** scene **3** lyrics **4** starred **5** stage **6** role

COMPOUND NOUNS/ADJECTIVES

2 Students match the words in the two columns. Ask them to say if each word is an adjective or a noun.

Answers

1 c, noun **2** f, noun **3** a, adjective **4** g, noun
5 b, adjective **6** e, noun **7** d, noun

MEDIA HABITS

3 Students reorder the letters in the words in red.

Answers

1 live stream **2** mobile device **3** transfer **4** stream, download **5** purchase **6** file-sharing sites

HOMEWORK

Assign students page 65 in their Workbook or the relevant sections of the Online Workbook.

8 Surviving disaster

KEY LEARNING OUTCOMES   CEF

Students will be able to:

- use different passive structures to talk about processes and procedures and to say what people say, know or believe
- understand written and spoken texts about natural disasters

- use a variety of verbs with the appropriate preposition
- use different words and expressions to talk about statistics
- use a variety of linkers in opinion essays

UNIT OVERVIEW

Vocabulary
Natural disasters
Words connected with natural disasters
PRONUNCIATION Word stress

Reading
Tsunami! A 21ˢᵗ century survival solution
CRITICAL THINKING Discussing how useful and practical an invention is

Grammar in context
The passive
The passive – verbs with two objects

Developing vocabulary
Prepositional phrases with verbs

Life skills
Citizenship: Helping a charity

Listening
The tsunami survivor who is an example to us all

Grammar in context
The passive with *say, know, believe*, etc.

Developing speaking
Talking about statistics

Developing writing
An opinion essay – 2

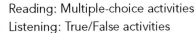
Exam success
Reading: Multiple-choice activities
Listening: True/False activities

DIGITAL OVERVIEW

Presentation Kit

- ▶ **Flipped classroom video Unit 8:** The passive with *say, know, believe*, etc. – 1
- ▶ **Life skills video Unit 8:** Helping disaster victims
- ▶ **Interactive versions of Student's Book activities**
- ▶ **Integrated audio and answer key for all activities**
- ▶ **Workbook pages with answer key**

Teacher's Resource Centre   TRC

- ▶ **Flipped classroom video Unit 8:** The passive with *say, know, believe*, etc. – 1
- ▶ **Life skills video Unit 8:** Helping disaster victims
- ▶ **Grammar communication activity Unit 8:** Passive pairs
- ▶ **Worksheets for this unit, including:**
  - – Grammar Practice worksheet Unit 8
  - – Flipped classroom video worksheet Unit 8: The passive with *say, know, believe*, etc. – 1
  - – Literature worksheet Units 7 and 8
  - – Culture worksheet Unit 8
  - – Life skills video worksheet Unit 8
  - – Everyday English worksheet Unit 8

Student's App
Gateway 2ⁿᵈ Edition wordlist for the award-winning Sounds App (available for download)

✔ TESTING AND ASSESSMENT

Resources for exam preparation and measuring student progress

- ▶ Test Generator Units 1–8
- ▶ Printable test Unit 8
- ▶ Gateway to exams Units 7 and 8 (end of Unit 8)

Vocabulary p96

Talking about natural disasters

You could ask students to do exercises 1a and 1b at home. They can look up any words they are not sure about in their dictionaries or the Macmillan Online Dictionary.

WARMER

In pairs, students discuss the meaning of the unit title *Surviving disaster* and what they think the unit is going to be about. Ask students: *What is a disaster?* (Something very bad that happens and causes a lot of damage or kills a lot of people.) *What is the difference between a natural disaster and a man-made disaster?* (A natural disaster is something that is created by a natural event, e.g. an earthquake, volcanic eruption, flood).

Natural disasters

1a Ask students to match the photos to the words. Remind them there are five extra words. Check their answers.

Answers

a earthquake **b** landslide **c** flood
d volcanic eruption **e** drought

>>> **FAST FINISHERS**

Elicit definitions of the five words in exercise 1a.
Answers

earthquake /ˈɜː(r)θˌkweɪk/ – a sudden shaking movement of the ground

landslide /ˈlæn(d)ˌslaɪd/ – a heavy fall of earth and rocks down the side of a mountain or steep slope

flood /flʌd/ – if water floods a place, it covers it

volcanic eruption /vɒlˈkænɪk ɪˈrʌptʃ(ə)n/ – if a volcano erupts, it explodes inside and flames, rocks and lava come out of the top

drought /draʊt/ – a long period of time when there is little or no rain and crops die

1b Ask students to match the extra words in exercise 1a with the definitions.

Answers

1 epidemic /ˌepɪˈdemɪk/
2 tsunami /tsuːˈnɑːmi/
3 avalanche /ˈævəˌlɑːntʃ/
4 forest fire /ˈfɒrɪst ˈfaɪə(r)/
5 hurricane /ˈhʌrɪkən/

2 **PRONUNCIATION** ▶ 38 Ask students to say where the stress goes in the words in exercise 1a. Then play the track for students to check their answers. Drill the words in open class.

Answers

avalanche, drought, earthquake, epidemic, flood, forest fire, hurricane, landslide, tsunami, volcanic eruption

TEACHER DEVELOPMENT: CLASSROOM TIPS AND PLANNING

Drilling

Drilling plays an important role in the classroom and is mainly used for modelling target language. In choral drills, where a whole class repeats a word or sentence in unison, the goal is accuracy. The teacher says a word or sentence out loud and students try to repeat it verbatim with the correct pronunciation, stress and intonation. You could write the word/sentence on the board using phonetic script and mark stressed syllables and rising or falling intonation. You could also tap out the rhythm of the stressed syllables as you say them.

3 **SPEAKING** In pairs, students discuss which parts of the world they associate with the natural disasters in exercise 1a and which ones could happen in their country.

Suggested answers

avalanches: snowy mountainous regions, e.g. the Alps

droughts: usually happen between 15 and 20 degrees latitude

tsunamis, volcanic eruptions, earthquakes: 80–90% of these happen in the Pacific Ocean's 'Ring of Fire'

epidemics: can occur anywhere, but most likely to occur in countries with poor health and hygiene standards

floods: most common in countries with monsoons (periods of very heavy rainfall) such as India, Bangladesh and Sri Lanka

forest fires: common in the western USA and Australia, sometimes in Mediterranean countries

hurricanes: the Atlantic Ocean (these same tropical storms are known as *cyclones* in the northern Indian Ocean and Bay of Bengal, and as *typhoons* in the western Pacific Ocean)

landslides: can occur anywhere in the world, but they are most likely to happen in places at the bases of steep slopes, at the bases of drainage channels and on developed hillsides

Words connected with natural disasters

4 **SPEAKING** Students work in groups of three. Each student reads one of the texts A–C and checks the words in red in a dictionary if necessary. Students then explain the words to the others in their group.

Answers

casualties – people who are injured or killed in an accident or military action

aftershock – a small earthquake (= occasion when the Earth shakes) that happens after a bigger one

victims – people who have been affected by a bad situation, such as an accident or an illness

survivors – people who are still alive after an event that could have killed or destroyed them

injuries – physical damage done to a person or a part of their body

collapsing – suddenly falling down

put out – to make something stop burning

tremors – movements in the Earth caused by an earthquake

ash – the grey powder that remains after something has burnt

molten lava – rock in the form of hot liquid

heading towards – moving in the direction of

panic – a sudden strong feeling of fear or worry that makes you unable to think clearly or calmly

spreading – affecting more people as it is passed from one person or place to another

refugees – people who leave their country or their homes, especially during a war or other threatening event

torrential (rain) – rain that falls fast and in large amounts

swept across – moved or spread quickly through an area

burst their banks – if a river bursts its banks, water rises above its sides and spreads over the surrounding area

evacuated – made to leave a building or area because it is not safe

mud – very soft wet earth

destruction – damage that is so severe that something stops existing or can never return to its normal state

5 Ask students to complete the sentences with the correct form of words in exercise 4.

Answers

1 evacuate   **2** sweeping   **3** heading   **4** spreading
5 ash   **6** survivors

6 **LISTENING** ▶ 39 Play the track for students to listen to three short reports on natural disasters and complete the notes. See pp178–179 for the audioscript for this exercise.

Answers

	1	2	3
Type of disaster	landslide	forest fires	tsunami caused by earthquake
Where	north-east Peru	Spain	Samoa
Casualties	28 people dead 25 people missing 50 people injured	4 firefighters dead	none
Damage	120 houses	serious damage to many houses	no material damage

7 **SPEAKING** In pairs, students talk about a natural disaster that has happened recently or that is very famous. Students use question words (*where, when, what,* etc.) to help them to think of what to say.

✚ EXTRA ACTIVITY

In pairs, students list as many different types of weather as they can in two minutes. Find out who has the longest list.

Suggested answers

breezy, cold, cool, damp, dry, foggy, freezing, frosty, hot, icy, mild, snowy, stormy, sunny, warm, wet, windy

HOMEWORK

Assign students page 66 in their Workbook or the relevant sections of the Online Workbook.

Reading p97

Reading for general and specific information

⟫⟫⟫ FAST TRACK

You could ask students to read the text in exercise 2 at home in preparation for in-class activities.

WARMER

Play *Noughts and crosses* with words from the previous lesson. See the instructions on p118.

1 **SPEAKING** In pairs, students look at the photo at the bottom of the page and discuss what they think it could be. Elicit answers from students around the class.

2 Ask students to read the article and answer the questions. Elicit answers from students around the class.

Answers

1 a Survival Capsule

2 to increase the chance of survivors being able to survive a tsunami; to protect people from both fire and flood

3 Ask students to read the text again and choose the best answer. Ask students to say where in the text they found their answers.

Answers

1 b (… had evacuation towers … The tsunami was much higher than expected …)

2 c (… many coastal areas with beaches have a similar landscape, with long, gradual slopes … it's impossible to get to sufficiently high ground fast enough.)

3 b (… (PSS) is designed to protect survivors not only in tsunamis, but also in hurricanes, earthquakes and tornadoes. … There are currently five versions of the capsule. They range in size from a basic two-person model … to one capable of holding ten adults …)

4 b (If the sea rises, the line tying the capsule to the ground gets longer.)

5 c (This is a small price to pay if, as Sharpe hopes, the Survival Capsules increase people's chances of surviving the next tsunami.)

✔ EXAM SUCCESS Students read about how to carry out multiple-choice reading activities. Tell students to turn to page 146 (Reading: Multiple-choice activities) for more ideas.

TEACHER DEVELOPMENT: STUDENT TRAINING

Multiple-choice reading activities

Remind students that only one of the four options in an exam question is correct, and distracters may deceive students deliberately by using words taken from the text. In order to improve students' skill at doing this type of activity, they could try the following techniques:

Treat each option as a true/false question and choose the 'truest' one.

Eliminate options you know to be incorrect. There should be at least two options that students can eliminate immediately.

Ask yourself if the answer is only partly true or true only under certain conditions. If students have to make assumptions in order for the option to be true, it is probably wrong. The correct option is the one that is obvious enough for most students to choose it.

Words like *only, never, always, usually,* etc. are very important and students need to pay special attention to them as the inclusion of one of these words may make an otherwise true sentence false.

4 **CRITICAL THINKING** Encourage students to say if they think the Survival Capsule is a useful, practical invention and give reasons why or why not.

Example answers

I think a Survival Capsule is a good idea because it can save lives in many types of disastrous situations.

I think it's a bad idea, because you can get trapped in the capsule. I also think they are very expensive and many people will not be able to afford to buy one.

5 Give students a few minutes to try to guess the meaning of the underlined words in the text from the context. Students then check their ideas in their dictionaries.

Answers

in anticipation of = if you do something in anticipation of an event, you expect it to happen and you prepare yourself for it

slopes = a straight surface that has one end higher than the other

range in size = vary in size

debris = the broken pieces that are left when something large has been destroyed, especially by an explosion, fire or accident

storage = space where things can be stored

recedes = moves back from a high point or level

6 **SPEAKING What about *you*?** In pairs or small groups, students discuss how they can prepare for a natural disaster. Elicit ideas from different students around the class.

ⓘ CULTURAL INFORMATION

In parts of the world where natural disasters may strike, schools often play an important role in identifying risk factors and teaching security procedures. Reopening schools, when safe, is a priority in disaster relief efforts. Children in crisis benefit from returning to normal life. Unfortunately, in many cases, educational facilities are destroyed and recovery is slow. In the aftermath of Hurricane Katrina, the first elementary school in New Orleans reopened three months after the storm. Similarly, as a result of the 2010 floods in Pakistan, an estimated 11,000 schools were destroyed and thousands more were used as sites for emergency shelters, further delaying school openings. Disaster preparedness goes a long way in reducing the impact of natural crisis on education. Following the massive 8.9 magnitude earthquake in Japan, where schools were physically destroyed and the lives of teachers and children lost, classes commenced a week after the disaster in disaster-proof and multi-hazard resilient buildings.

In Japan, the tactical use of education to prepare children and their families for natural disasters is an example for the rest of the world. In addition, education can play an important role in promoting disaster risk reduction and teaching basic scientific concepts related to climate change and sustainable practices.

✚ EXTRA ACTIVITY

Students investigate one type of natural disaster from the Vocabulary lesson in depth and present their findings to the other students in the next class.

HOMEWORK

Assign students page 67 in their Workbook or the relevant sections of the Online Workbook.

Grammar in context pp98–99

Using different passive structures to talk about processes and procedures

⟩⟩⟩ FAST TRACK

You could ask students to do exercises 1 and 2 at home.

Test before you teach

Write the following sentences on the board. Ask students to complete the sentences with the correct form of the verbs given:

1 Many coastal towns in Japan _____ by the tsunami in 2011. (destroy)
2 Sugar _____ to make caramel. (heat)
3 If you lie there too long, you _____ by the sun. (burn)

If the students are familiar with the form and use of the passive, move through the Grammar guide exercises quickly in open class.

Answers

1 were destroyed **2** is heated **3** will be burnt

The passive

1a Students look at sentences a–d and answer questions 1–4.

Answers
1 Yes, they are all passive.
2 **a** past simple passive (*was/were* + past participle)
   b present simple modal passive (modal + *be* + past participle)
   c present simple passive (*am/is/are* + past participle)
   d present perfect passive (*have* + *been* + past participle)
3 subject (+ modal) + *be* + past participle (+ *by* + agent)
4 *By* introduces the 'agent' of an action, i.e. the person or the thing that does the action.

TEACHER DEVELOPMENT: LANGUAGE

The passive
Remind students that to make the passive we use the appropriate form of the verb *be* + the past participle of the verb, e.g. *I was born in 1999.* We change the verb *be* to agree with the subject and put it in the appropriate tense, e.g. *The baby will be born in May.*

1b Students decide if the statements are True (T) or False (F).

Answers
1 T **2** T **3** T

TEACHER DEVELOPMENT: PRONUNCIATION

Word stress – the passive voice
Tell students to look at the sentences in exercise 1a and decide which words are stressed in each sentence. Elicit the words and ask students to explain why they are stressed (the content words are stressed, i.e. the words that carry the meaning of the sentence). Elicit what happens to the verb *be* and why (it is not stressed because it is an auxiliary verb).

TEACHER DEVELOPMENT: LANGUAGE

by + agent
In many cases, there is no need to include *by* + agent after the verb. Encourage students to omit the agent wherever possible as it often sounds wrong and adds no extra information to the sentence, e.g. *This invention has been used since 1908 (by people).*

2 Ask students to complete the sentences with the correct passive form of the verbs given.

Answers
1 was hit **2** have been destroyed **3** will be controlled **4** be seen **5** is measured **6** be built **7** were not warned

3 Ask students to find the mistakes in the sentences and rewrite them correctly. Ask students to compare their answers in pairs before you check them in open class.

Answers
1 Some areas of Africa have **been** affected by a terrible drought./Some areas of Africa **are being affected** by a terrible drought.
2 Twenty people were **saved** in the mountains by a rescue team yesterday.
3 A huge landslide **hit** a small town in Peru last week.
4 Some people think that one day the Earth will be destroyed **by** a big meteorite.
5 Our house **was** damaged by torrential rain last year.
6 More hurricanes have **been** predicted for this summer.
7 Have **any people been** injured in the fire?
8 In rescue situations I think children must **be** helped first.

The passive – verbs with two objects

4a Students look at the sentences and read the explanation.

4b Students decide if it is more common to use the thing (2a) or the person (2b) as the subject.

Answer
It is more common to use the person (the indirect object) as the subject of passive sentences – 2b.

4c Ask students to look at the common verbs that can be followed by two objects and check their meanings in a dictionary if necessary. Elicit definitions of the verbs.

5 Students decide which sentence in each pair is more natural. When checking answers, point out that in sentence 4, the urgent message is the preferred subject, not the person, because it is more natural to stress this by putting it at the start of the sentence.

Answers
1 a **2** b **3** a **4** b **5** b

6 Ask students to rewrite the sentences using the passive. Remind students to use the person or people as the subject. Focus students' attention on the example sentence.

Answers
2 The president of the company was paid $40,000 for two Survival Capsules.
3 The survivors are being offered financial aid.
4 I have been given information about surviving earthquakes by my teacher.
5 Perhaps the casualties will be offered medical help.
6 She was told the news when she arrived.
7 The refugees are not going to be refused entrance into the country.
8 The scientists have been promised money for research by the government.

7 SPEAKING Draw students' attention to the first square and elicit the question they need to ask (*Have you ever been given a prize?*). With less confident classes, give students time to make a note of the questions for the other squares before they start. Then have them move around the classroom to find someone in the class for each of the squares and write their name. Point out that they cannot use the same person twice. Tell them to ignore the 'Details' section at this point.

8 SPEAKING With less confident classes, you could tell students that you received a prize one day, and encourage them to ask questions to find out more details about this. Draw attention to the example questions. Then ask them to talk to each of the people they wrote in the squares and make brief notes about what happened.

Find someone who ...

This is a classic communication activity. Students mingle, forming questions, giving short answers and writing the names of people who say 'yes'. This activity gives students an opportunity for meaningful speaking and listening practice, and they are often motivated by finding out more about their classmates. It is a good idea to put some background music on to help students lose their inhibitions.

✚ EXTRA ACTIVITY

Students write sentences about each activity from the *Find someone who ...* task, giving the name of the person and details, e.g. *Lucia has been given a prize for scoring the most goals in her football team.* Students then choose the most interesting information and compare it with others in small groups.

Refer students to the Grammar reference on page 106 if necessary.

HOMEWORK

Assign students page 68 in their Workbook or the relevant sections of the Online Workbook.

Developing vocabulary p99

Using prepositional phrases with verbs

⟫⟫ FAST TRACK

If students are familiar with the target vocabulary, you could do exercises 1 and 2 as a class activity by inviting individual students to read out the sentences and checking if the rest of the class agrees.

Prepositional phrases with verbs

1 Ask students to look at the verbs in the sentences and decide which prepositions they need.

Answers

1 on **2** from

2 Ask students to complete the sentences with the prepositions in the box. Encourage less confident students to cross off each preposition as they use it. Give them time to compare their answers in pairs.

Answers

1 to **2** with **3** in **4** on **5** for **6** about **7** of **8** for **9** to **10** on

Preposition + gerund

Remind students that if a verb comes after a preposition, we use the gerund. A gerund is the form of the verb that ends in *-ing* and functions as the object of the preposition, e.g. *She apologised for forgetting my birthday.*

3 Ask students to complete the sentences so that they are true for them. Remind them to use a preposition.

Example answers

1 I occasionally spend money on designer clothes.
2 I hate waiting for the bus.
3 For the future, I dream of travelling around Peru.
4 I know I can rely on my family and friends.
5 I never listen to heavy metal.
6 Once I had to apologise for being late for school.
7 I nearly always agree with what that TV presenter says.
8 I don't usually complain about having a headache.

4 SPEAKING In small groups, students compare their sentences in exercise 3. Students then tell the class any sentences they have in common.

✚ EXTRA ACTIVITY

Play *Preposition tennis.* In pairs, one student says a verb from exercises 1 or 2 for the other player to say the correct preposition, e.g. A: *rely*; B: *on*. If correct, Student B scores a point (use the traditional scoring for tennis: 15, 30, 40, Deuce, etc.). Play then continues by Student B saying a verb, and so on.

HOMEWORK

Assign students page 69 in their Workbook or the relevant sections of the Online Workbook.

Gateway to life skills pp100–101

Helping a charity

To learn about the work of a humanitarian organisation, to consider reasons for helping with charity work and to investigate a current disaster or problem and how we can help

⟫⟫ FAST TRACK

Students could do research into a current or recent disaster or a typical problem affecting people in any part of the world in preparation for the Life task.

In the UK, there are over 160,000 charities with a combined income per year of around £37bn, alongside more local, sponsored initiatives with people raising funds in a variety of ways from car boot sales to sponsored swims. Charity shops are largely a British institution. There are an estimated 10,500 shops in the UK. The first of these was opened by Oxfam in 1947 and is still in operation today. They are retail outlets selling mainly second-hand donated goods to raise funds for their parent charities. Many people visit charity shops to pick up retro and vintage clothing in particular.

In the UK, the major charities include health charities, such as Cancer Research UK and Macmillan, global development groups such as Save the Children, Oxfam and the British Red Cross, and animal charities such as the RSPCA and the RSPB. A good example of a charity organisation that has become something of a British institution is Comic Relief – founded in 1985 in response to famine in Ethiopia. The highlight of Comic Relief's appeal is Red Nose Day – every two years people in the UK get together and do something funny for money at home, school and work. Comic Relief spends the money raised by Red Nose Day to help people living tough lives across the UK and Africa.

WARMER

Ask students to brainstorm disaster movies they know. Disaster movies are often about impending or actual disaster on an epic scale. Examples of different kinds of disaster movies include: Environmental disaster: *Earthquake* (1974), *The Core* (2003), *Waterworld* (1995), *Deep Impact* (1998), *Armageddon* (1998), *2012* (2009), *The Day After Tomorrow* (2004); Pandemic: *Twelve Monkeys* (1995), *Outbreak* (1995), *I Am Legend* (2007), *Contagion* (2011) and *The Epidemic* (2015). Ask students to read through the Key concepts and check any vocabulary they don't understand.

1 SPEAKING In pairs, students discuss what they know about Ebola and the organisation *Médecins Sans Frontières/ Doctors Without Borders* (MSF). Elicit some answers from different students around the class.

2 Ask students to look at the poster about Ebola created by MSF. Direct them to the introduction at the top and ask them to read it and answer the questions. Remind students that they can refer to Key concepts for definitions of words they are not sure about. Elicit answers from students around the class.

Answers

1 Ebola is a haemorrhagic fever. It is highly infectious and deadly, so patients need to be treated in isolation by staff wearing special protective clothing.

2 MSF has set up three specialised treatment centres in the worst-hit areas.

3 In the rest of the poster, there will be detailed information about how the treatment centres are set up.

3 SPEAKING In pairs, students look at the map of the centre and discuss the questions.

Suggested answers

1 (see text on poster)

2 Purple route = high-risk zone for confirmed cases: On the purple route, staff change into protective clothing, enter the wards in the high-risk zone to monitor suspected cases and treat confirmed cases in the treatment wards. They then leave the high-risk zone and go to the laundry, to wash and recycle their clothes.

3 They want people to know that the special equipment is a significant cost and they want people to know what they are going to buy with their donations.

4 The poster helps people understand how complex treating Ebola is, what the process involves and to visualise how donations will be used.

4 Ask students to read texts 1–12 and answer the questions.

Answers

1 Staff are not allowed to touch each other to prevent infection.

2 They plan exactly what they are going to do and what equipment they need.

3 They remove their suits and disinfect themselves.

4 To prevent the spread of Ebola to people who have other diseases with similar symptoms.

5 They have to have had two negative lab tests in a row, they shower in chlorinated water and receive clean clothes and a food/vitamin pack.

6 They continue to get support from psychologists and health promoters.

5 SPEAKING In pairs, students discuss if they think the poster is successful and give reasons why or why not.

Example answers

I think it is a successful poster because it is very informative on a general and specific level about what Ebola is and how it can be cured,

VOCABULARY FOCUS

The video contains some useful colloquial language about charities and fund raising that students may not be familiar with. You might want to pre-teach these words and phrases with students before watching:

hold/put on events [phr v]: organise and manage events

bake/cake sale [n]: an occasion where people sell homemade cakes for charity

carols [n]: traditional songs sung at Christmas

care home [n]: a place where old or sick people can be looked after which is not a hospital

human interaction [n]: the relationships between people

harassing [v]: to keep annoying or irritating someone

raise awareness (of/about) [phr v] : to bring a matter to people's attention

ethical [adj]: involved in the principles of deciding what is right or wrong

vulnerable [adj]: being unable to look after or defend oneself

6 **LISTENING** ▶ 40 Tell students they are going to watch or listen to four speakers discussing charity fundraising. Play the video or audio track for students to note which speakers agree or disagree with the four statements in exercise 6. They answer the questions by ticking a–d in the table. See the Teacher's Resource Centre for the audioscript/videoscript for this exercise.

Answers

Sam: –   Bea: a, c, d   Vanessa: a, b   Chris: a, d

7 ▶ 40 Play the video or audio track again for students to note down what each speaker says about their own experiences of raising money for charity. Students then discuss their answers in pairs. Check answers and ask students to give examples in open class.

Answers

Sam: spent a day raising money for an environmental charity at his school, sold cakes, held events, a fun day

Bea: has done a lot of fundraising for different charities, cancer and disaster charities, organised fun runs and cake schools with her school, a few summers of door-to-door fundraising, fantastic

Vanessa: a fundraising event for a health charity, children from local village did a bake sale and put on a performance

Chris: dressed in fancy dress with a few friends and sung Christmas carols in a local shop, a lot of fun, raised quite a lot of money for a care home for the elderly

---

LIFE TASK 🏃

Tell students that they are going to investigate a problem and ways they can help. Divide the class into groups and ask them to follow the plan:

- *Step 1*

  Ask students to choose a current or recent disaster or a typical problem affecting people in any part of the world.

- *Step 2*

  Students then research the problem and find out the causes, effects and importance of the problem. Encourage them to divide the topics among the members of the group and arrange to report back to each other and share their notes.

- *Step 3*

  Ask students to find out what type of help could be given to the people suffering the problem, if any, and what kind of help they need.

- *Step 4*

  Students then make a poster to inform members of the public about the problem and how they can help.

Listening p102 🎧

Making predictions and listening for specific information and gist

WARMER

Brainstorm the names of charities students know. In pairs, students tell each other if they have participated in a charity event, and explain what the charity was and what they did to raise money. Elicit from the class different ways money can be raised for charity (a raffle, a lottery, a sponsored run, auction, etc.).

1 **SPEAKING** In pairs, students look at the photo and caption and answer the question. Encourage them to share their ideas with another pair.

2 **LISTENING** ▶ 41 Tell students they are going to listen to a radio programme about the woman in the photo. Play the track for students to check the predictions they made in exercise 1. See p179 for the audioscript for this exercise.

3 ▶ 41 Play the track again for students to listen and decide if the statements are True (T), False (F) or the information is Not Mentioned (NM). Elicit from students which phrases in the listening text helped them to decide on their answers.

Answers

1 T (Her friend's body was only found three months later.)
2 T (The idea of this organisation is to rebuild schools in areas around the world ...)
3 T (It's thought that Tilly saved around a hundred lives ...)
4 NM (The text says that Petra's known to have been very impressed by Tilly, but it doesn't say that she has met her.)
5 F (She uses her status as a supermodel to get support from big companies that work in the world of beauty and fashion.)
6 NM (There is no reference to this in the listening text.)
7 T (… her organisation has become a specialist in helping out two or three months after a disaster strikes.)
8 NM (There is no reference to this in the listening text.)

✔ EXAM SUCCESS Students read about how to do exercises where there are three possibilities: *True/False/Not mentioned*. Tell them to turn to page 146 (Listening: True/False activities) for more ideas.

TEACHER DEVELOPMENT: STUDENT TRAINING

Listening – True/False/Not Mentioned

Students should read all the statements first before they listen. It can be helpful to point out to students that the answers usually appear in the listening text in the same order as the questions. At this stage they should identify key words in the statements and listen out for similar vocabulary. If, at the end of the activity, they are still not sure, remind students to choose an answer (there is a 33% chance they will be correct!).

4 SPEAKING **What about *you*?** Students discuss what they think of the story of Petra Němcová. Encourage them to share their thoughts with the class.

✚ EXTRA ACTIVITY

In pairs, students correct the false statement in exercise 3 (5).

Answers

1 (She was ... with a friend of hers ...)
5 F (Petra uses her contacts in beauty and fashion to raise money.)

HOMEWORK

Assign students page 69 in their Workbook or the relevant sections of the Online Workbook.

Grammar in context pp102–103 Ⓖ

Using different passive structures with say, know, believe, etc.

⟫⟫ FAST TRACK

Students could do exercises 1 and 2 at home. Check their answers and start the class on exercise 3.

 Test before you teach: Flipped classroom
Set the Flipped classroom video and tasks for homework <u>before the lesson</u>. This will allow you to assess the needs of the students before the class. Students can then move on to the relevant grammar practice activities.

The passive with say, know, believe, etc. – 1

1a Students look at sentences a–d and answer questions 1–3.

Answers

1 *It* is the subject in the first part of the sentences.
2 We use the passive in the first part of the sentence because we want to make a general statement about people's views, beliefs or opinions.
3 The different tense shows if we are talking about a present or past belief, thought, claim, expectation or knowledge.

TEACHER DEVELOPMENT: LANGUAGE

The passive with *say, know*, etc.

We use this structure to talk about what people in general say, know or believe about something. These structures are common in the impersonal style of news reports. Encourage students to use them in formal writing, for example opinion or for-and-against essays.

1b Students check they know the meanings of the verbs in the box, which are frequently used in the passive. Encourage students to look them up in their dictionaries if necessary.

Answers

believe – to think that a fact is true
claim – to say that something is true, even though there is no definite proof
expect – to think that something will happen
know – to have learnt or found out about something
report – to provide information about something that exists or has happened
say – to think something, or to have a particular opinion
think – to believe something based on facts or ideas

2 Students write complete sentences using the structures in exercise 1. Draw their attention to the example sentence.

Answers

2 It was thought that the Earth was flat.
3 It is claimed that natural disasters are becoming more frequent.
4 It has been said that an asteroid will destroy the world one day.
5 It is expected that a big volcano will erupt in Iceland soon.
6 It is known that volcanic ash can have a terrible effect on planes.
7 It was reported that people heard the eruption of Krakatoa over 3,000 km away.
8 It is said that one day an enormous earthquake will strike Los Angeles.

The passive with say, know, believe, etc. – 2

3 Students look at sentences a–e and decide if statements 1–5 are True (T) or False (F).

Answers

1 T   **2** T   **3** T   **4** T   **5** T

4 Ask students to rewrite the sentences. Ask different students around the class to read out their sentences.

Answers

1 Toads are said to sense earthquakes.
2 Bees are known to be very important for the environment.
3 Global warming is claimed to be responsible for many natural disasters.
4 Many people were reported to have gone missing after the eruption.
5 The Titanic was believed to have been unsinkable.
6 Everest wasn't known to be the highest mountain until 1852.
7 Pompeii is said to be one of the most popular tourist attractions in Italy.
8 A meteorite is believed to have caused the extinction of dinosaurs.

5 Ask students to read the text and choose the correct alternative. Check answers in open class by asking different students to read out a section of the text.

Answers

a have died   **b** it was   **c** reported   **d** thought
e Some animals are known   **f** that animals are
g is   **h** claimed

Write these sentences on the board and ask students to say if they are true or false.

The 2004 tsunami flooded a national park in Thailand. (F – Sri Lanka)

Only a few animals could detect the tsunami before it arrived. (F – Most animals ...)

All the water buffalos survived. (F – The only animals that died were two or three water buffalos.)

Elephants can detect small movements of earth. (T)

The writer says that humans may once have had a 'sixth sense'. (T)

6 Ask students to complete the sentences in a logical way. You could allow less confident students to do this exercise in pairs.

Example answers

1 People from my country are said to have a good sense of humour.

2 It's well known that eating too much salt is bad for your health.

3 In the past, it was believed that the sun revolved around the Earth.

4 Last week in the news it was reported that the number of robberies had gone up.

5 Students are expected to do their homework.

6 Sometimes I'm known to be a bit forgetful.

7 **SPEAKING** Students compare their sentences with a partner and see if they agree with their partner's sentences.

Refer students to the Grammar reference on page 106 if necessary.

HOMEWORK

Assign students page 70 in their Workbook or the relevant sections of the Online Workbook.

Developing speaking p104

Talking about statistics

>>> FAST TRACK

You could ask students to do exercises 1 and 2a at home in preparation for the listening activity.

WARMER

Think of a famous natural disaster that students are familiar with, e.g. Pompeii, the 2011 Japan earthquake/tsunami and play *20 questions*. Students can ask up to 20 Yes/No questions to find out which disaster you are thinking of. You can only answer *yes* or *no*. When they have guessed the answer, students play again in small groups.

1 Students look at the pie chart and decide if the statements are True (T) or False (F).

Answers

1 T **2** F **3** T **4** T **5** T **6** F

2a Students rewrite the fractions as percentages and vice versa.

2b **LISTENING** 42 Play the track for students to listen and check. Students then practise saying the fractions and percentages. See p179 for the audioscript for this exercise.

Answers

1 25% **2** $\frac{1}{5}$ **3** $\frac{1}{10}$ **4** $\frac{2}{3}$ **5** 50% **6** $\frac{4}{5}$

3 Ask students to look at the graph and read the text. Encourage students to check the meaning of the words in bold, looking them up in their dictionaries if necessary.

Answers

rose gradually – went up slowly

a sharp increase – a very quick rise

tripled – multiplied by three

fell sharply – went down quickly and by a large amount

a slight increase – a small rise

fluctuated – changed frequently

stayed the same – did not change

a dramatic rise – a large increase

a significant decrease – an important fall

4 Ask students to find a word or words in the Speaking bank to match the definitions. Have them compare their answers in pairs before you check them in open class.

Answers

1 rise, increase

2 rise significant(ly)/sharp(ly)/dramatic(ally)

3 fall significant(ly)/sharp(ly)/dramatic(ally)

4 a third

5 steadily

6 significant

7 significant(ly), sharp(ly), dramatic(ally)

8 the majority

PRACTICE MAKES PERFECT

5a **SPEAKING** Divide the class into A and B pairs. Ask Student A to describe the pie chart to their partner using words and expressions in the Speaking bank.

Suggested answer

The pie chart shows different types of natural disasters. If we relate the effects of these disasters to the population of a place, we can say that over one third of people were affected by storms. Over one quarter of people were affected by droughts and a similar number of people were affected by floods. Over one in twenty people were affected by earthquakes. Only about three in every hundred people were affected by extreme temperatures and just over one per cent by epidemics.

5b Now ask Student B to describe the graph to their partner using words and expressions in the Speaking bank.

Suggested answer

This graph shows how the number of floods around the world rose gradually between 1980 and 1999. Then there was a sharp increase in the number of floods between 2000 and 2003. Between 2000 and 2004, the number of floods increased by over 50%. In 2004 there was a significant decrease, but in 2005, the number of floods rose sharply. The highest point was in 2006 when there were over 200 floods around the world. The number of floods then dropped and fluctuated between 2006 and 2008.

5c Students compare the two pie charts on the page and then the two graphs. Ask them to discuss what information they find surprising, interesting or worrying. Elicit opinions in open class and try to develop a discussion. For students who are less confident, photocopy the model dialogue below, and either read it aloud yourself, or ask a strong student to read it with you. Students can then use this as a guide for their discussion.

Model dialogue

A: Well, the graphs and pie charts all relate to natural disasters since the 1980s.

B: Yes, they all show the different types of disasters around the world and how many people were affected in each part of the world.

A: The first pie chart shows that almost two-thirds of the disasters in Oceania are caused by drought and extreme temperatures. Over 40% of people are affected by droughts.

B: Yes, that's very interesting because in the Americas, flooding is a problem that affects over a quarter of people, but only three in every hundred in Oceania. In the Americas, over a quarter of people are also affected by drought, but it is worse in Oceania.

A: I think it's interesting that storms have affected over a third of people in both Oceania and the Americas.

B: And what surprises me is that earthquakes and epidemics don't affect people in Oceania and people in the Americas haven't been affected by volcanoes.

A: Yes, and I think the significant difference in floods and extreme temperatures is really surprising. Floods don't affect Oceania much, but they suffer from extreme temperatures. In the Americas, it's the other way round.

B: And what about the graphs that show the number of floods and storms around the world between 1980 and 2011?

A: It seems to me that the number of storms rarely stays the same, but it decreased in 2006 after a dramatic rise in numbers. However, the number of floods rose dramatically and although there was a sharp decrease in 2008, it is still much higher than the number of storms.

B: That's true, the number of floods reached over 200 in 2004–2005 and then dropped to 150, but the number of storms never reached more than 150 a year. In my opinion this is a significant and surprising difference.

A: Yes, and many of the disasters are related to weather. Climate change is likely to cause a significant increase in the number of these disasters, which could have a dramatic financial impact on many parts of the world.

➕ EXTRA ACTIVITY

In pairs, students write five to ten words from the unit on slips of paper and give them to another pair. Each pair divides the slips of paper between them and takes it in turn to describe their words for their partner to guess, e.g. A: *when the ground moves a lot*; B: *earthquake.* Encourage students to use synonyms, to paraphrase and give examples in both asking and guessing the words.

HOMEWORK

Assign students page 71 in their Workbook or the relevant sections of the Online Workbook.

Developing writing p105

Writing an opinion essay using linkers

≫ FAST TRACK

You could ask students to prepare ideas for exercise 1 at home in preparation for the writing activity.

WARMER

Write this question on the board: *Should we give money to charity? Why/Why not?* Ask students to discuss the question in small groups and share their ideas with the class.

Example answers

I think we should all give money to charity, if we can, as people who can afford to should share their money with people who need help.

I don't give money to charity because it all gets spent on administration and people's salaries. The people who need help don't see very much of the money.

1 **SPEAKING** In pairs, students read the task and discuss at least two ideas for each of the points 1 and 2. Then ask them to decide on a third point that they consider important, and to think of two more relevant ideas.

2 Ask students to read the essay to see if it includes any of their ideas in exercise 1. Then ask them to make some brief notes about whether they agree or not with the writer.

3 Ask students to read the essay again and decide on the purpose of each paragraph. Check their answers.

Answers

Paragraph 1: Introduction. General statement on the topic and opinion
Paragraph 2: First and most important reason for opinion
Paragraphs 3 and 4: One or two other reasons for opinion
Paragraph 5: Summary and conclusion. Restate opinion

4 Ask students to categorise and write the underlined words and expressions in the text in the correct list.

Answers

Expressing opinions: In my opinion, I believe that
Adding ideas: What is more, Another thing to bear in mind is that, Furthermore
Putting ideas in order: The first point to make is that
Contrasting ideas: However, Although
Concluding: In conclusion

5 Ask students to look at how *although, even though* and *however* are used in the text. Elicit which word(s) join two halves of a sentence and which word(s) introduce a new sentence. Students then check their answers by reading the information in the Writing bank and check that they understand the meaning of all the linkers.

PRACTICE MAKES PERFECT

6a In pairs, students read the task carefully and think about ideas and information they could include.

TEACHER DEVELOPMENT: STUDENT TRAINING

Brainstorming

It is important to spend time on this brainstorming stage as it makes the next steps easier. Students can then select and order their ideas to write a first draft of their text. Their goal at this point is to include the main points from the brainstorming phase in one text. Students should not rewrite, revise or edit at this stage. In the first draft, spelling, grammar, punctuation or word choice are not important.

6b Ask students to write their essay. Remind them to include appropriate linkers and to refer to the information in the Writing bank. They can also follow the advice in the Writing bank on page 151. For students who are less confident, photocopy the model text below for extra support during the writing task.

Model text

All around the world, we can see changing weather conditions. Countries are suffering from massive droughts, floods and fluctuating temperatures. <u>In my opinion</u>, it is strange that hardly anybody is doing anything to slow down and stop the damage, <u>even though</u> we all know it's happening. <u>I believe</u> people are not informed enough about the dramatic consequences. <u>The first point to make</u> is that people need to be educated about how changing weather conditions impact on our planet. <u>However</u>, many people don't trust scientists and politicians and don't believe that making sacrifices now will make a difference in the future. <u>What's more</u>, some people think that global warming is a good thing because of the warmer weather.

<u>Another thing to bear in mind</u> is that most people think changing weather conditions will not seriously affect them in their lifetime so it is not their problem. <u>Although</u> people read and hear about the terrible effects of weather every day, they always seem to have other problems in their lives, which seem more urgent and important.

<u>In conclusion</u>, I believe that very few people are prepared to change their lifestyle to help the situation even though there could be disastrous consequences. Unless we fight for society to wake up, the situation will get worse and it will be too late.

TEACHER DEVELOPMENT: STUDENT TRAINING

Editing

Once they have written a first draft, students should proofread their text for spelling, grammar and punctuation mistakes and make sure they have used a variety of structures. Editing is the revision process when students take a global look at their text and decide if the text flows in a clear, well-organised way. Students should concern themselves with clarity, coherence and unity. Tell students to reread the essay, out loud if possible, to make sure that it flows well and that it makes sense as a whole. Repetitive sentences are irritating and distract the reader's attention from content – students should ask themselves if everything in their essay is there for a reason.

✛ EXTRA ACTIVITY

In pairs, students read out their texts to each other for their partner to comment on their ideas and correct any errors they hear. Encourage them to do this constructively.

HOMEWORK

Assign students page 72 in their Workbook or the relevant sections of the Online Workbook.

Language checkpoint: Unit 8

>>> FAST TRACK

The extra support provided in the Grammar and Vocabulary reference sections makes the Grammar and Vocabulary revision sections ideal for setting as homework. You could get students to complete the whole revision page or just certain exercises for homework.

Grammar revision p107

The passive

1 Students rewrite the sentences to change the form from active to passive or passive to active.

Answers

1 The boy and girl were rescued by a boat.
2 The damaged towers are going to be rebuilt by a Japanese company.
3 A famous architect had designed the airport.
4 The port won't have been destroyed by the waves.
5 The awards are being presented by Petra Němcová tonight.
6 A report should have been written about the catastrophe.
7 A local politician might open the school.

The passive – verbs with two objects

2 Students put the words in the correct order and then make the sentences active. Draw students' attention to the example sentence.

Answers

2 I was given a camera for my birthday. They gave me a camera for my birthday.
3 They are being shown a film about natural disasters. They are showing them a film about natural disasters.
4 Young children are often told stories by their parents. Parents often tell their young children stories.
5 The actor has been paid a million dollars. They have paid the actor a million dollars.
6 I was lent some money by my sister. My sister lent me some money.
7 We were taught mathematics by a new teacher. A new teacher taught us mathematics.
8 He has been offered a job by the government. The government has offered him a job.

The passive with say, know, believe, etc.

3 Students find the mistakes in the sentences and rewrite them correctly.

Answers

1 It is often claimed **that Paris is** one of the most beautiful cities in the world./**Paris is often claimed** to be one of the most beautiful cities in the world.
2 Galileo Galilei is said to **have invented** the telescope.
3 **An accident** was reported to have started the fire./The fire was reported to **have been started** by an accident.
4 Avalanches are said **to be** caused by loud noises.
5 A long time ago the Moon **was** believed to be made of cheese.
6 The eruption of Krakatoa in 1883 is thought to **have turned** the skies orange.

Vocabulary revision p107

NATURAL DISASTERS

1 Students write simple definitions or explanations for the words.

Suggested answers

1 If water floods a place, it covers it.
2 a situation in which a disease spreads very quickly and infects many people
3 a heavy fall of earth and rocks down the side of a mountain or steep slope
4 a long period of time when there is little or no rain and crops die
5 when a large area of land and trees is burnt

WORDS CONNECTED WITH NATURAL DISASTERS

2 Students match the definitions to the words in the corresponding section on page 106.

Answers

1 torrential **2** casualty **3** put out **4** spread
5 head towards **6** evacuate **7** collapse **8** ash

PREPOSITIONAL PHRASES WITH VERBS

3 Students match the verbs and prepositions.

Answers

1 e **2** b **3** d/g **4** a **5** f **6** c **7** d/g

HOMEWORK

Assign students page 73 in their Workbook or the relevant sections of the Online Workbook.

Reading p108

1 SPEAKING In pairs, students discuss if they would go on holiday to an area where a natural disaster is happening and say why or why not. Elicit some answers from different students.

2 Students read the text and choose the best answer. Ask students to identify the sentences that helped them decide on their answers.

Answers

1 b (By 9 o'clock on Sunday morning our team was in the office, making sure everyone travelling with us in Iceland and those who were about to travel were fully briefed on the situation.)

2 a (On the Monday we contacted all those on our Volcano Hotline and started making travel plans for those wanting to see the eruption.)

3 a (Ten days later I found myself on a plane bound for Keflavik with two of my children Ben (16) and Gemma (13) – we had also been bitten by the volcano bug.)

4 b (Just after lunch the next day we took one of the helicopters based at the hotel for the most amazing flight I have ever experienced in my life.)

5 b (All too soon it was time to go and the helicopter returned to collect us.)

6 b (Driving Superjeeps is an Icelandic art and our driver, Ragnar, was both skilled and great company.)

Listening p109

3 LISTENING ▶ 43 Play the track for students to listen to two people talking about different rescue services in the US and decide if the statements are True (T), False (F) or the information is Not Mentioned (NM). Encourage students to correct any false statements. See pp179–180 for the audioscript for this exercise.

Answers

1 F (It's basically a private jet company. … you hire a plane…)

2 NM

3 T

4 NM

5 T

6 T

7 F (They promise to supply you with generator-produced electricity … So that if you have a business, you can keep it running despite the storm.)

4 SPEAKING In pairs, students say what they think of the services they talk about in the listening. Students discuss if they are fair and say why or why not. Elicit some ideas and have a discussion in open class.

Writing p109

5 **SPEAKING** In pairs, students look at the notice and decide which film they would choose to recommend. Ask them to explain why.

6 Individually, students write a review. Remind them to follow the paragraph plan and use linkers to introduce and sequence arguments and make contrasts. Refer them to the Writing bank on page 105. For students who are less confident, photocopy the model text below for extra support during the writing task.

Model text

A film that I would recommend to all my friends is *Jurassic World*, the latest film in the Jurassic Park series by the famous director Steven Spielberg. It's an epic action-adventure based on characters created by Michael Crichton.

A dinosaur theme park, Jurassic World, has opened on Isla Nublar. However, after ten years of operation, visitor rates are falling and the company needs to provide a new attraction to re-spark visitors' interest. Unfortunately, this goes terribly wrong. A genetically modified dinosaur-hybrid named *Indominus rex* escapes and many visitors and some of the main characters are killed.

What I liked about the film is the awesome special effects and the incredible computer animation. The dinosaurs are very realistic, although palaeontologists criticise the film-makers and say that they do not reflect recent scientific discoveries.

I would recommend the film to anybody who likes to see many intense scenes of sustained terror and suspense. I think teens who are fans of suspense and action (and still like dinosaurs) will love it.

Speaking p109

7 Students look at the expressions and decide which we use for giving emphasis and which we use to give examples.

Answers

Giving emphasis: You have to remember that …; I really do think that …; You can't deny that …

Giving examples: Take …, for instance; You only have to think of …

8 Students look at the statement, decide what their opinion is and make notes with ideas and examples.

9 **SPEAKING** In groups of three, students discuss their opinions. Remind them to use expressions to give emphasis and examples.

HOMEWORK

Assign students pages 74–75 in their Workbook or the relevant sections of the Online Workbook.

1 Ask students to mark from 1–4 how well they feel they can do each thing in English.

2 Ask students to look at their marks and decide what they need to do to improve. Elicit ideas from students around the class.

9 Digital world

UNIT OVERVIEW

Vocabulary
Everyday technology
Verbs connected with technology

Reading
Gen Z: A generation of 'screenagers'
CRITICAL THINKING Discussing the profile of a typical Generation Z teenager

Grammar in context
Relative clauses

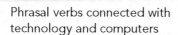

Developing vocabulary
Phrasal verbs connected with technology and computers

Life skills
ICT: Using technology for study

Listening
Solving problems

Grammar in context
Gerunds and infinitives – 2

Developing speaking
Discussions – 2
PRONUNCIATION Stress in questions and sentences

Developing writing
A report

Exam success
Use of English: Cloze activities
Writing: Reports

DIGITAL OVERVIEW

Presentation Kit
- ▶ **Flipped classroom video Unit 9:** Gerunds and infinitives – 2
- ▶ **Life skills video Unit 9:** Using technology for study
- ▶ **Interactive versions of Student's Book activities**
- ▶ **Integrated audio and answer key for all activities**
- ▶ **Workbook pages with answer key**

Teacher's Resource Centre TRC
- ▶ **Flipped classroom video Unit 9:** Gerunds and infinitives – 2
- ▶ **Life skills video Unit 9:** Using technology for study
- ▶ **Grammar communication activity Unit 9:** Invention or no invention?
- ▶ **Worksheets for this unit, including:**
  - – Grammar Practice worksheet Unit 9
  - – Flipped classroom video worksheet Unit 9: Gerunds and infinitives – 2
  - – Literature worksheet Units 9 and 10
  - – Culture worksheet Unit 9
  - – Life skills video worksheet Unit 9
  - – Everyday English worksheet Unit 9

Student's App
Gateway 2nd Edition wordlist for the award-winning Sounds App (available for download)

✓ TESTING AND ASSESSMENT

Resources for exam preparation and measuring student progress

- ▶ Test Generator Units 1–9
- ▶ Printable tests Unit 9/Review
- ▶ Gateway to exams Units 9 and 10 (end of Unit 10)

Vocabulary p110

Talking about technology

>>> **FAST TRACK**

You could ask students to do exercises 1 and 2 at home. They can look up any words they are not sure about in their dictionaries or the Macmillan Online Dictionary.

WARMER

Discuss the meaning of the unit title *Digital world* and what they think the unit is going to be about. Elicit examples of digital technology, e.g. MP3 player, smartphone, Internet broadband, etc.

Everyday technology

1 SPEAKING In pairs, students match the words in the columns to make everyday items and decide what we use each thing for.

Answers

1 f *dishwasher* – a machine that washes dishes

2 j *washing machine* – a machine that washes clothes

3 l *webcam* – a camera connected to a computer that produces images that can be seen on a website

4 a *remote control* – a piece of equipment that you use for controlling a machine, such as a television or stereo system, from a short distance away

5 e *headphones* – a piece of equipment that you wear over your ears to listen to something without other people hearing it

6 k *flash drive* – a small plastic disk drive that stores information and that you can carry around with you. You connect the flash drive to a computer when you want to use the information

7 c *microwave* – an oven that cooks food very quickly by passing electricity through it, instead of using heat

8 g *vacuum cleaner* – a piece of electrical equipment that cleans floors by sucking up dirt

9 b *food processor* – a piece of electrical equipment used for cutting food into very small pieces or mixing different foods together

10 i *digital camera* – a camera that takes and stores pictures in the form of electronic signals

11 h *satnav* – satellite navigation: a system for finding the best way to a place using information from satellites. It is often found in cars

12 d *keyboard* – a piece of computer equipment with keys on it, used for putting information into a computer

2 Ask students to match the words with the definitions 1–10.

Answers

1 device   **2** network   **3** touch screen   **4** charger
5 broadband   **6** wireless   **7** coverage
8 drop-down menu   **9** glitch   **10** plug

>>> **FAST FINISHERS**

Students think of more words connected to the unit theme, e.g. *scanner, e-book, software, emails* and write a short definition for each one. When the class has finished the previous activity, they read out their definitions for the others to guess the word.

Verbs connected with technology

3 In each sentence, students choose the correct alternative and then say what the other word means. Remind students that in two cases, both alternatives are correct.

Answers

1 both correct

2 gone dead (*recharge* – to put more power into a battery)

3 insert (*plug in* – connect a piece of equipment to an electricity supply)

4 both correct

5 upgrade (*install* – to put a new program or piece of software into a computer so that you can use it)

6 set (*delete* – to remove information stored in a computer)

7 select (*adjust* – to change something slightly in order to make it better, more accurate or more effective)

8 pinching (*swipe* – to move your finger across the screen of a smartphone or tablet)

9 disconnect (*connect* – to join two things together)

10 hold (*tap* – to touch something gently)

TEACHER DEVELOPMENT: PRONUNCIATION

Word stress – nouns and verbs

Point out to students that there are many two-syllable words in English whose meaning and class change with a change in stress. In two-syllable verbs, the stress is usually on the second syllable. In two-syllable nouns, the stress is usually on the first syllable, e.g. *I want to down*load *this song. The* down*load didn't work.*

4 LISTENING ▶ 44 Play the track for students to listen to somebody giving instructions and decide what exactly the instructions are for. See p180 for the audioscript for this exercise.

Answer

The instructions are for setting the day, date and time on a computer.

5 Individually, students write the complete instructions to describe the steps they need to take to call a friend if their mobile phone is switched off and the battery is dead. Draw attention to the example sentences.

Example answer

Then turn the mobile on. Type in your pin code and wait for the phone to get a signal. Select your friend's name from your contacts list and press the 'call' button. Put the phone to your ear and wait for your friend to answer.

TEACHER DEVELOPMENT: LANGUAGE

Giving instructions

Instructions are usually written with the imperative form of the verb, e.g. *Switch on the computer.* Sequence is also important so we often use words such as *first, then, next,* etc.

6 **SPEAKING** In pairs, students read their instructions to their partner and compare them to see if they are similar.

7 **SPEAKING** In pairs, students think of something that they typically do with their phone or tablet and prepare instructions to describe the process. Ask students to read out their instructions to the class for other students to identify what the action is.

✚ EXTRA ACTIVITY

Students write instructions for how to play a DVD or how to heat food in a microwave.

HOMEWORK

Assign students page 76 in their Workbook or the relevant sections of the Online Workbook.

Reading p111

Reading for gist and specific information

⫸ FAST TRACK

You could ask students to read the text at home in preparation for the in-class activities. They can look up any words they are not sure about in their dictionaries or the Macmillan Online Dictionary.

WARMER

In pairs or small groups, students discuss which everyday item from page 110 they use most and which they never use, and say why. Then have them think about their parents and answer the same questions.

Example answers

The everyday item I use most is a mobile phone because I use it several times a day to call or text my friends and family.
I never use a satnav because I can't drive.

1a **SPEAKING** In pairs, students look at the photo and the title of the article and say what they can see and what they think a 'screenager' is. Elicit ideas from students around the class.

Example answers

I can see a group of young people relaxing while using different technology. I think a screenager is a teenager who spends a lot of time online.

1b **READING** Ask students to read the text through, ignoring the spaces, in order to check their ideas about 'screenagers' in exercise 1a.

ℹ CULTURAL INFORMATION

The word *screenager* is a blend of *screen* and *teenager*; coined by the author Douglas Rushkoff. 'Screenager' signifies a teenager who spends time in front of the screen of a personal computer or video game console (TV still rates as the screen teenagers spend the most hours in front of). Generation Z are the world's first 'screenagers'. While previous generations had to learn to incorporate technology into their lives, this generation was born into a digital world. Generation Z teenagers spend up to ten hours a day in front of a TV or computer screen, mobile phones or playing video games, and number over two billion people worldwide. Global social media combined with crowdsourcing, open-platform education and sharing provide this generation's inventors with unprecedented influence and opportunities.

2 Ask students to read the text again and complete the gaps with sentences A–G. Give them time to compare their answers in pairs before you check them in open class.

Answers

1 E **2** C **3** B **4** F **5** A **6** G **7** D

3 **CRITICAL THINKING** Give students time to note down a very brief response saying if they agree with the description of Gen Z and saying why or why not. Then encourage a class discussion.

Example answers

I agree with the description of Gen Z. We can quickly sort through and assess enormous amounts of information. If we are interested in something, we are very committed and focused.
I don't agree with everything in the text. It implies that we are very different from previous generations, but I think we still have to be able to communicate clearly in person, and this is the number-one skill for our future success. This is the same for every generation.

4 Ask students to try to work out the meaning of the underlined words in the text by looking at the context. They then look up the words in their dictionaries to check their answers.

Answers

at the heart of = something central or important
the norm = something that is usual or expected
ingenious = uses new or clever ideas
recession = a period when trade and industry are not successful and there is a lot of unemployment
burying their heads in = to give all your attention to something

5 **SPEAKING** **What about *you*?** In pairs or small groups, students discuss how long they spend looking at a screen per day and what device they use the most and what they use it for. Elicit answers from students around the class and try to develop a class discussion about reasons to reduce screen hours.

Assign students page 77 in their Workbook or the relevant sections of the Online Workbook.

Grammar in context pp112–113

Using defining and non-defining relative clauses

>>> **FAST TRACK**

You could ask students to do exercises 1 and 2 at home. Check the answers to exercise 1 in open class and allow students to compare their answers to exercise 2.

Test before you teach

Divide the class into two teams. Team A is noughts (0) and Team B is crosses (X). Draw a 3 x 3 grid on the board and write relative pronouns (*which, who, that, whose, when, why*) in the spaces (some will appear more than once). Add a question mark (?), plus sign (+) or minus sign (-) next to each pronoun depending on whether you want students to form an interrogative (?), affirmative (+) or negative (-) sentence. Teams take it in turns to choose a square and say a correct sentence using the relevant relative pronoun, e.g. *which (?): Have you ever been to a cinema which has ten screens?* If their sentence is correct, write a 0 or an X in that square. The first team to win three squares in a row (horizontally, vertically or diagonally) wins the game.

If the students are familiar with relative clauses, move through the Grammar guide exercises quickly, eliciting answers from students in open class.

1 Ask students to look at the sentences and answer the questions.

Answers

1 a, c, d. They do not have commas.
2 b, e, f. They have commas.
3 We use *which* with things. We use *who* with people.
4 We use *whose* for possessions, *when* for times, *where* for places and *why* for reasons.
5 Yes, we can replace *which* with *that* in defining relative clauses.
6 No, we can't replace *which* with *that* in non-defining relative clauses.
7 No, we can't omit the relative pronoun in non-defining relative clauses.
8 No, we can't omit the relative pronoun in sentences a or d because *which* and *who* are followed by verbs.
9 Yes, we can omit the relative pronoun in sentence c because it is followed by a noun/pronoun.

Relative clauses

Defining relative clauses give essential information to define or identify the person or thing we are talking about. Some key points about this kind of relative clause are:

Commas are not used in defining relative clauses, e.g. *The house which is on the hill is very big.*

Who, whom and *which* can be replaced by *that*. This is very common in spoken English, e.g. *The house that is on the hill is very big.*

Whom is very formal and is only used in written English, e.g. *The candidate whom I recommended for the job was Mexican.*

The relative pronouns *who, which* and *that* can be omitted when followed by a noun or a pronoun. This is especially common in spoken English, e.g. *The boy we spoke to last night was very good-looking.*

Relative clauses with *who, which, that* as subject pronouns can be replaced with a participle. This makes the sentence shorter and easier to understand, e.g. *I told you about the boy who lives next door.* → *I told you about the boy living next door.*

Non-defining relative clauses give extra, non-essential information. It can help students to think that this information might be followed by the words 'by the way', i.e. it is additional information and could be presented as two separate statements. Some key points about this kind of relative clause are:

Non-defining relative clauses are always separated from the rest of the sentence by commas. The commas have a similar function to parentheses, showing the information is not vital to the sentence, e.g. *The house on the hill, which is 150 years old, is very big.*

We can't use *that* instead of *who, whom* or *which* and we can't leave out the relative pronoun, even when it is the object of the verb in the relative clause, e.g. *He gave me the present, which was wrapped in pink paper. He gave me the present, which I opened immediately.*

Non-defining relative clauses can be introduced by expressions like *all of, many of* + relative pronoun, e.g. *I've got a lot of friends in my class, many of whom I have known for years.*

2 Students decide if the sentences are correct and rewrite the incorrect sentences. Give them time to compare their answers before you check them in open class.

Answers

1 My tablet, **which** I bought last week, is already broken!
2 I think that's the phone that I saw ~~it~~.
3 correct
4 correct
5 They're the two people **whose** invention became really popular.
6 correct
7 correct
8 This is the friend **who/that/–** I told you about.

3 Students omit the relative pronouns where possible. Elicit why it is possible and not possible in each case.

Answers

The relative pronouns can be omitted in: a, d, h and l, because these are all defining relative clauses where the relative pronoun is followed by a noun or pronoun.
(b, c, e, i, j, k are also defining relative clauses but the relative pronouns are followed by a verb. f and g are non-defining relative clauses.)

4 Ask students to rewrite the sentences as one sentence using a non-defining relative clause. Do the first one as an example with the class. Point out that in some cases there is more than one correct way to do this.

Answers

1 The inventor of the remote control, whose name was Robert Adler, didn't like watching TV.
2 Remote controls, which first appeared in 1956, were originally called 'space commands'.
3 Robert Adler went to university in Vienna, where he was born./Robert Adler, who was born in Vienna, went to university there.
4 Adler, who invented more than 180 different things, was a brilliant physicist./Adler, who was a brilliant physicist, invented more than 180 different things.
5 Adler, whose most successful invention was the remote control, was especially proud of his work on touch screens.
6 His remote control, which was replaced by infrared systems in the 1980s, used ultrasonic frequencies.
7 In 2007, when he was ninety-three, Robert Adler died./Robert Adler died in 2007, when he was ninety-three./Robert Adler, who was ninety-three, died in 2007.
8 Adler wasn't very interested in his own invention, which changed the way we live./Adler, whose invention changed the way we live, wasn't very interested in it himself.

5 Ask students to read the text and say who the boy in the photo is and what he did. Elicit from students what was so surprising about what he did.

Answers

The boy in the photo is Adam Cudworth. He sent a camera up into space. The photos that Adam took look like they could be images from NASA.

6 Ask students to read the text again and choose which answer (A, B, C or D) best fits in each gap. Check their answers.

Answers

1 B **2** B **3** D **4** B **5** B **6** C **7** B **8** C **9** A **10** B

✔ EXAM SUCCESS Ask students to read the tip about multiple-choice cloze activities. Tell them to turn to Exam success on page 147 for more tips (Use of English: Cloze activities).

✚ EXTRA ACTIVITY

Hold a *Sentence auction*. Divide the class into three teams: Teams A, B and C. Each team writes three correct and three incorrect sentences with relative clauses and then hands their sentences to you. Tell each team they have €1,000 to spend at the *Sentence auction* and the aim is to buy correct sentences. Read out one of Team A's sentences for Teams B and C to decide if the sentence is correct. If they think it is correct, they must bid for the sentence. To buy the sentence, a team must offer more money than the other team. Every time they win a bid, they must write down the amount they paid. Read out each team's sentences for the other two teams. At the end of the auction, students subtract the amount they spent from their €1,000 total to get their new total. Ask a member of each team to read out the sentences they bought for the class to decide if they are correct or incorrect. If it is correct, students add the amount they paid for that sentence to their new total. If it is incorrect, they subtract the amount they paid. The team with the most money is the winner.

Refer students to the Grammar reference on page 120 if necessary.

HOMEWORK

Assign students page 78 in their Workbook or the relevant sections of the Online Workbook.

Developing vocabulary p113 (Aa) (Bb)

Using phrasal verbs connected with technology and computers

⋙ FAST TRACK
Students could do exercise 1 at home.

Phrasal verbs connected with technology and computers

1 Students look at the sentences and match the phrasal verbs in red with their meanings a–j.

Answers
1 g **2** b **3** e **4** h **5** d **6** c **7** j **8** a **9** f **10** i

2 **SPEAKING** In pairs, ask students to look at the pictures and answer the questions using a phrasal verb.

Answers
1 to scroll up/down **2** to print something out
3 It zooms in. **4** It isn't picking up a signal.
5 The battery's running out. **6** The alarm is going off.

⋙ FAST FINISHERS
Students draw a picture to illustrate another phrasal verb from exercise 1 and get another student to guess the word.

Assign students page 79 in their Workbook or the relevant sections of the Online Workbook.

Gateway to life skills pp114–115 🏃

Using technology for study

To reflect on the uses of technology for study, to consider some advantages and disadvantages of using technology in your studies and to plan how to integrate technology into your future study plan

⟫⟫ FAST TRACK

Students could do the questionnaire in exercise 3 at home in preparation for the speaking activity in exercise 4.

ⓘ BACKGROUND INFORMATION

To study effectively on an online course, you need self-discipline and initiative. Online courses currently have a high drop-out rate, possibly because of a lack of sufficient student support. In face-to-face classes, students have their classmates, learning centres and tutors to support and help them with their various learning needs. These resources guide them, clarify and reinforce the material, and allow them to succeed in their education. As online courses become more popular, developers and instructors are challenged with finding new ways to provide support and effectively translate the material from the traditional classroom setting to a digital environment so that messages and meaning are not lost. The sound practices we have developed in the traditional classroom setting have to be creatively transformed to fit the online medium.

In this lesson, students reflect on technology for study skills, tips and techniques that will promote various aspects of their overall learning and study skills.

WARMER

Individually, students note down advantages and disadvantages to studying online. Tell students to refer to Key concepts for ideas and help with vocabulary. In pairs, students then compare their ideas and discuss any similarities or differences. Elicit ideas in open class and encourage students to write their ideas on the board so that they can be referred to later on in the lesson.

Suggested answers

Advantages
can offer educational access to all
convenient
cheaper
increased time on task

Disadvantages
impersonal
less interaction with students
less access to resources
more written texts
lack of immediate feedback

1 READING Ask students to look at the statistics about university students and technology and discuss if any of the statistics surprise them and if so, which ones and why. Elicit answers from students in open class.

2 SPEAKING In pairs, students answer the questions. Elicit from students if their answers coincide with the most common answers in exercise 1.

3 Individually, ask students to do the questionnaire on the phone screen.

4 SPEAKING In pairs, ask students to compare their answers in exercise 3 and discuss points 1–3. Elicit the answers from students around the class.

5 In pairs, ask students to make two lists, one with the advantages of using technology for study and one with the disadvantages.

ⓠ VOCABULARY FOCUS

The video contains some useful colloquial language about using technology for studying that students may not be familiar with. You might want to pre-teach these words and phrases with students before watching:

entire [adj]: extensive or complete
type up [phr v]: to transform handwritten notes into text on a keyboard
aid [v]: help or assist
hugely [adv]: very/very much
presentation slides [n]: images projected on a screen during a talk or lecture
become reliant (upon/on) [phr v]: to start depending on someone or something
enhance [v]: to make better
highly doubt [adv/v]: doubt very much
cater to [v]: to provide something people want or need
thrive [v]: to get stronger and grow
immersive [adj]: creating a 3D image which appears to surround you (computing)

6 LISTENING ▶ 45 Tell students they are going to watch or listen to four students talking about using technology for study. Play the video or audio track for students to note down if the students mention any of their ideas in exercise 5. See the Teacher's Resource Centre for the audioscript/videoscript for this exercise.

7 ▶ 45 In groups of four, students choose one speaker each (Sam, Vanessa, Bea or Chris). Play the video or audio track again for students to write notes on what the speaker they chose says about the questions. Students then compare their notes and discuss whether they agree more with their speaker or with the other speakers, explaining why or why not.

Answers

Sam: 1 university has online system of resources, types up essays and communicates with lecturer on computer; **2** variety of resources online; **4** doubt face-to-face teaching will disappear – people learn more from human teachers; **5** a reliable digital word- or essay-checker to improve writing and take work away from teachers

Vanessa: 1 phone, but mostly laptop; **2** saving copies, editing documents, sending information; **3** too reliant on the Internet; **4** face-to-face interaction is how we thrive; **5** a gadget to allow data to be downloaded straight into your brain

Bea: 1 Internet, university's database; **2** all the information at your fingertips; **3** spelling and grammar suffer; **4** face-to-face teaching will continue; **5** a virtual helmet for an immersive learning experience

Chris: 1 coding course – software and hardware he needs; **2** access presentation slides after lectures; **3** no disadvantages; **4** face-to-face teaching won't disappear – certain things need experts for; **5** free wi-fi for everybody

8 SPEAKING In pairs, students take it in turns to ask and answer the questions. In open class, elicit students' opinions on the advantages and disadvantages of using technology mentioned in exercise 7 and encourage students to think of solutions to the problems mentioned.

✦ EXTRA ACTIVITY

Play a section of the video or audio track of one of the four students and do a *Dictogloss* activity. Ask students to listen intensively and write down as many words as they can. Then, in pairs, students try to combine their versions to get the version as close to the original as possible. Play the section one more time. Then give students two minutes to write their final version. Ask pairs to combine to make groups of four to work together on the final version. Groups swap texts to peer correct any mistakes they see (misspelled words, bad punctuation, etc.) and count them. The team with the fewest mistakes is the winner.

ACADEMIC TASK

Divide the class into groups and tell them they want to integrate technology into their English studies. Ask them to follow the plan:

■ *Step 1*

Discuss which hardware, programs or websites they could use to study English, either in the classroom or out. Remind them to use the general ideas from this lesson for ideas.

■ *Step 2*

Ask students to research which topics, areas and tasks they are going to do in English in the next two or three weeks.

■ *Step 3*

Ask students to write up a plan with suggestions for using technology to help with the tasks and try some of their suggestions out. Ask students to evaluate how successful each experience is and why. Students could write a short report or give a short presentation to the class about their experiences.

Listening p116

Listening for gist and specific information

WARMER

In pairs, students try to think of a word connected to technology for each letter of the alphabet (except Q, X and Y). Set a time limit of three minutes. The pair with the most correct words is the winner.

Example answers

antenna, browser, chat room, disk drive, email, firewall, gateway, hard disk, Internet, JPEG, keyboard, laptop, modem, network, online, PDF, ROM, scanner, television, URL, virus, website, zip

1 SPEAKING In pairs, students look at pictures a–d and discuss what the problem could be in each situation. Elicit opinions from different students around the class and what they could or should do in each case.

2 LISTENING ▶ 46 Play the track for students to listen and match the problems a–d to speakers 1–4. Check answers and elicit if any of the ideas are similar to students' ideas in exercise 1. See p180 for the audioscript for this exercise.

Answers

Speaker 1: b
Speaker 2: c
Speaker 3: d
Speaker 4: a

3 46 Play the track again for students to listen and decide which problem the statements refer to. Check their answers.

Answers

1 b **2** d **3** a **4** c **5** d **6** b **7** b **8** a **9** a **10** d

4 SPEAKING ▶ 46 In groups, ask students to make notes about one of the problems. They then explain it to the rest of the class. Ask if everybody agrees that the information is correct. Students can listen again to check if necessary. Make sure that all four problems are selected.

5 SPEAKING **What about *you*?** In pairs or small groups, students discuss their own experiences and answer the questions. Elicit answers in open class.

HOMEWORK

Assign students page 79 in their Workbook or the relevant sections of the Online Workbook.

Grammar in context pp116–117

Using gerunds and infinitives

>>> FAST TRACK

Students could do exercises 1a and 1b at home. Check their answers and start the class on exercise 2.

Test before you teach: Flipped classroom
Set the Flipped classroom video and tasks for homework <u>before the lesson</u>. This will allow you to assess the needs of the students before the class. Students can then move on to the relevant grammar practice activities.

1a Students read the pairs of sentences and say in which pair the two sentences have the same meaning.

Answer

sentences 2a and 2b

1b Ask students to match the verbs + gerund/infinitive with the correct meaning (a or b).

Answers

1 a **2** b **3** b **4** a **5** a **6** b **7** b **8** a

TEACHER DEVELOPMENT: LANGUAGE

Gerunds/Infinitives

Some verbs are followed by either a gerund or an infinitive with a change in meaning. This grammar point is often tested in examinations at this level. Point out to students that after these verbs, a to-infinitive refers to the future, while a gerund expresses an earlier action, relative to the time of the verb in the main clause.

2 Ask students to choose the correct alternative. Elicit answers from different students around the class.

Answers

1 playing **2** to do **3** to go **4** to eat **5** to bring **6** to give **7** eating **8** to get

3 Ask students to complete the second sentence so that it has a similar meaning to the first sentence, using the word given. Remind students that they mustn't change the word given and they can only use between two and five words including the word given. You could do the first one together as an example.

Answers

1 forgot to send that email **2** likes to wear a tie **3** stop interrupting me **4** I remembered to send **5** like making **6** work to have **7** remember losing **8** remember to meet me **9** stopped talking **10** never forget spilling orange juice

4 Ask students to decide if the sentences are correct and rewrite the incorrect sentences.

Answers

1 I have to go back home because I forgot **to switch** the oven off.
2 Can you remember **to bring** me my book tomorrow because I need it?
3 correct
4 Stop **playing** that song because it's awful.
5 I like **to get up** early when I have an exam.
6 correct
7 I'll always remember **meeting** you for the first time last summer.
8 correct

5 Ask students to write complete sentences about the different things. Monitor and give help as necessary as they work.

6 SPEAKING In pairs, ask students to compare their sentences and encourage them to develop a conversation by asking follow-up questions. Draw students' attention to the model dialogue.

✚ EXTRA ACTIVITY

Play the game of consequences. Give each student a piece of blank paper where you dictate the first part of a story and they complete it. Everyone then folds over the paper so that the writing is hidden and passes it to the person on their right. Dictate the second part of the story for students to complete before folding over the paper and passing it on again. Once the story is finished the last student unfolds the paper and reads the often funny story. Remind the students before the exercise that they are practising verbs followed by *-ing* forms or infinitives.

Once upon a time (students write the name of character one) *was walking in the park when he/she* (student then folds the paper concealing their writing and the paper is then passed to the next person)

... met (students write the name of character two) and they started ...
They liked ...
but then they stopped ...
They forgot ...
Finally, they remembered ...

Refer students to the Grammar reference on page 120 if necessary.

HOMEWORK

Assign students page 80 in their Workbook or the relevant sections of the Online Workbook.

Developing speaking p118

Clarifying and checking understanding

>>> **FAST TRACK**

Students could prepare their arguments for and against smartphones in exercise 2a at home in preparation for the speaking activity.

WARMER

Write these questions on the board: *Do you have a mobile phone? What kind of features does your mobile phone have? Who is the youngest person you know who has a mobile phone? How long have you had a mobile phone? Could you live without your mobile phone? How much do you spend a month on your mobile phone? Have you ever lost your phone? Has your phone ever been stolen? Has your mobile phone ever broken?* In small groups, students take turns to ask and answer the questions. Ask different students to share any interesting information they found out about their partners with the class.

1 **SPEAKING** In pairs, students compare and contrast the two photos. Elicit descriptions from students around the class and ask what they think is happening in each photo.

2a In pairs, students draw a simple two-column table in their notebooks and make two lists – one with arguments in favour of using smartphones in the classroom and one with arguments against.

2b In open class, elicit from students if they have more arguments for or against smartphones in the classroom and encourage them to express their overall feelings as to whether they think it is a good idea or a bad idea.

Example answers

For:

- Times have changed and schools should be making the most of modern technology.
- It is more important for pupils to use the latest technology than learn dates in history: use smartphones to create apps or record videos.
- In class we should use the good things that smartphones can offer – applications and access to the Internet.
- It's fun: smartphones motivate students.
- Students look after smartphones.
- Not every classroom offers students access to a computer, so devices like smartphones, even if you have to pair up, are very useful.

Against:

- Smartphones are easily lost or stolen.
- They distract students' attention.
- There can be a misuse of technology: cyberbullying, texting friends in class, etc.

3 **LISTENING** 47 Tell students they are going to listen to two people discussing whether students should be allowed to take mobile phones into class. Ask them to note down each person's opinion. Elicit what the two people say to justify their opinions. See pp180–181 for the audioscript for this exercise.

Answers

The man is for the idea of students taking smartphones into class and the woman is against it.

Man: They're a part of daily life now … use your phone as a dictionary in English lessons … Or … connect to a map if you're studying geography … smartphone … like a pen.

Woman: They can do that at the weekend … take a photo instead of copying the information down … lazy … students will forget how to write … take photos or video teachers, or other students … cheat in exams.

4 Ask students to read through the expressions in the Speaking bank and complete the headings with options a and b.

Answers

1 checking someone has understood you
2 asking someone to clarify something

5a **PRONUNCIATION** Students look at the first sentence from the Speaking bank and discuss what they think the circles represent. Drill the question with the class.

Answer

The circles mark where the stress falls in the sentence.

5b Students mark where they think the stress should go in the other sentences in the Speaking bank. Ask them to compare their answers in pairs.

5c **LISTENING** 48 Play the track for students to listen and check their answers.

Answers

Do you <u>get</u> what I'm <u>saying</u>?
Are you <u>foll</u>owing me?
Are you <u>with</u> me?
What I <u>mean</u> is …
Yes, that's <u>exactly</u> what I mean.
No, that's not <u>quite</u> what I mean.
Are you <u>saying</u> that …?
If I under<u>stand</u> you cor<u>rect</u>ly, …
In <u>other</u> words …
What do you <u>mean</u> when you <u>say</u> …?
I'm not <u>sure</u> what you <u>mean</u> by …
<u>Could</u> you go over that a<u>gain</u>?
<u>Sorry</u>, I'm not <u>with</u> you.
I <u>don't</u> under<u>stand</u> what you're <u>gett</u>ing at.

5d 48 Students listen again and repeat, paying attention to the stress and intonation.

PRACTICE MAKES PERFECT

6 Ask students to look at the statement and prepare some notes, giving their opinion and arguments to support it.

7 **SPEAKING** Divide the class into small groups and ask them to discuss the statement in exercise 6. Remind them to use expressions from the Speaking bank.

For students who are less confident, photocopy the model dialogue below, and either read it aloud yourself, or alternate the roles with you and two strong students. Then instruct students to read aloud in groups of three, alternating between roles A, B and C. Students then use the dialogue as a guide for their own discussion.

✂- -

Model dialogue

A: I don't think students should spend so many hours a day in front of the screen. It's bad for your eyes and you are sitting in a chair for too long. Are you with me?

B: I agree with you. It's very bad for your back. Another thing is that screens produce radiation and that's a health risk.

C: Are you two saying that you don't spend hours every day on a screen? Life has changed and most people need to be connected for many hours a day. I don't think it's a problem if you take regular breaks. Do you see what I mean?

B: If I understand you correctly, it's fine to spend hours in front of the screen as long as you get up for ten minutes every four hours!

C: No, that's not quite what I meant. What I meant is that we can compensate for the physical effects by taking breaks and doing sport.

A: I don't understand what you're getting at. Screen time is not just a physical problem, it's a psychological one, too. Are you following me?

B: In other words, screen time doesn't just damage your health, it also affects your social life. You can become very isolated.

C: What do you mean when you say 'very isolated'? I have friends from around the world and a really big circle of contacts. Do you see what I mean?

A: Well, it would be interesting to try to spend less time in front of the screen and go out with friends that are not just virtual.

B: Yes, I think you have to find a balance – you can have the best of both worlds.

- -

✚ EXTRA ACTIVITY

Students write a short text about the advantages and disadvantages of having smartphones in class.

HOMEWORK

Assign students page 81 in their Workbook or the relevant sections of the Online Workbook.

Developing writing p119

Writing a report

⟫⟫ FAST TRACK

You could ask students to read the report in exercise 3 at home in preparation for the writing activity.

WARMER

Write these questions on the board: *1 Do you think it is OK for a teenager to spend ten hours a day in front of a screen? 2 Do you think every student should have a smartphone or tablet to use in the classroom as standard equipment?* Ask students to choose one of the questions and to go round and ask ten classmates. Then have them write a sentence to explain their results, e.g. *The majority of/70% of/ Seven out of ten students think/don't think that …* Ask students to read out their results to the class.

1 **SPEAKING** In pairs, students discuss the answers to the questions. Invite them to share any interesting comments or ideas with the class.

2 Students read the writing task and discuss if they should use a formal or informal style for the task.

Answer

The style should be formal because it is a report for the head of the school.

3 Ask students to read the student's report and decide what style it is written in. Elicit if the student mentions any of the things they talked about in exercise 1.

Answer

The report is in a formal style.

✔ **EXAM SUCCESS** Students read about writing a report. Tell them to turn to page 147 for more ideas.

TEACHER DEVELOPMENT: STUDENT TRAINING

Writing a report

A report has to be formal. In their reports, students should include a title and subtitles:

Title: *Report on …*
Introduction: *The aim of this report is to …*
The current situation/findings: *At the moment …; Currently …; My findings show that …; The current situation is that …*
Our opinion/recommendation(s): *I would like to recommend you …; It would be ideal if …; I would suggest …; My suggestion would be …*
Conclusion: *To conclude …; In conclusion …; To summarise …*

4 Students decide if the words in orange are used correctly and rewrite the incorrect sentences. Remind them to use the helpful information in the Writing bank.

Answers

1 Each **student thinks** that it is important.
2 correct
3 None **of the** students wanted to visit the website.
4 correct
5 A good website needs **a lot of/lots of** time and effort.
6 correct
7 correct
8 Most of the people in our class **find** the website boring.

PRACTICE MAKES PERFECT

5 Ask students to read the task and write their report. Remind them to use words and expressions from the Writing bank. They can also follow the advice in the Writing bank on page 157. For students who are less confident, photocopy the model text below for extra support during the writing task.

Model text

Websites that teenagers like and why they like them

Introduction

The aim of this report is to explain which websites teenagers I know like and what it is they like about them. This report will detail what types of websites are most popular amongst teenagers in my country and how we enjoy visiting them.

The most popular websites

We visit websites to help us with our homework like Wikipedia and the Internet Public Library. We like sites that let us write, share, chat and meet new friends. We also like websites where we can micro-blog like Tumblr. We often visit Google Maps to find out about how to get to places. We also visit sites related to our hobbies or other special interests, including learning new skills or finding fun activities. We like websites that offer entertainment, including music and games and news about our favourite celebrities. Most teenagers also visit websites where we can find out about the news and current events. A large number of teenagers like to do their shopping on the Internet.

What we like about these sites

It may seem more complicated for older generations, but we are Generation Z and we like to post secrets on Whisper and share jokes on Twitter. All of the teenagers I know like to visit mobile chat services like WeChat, and photo-sharing apps like Instagram and Snapchat. It's a way for us to share funny moments without the risk of having them go public. They also send and load much faster than email or text. We like to visit sites where we can share, exchange videos or listen to songs. We also visit sites where we can watch films on the Internet.

Conclusion

In conclusion, what's cool with teens is constantly changing and new websites are being created daily. Some years ago, everybody liked Facebook, but now we use Snapchat or Instagram to keep up with friends. Every teenager I know visits a lot of different websites, but they bookmark their favourites so they don't forget the good ones!

✚ EXTRA ACTIVITY

In pairs, students read out their texts to each other for their partner to comment on their ideas and correct any errors they hear.

HOMEWORK

Assign students page 82 in their Workbook or the relevant sections of the Online Workbook.

Language checkpoint: Unit 9

>>> FAST TRACK

The extra support provided in the Grammar and Vocabulary reference sections makes the Grammar and Vocabulary revision sections ideal for setting as homework. You could get students to complete the whole revision page or just certain exercises for homework.

Grammar revision p121

Relative clauses

1 Students choose the correct alternative. Remind them that if they think both are possible, they should choose both.

Answers

1 who **2** when **3** which **4** which **5** that/–
6 whose

2 Students write definitions with defining relative clauses for the people, places, times or things.

Example answers

1 Argentina is a country where you can find lots of natural wonders.
2 2014 was the year when Germany won the World Cup for the fourth time.
3 Caviar is a type of food which/that comes from a fish called a sturgeon.
4 Ice hockey is a sport that/which is played in Canada.
5 Marie Curie was a scientist who created the theory of radioactivity.
6 Tea is a drink which/that can be drunk hot or cold.
7 Glass is a material which/that breaks easily if it's dropped.

Gerunds and infinitives – 2

3 Students complete the sentences with the correct form of the verbs.

Answers

1 to switch **2** painting **3** writing **4** to go
5 seeing **6** to do **7** playing

Vocabulary revision p121

EVERYDAY TECHNOLOGY

1 Students complete the words.

Answers

1 network **2** drop-down menu **3** webcam
4 headphones **5** broadband **6** wireless

VERBS CONNECTED WITH TECHNOLOGY

2 Students match the words with the definitions. Remind them there are four extra words.

Answers

1 press **2** pinch **3** insert **4** freeze **5** adjust
6 delete **7** recharge

PHRASAL VERBS CONNECTED WITH TECHNOLOGY AND COMPUTERS

3 Students choose the correct alternative.

Answers

1 up **2** pick **3** out **4** popped **5** on **6** in **7** off

HOMEWORK

Assign students page 83 in their Workbook or the relevant sections of the Online Workbook.

10 News feed

KEY LEARNING OUTCOMES

Students will be able to:

- talk about the future in the past using a variety of tenses and expressions
- use indirect questions to be polite
- understand written and spoken news stories
- present and respond to opposing views when giving oral presentations
- write structured magazine articles

UNIT OVERVIEW

Vocabulary
News sections
News headlines

Reading
News 24/7
CRITICAL THINKING Discussing if news stories judge events or simply say what happened

Grammar in context
Future activities in the past
Mixed conditionals

Developing vocabulary
Collocations connected with the news

Life skills
Critical thinking: Analysing news stories

Listening
Was the mystery artist Bootsy?

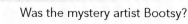

Grammar in context
Indirect questions
Question tags
PRONUNCIATION Intonation in question tags

Developing speaking
Presentations – 2

Developing writing
An article – 2

Exam success
Reading: True/False activities
Listening: Multiple-choice activities

DIGITAL OVERVIEW

Presentation Kit
- ▶ Flipped classroom video Unit 10: Indirect questions
- ▶ Life skills video Unit 10: Citizen journalism debate
- ▶ Interactive versions of Student's Book activities
- ▶ Integrated audio and answer key for all activities
- ▶ Workbook pages with answer key

Teacher's Resource Centre
- ▶ Flipped classroom video Unit 10: Indirect questions
- ▶ Life skills video Unit 10: Citizen journalism debate
- ▶ Grammar communication activity Unit 10
- ▶ Worksheets for this unit, including:
  - Grammar Practice worksheet Unit 10
  - Flipped classroom video worksheet Unit 10: Indirect questions
  - Literature worksheet Units 9 and 10
  - Culture worksheet Unit 10
  - Life skills video worksheet Unit 10
  - Everyday English worksheet Unit 10

Student's App
Gateway 2nd Edition wordlist for the award-winning Sounds App (available for download)

✓ TESTING AND ASSESSMENT

Resources for exam preparation and measuring student progress

- ▶ Test Generator Units 1–10
- ▶ Printable tests Unit 10/End of year
- ▶ Gateway to exams Units 9 and 10 (end of Unit 10)

Vocabulary p122

Understanding and talking about news stories

>>> FAST TRACK

You could ask students to do exercises 3 and 4 at home in preparation for the speaking activity in exercise 5.

WARMER

In pairs, students discuss the meaning of the unit title *News feed* (a data format used for providing users with frequently updated content) and what they think the unit is going to be about (newspapers and magazines). Elicit from students what the expression *breaking news* means (a current event that broadcasters feel is important enough to interrupt scheduled programming in order to report its details) and if they remember a breaking news story that made an impact on them.

News sections

1 **SPEAKING** In pairs, students look at the different sections that often appear on a news website or in a newspaper and discuss what they think each one is. Ask them to group any that they think are similar. Provide dictionaries if necessary for students to check their answers.

>>> FAST FINISHERS

Students write a description for these sections: arts/business/editor's blog/opinion/sport/weather forecast/world news in exercise 1. When the rest of the class have finished, they read out their definitions for the other students to guess the word.

Answers

arts – news and articles about theatre, cinema, music, visual arts, literary events and the world of entertainment in general

business – news and articles about national and international events in business, finance and IT

editor's blog – a section where the newspaper editor writes about their thoughts and opinions

opinion – in this section there are usually two or three articles on current events which reflect the viewpoint of the paper's publishers and editors

sport – news and articles about national and international events in the sporting world

weather forecast – predictions for the weather for today and tomorrow

world news – news from different countries around the world

2 **SPEAKING** In pairs, ask students to discuss the questions. Elicit answers from students around the class.

News headlines

3 Ask students to look at the headlines and read about how the grammar and vocabulary in newspaper headlines helps catch people's attention.

4 Ask students to match headlines 1–4 with topics a–d.

Answers

1 a **2** c **3** d **4** b

5 **SPEAKING** In pairs, students read the headlines and explain what they think the newspaper stories are about.

Answers

a A (new) government plan has been supported by universities.

b A football star has resigned after a disagreement with his manager.

c People are worried about a new virus.

d Police are holding an investigation into possible/suspected corruption.

e There is a connection between a spy mystery and an explosion in the city centre.

f The government is taking a step towards making fast-food advertising illegal.

g An important politician has been involved in a tense situation on a plane.

6 **LISTENING** 49 Play the track for students to listen to three stories and match each story to a headline in exercise 5. See p181 for the audioscript for this exercise.

Answers

1 c **2** b **3** d

7 **SPEAKING** In pairs, students invent a headline using the vocabulary and grammar from exercise 3. Ask them to write a short explanation of their news story. Students then read out their explanations to another pair for them to guess the headline.

HOMEWORK

Assign students page 84 in their Workbook or the relevant sections of the Online Workbook.

Reading p123

Predicting content and reading for gist and specific information

>>> FAST TRACK

You could ask students to read the texts at home in preparation for the in-class activities. They can look up any words they are not sure about in their dictionaries or the Macmillan Online Dictionary. Ask them to look at the headlines and predict what each story will be about before they read the texts.

WARMER

Before the class, find some headlines from British newspapers or news websites and cut them out. Give headlines to students in small groups and ask them to discuss what they think each story is about. Ask students to share their ideas with the class and tell them if they were correct or not.

1 **SPEAKING** In pairs, students look at the headlines and predict what they think each news story will be about.

2 Students read the news stories to find out if they are similar to their predictions in exercise 1. Tell them not to worry about any unknown vocabulary at this point.

3 Students read the news stories again and decide if the statements are True (T), False (F) or the information is Not Mentioned (NM). Ask students to identify the sentences which helped them decide on their answers.

Answers

1 NM
2 F (PETA argue that although students may get rid of their stress with a petting zoo, these zoos actually cause stress for the animals in them.)
3 T (They believe that if students knew the facts, these zoos wouldn't have become so popular on campuses.)
4 T (Travel, confinement to small cages and rough handling cause animals intense stress.)
5 F (The students got excited. Reese already had plans – he was going to buy a car for his mum, and a boat!)
6 T (The students knew that they hadn't earned the money …)
7 NM

✔ EXAM SUCCESS Students read about how to approach True/False reading activities in exams. Tell them to turn to page 147 (Reading: True/False activities) for more information.

TEACHER DEVELOPMENT: STUDENT TRAINING

True/False reading activities

Remind students that every part of a true sentence must be true. If any one part of the sentence is false, the whole sentence is false. Students should only choose 'not mentioned' if they can find no reference to the statement in the text.

4 **CRITICAL THINKING** Individually, students contemplate whether the news stories judge people's actions or whether they simply say what happened. Ask students to compare their ideas with the rest of the class.

Example answer

The texts outline the events as they happened and appear not to judge people's actions. In the first text, it is clear that PETA disapproves of petting zoos and there are no arguments in favour so we are encouraged to criticise wrong behaviour. However, in the second text, we are encouraged to value the college students' right behaviour.

5 Encourage students to work out the meaning of the underlined words in the texts by looking at the context. They then use their dictionaries to check their answers.

Answers

a bad bet = a bad idea
confinement = forced to stay in a place, especially a prison or a cage, and not allowed to leave
bouncy castles = large plastic structures filled with air, and often in the shape of a castle. Children play on them by jumping up and down, for example at a party or a funfair.
smelly = with an unpleasant smell
pick = select
empty-handed = without getting anything for your effort

6 **SPEAKING** What about *you*? In pairs or small groups, students say what comment they would add for each story.

Example answers

Text 1: It's really cruel. I think we should start a campaign to boycott petting zoos.
Text 2: They did the right thing. Your actions, whether good or bad, will often have consequences that you can't predict.

✚ EXTRA ACTIVITY

Write these questions on the board for students to discuss in pairs or small groups: Text 1: *Are there any animal protection organisations, like PETA, in your country? What do you think of these organisations?* Text 2: *What would you have done if you had been in the students' position? Do you think the woman should have given them more money? Why/Why not?*

HOMEWORK

Assign students page 85 in their Workbook or the relevant sections of the Online Workbook.

Grammar in context pp124-125

Talking about future activities in the past and using mixed conditionals

⟫ FAST TRACK

You could ask students to do exercises 1 and 2 at home.

Test before you teach

Write the following sentences on the board and ask students if they are each talking about the past, present or future (future):
1 *They are going to sell their house.*
2 *I'm leaving tomorrow.*
3 *My parents will be home soon.*
Now elicit the same sentences in reported speech and ask the same question. Elicit that they are talking about future activities in the past. Have students say or write some more examples using a variety of tenses. If they seem to be familiar with this structure, move through the Grammar guide exercises quickly in open class.

Future activities in the past

1 Ask students to read the explanation about structures used to talk about future activities in the past. Tell them to read the sentences and find the structures with this function. Elicit answers from students around the class.

Answers

1 were about to **2** was going to **3** was to turn to
4 would have **5** was opening

TEACHER DEVELOPMENT: LANGUAGE

Future in the past

We use structures to talk about future activities in the past when we want to express the idea that in the past we thought something would happen in the future. It does not matter if we are correct or not. *Would* is used to volunteer or promise, and *was going to* is used to plan. Moreover, both forms can be used to make predictions about the future. Like all future forms, these 'future in the past' structures cannot be used in clauses beginning with time expressions such as *when, while, before, after, by the time, as soon as, if, unless,* etc.

2 Ask students to complete the text with the words and expressions in the box. Have students compare in pairs before you check answers in open class.

Answers

a playing **b** about **c** going to **d** would **e** to
f would survive **g** were

3 Ask students to decide if the sentences are correct and rewrite the incorrect sentences. Check their answers.

Answers

1 The sky went black and it looked like it was about **to** rain very soon.
2 correct
3 They were to **get** an incredible surprise the day after.
4 They thought it **would snow/was going to snow** the next day, but it didn't.
5 correct
6 They went to bed early because the next day was **going** to be very busy.

4a Ask students to use their imagination to complete the sentences.

Example answers

1 I knew it was going to be a great day because the sun was shining.
2 I was going to do my homework when the phone rang.
3 I never thought it would happen, but one day it did.
4 I was meeting my friends the next day, but I came down with a cold.
5 I was going to call my parents when suddenly they called me.
6 The car was about to hit the dog when it swerved at the last moment.

4b SPEAKING Encourage students to compare their sentences in groups and choose the best sentence for each situation. Ask them to read their best sentences out to the class.

Test before you teach

Ask students the following question: *Where would you be today if your parents had decided to go to live abroad?* Elicit some answers from different students and then write the question on the board and elicit that this is a mixed conditional (it combines the second conditional and the third conditional). If students are familiar with this type of sentence, ask them to write one or two more mixed conditional sentences, then move through the Grammar guide exercises quickly in open class.

Mixed conditionals

5 Ask students to look at the sentences and answer the questions. Check their answers.

Answers

1 Mixed conditionals are a mixture of second and third conditionals.
2 a
3 b

TEACHER DEVELOPMENT: LANGUAGE

Mixed conditionals

Mixed conditionals are conditional sentences that combine two different types of conditional patterns. These combinations are very frequent, but the most common combination is the third conditional in the *if*-clause (*if* + past perfect) followed by a second conditional (*would* + infinitive) in the main clause. We use this combination to contrast an imagined or real event in the past with the present result. We use this type of conditional when we regret a past action or inaction. The second, less common type of conditional is when we have a second conditional in the *if*-clause (*if* + past simple) followed by a third conditional (*would've* + past participle) in the main clause. Here we describe ongoing circumstances in relation to a previous past event.

6 Ask students to decide which sentence endings are possible and how the meaning of each sentence is different. Elicit answers from students around the class.

Answers

1 b, c (In b, the speaker would currently take photos; in c, they would have taken photos in the past, but not now.)
2 b, c (In b, the speaker doesn't like science fiction movies now; in c, they didn't like science fiction movies at that time in the past.)
3 b, c (In b, she currently/regularly takes the medicine that helps her; in c, she took the medicine in the past.)
4 b, c (In b, it focuses on the present situation – people would still be dying; in c, it refers to people in the past.)
5 b, c (In b, the speaker is talking about a hypothetical future; in c, it refers to a possible lie in the past.)

7 Ask students to look at the situations and complete the sentences using mixed conditionals.

Suggested answers

1 If Jenna didn't love taking photos, she wouldn't have joined a camera club.

2 If Sam hadn't spent lots of time studying, he wouldn't be a journalist now.

3 If they hadn't spent years making their new film, it wouldn't be great.

4 If they knew where the key was, they would have opened the door.

5 If they could speak English, they would have interviewed the actor.

6 If I had known you were coming, I would have something for you to eat.

7 He wouldn't have a new phone if he hadn't lost his old one.

8 If I had remembered to do my homework yesterday, I wouldn't have to do it now.

Refer students to the Grammar reference on page 132 if necessary.

HOMEWORK

Assign students page 86 in their Workbook or the relevant sections of the Online Workbook.

Developing vocabulary p125

Using collocations connected with the news

FAST TRACK

You could ask students to do exercises 1 and 2 at home.

Collocations connected with the news

1 **SPEAKING** In pairs, students look at the expressions in red in the sentences and discuss what they think they mean. Elicit their ideas in open class.

2 Ask students to match the expressions in red in exercise 1 with their meanings a–i.

Answers

a news item   **b** hold a press conference   **c** make the headlines   **d** news updates   **e** breaking news
f front-page news   **g** newsflash   **h** turn of events
i keep you informed

TEACHER DEVELOPMENT: LANGUAGE

Collocations

Students may already be aware of the importance of collocations for learning English. Students need to familiarise themselves with combinations of words and the many different types of collocations, e.g. adjective + noun (*hot news*), verb + noun (*make headlines*). There is no grammatical reason for collocations so there are no rules for students to learn. Students should make sure they write down collocations and learn them whenever they can.

3a Ask students to complete the sentences with the words in the box. Check their answers.

Answers

1 informed   **2** newsflash   **3** press   **4** front
5 headlines   **6** items   **7** breaking

3b **SPEAKING** In pairs, students discuss the questions in exercise 3a. Elicit their answers and try to develop an open-class discussion.

✚ EXTRA ACTIVITY

Bring in some English-language newspapers for students to look at. Tell them to discuss questions 4–7 in exercise 3a again using the newspapers to refer to.

HOMEWORK

Assign students page 87 in their Workbook or the relevant sections of the Online Workbook.

Gateway to life skills pp126–127

Analysing news stories

To learn how to analyse news stories, to consider the advantages and disadvantages of citizen journalism and to practise analysing news stories from different sources and compare their treatment

FAST TRACK

Students could read the guide in exercise 2 to help them analyse the news stories in exercise 3.

WARMER

Write these questions on the board for students to discuss in pairs: *What is the biggest news item so far this year? Who owns the newspapers and TV stations in your country? Do you think this has an effect on the news that you receive? Do you think journalists should report everything? What do you think about news censorship? Do you think the media is objective? Why/Why not?* Ask students to read through the Key concepts and check any vocabulary they don't understand.

1a **SPEAKING** In pairs, students discuss the popular saying: '*Don't believe everything you read in the news.*' Ask them to say if they agree with the statement and give reasons why or why not.

Example answer

I agree with this statement. Some newspapers run stories without checking if they are true or not. There are people who make a living by inventing stories and selling them to newspapers. Many newspapers print them and then other newspapers print the same story. That's how stories spread around the world very quickly, whether they are true or not.

1b Ask students to make a list of questions that they could ask about a news article to help them to decide whether to believe it or not. Draw students' attention to the example question. Allow them to compare their questions in pairs or small groups.

2 READING Ask students to read through the guide to help students analyse news articles in order to see how many of the questions they thought of in exercise 1b. Refer them to the definitions in Key concepts to help with difficult vocabulary.

3a Ask students to use the questions in the guide to analyse the news stories on page 123.

3b SPEAKING In pairs, students compare their answers in exercise 3a. Elicit answers in open class.

4 SPEAKING In pairs, students discuss the questions. Elicit in open class why students think it is important to analyse news stories in this way and which three questions in exercise 2 they consider to be the most important.

5 In pairs, ask students to read the explanation of 'citizen journalism' and make two lists of the advantages and disadvantages of citizen journalism. Draw two columns on the board and ask students to come up and write in their answers.

🔍 VOCABULARY FOCUS

The video about citizen journalism contains some useful vocabulary that students may not be familiar with. You might want to check these words and phrases with students before watching:

hyperspeed [n]: extremely fast speed

live feeds [n]: (TV) transmissions being shared through the Internet

footage [n]: recorded film or video (once measured in feet)

factually correct [adj]: accurate and true to life

background checks [n, pl]: research done to verify something

spewing out [v]: producing a lot of something (like vomiting)

scoop [n]: a news story that hasn't been made public before

mindset [n]: an established set of ideas or values

snippet [n]: a very small quantity or particle of something bigger

(to go) viral [phr v]: to be seen by many people on the Internet

swing it [v]: to move from one opinion or attitude to another

non-biased [adj]: without prejudices or strong opinions

sob story [n]: a very sad human story (usually used ironically)

prey on [v]: to make a victim of or have a bad influence on someone

vigilante justice [n]: where the public try to take the law into their own hands and out of the hands of the police

6 🎬 **LISTENING** ▶ 50 Tell students they are going to watch or listen to four students in a media studies class who are debating whether citizen journalism is a good thing. Ask students to note down which of their ideas in exercise 5 they mention. Ask students to decide who they would vote for at the end of the debate. See the Teacher's Resource Centre for the audioscript/videoscript for this exercise.

7 ▶ 50 Play the video or audio track again for students to complete each sentence with between one and three words. Encourage students to compare in pairs before you check in open class.

Answers

1 live feeds   **2** reliable   **3** sources   **4** shot
5 personal gain   **6** speculation

8 SPEAKING In pairs, students discuss if they agree with the statements in exercise 7 and give reasons why or why not. Elicit students' opinions in open class.

➕ EXTRA ACTIVITY

Ask students to dub the video. Prepare copies of a section or all of the audioscript and divide the class into pairs. Students take it in turns to read sections of the video and try to synchronise their speaking with the video. Play the video with the sound down.

21ˢᵗ CENTURY TASK

Tell students they want to analyse a news story from different sources. Divide the class into small groups and ask them to follow the plan:

- *Step 1*
  Students discuss and choose a story that has been in the news recently.

- *Step 2*
  Ask students to find two different sources for this story, e.g. two different newspapers, or a newspaper and a news website.

- *Step 3*
  Ask students to analyse if the stories receive the same amount of space or attention and if the journalists give the same facts or comment on the news in the same way. Remind them to use the questions in the guide on page 126 to help them.

- *Step 4*
  Ask students to work with their group and compare their opinions.

- *Step 5*
  Students write a report with their conclusions. Encourage them to work together to edit their report. Remind them to refer to the Writing bank on page 157 if necessary.

- *Step 6*
  Students present their report to the class.

Listening p128

Listening for general and specific information

WARMER

In pairs or small groups, students try to think of the name of internationally recognised media for each letter of the alphabet (except J, K, P, Q, X and Z), e.g. names of magazines, newspapers, TV stations, websites. Set a time limit of three minutes. The pair/group with the longest list of correct words is the winner.

Example answers

Amazon, BBC, CNN, Daily Telegraph, The Economist, Facebook, Google, Hotmail, The Times of India, Living TV, MTV, Ning, The Observer, Reuters, Skype, Twitter, UKTV, Virgin Media, Wikipedia, YouTube

1 SPEAKING In pairs, students read the headline and make a list of questions they would ask the teenager to find out the full story of what happened. Elicit questions from different students around the class.

2 LISTENING 51 Tell students they are going to listen to two journalists interviewing the teenager in the headline. Play the track and ask students to tick any of their questions from exercise 1 which they hear. Ask students how many questions they ticked. See pp181–182 for the audioscript for this exercise.

3 51 Ask students to read through the questions. Then play the track again for them to listen and choose the correct answers. Check their answers. Ask students to say which parts of the listening text helped them decide on their answers.

Answers

1 b (His clothes certainly weren't very smart. I specially remember that his jacket was small and didn't go over his arms.)

2 b (… it was a print … He signed it … And he added colours at the top.)

3 a (He actually said to me 'This will be worth about £20,000.' I didn't really believe that at first, which is why I looked him up on the Internet when I got home.)

4 a (But what we've decided to do now is … my dad is going to take the picture and get some experts to examine it, and see what they say.)

5 b (It's great to see somebody getting an immediate reward for a simple act of kindness.)

✔ EXAM SUCCESS Students read the tip on how to do well in multiple-choice listening activities. Ask them to turn to Exam success on page 147 for more ideas (Listening: Multiple-choice activities).

TEACHER DEVELOPMENT: STUDENT TRAINING

Multiple-choice listening activities

Students should read the options carefully before they listen. When students listen for the first time, encourage them to relax and listen without taking notes. If they write notes as they listen, they may lose the sequence of answers and start to panic. Remind students that the speaker sometimes says one thing and then changes it or adds new information.

After they listen, students should try to choose the best answer. Students should note which answers they are not sure about so they can listen out for these when they hear the recording a second time.

4 SPEAKING What about *you*? In pairs or small groups, students discuss what they would do if this happened to them – would they keep the picture or sell it? Elicit answers in open class.

HOMEWORK

Assign students page 87 in their Workbook or the relevant sections of the Online Workbook.

Grammar in context pp128-129

Using indirect questions to be polite and using question tags

⟫ FAST TRACK

Students could do exercises 1a and 1b at home. Check their answers and start the class on exercise 2.

Test before you teach: Flipped classroom Set the Flipped classroom video and tasks for homework <u>before the lesson</u>. This will allow you to assess the needs of the students before the class. Students can then move on to the relevant grammar practice activities.

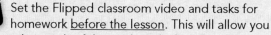

1a Ask students to look at the indirect questions and write the direct questions.

Answers

a What did the man look like?
b What did he do then?
c What was your reaction when you found out?
d Why did he give you the picture?
e Would you sell it?
f What would you do with the money?

1b Ask students to answer the questions about sentences a–f.

Answers

1 The subject comes before the verb (like in a statement).
2 We use question marks when the first part of the sentence is a question.
3 Indirect questions are usually more formal and polite.

2 Ask students to complete the second sentence so that it has a similar meaning to the first sentence, using the word given. Remind students to use between two and five words.

Answers

1 long it took you **2** know whether he was talking **3** any idea why he doesn't **4** wonder what other artists think **5** if this is the **6** why you decided to give **7** he does each year

3 Students write indirect questions using the words given. Check answers in open class paying attention to the final punctuation – full stop or question mark.

Answers

1 I'd like to know how long you have lived in this area.
2 Can you tell me what you think of graffiti?
3 Have you any idea what you are going to do this summer?
4 Can I ask how often you watch the news on TV?
5 I wonder if you could tell me if you are interested in sport.
6 Do you know how many people read showbiz news?
7 I'd like to ask if you have ever met somebody famous.

4 **SPEAKING** In pairs, students take it in turns to ask and answer the indirect questions in exercise 3.

5a **SPEAKING** In pairs, students look at the news headline and, in the role of reporters, write six indirect questions to ask the teenager.

5b One student in each pair is the reporter and the other is the teenager from the story. Students role-play their conversation for the class. If time is short, divide the class into several large groups and ask the pairs to role-play their conversation for their group.

Test before you teach

As a class, ask several questions using question tags to different students around the class, e.g. *You've had your hair cut, haven't you? You live near the school, don't you?* Encourage some more confident students to ask similar questions. Then say some sentences and ask students to call out the question tag ending, e.g. *Manchester United won't win the league this year, _____? (will they); Inside Out was a great film _____? (wasn't it).* If students seem familiar with the use of question tags, move through the Grammar guide exercises quickly in open class.

6 Students look at sentences a–g and the question tags they contain. Ask students to decide if statements 1–6 are True (T) or False (F).

Answers

1 T **2** T **3** T **4** T **5** F **6** T

TEACHER DEVELOPMENT: LANGUAGE

Question tags

We use question tags to change a statement into a question. We use pronouns, not names or nouns. If there is not an auxiliary or modal verb in the first part of the sentence we use *do*. Remind students that we reply to question tags using the auxiliary or modal verb, not the main verb, e.g. *You like classical music, don't you? Yes, I do./No, I don't.*

7 Ask students to match sentences 1–8 with the correct question tags a–h.

Answers

1 h **2** b **3** a **4** g **5** e **6** c **7** f **8** d

8 Ask students to complete the sentences with question tags.

9 **LISTENING** ▶ 52 Play the track for students to listen and check their answers. See p182 for the audioscript for this exercise.

Answers

1 don't they **2** aren't I **3** shouldn't we **4** won't it
5 aren't we **6** didn't you **7** does she **8** haven't we

10a **PRONUNCIATION** ▶ 53 Play the track for students to listen to a sentence said twice and identify the difference in pronunciation. Elicit in which case the speaker seems very certain that he knows the answer to the question.

Answers

1 falling intonation on question tag
2 rising intonation on question tag
The speaker sounds more certain in sentence 1 (falling intonation).

10b ▶ 52 Play the track again for students to listen to the sentences in exercise 8 and decide if the intonation goes up or down.

Answers

1 Everybody likes the summer, don't they? ↗
2 I'm right, aren't I? ↘
3 We should use question tags, shouldn't we? ↘
4 The news will be on soon, won't it? ↗
5 We're going to be on TV one day, aren't we? ↗
6 You read the news yesterday, didn't you? ↘
7 She never comes late, does she? ↘
8 We've got homework tonight, haven't we? ↗

10c ▶ 52 Play the track again for students to listen and repeat, paying special attention to the intonation.

TEACHER DEVELOPMENT: PRONUNCIATION

Intonation

Intonation is about how we say things, rather than what we say. Speech is divided into phrases, also known as 'tone units', and in each tone unit the pitch moves up and down, within a 'pitch range'. English has a particularly wide pitch range. The pitch movement (a rise or fall in tone, or a combination of the two) takes place on the most important syllable known as the 'tonic syllable'. The tonic syllable is usually a high-content word, near the end of the unit. It is helpful to teach predictable intonation patterns which are associated with some key grammar areas, e.g. falling intonation in *Wh*-questions, rising intonation in *Yes/No* questions.

11a SPEAKING Ask students to write three sentences about their partner that they know or think they know, and three things that they aren't sure about. Draw attention to the example sentence.

11b Ask students to add a question tag to each sentence. Refer students to the example sentence.

11c In pairs, students take it in turns to ask each other their questions, remembering to use falling intonation when they are quite certain of their partner's answer and rising intonation when they aren't so sure.

✚ EXTRA ACTIVITY

Elicit 15 personal questions and write them on the board, e.g. *When is your birthday? What time did you go to bed last night? Where did you go last weekend?* Try to get a variety of tenses. Students then ask each other the questions in pairs, without taking notes. When they have asked all the questions, they check they have remembered their partner's answers by using question tags, e.g. *Your birthday is in February, isn't it?* Remind them to use rising intonation if they're not sure and falling intonation if they are sure.

Refer students to the Grammar reference on page 132 if necessary.

HOMEWORK

Assign students page 88 in their Workbook or the relevant sections of the Online Workbook.

Developing speaking p130

Giving your point of view in presentations

⟫⟫ FAST TRACK

Students could prepare arguments for and against one of the statements in exercise 5 at home in preparation for the speaking activity.

WARMER

Say to students: *I wonder if you would like to be famous.* Ask them to discuss the question in pairs or small groups. Elicit ideas from different students around the class and ask students to identify the advantages and disadvantages of being famous.

1 SPEAKING In pairs, students discuss the questions. Encourage students to share any interesting ideas with the class.

2 SPEAKING In pairs, students look at the statement and think of arguments for and against it.

3 LISTENING ▶ 54 Tell students they are going to listen to somebody giving a presentation on the topic in exercise 2. Play the track for them to listen and decide if they agree with what the person says. Elicit why or why not. See p182 for the audioscript for this exercise.

4 ▶ 54 Play the track again for students to listen and complete the expressions in the Speaking bank.

Answers

There's no **denying** that …
You can't **argue** with the fact that …
Let's not **forget** that …
Having **said** that,

5 Ask students to choose one of the statements and think of arguments for and against it. Then encourage students to decide what their opinion is.

6 Ask students to make notes for a presentation on the statement they chose in exercise 5. Ask them to follow the guide.

7 Ask students to think of expressions that are useful at each stage of their presentation and make notes. In a less confident class, you could brainstorm expressions together as a class and write them on the board.

Suggested answers

Introducing and sequencing arguments: I'd like to begin by saying; Firstly; Secondly; Finally
Stating your opinion: I think (that); I don't think (that); Personally, I think; As far as I'm concerned; In my opinion; From my point of view
Adding arguments: Furthermore; What's more; In addition
Making contrasts: On the one hand; On the other hand; In contrast; However
Concluding: In conclusion; To sum up

PRACTICE MAKES PERFECT

8 **SPEAKING** Students give their presentation to the class. Remind them to use expressions from the Speaking bank and exercise 7.

For students who are less confident, photocopy the model text below, and either read it aloud yourself, or ask a strong student to do so. Students can then use this as a guide for their presentations.

Model text

I'd like to begin by saying that not all famous people should suffer the same lack of privacy. As far as I'm concerned, writers have more right to privacy than famous actors, singers or politicians for the reasons I am now going to explain.

In the first place, famous actors or singers are part of the entertainment world. There's no denying that when people become famous stars, people like to know everything about their appearance and personality. It is true that this can be annoying and intrusive. However, you can't argue with the fact that famous actors and singers invite publicity, especially at the beginning of their careers and they get paid a lot of money in exchange for losing their privacy. What's more, politicians trade privacy for power. In a democratic system, accountability justifies some loss of privacy.

However, famous writers should have more right to privacy. We should only be interested in their written work and respect their personal privacy as much as possible. Having said that, I would also like to say that everyone has the basic right to privacy and even famous actors, singers and politicians have these rights. That doesn't alter my opinion that they give up some of these rights in exchange for fame. To sum up, a complete lack of privacy is unacceptable, whoever you are.

TEACHER DEVELOPMENT: STUDENT TRAINING

Giving a presentation

Learning to speak in front of others is a skill that will be of lifelong benefit to students and one that will help them become active and autonomous learners.

Experience builds confidence, which is the key to an effective oral presentation, so it is a good idea for students to practise in pairs before they present their topic to the class. Students may feel more comfortable if they know the assessment criteria beforehand so, if possible, hand out the grading criteria to the students before they do the activity. Ask the class to grade each other's presentations using the assessment criteria and give feedback at the end of each presentation.

Example assessment criteria:

- Is the organisation logical with a clear introduction and conclusion?
- Is the content interesting and engaging?
- Does the speaker seem confident, use eye contact and speak clearly and slowly?
- Does the speaker talk fluently and without hesitation?

TEACHER DEVELOPMENT: CLASSROOM TIPS AND PLANNING

Speaking assessment

Student presentations are an excellent way to document their learning experiences. They can be recorded and collected as part of the *Language Dossier*. You could use this pro forma (or one of your own choice) to encourage students to reflect on what they have learnt and how they can improve their performance the next time they do a presentation:

Name: _____

Presentation date: _____

Topic: _____

Resources: _____

_____

What did you like best about your presentation?

_____

_____

What are some ways to improve your presentation?

_____

_____

Did you learn anything new? What could you do differently in the future?

_____

_____

_____

✚ EXTRA ACTIVITY

Students write a short text to summarise their presentation.

HOMEWORK

Assign students page 89 in their Workbook or the relevant sections of the Online Workbook.

Developing writing p131

Writing a magazine article

>>> FAST TRACK

You could ask students to read the article in exercise 3 in preparation for the writing activity.

WARMER

In groups, students play *20 questions*. Student A thinks of a news story that people are talking about now and the other group members ask 20 *Yes/No* questions to try to discover what it is. Student A can only answer *yes* or *no*. When somebody guesses correctly, they take a turn to answer questions.

1a SPEAKING In groups, students brainstorm any people, stories or events that teenagers in their countries are talking about right now.

1b Encourage students to compare their answers with the rest of the class to see if they have chosen similar things.

2 Students read the writing task carefully and find the key information that they need to include in their article.

Answers
… who or what, in your opinion, people are talking about right now.

… why you think people are talking about them …

…. give us your own opinion …

3 Ask students to read the article and decide if it includes all the necessary information. Elicit the answer and what stories the article talks about.

Answer
Yes, it includes the necessary information.

4 Ask students to look again at the article and choose the correct alternative. Ask them to think about the meaning of the words and how they function in a sentence.

Answers
a Despite the fact that **b** At first **c** since
d However **e** as **f** As far as I am concerned **g** as

5 Ask students to read the lists of linkers in the Writing bank and put the titles in the correct places.

Answers
2 f **3** a **4** b **5** e **6** c

6 In pairs, students put the stages of writing a text in order.

Answers
2 b **3** a **4** d **5** c **6** f

TEACHER DEVELOPMENT: STUDENT TRAINING

Improving writing

Students could use this writing checklist before they hand in their written work:

- Does the text answer the task and is it relevant?
- Is the style appropriate: correct format and register, suitable for the audience?
- Is the text logically arranged, with good use of linkers and time expressions to help the reader follow it?
- Does the text have good paragraph organisation?
- Is it the right length for its purpose?
- Is the grammar, punctuation and spelling acceptable?
- Is the text interesting with a wide variety of vocabulary and structures?
- Is it neat and legibly written?

PRACTICE MAKES PERFECT

7 Individually, students write an article for the task in exercise 2. Remind them to use linkers from the Writing bank and to follow the correct procedure outlined in exercise 6. They can also follow the advice in the Writing bank on page 153. For students who are less confident, photocopy the model text below for extra support during the writing task.

Model text

Whether it is books, films, music or video games, there is always a new trending topic to get excited about. Despite the fact that it can be impossible to keep up with the constant change – what I am going to talk about today will be different tomorrow – I am going to tell you about two trending topics this week and what I think about them.

Despite the fact that I don't actually like this kind of film, a lot of teenagers are talking about the new film *Minions*. It's about these yellow organisms who serve evil masters and it's really popular. Firstly, it has a lot of cute characters and secondly there's the Academy Award-winner Sandra Bullock, who plays a super-villain. I wasn't particularly interested in this kind of film since they don't really appeal to me. However, I've seen the trailer and I must say it looks quite good.

The other topic that many teenagers are talking about is a new type of trainer in stores now. You can blow up the inside sole with a small pump on the side. It means that the trainer adjusts better to your foot so that it's more comfortable and you can run faster. People are talking about how good they are and where you can get them.

➕ EXTRA ACTIVITY

Students check each other's texts using the writing checklist in exercise 6 and give each other feedback on their writing.

HOMEWORK

Assign students page 90 in their Workbook or the relevant sections of the Online Workbook.

Language checkpoint: Unit 10

>>> FAST TRACK

The extra support provided in the Grammar and Vocabulary reference sections makes the Grammar and Vocabulary revision sections ideal for setting as homework. You could get students to complete the whole revision page or just certain exercises for homework.

Grammar revision p133

Future activities in the past

1 Students complete each sentence with one of the words in the box. Remind them they can only use each word once.

Answers
1 would 2 going 3 to 4 was 5 to

Mixed conditionals

2 Ask students to put the verbs given in the correct form.

Answers
1 would be 2 had passed 3 would have called
4 had won 5 would have finished

Indirect questions

3 Ask students to put the words in the correct order and add a question mark at the end of the sentence if necessary.

Answers
1 Can you tell me what you want?
2 I would like to know how you are.
3 Do you know what time it is?
4 Have you any idea whether he drinks coffee?
5 I want to know how you did that.

Question tags

4 Ask students to choose the correct alternative.

Answers
1 do they 2 do 3 hasn't 4 am 5 there

Vocabulary revision p133

NEWS SECTIONS

1 Ask students which section of the newspaper they would look at if they wanted to read or find out about the things in 1–6.

Answers
1 obituaries 2 gossip 3 weather forecast
4 entertainment 5 have your say 6 features

NEWSPAPER HEADLINES

2 Ask students to match the headline words (1–8) with their common equivalents.

Answers
1 f 2 e 3 c 4 h 5 a 6 g 7 b 8 d

COLLOCATIONS CONNECTED WITH THE NEWS

3 Ask students to choose the correct alternative.

Answers
1 press conference 2 events 3 news item
4 updates 5 informed 6 front page

HOMEWORK

Assign students page 91 in their Workbook or the relevant sections of the Online Workbook.

Reading p134

➤ **TIP FOR READING EXAMS**

Students read the tip for doing True/False/Not mentioned activities in reading exams. Tell students to look at Exam success on page 147 for more ideas.

1 SPEAKING In pairs, ask students to look at the headlines and invent a short newspaper story that could fit each one. When they finish, students compare stories in open class.

2 READING Ask students to read the real newspaper stories to see if they are similar in any way to their invented stories.

3 Ask students to read the stories again and decide if the statements are True (T), False (F) or if the information is Not Mentioned (NM). Ask students to identify the lines in the text which helped them decide on their answers.

Answers

1 NM
2 F (After looking at Cent's records they found out …)
3 T (… because we are of Polish origin, his story really stuck with us.)
4 NM
5 NM
6 T (A website set up in his honour has so far received donations of over $14,580 to reward him.)
7 T (Thanks to another offer, the taxi driver could have recorded an album if he was interested in starting a music career.)
8 F (Immediately after finding the money, Gori began to look for the couple. … He always knew he wouldn't take the money for himself.)

4 SPEAKING **What about *you*?** In pairs, ask students to discuss if they think there are enough 'good news' stories in the news today or not.

Listening p135

➤ **TIP FOR LISTENING EXAMS**

Students read the tip about how to do multiple-choice activities in listening exams and then look at Exam success on page 147 for more ideas.

5 SPEAKING In pairs, students read the headline and say what they think actually happened. Elicit some ideas from students in open class.

6 LISTENING ▶ 55 Tell students they are going to listen to some journalists interviewing the shop owner from the headline. Play the track for students to listen and choose the correct answer. Check answers in open class. See p182 for the audioscript for this exercise.

Answers

1 b **2** c **3** a **4** b **5** a **6** b **7** a

Use of English p135

➤ **TIP FOR USE OF ENGLISH**

Students read the tip for doing cloze activities in Use of English. Tell students to look at Exam success on page 147 for more ideas.

7 Ask students to read the news story and invent a good headline for it. Tell them to ignore the gaps for the moment.

Example answer

Criminals Beware! GPS tracking app catches gang of robbers

8 Ask students to read the text again and decide which answer best fits each gap (A, B, C or D).

Answers

1 D **2** B **3** D **4** C **5** A **6** D **7** C **8** D

Writing p135

➤ **TIP FOR WRITING EXAMS**

Students read the tip for writing reports and turn to Exam success on page 147 for more ideas.

9 Students read the task carefully and decide what headings and how many paragraphs they will have in their report. Then they write their report. For students who are less confident, photocopy the model text below for extra support during the writing task.

Suggested answer

Introduction
Findings
My opinion
Conclusion

✂ -

Model text

Report on how interested young people are in the news

Introduction

The aim of this report is to discuss how interested young people are in the news. This report will also detail how they follow the news (TV, the Internet, newspapers, etc.) and what sections young people are most interested in. I will also suggest that young people are growing less interested in the news, regardless of how it is delivered.

Findings

Having spoken to a number of students about how they follow the news, the most popular way nowadays is via the Internet or the TV. None of the young people I spoke to buys a newspaper. Most students read the entertainment and sports section first. Some students read about world news, but most students are interested in news stories that affect them in their everyday lives.

My opinion

I think most young people like to read an e-newspaper because they can enjoy the interactive features these websites offer. It is easy to contrast information and find out more about a story when you read the news on the Internet. When young people watch the news on the TV, it is usually because there is something important that catches their attention and they want to watch.

Conclusion

In conclusion, the news business faces the most difficult time in its history. Thousands of journalists have lost their jobs and newspapers have closed down. The transformation of media in the digital age has changed the way that young people access information. However, evidence suggests that, compared to previous generations, young people are just not as interested in the news.

- -

HOMEWORK

Assign students pages 92–93 in their Workbook or the relevant sections of the Online Workbook.

1 Ask students to mark from 1–4 how well they feel they can do each thing in English.

2 Ask students to look at their marks and decide what they need to do to improve. Elicit ideas from students around the class.

Unit 1

Vocabulary p6

4 01

1 What subject do you study at university if you want to take care of animals?
2 Where are there more students, in a lecture or in a tutorial?
3 Which word is similar to *grade: note* or *mark*?
4 What is the name of a student who doesn't already have a degree?
5 What is the name of a person who teaches students?
6 What is a name for a piece of work you do as part of your course?
7 Which university subject studies the human mind?
8 What can you sometimes do if you fail an exam at university?

Listening p12

2 and 3 ⏵ 04

Boy: Hi, Scott. Are you OK? You don't look very well.
Scott: I'm not brilliant, no. I was up late last night studying for the history exam we've got this afternoon. I probably drank about five cups of coffee and didn't go to sleep until half three.
Boy: I can't do that. It just makes me too tired to think on the day of the exam.
Scott: The problem is that I only started studying for the exam yesterday.
Boy: Why? Scott, we've known about it for a month!
Scott: I know, but I hate revising. I prefer to leave revision to the last minute.
Boy: Really? I remember more if I study for short periods every day.
Scott: The problem is that I never have time to study. I've got basketball practice three times a week so I don't have time to study at all on Mondays, Wednesdays and Fridays. And I always have a match on Saturday. And then I often play football on Sundays.
Boy: Well, last night did you have time to revise all of the seven different topics that come up in the exam?
Scott: Seven? I thought there were only five! Anyway, I only studied three of the topics, because I haven't got any notes for some of them. I don't know if I've lost them or if I just didn't write anything down in the first place. Anyway, there are only three questions in today's exam, aren't there?
Boy: Yes, but what if the questions are about the topics you haven't studied?
Scott: I looked at last year's exam and chose the topics that didn't come up last year. Anyway, if I do two questions really well, I can pass.
Boy: But Scott! Didn't you hear what the teacher said? He said that in this exam you have to answer everything.
Scott: Did he? I don't remember that! Oh dear, I'm going to fail, aren't I?
Boy: Look, the exam's after lunch. You can study some of the other topics during the lunch break.
Scott: Yes, in theory, I could. But Mum brought me to school in her car this morning because I was so tired and I left my books and papers in the car. She goes home for lunch, but it'd take too long to go home and come back again.
Boy: Listen, Scott, the only good thing is that this is the first exam of the term. There are lots of exams this year so you can try to get a higher mark next time.

Developing speaking p14

2 and 3 ⏵ 05

Student A:
I need to think about this question at the moment because this is my last year at school. I really like studying languages. I study English and French at school and I also study German outside school. I think I'd like to study languages at university. My parents would rather I studied music because I play the piano really well. But I'd prefer to be a translator or an interpreter than a musician.

Student B:
I enjoy enjoy doing sport. I don't have much time during the week, but on Saturday or Sunday I play football or basketball. I'm in a youth football team, so it's important I practise a lot. Sometimes I watch movies at home, you know, sci-fi movies, they're my favourite.

Student C:
Yes, I do. I like books … Yes, I like reading.

Student D:
It depends. I like doing projects and things like that with other people. But when I have exams, I prefer revising alone because I find it easier to concentrate when I'm on my own. You have a good time when you work with other people, but sometimes you don't do much work.

Student E:
I prefer doing mental work. That's because I'm not very strong, and I don't really like sport. My parents would prefer me to do more exercise because they say I'm always reading or playing computer games. The thing is I don't mind spending hours reading at the weekend. But when my mum makes me do chores I get bored really quickly.

Student F:
Hmm. It's quite a small place and so I like being able to walk everywhere. For example, I can walk to school; I don't need to catch a bus or anything. But it can be a bit boring too because there aren't many places to go. At least we live quite close to a big city so we can go there quite easily, at the weekend for example. But personally I think I'd rather not live in a small town, I'd rather live in a city.

Unit 2

Vocabulary p18

4 06

Speaker 1:
I work indoors. My job is not very stressful. I deal with students but also with all the people who work here. It's mostly manual work. I'm responsible for fixing things that are broken. Sometimes I do photocopies. I also check who comes into the school building. Really I do a variety of things.

Speaker 2:
My job can be quite stressful. You need special qualifications and training to do it. I'm responsible for designing special computer systems for my customers. Sometimes I work for banks or big offices. The salary isn't bad when you work for big companies.

Speaker 3:
Well, my boss says I'm a really important employee. Without me, she says she couldn't survive. I'm responsible for arranging meetings, taking calls, writing letters. I deal with all my boss's paperwork and with the people who want to speak to her.

Speaker 4:
I help people who've had injuries. I get them moving again using special physical exercises. My salary isn't the same as a doctor's, but it isn't bad. And it's very satisfying to help somebody walk or run again.

Vocabulary p18

8b ⏵ 07

1 look for a job
2 apply for a job
3 be offered a job
4 sign a contract
5 get a promotion

Grammar in context p20

2b ⏵ 08

cried	developed
happened	hated
mentioned	occurred
planned	preferred
stepped	stopped
studied	travelled
tried	visited

Listening p24

2 10

Speaker 1:

I needed money to help me to pay for university so I looked for a job in my home town. It's a small town and the only work I could find was in a restaurant. I'd never worked in a restaurant before and I didn't enjoy it much. But in some ways that was a good thing. I realised that I never wanted to do a job like that again. It motivated me to study hard at university, so that I could get ahead. It's really difficult to get interesting, creative jobs nowadays, but now I know what the alternative is. Also, the other plus side was that I'd been working really hard for almost 11 months when I had an idea. As I'd saved up a lot of money, I decided to use a small amount to pay for a holiday. When I'd finished my job at the restaurant, I went to Japan for a month.

Speaker 2:

I didn't plan my gap year at all. First, I worked in a supermarket to make some money. I didn't really know where I wanted to go, but I knew I wanted to travel. When I'd earned enough money I decided to go skiing in France. I found a job working in a restaurant there and spent six months skiing, learning French and making friends. After all that snow I wanted to see the sun so I went to Spain. I learnt basic Spanish and travelled around the country. When my gap year finished I'd learnt how to become independent.

Speaker 3:

For my gap year I wanted to experience something totally new. I contacted an organisation that works in India, helping poor children who live on the streets. It was hard work because of the problems that these children had to face. But the children we were helping lived in such terrible conditions, so we just kept at it. Now, when I'm studying at university and I have a problem, I think about those children and remember how lucky I am. The work I'd been doing in my gap year really made a difference to them. I decided then that when I finish uni, I want to do a job where I can help others.

Speaker 4:

My gap year had two very different parts. For the first six months I worked as a waitress to make some money, doing overtime most weeks. When I'd done that I found an organisation that does scientific research in Madagascar. I applied and was offered the job. The whole experience was amazing. We were living in a tent for three months and conditions were quite basic, but I loved the bush life. I saw species of plants and animals that you just can't see anywhere else in the world. I worked with people from totally different places. That trip was the start of a new life for me. I'm seriously considering a career in development work abroad when I graduate.

Speaker 5:

I knew exactly what I wanted to do in my gap year. I'd been dreaming about it for years.

When I'd finished school I bought a ticket to travel round the world. It cost £1,800 and included all the various flights and train and bus fares … There were so many highlights! Riding an elephant in Thailand, swimming with dolphins in Australia, doing adventure sports in New Zealand! I went to places that everybody wants to visit one day, but they start university and then work and they never find the time.

Developing speaking p26

2 and 3 11

Examiner: Hello. I would like you to discuss how dangerous the jobs on the diagram are.

Girl: OK. What do you think about being a pilot?

Boy: Well, I think it's quite a dangerous job because, of course, you can have an accident, and air accidents are always serious.

Girl: Maybe, but I don't think they are very common. I think flying is usually a very safe thing to do.

Boy: What about firefighters?

Girl: I think that's a very dangerous job. They always work in very difficult situations and they could easily have an accident when there's a big fire.

Boy: Yes, I agree. What about police officers?

Girl: I think it depends. Their job can be very dangerous at times, but I don't think they're dealing with dangerous criminals every day. Do you agree?

Boy: Yes, I think you're right. Sometimes they just do paperwork or stop non-violent crimes.

Girl: And what about construction workers?

Boy: I think they do a lot of hard, manual work. But I don't think it's a very dangerous job, really.

Girl: Yes, but they often work high up, and accidents are quite common. You know, in some countries people don't have to wear helmets, so that's very dangerous.

Boy: I see what you mean. And Formula 1 drivers?

Girl: I think that's a really dangerous job, too. There's lots of technology to prevent accidents, but accidents still happen when you travel so fast.

Examiner: Now you have a minute to decide which of those jobs you think is the *most* dangerous.

Boy: I think being a Formula 1 driver is the most dangerous. In the last few years there have been some terrible accidents in races.

Girl: I agree up to a point, but firefighters have to take risks nearly every day, not just from time to time in a race.

Boy: That's true. And being a firefighter is definitely more dangerous than being a construction worker or a police officer.

Girl: Yes, because normally those jobs aren't particularly dangerous, only once in a while. And we said that plane accidents aren't so common.

Boy: OK, so why don't we choose the firefighter?

Girl: Sure, let's do that.

Gateway to exams: Units 1–2

Listening p31

9 12

Speaker 1:

I'm 26. I've got a job in a clothes shop and I live alone in a small flat. The thing is that my mum is constantly calling me. In some ways, it's great because I know she loves me and I find out what she's doing and if she's OK. But she will tell me what to do all the time. She's forever offering to help me at work. She says that if one day I can't go to work because I'm ill, she can call my boss for me. I know she's just trying to help me but … I'm an adult now! I stopped being a child when I left school. It's true, it isn't always easy being an adult, but I think I need to try doing things my own way, even when it's the wrong way.

Speaker 2:

I'm a history tutor at the university here. I've worked here for 30 years and I can't remember seeing so many parents as this year. They'll come to talk about their son's exams or their daughter's assignments. They'll ask why I gave this mark and why it wasn't a higher mark. One student forgot to come for an exam and his mother came and asked why her son couldn't do the exam another day. Well, I explained that her son needed to start taking responsibility for himself and for his own mistakes. Parents have started doing everything for their children and now children aren't doing anything for themselves. It didn't use to be like that.

Speaker 3:

I don't think it's fair to call me and my wife helicopter parents. We have two children, one at university and one who's just started work. When I was in their situation, parents behaved differently. I often wanted my parents to help me at school, university or even work, but they didn't use to have time. We're lucky. We've got time to help our children, to find good courses and jobs for them, to do work for them if necessary. I like to make life easy for my kids. That's only natural, isn't it?

Speaker 4:
I couldn't believe it. I was doing something important, but I stopped to prepare myself for an interview with a 23-year-old science graduate. There was a knock on my door and there was the graduate ... with his mother! She wanted to be with her son at the interview. She said she had some questions to ask me. I explained it to her very clearly. To do this job, you need to be independent, responsible and want to get ahead. Having your mum with you at a job interview doesn't really show that you have those qualities. And that was it, I said goodbye to them and closed the door!

Speaker 5:
I've never really tried influencing our son's decisions. When he left school, he said he didn't want to go to university. I wasn't happy, but I didn't stop him. He tried doing three or four different jobs, but he really didn't like them. Then he decided that he wanted to go to university after all. He applied for a course in business management. They offered him a place and he's there now and he loves it. I think everyone needs to live their own life and make their own mistakes. When you try to make somebody do what you want, not what they want, it can be a big mistake.

Unit 3

Vocabulary p32

3 13

1 The train now approaching Platform 3 does not stop here. Will passengers please stand well away from the edge of Platform 3? Thank you.
2 The next train at Platform 5 is the 17.40 service to Newcastle, calling at Oxford, Birmingham New Street, York and Newcastle. At Platform 5, the 17.40 service to Newcastle.
3 Will passengers on the platform please let people get off the train before trying to board the train? Please let passengers get off the train before boarding. Thank you.
4 Due to engineering work, this train will *not* be stopping at West Kensington. We repeat, the train will *not* be stopping at West Kensington due to engineering works. We apologise for any inconvenience.
5 Last call for passengers on flight Jet 325 to Manchester. Please proceed urgently to gate number D34. Flight Jet 325 now boarding from gate number D34.
6 Passengers are reminded not to leave luggage unattended. Please do not leave luggage unattended.

Developing vocabulary p35

3b and 3c ▶ 14

disadvantage	disagree
unbelievable	incapable
incomplete	unexpected
unlikely	illogical
unnecessary	disobey
impatient	impossible
irregular	irresponsible
unsuccessful	invisible

Listening p38

2 and 3 ▶ 16

Kim: Hello and welcome to *Future World*, the programme that looks at new technology and how it's changing our world. Today we're looking at something that is already starting to have a great impact on our lives, drones. With us is our expert Scott Wilson. Scott, you've just come back from an annual 'drone conference' in Washington in the US. What can you tell us about the latest developments, and where drones are going next?

Scott: Hi, Kim. Well, the first thing I discovered is that the industry doesn't like calling them drones. At the conference people usually talk about UAVs.

Kim: UAV? What do those letters stand for?

Scott: Unmanned, or Unpiloted, Aerial Vehicle. So, anything that flies without an actual human being on board. The thing is that when people think of drones they usually think of war and missiles. In fact, by February next year, the US army will have been using drones for 42 years already. But in the future UAVs will be doing millions of different jobs, and many of those jobs will be helping the world, not destroying it.

Kim: Can you give me an example?

Scott: Sure. In a big national park in Namibia they're using UAVs to patrol the park, to protect rhinos there.

Kim: Really? How do they protect them?

Scott: Well, if a UAV finds any hunters, a team is immediately sent to that area to stop them.

Kim: So UAVs can actually help to protect wild animals?

Scott: That's right. And then, take natural disasters. Very soon, it will have become normal for rescue services to send UAVs to the sites of natural disasters, like earthquakes, floods or tsunamis.

Kim: OK, but what will the UAVs do there? They won't be able to help anyone, will they?

Scott: Yes, they will. They'll be able to examine the site and get a detailed idea of the situation. And they'll also be able to take medicine, water or food to the victims. That'll be particularly important in remote areas, or areas that are difficult to get to for one reason or another.

Kim: I've heard that some film studios are using UAVs to make movies.

Scott: That's right. It's easy to send a camera up on a UAV, and you can get spectacular images from the air.

Kim: In the 2014 Winter Olympics the TV companies started using UAVs to film skiing and other events, didn't they?

Scott: Yes. I think soon we'll be seeing UAVs flying over the heads of football players or at tennis matches. We'll be able to have really spectacular reporting of sports events.

Kim: Isn't that expensive, though?

Scott: Well, at the moment, one company sells UAVs to film studios for $30,000. But in five or ten years the price will have dropped as more and more people buy them. By 2025 the world of the UAV will have become incredibly big business. The world will be spending billions of dollars on UAVs. And thousands of normal people will be using them.

Kim: But, of course, a big problem with that is privacy, isn't it? What happens when people start using drones to film normal people at home, or use them to spy on you and find out what you're doing or where you're going?

Scott: Yes. That *is* a very important question. I think governments will need to think hard about new laws for why, how and when we can use UAVs. Many people are already completely against them.

Kim: Hmm, there's certainly a lot to think about as far as UAVs are concerned. Scott, thanks for coming in and telling us about them.

Developing speaking p40

2 and 3 ▶ 17

Both photos show people travelling in a city. In the first photo the people are using the Underground, whereas in the second photo the woman is cycling in the road. One big difference between the photos is that the first photo shows a big crowd of people waiting on the platform while in the second one the woman seems to be alone and is on the move. Compared with the cyclist the people in the station seem unhappy – maybe they're impatient to get home. Another important difference is that in the Underground there can't be much fresh air, while the cyclist is outdoors and so the air is probably better.

One similarity is that there are problems with both ways of travelling around the city. In the Underground you don't have much space and it's probably quite difficult to sit down when it's busy. But I think it can be very dangerous cycling in a big city. At least the woman in the photo is wearing a helmet though. Also, when it rains it isn't nice to be cycling.

Vocabulary p44

7 18

Speaker 1:

I like working with Joe, but not everybody does. The thing is, he likes being in control. He tells everybody what they need to do. Some people get annoyed, but I think he's efficient because everybody knows where they are. He's definitely the boss, but I think that's OK because when you work in a group, somebody needs to be the boss. The other good thing about Joe is that he believes in himself. He knows he can do the job, and he knows that he can do it well. You know, you don't want the leader of the group to be insecure and worried all the time, do you?

Speaker 2:

You know, I was really angry with Lily last week. When she saw me, do you know what the first thing was that she said to me? She said, 'Oh, you look terrible. Where did you get those jeans? They don't look good on you.' I couldn't believe it! I mean, I know that *she* thinks she's just perfect and that her clothes are the best and she's the only person whose opinions are important, but she needs to be a bit more modest because one day she's going to end up with no friends.

Speaker 3:

You know, sometimes Matthew really gets on my nerves. Once he makes a decision it's impossible to get him to change his mind. Last week he had an argument with Oliver and now he won't speak to him. He says *nothing* can make him change his mind. The thing is that they argued about a maths exercise. You know that Oliver is a really gifted mathematician. He explained the exercise *five* times to Matthew and Matthew just couldn't understand. The thing is the exercise wasn't difficult, but, well, you know, Matthew is bottom of the class in maths. He finds it really difficult.

Listening p50

2 and 3 20

Presenter: And now it's time to look at the world of TV. Sue Wilson is here to tell us about her programme of the week. Hi, Sue. What do you have for us this week?

Sue: Well, it hasn't exactly been a brilliant week for TV to be honest. There was just one programme that stood out for me. The programme was the first in a new series on Channel 4 called *Hidden Talent*.

Presenter: *Hidden Talent*? Is that another one of those talent programmes with pop singers and bands?

Sue: No, no, but that's what I thought too, at first. But it's much more original than that. The basic idea of the programme is that many people have a special talent, but they don't know what it is. So they invited 900 normal people to do nine different tests, and then they looked at who did the tests well. The programme then shows how they train those people to develop their talents.

Presenter: What sort of talents are we talking about?

Sue: Well, in the first programme on Wednesday night the two talents were rock climbing and lie-detecting.

Presenter: And did they find anybody with those talents?

Sue: They certainly did. For rock climbing they discovered a nurse in her forties called Maggie Reenan who had never climbed before in her life! They gave her a really difficult task.

Presenter: What was it?

Sue: It was to climb a 60-metre rock surrounded by water off the coast of Scotland. It's hard enough to climb it in good weather conditions, but this place is known for being extremely windy and rainy, and it can be quite a scary experience. In fact, it's such a difficult climb that you usually need many years of experience to try it. But Maggie had just 18 *days* of training! She was so calm about it, too. When she was climbing her heartbeat was slower than the person who was monitoring her heartbeat! Maybe her work experience helped her because when nurses treat patients in emergencies they need to stay calm.

Presenter: Amazing! And did she do it in the end?

Sue: Yes! She did it *so* well! She was brilliant!

Presenter: And what about lie-detecting?

Sue: That was interesting, too. They say that only one in 400 people is good at identifying liars. But in the first test, a 63-year-old woman called Brenda Chamberlain identified 16 out of 20 lies. She was much better than the rest.

Presenter: So how did they train her?

Sue: She did a course with some experts from the FBI. They taught her to watch body language carefully, for example. And to notice the typical things we say when we're nervous.

Presenter: What was her final task?

Sue: One person out of a group of five took some money and she had to identify who it was by asking them questions.

Presenter: And was she good enough to do it?

Sue: Yes, she was!

Presenter: So these really are just normal people with hidden talents?

Sue: Yes. The programme really made me think … It's such a pity that we can spend our lives without realising we have a special talent. Maybe you could be the best diver in the world, for example, and never know it. Take Maggie Reenan, the rock climber. As a grandmother she'd always been too busy with her family to be able to do something like this. So it was inspiring to watch her perform something amazing that she never knew she could do.

Presenter: Thanks, Sue! I'll be sure to watch out for *Hidden Talent* next week!

Developing speaking p52

4 and 5 21

I'd like to begin by saying that I disagree with the statement that there are no heroes in today's world and I'm going to give you some reasons why I disagree.

First of all, I believe that it is true that nowadays people use the word *hero* too often. Some newspapers talk about the hero in a football match just because they scored a goal. Or maybe a teenager says that a new pop star or actor is their hero because they really like their songs or films. But I think a hero is much more than just an entertainer or a sportsperson.

In my opinion, a real hero is somebody who makes a sacrifice to help others, somebody who makes a big difference to other people's lives in difficult situations. So, for example, I believe that doctors or firefighters are heroes when they put themselves at risk to try to save somebody's life. Doctors or firefighters don't do this to become famous or rich. They do it because they believe that we should help others. What's more, people like this are true heroes because they may save lives not just once or twice but perhaps many times.

It's also true that there are some celebrities who can be called heroes because they inspire people and help make the world a better place. One person who I think is a real hero is the actress Emma Watson. She is young and famous, but she has always worked closely with different charities, particularly to help children and young people. Furthermore, she has worked as a Goodwill Ambassador for the United Nations for a number of years and has made very inspiring speeches asking boys and men to do more to achieve equal rights for women around the world.

To sum up, I think that we should be careful when we use the word *hero*. A hero is not just somebody who does something funny, entertaining or exciting. I believe that a hero is somebody who does something extraordinary to save lives or to help and inspire others. In short, in the past there have always been people prepared to do heroic things in difficult situations, and I believe that today is no different.

Unit 5

Vocabulary p58

5 ▶ 22

1 If a jacket originally costs £50 and there is a ten per cent discount, how much does it cost now?

2 You want to buy a CD that costs £13 and you pay with a £20 note. How much change do they give you?

3 You have seen a pair of jeans that cost £55, but now they cost £60. Is that a bargain?

4 You usually buy one-litre bottles of orange juice that cost £1.20. Now there is a special two-litre bottle that costs £2. Is that good value for money?

5 You want to buy two books that cost £12. You have £30 with you. Can you afford the books?

6 You have £200 in a savings account. The bank gives you two per cent interest each year. How much interest do you have after one year?

7 You have £250 in your current account. You have to pay three bills, one for £70, one for £120 and another for £80. Are you going to get into debt?

8 You have £10,000 in your bank account and you want to buy a car that costs £8,000. Do you need an overdraft?

Listening p64

4 ▶ 25

Presenter: In the past, all sorts of objects have been used as money – cows, cocoa beans, and, of course, coins made from precious metals. But there are some experts who say that it can't be long before physical forms of money disappear completely. That may or may not be true. But there's already one type of virtual money that more and more people are talking about … and using. It's called the Bitcoin and here to tell us about it is Sarah Gould. Sarah, what is Bitcoin exactly?

Sarah: Bitcoin is a new type of money which is 100% digital. In fact, you do sometimes see physical Bitcoins, but they're actually worthless without the private codes printed inside them.

Presenter: So, if there are no physical Bitcoins, how do they exist?

Sarah: Each Bitcoin is basically a file which you keep in your smartphone or computer.

Presenter: And how do you get Bitcoins?

Sarah: There are three different ways. Firstly, you can buy them with 'real' money. Or you can sell things and let people pay for them with Bitcoins. Or you can actually create your own with a computer.

Presenter: Really? It must be easy to become a millionaire if you can make money yourself.

Sarah: No, no, it's actually quite complicated. There's a process called mining. To mine Bitcoins, your computer has to do incredibly difficult mathematical problems. When your computer finally solves the problem, they give you a Bitcoin. But the problems are becoming more and more difficult because they don't want too many bitcoins to exist.

Presenter: So it could take years to get just one Bitcoin?

Sarah: That's right. Some people have actually built special computers to generate Bitcoins. But you have to remember that they would lose their value if there were lots and lots of them.

Presenter: Not everybody's happy about Bitcoins, though. There are some people who think that they might not be such a good idea, aren't there? What are some of the problems with them?

Sarah: No bank or government controls the Bitcoin. With no central control, the value of Bitcoins often changes dramatically. It could be worth a lot today but almost nothing tomorrow.

Presenter: I've heard that criminals use Bitcoins, too. Is that true?

Sarah: Yes, that's quite worrying. Because there's no government control, and because it's difficult to know who exactly is sending and receiving money, some people are able to use Bitcoins for illegal operations.

Presenter: Now, one of the curious things about Bitcoins is that nobody knows exactly who created them, do they?

Sarah: Well, we know that he used the name Satoshi Nakamoto, so, logically, you would think that it must be a Japanese man. But a lot of people think he might have used a Japanese

pseudonym, just to confuse people.

Presenter: Have they ever found someone with that name?

Sarah: Yes, journalists found a man called Satoshi Nakamoto in California. At first, they thought he may have been the inventor because he knew about computer programming. But this Satoshi was 64 and he claimed it can't have been him because he'd been suffering from an illness and didn't even know what Bitcoins were until his son told him! What's clear is that, right from the beginning, their inventor must have wanted to remain anonymous because he was careful never to give away any information about his identity. Anyway, he must have made a lot of money from Bitcoins. Some people calculate that he has billions of dollars worth of Bitcoins.

Presenter: Wow! Not bad!

Developing speaking p66

3 ▶ 26

Let me think. Both photos show people shopping, but in the first photo the people are at a second-hand sale outside in the country, because there are lots of trees in the background. There's a table in the foreground covered in lots of things, whereas in the second photo there's a real shop, a clothes shop, with shelves and lights in the background. In both photos the people seem as if they're happy and enjoying themselves. But one big difference is that in the second photo we know what they're interested in buying because we can see all the different T-shirts in the foreground on the left. But in the first photo they're looking at a model plane and a hat, but they may be looking for something completely different – you don't know what they're going to buy in the end!

I think people like shopping in these different ways because they both have some advantages. I mean, in a clothes shop it's fun because you can try the clothes on and you can see what they look like on you. I think it's better to buy clothes like this because you know exactly what you're buying. On the other hand, it's interesting to walk round a second-hand sale because you don't know what you'll find and you might come across something really unusual. The other advantage of shopping at a second-hand sale is that nothing costs too much money and you could find a bargain, whereas the shop in the second photo looks quite trendy and the clothes are probably expensive. Also, in my opinion, shopping in a real shop is more tiring and stressful than wandering round an outdoor sale, as in most real shops there are usually big crowds of people, especially at the weekend, and sometimes you might queue for a long time to pay. Personally, I enjoy both ways of shopping, but above all I think it depends on what you want to buy.

Unit 6

Vocabulary p70

4b 27

A I think that generally I have quite a healthy lifestyle. I take regular exercise. I work out in a gym three or four times a week. I also have a balanced diet, including fresh fruit and vegetables. I go to the doctor's for a check-up every six months and I take my blood pressure regularly, too. The only problem I have is that I'm allergic to pollen, but I have a special injection from time to time and it relieves all the symptoms.

B Last year the doctor told me to stop eating so much fatty food and processed food that's high in salt and sugar. I was putting on a lot of weight and the doctor said I was in danger of becoming obese. My diet was increasing the risk of heart disease. To be honest, I think I was becoming addicted to junk food because I was eating it all the time, but I was able to stop and now I'm back to my ideal weight.

C Last week I picked up some sort of throat infection. I had a temperature and felt dizzy all the time. I couldn't stop shivering either. My doctor treated me for the illness. He wrote me a prescription which I took to the chemist's. As soon as I started taking the medicine, I got over the illness.

D Last month I fell down the stairs and injured myself quite badly. I twisted my ankle, sprained my wrist and dislocated my shoulder. The only good news was that I didn't fracture or break any bones and I didn't need an operation or anything. But it was still really painful, as you can imagine.

Listening p76

2 and 3 30

Speaker 1:

I only started swimming seriously last year. The thing is, I used to run five times a week, but my knee started giving me problems. My doctor told me I shouldn't run so much because the impact was bad for me. He recommended swimming. I wasn't mad about the idea at first, but I found that I really enjoyed it. The only thing is, I wish I'd learnt to swim properly when I was a kid because it's difficult to change bad habits when you're older. If I'd started to swim when I was younger, I'd be a much better swimmer now. But at least when I swim I know that I'm exercising my whole body – arms, legs, chest, stomach. It's really complete and very tiring.

Speaker 2:

When I was eight, I started playing basketball at school, in a team. I found that I was quite good. I got better and better and became the captain of the team. I played most days of the week and only ever thought about basketball. The only problem is that I wasn't very tall. In fact, I'm still not very tall. I wish I was taller. It makes a big difference in basketball. When I got older, I was still good with the ball, but I couldn't get past the defence because they were all taller than me. But that's when I realised that I didn't care anymore about being the best or about winning matches. I just wanted to play to keep fit and be with my friends. Now I wish I had just played for enjoyment when I was younger. I still play in a team now, but just for fun.

Speaker 3:

I love water sports, even though I'm not actually a very good swimmer. I love doing sport on the water rather than in it. Surfing and windsurfing are my favourite sports. Just that feeling of being free and in touch with nature, it's magic. It takes me two hours to get to the sea from where I live. That's why I only started surfing and windsurfing when I was 16. If I'd lived closer to the sea, I would have begun much earlier, I'm sure. But I soon learnt and people say I'm really good at it. It's quite an expensive sport because you need to buy all the equipment and to pay for accommodation and actually getting to the coast.

Speaker 4:

My favourite sport is called pilates. I saw a TV programme about it once and thought it looked interesting. Maybe people don't take it seriously because you use big rubber balls and bands and do a lot of exercises on mats on the floor. The idea is that it improves strength and flexibility by controlling your breathing. You don't sweat much, but you use muscles you didn't know you had! I wish people wouldn't make fun of pilates. People ask me why I do it. Obviously, the main reason is I enjoy it. If I didn't like it, I would have stopped a long time ago. And you aren't just sitting around doing nothing. You don't seem to be making much effort, but you are, believe me!

Speaker 5:

One year my parents gave me a special present. They paid for me to do a diving course because I'd passed all my exams and got really good marks. If I hadn't passed, they wouldn't have let me do it, I'm sure. In fact, I was the only teenager on the course, the rest were all between 25 and 50. You can't just go and dive in the sea straight away. You have to study some theory first, to know how to calculate how much oxygen you have and how much time you can stay underwater. Then we went to a swimming pool where we were only one metre under the water, but some people got really nervous. I was just the opposite. Anyway, after five pool dives, we finally went into the sea and did four dives there. On the last dive we went 20 metres down. I loved every minute of it and was really proud to get my certificate.

Developing speaking p78

3 31

Examiner: I'd like you to imagine that your school wants to encourage students to live healthier lives. Here are some ideas that they are thinking about and a question for you to discuss. Talk to each other about how these ideas could encourage students to live healthier lives.

Girl: OK. What do you think about cookery classes?

Boy: Well, I think they could be really useful because they could help us to prepare healthy meals.

Girl: I agree. We'd have a better idea about which food and ingredients are good or bad for us. And if we cooked our own meals, we wouldn't eat so much junk food.

Boy: Yes. What about the idea of having a school sports day?

Girl: It depends what that means exactly. I suppose if everybody took part, it would help them to get some exercise.

Boy: That's true. And maybe some people would realise that they aren't as fit as they should be, and that might encourage them to do more sport, which is really important for a healthy life.

Girl: Yes ... I think that a talk by a doctor could be useful too, because a doctor can explain how your body works and what happens when you don't eat a balanced diet or take exercise.

Boy: Yes, I think you're right. Maybe they could explain about the risks of heart disease and things like that. And what about a weekend in the country?

Girl: I'm not sure. I suppose it could be useful because it's quite relaxing and it's good to get fresh air.

Boy: Yes, as long as the idea is to spend the time outdoors, walking or doing sport. And what about the last one, free membership of a gym or sports club?

Girl: That could be really useful because you could try out different sports or exercises and see what activities you like.

Boy: Yes, and if you enjoy doing that, you can carry on afterwards. I think that would definitely encourage you to have a healthy lifestyle.

Examiner: Now you have a minute to decide which two ideas you think are the best.

Girl: I think we should choose a talk by a doctor. I think that would be really useful because doctors are experts in anything connected with your health.

Boy: I see what you mean, but some students might not find it interesting enough. It might be too technical or scientific. In my opinion, cookery classes might be a better choice because they're really practical and it would be different from our usual classes.

Girl: Yes, you're right. I think another good choice is the free membership to a gym or sports club. That would give everybody a chance to try out a sport. What do you think?

Boy: Yes, that's a great idea. That way we'd have one choice that helps with diet and another that helps with exercise and sport.

Girl: Yes, because a lot of people already go to the country for the weekend. And a week's free membership of a sports club is better than just one day of sport at school.

Boy: OK, let's choose the cookery classes and membership of a gym.

Girl: Sure.

Examiner: Thank you.

Gateway to exams: Units 5–6

Listening p82

8 32

Presenter: On *Healthy Living* today we're looking at energy drinks, and here to tell us more about them is our expert, Norma Robins. Norma, energy drinks have become very popular in the last ten or so years, but there's a bit of a mystery surrounding them, what they contain, and whether they're any good for us. Can you help to clarify some of the mystery for us?

Norma: Well, I'll try, but one of the problems is actually deciding what an energy drink is. Personally, I would make a clear distinction between energy drinks and sports drinks. Sports drinks are drinks which help with hydration. They help to keep your liquid level up and they replace carbohydrates and minerals that you use up when you do sport and physical activity. We know that these drinks do help you to keep up your strength when you're physically active and they're safe. Top professional sports people use them, for example.

Presenter: And energy drinks?

Norma: Right, well, there are lots of different energy drinks and their contents are not always exactly the same. But what they do all generally have in common is caffeine, some have a bit more, some a bit less, but generally they all have a lot of caffeine.

Presenter: And is that good or bad?

Norma: First of all, that depends on your age. Until you're 16 there might be a danger, but certainly if you're under ten then a lot of caffeine is clearly harmful. Each energy drink is more or less the equivalent of a strong cup of coffee or two cola drinks. For young children, that's going to cause sleep problems and probably make them irritable and anxious. But for older people it can be a problem, too. And one major effect of caffeine we haven't talked about is that it dehydrates you. In that sense, energy drinks and sports drinks are almost opposites because energy drinks contain caffeine, but sports drinks don't.

Presenter: In fact, drinking energy drinks when you do exercise can be really dangerous, can't it?

Norma: Not *everybody* agrees, but I think they are dangerous, yes. An 18-year-old boy died when he drank four cans of an energy drink and then played basketball. Maybe it was a coincidence, but I think it's safer not to mix energy drinks and sport.

Presenter: And, of course, drinking four cans was probably excessive.

Norma: Yes, like everything, moderation is important. I think one can is probably not going to be too harmful, but because there's so much caffeine in them, drinking two or three cans in one day is, in my opinion, not a good idea.

Presenter: Of course, some young people drink energy drinks, not to do sport, but to keep awake and alert to study more. Do you think that works?

Norma: Well, caffeine in general can have that effect. I read a report which suggested that an energy drink could help drivers to maintain concentration on the road. But, of course, the effect is only short term. And remember, as I said before, caffeine can also make you irritable and anxious. The other thing to bear in mind is that most energy drinks don't just contain caffeine, they also contain a lot of sugar. Some have the equivalent of five teaspoons of sugar in one 250 millilitre can.

Presenter: What else do they contain?

Norma: Well, it depends on the drink, but most contain a substance called taurine.

Presenter: Taurine?

Norma: Yes, spelt T-A-U-R-I-N-E. It's an amino acid which occurs naturally in the body. Amino acids help to build protein. We think that they also help to take away harmful substances from the body, to eliminate waste. When you're tired or stressed, your body often has less taurine so some people drink energy drinks to replace it.

Presenter: And does it work?

Norma: Hmm. People are investigating this at the moment. To be honest, at the moment we just don't know enough to be certain. One thing that worries me, personally, is that substances like taurine exist in the body, but energy drinks contain much higher doses. Too much of something can be as bad as too little. And really if you have a healthy, balanced diet, you shouldn't need to take anything else.

Presenter: Norma, thank you.

Unit 7

Vocabulary p84

3 33

1 It's where you can watch and listen to music being played.

2 Correct

3 This word means that you hear the musicians at the actual moment that they're playing.

4 This is a group of people watching a performance, or a film.

5 This is another word for the different songs on a CD, for example.

6 This is a moment in a film where the events all happen in the same place.

7 This is what a musician does in a studio to make a CD.

8 This is a word for the music in a film or a CD of that music.

Listening p90

2 and 3 36

Presenter: The worlds of art, culture and entertainment would be nothing if it wasn't for the passion of the fans who follow them. Today on *Media Watch*, instead of looking at singers, writers or artists, we're looking at their fans, or rather, superfans, people who love something so much that they dedicate most of their time, thought, and often money, to their passion. Here to tell us about three unusual superfans is Andrew Lloyd. Andrew, what sort of things can turn normal people into superfans?

Andrew: It can be anything, really. For example, in the case of Ahmed bin Fahad, a police employee from Dubai, it's computer games.

Presenter: A lot of people love computer games.

Andrew: Yes, I know, but Ahmed is a fan of computer games made by one company.

Presenter: Oh? Which one?

Andrew: Nintendo. He's in the *Guinness Book of Records* for his massive collection of Nintendo games. Would you believe, he's got every edition of Super Mario ever made, as well as many other games made by Nintendo.

Presenter: How old is he? Has he been collecting a long time?

Andrew: He's 33 or 34. Actually, one thing I've discovered about superfans is that they usually start young. In the case of Ahmed, he started when he was just five, when his parents gave him a console as a gift.

Presenter: How expensive is it to collect old computer games?

Andrew: *Very* expensive. Just imagine. He has about 8,000 items in his collection. And don't forget that collectors often buy two copies of each game – one for playing and the other for their collection.

Presenter: You said superfans usually start young. Could you give us another example?

Andrew: There's a Harry Potter superfan who's spent £40,000 on her Harry Potter collection. Her name's Katie Aiani and she started when she was just 11.

Presenter: Oh, so Katie started her collection much later than Ahmed. But that's the usual age to start reading the Harry Potter books, I suppose.

Andrew: Yes, although the unusual thing is that at first she made fun of her sister for reading the first Harry Potter book. But then her sister forced her to read it. She finished the whole book in one night and then became a superfan.

Presenter: What's the most unusual object in her collection?

Andrew: Probably a personal letter that the author JK Rowling wrote to her. She actually tattooed some of the words from the letter onto her arm!

Presenter: That's the thing with superfans, isn't it? They're so passionate they sometimes do crazy things.

Andrew: Yes, like Sarah M.

Presenter: Sarah M? Who's she?

Andrew: They say that Sarah M is the world's most famous superfan. She takes photos with famous people – actors, singers … She has over 6,000 photos with different celebrities.

Presenter: That's a lot of famous people! Who does she appear with?

Andrew: Basically anybody and everybody who's famous. Lady Gaga, Harry Styles, Miley Cyrus … There are lots of famous people who know her really well by now.

Presenter: How old is she?

Andrew: Eighteen, I think. And she started young too, when she was 12.

Presenter: So, how does she do it? Usually stars don't like fans coming up and asking for photos.

Andrew: People always ask her that. And she tells them that you have to be polite and respectful. She always asks the celebrity first if they're happy for her to take the photo. If they say no, she immediately leaves them alone. She never tries to force them.

Presenter: That's good.

Andrew: Yes. Another thing she does is say positive things about famous people, you know, she doesn't spend her time criticising them. Also, she never tries to sell her photos. She just likes collecting them.

Presenter: But how does she know where the famous people are going to be?

Andrew: Well, she lives in Los Angeles, which helps. She knows the city and area well, so she knows where all the famous people stay and hang out. And she's also friends with lots of professional photographers. But she works hard. For example, if a British singer comes to LA she finds out what time the plane arrives, what time the concert is, which hotel they're going to stay at ... so it isn't just a question of luck. Another thing about her is that she finds out about lots of young actors and singers who aren't incredibly famous yet, and then gets photos before they become mega-famous.

Presenter: I suppose that's what you have to do if you want to be the world's biggest superfan.

Andrew: Yeah. The strange thing is that by appearing in so many photos with so many different people, she's become famous herself! Lots of teenagers ask *her* for photos and autographs!

Developing speaking p92

3 and 4 37

Boy: So what do you think about this article, then?

Girl: Personally, I'm totally convinced that most films don't give enough importance to women. For instance, right now in the cinema there are only one or two films that star women.

Boy: I agree. You only have to think of superhero movies or action films. There are always a lot more male heroes than female ones. But you can't deny that the situation is changing. Take *The Hunger Games*, for example.

Girl: Yes, that's true. But don't forget that *The Hunger Games* books were written by a woman. Maybe that's what the movie business needs, more female writers and directors.

Boy: I'm not sure that makes much difference. What about the case of Harry Potter? Those books were written by a female writer.

Girl: Yeah …

Boy: Anyway, maybe there are more male stars such as George Clooney and Brad Pitt because people just expect the star to be male, because it's always been that way.

Girl: But there's no doubt in my mind that female stars can be just as popular and successful as male stars. Look at Sandra Bullock in *Gravity* and Anne Hathaway in *Interstellar*.

Boy: I agree. I really do think it's time that the situation changed. I think they should use the test to evaluate a new film when they're writing the screenplay.

Girl: Yes. That way they could make sure that there are enough female characters and that there are more female stars.

Unit 8

Vocabulary p96

6 39

News reader 1:
Torrential rain has caused a new landslide in the north-east of Peru. At least 28 people have died, but 25 more are missing. Fifty people have received injuries. The landslide has also damaged 120 houses.

News reader 2:

The high temperatures and strong winds have made conditions particularly favourable for forest fires in Spain at the moment. Right now there are 25 separate fires all burning in different points of the country. In one of the fires, four firefighters have died, but so far there have been no civilian victims. However, thousands of people have been evacuated and there has been serious damage to many houses.

News reader 3:

A massive earthquake off the South Pacific island nation of Samoa has caused a terrible tsunami, forcing the population to evacuate the coast and head for higher ground. Waves have been as high as three metres. Luckily, there have been no victims thanks to the early warning, and no material damage. The inhabitants of Samoa are used to training for disasters of this type since the island is very low and in an area where earthquakes are common.

Listening p102

2 and 3 ▶ 41

Presenter: Next month is the anniversary of the terrible tsunami that hit Thailand in 2004. More than 280,000 people are believed to have died as a consequence of this natural disaster. But today we're looking at one famous survivor who has used her experience to help thousands of others. Her name is Petra Němcová, and here to tell us about her is Amy Sinclair. Amy, first of all, who exactly is Petra Němcová and how did she survive the tsunami?

Amy: Petra is a top model who was born in the Czech Republic. She was on holiday on a beautiful island in Thailand at the time of the tsunami. She was actually with a friend of hers, who was a fashion photographer. They were inside the hotel when the first wave hit them. The water carried them both away. Petra suffered terrible injuries but managed to hold onto a tree. She was found and rescued eight hours later. Her friend's body was only found three months later.

Presenter: Oh dear. That's awful.

Amy: Yes. But after suffering this tragic experience, Petra decided to do something positive to help areas affected by natural disasters. She'd always wanted to work with children, and it's believed that children are often the worst-affected victims of natural disasters. So she began a charity called the Happy Hearts Fund. The idea of this organisation is to rebuild schools in areas around the world affected by tsunamis, floods, earthquakes and so on.

Presenter: How many schools has she helped to rebuild?

Amy: In the first ten years after the tsunami they'd already rebuilt 107 schools! And in many different countries – Thailand, of course, but also Colombia, Peru, Haiti, the US, for example in New Orleans after Hurricane Katrina.

Presenter: Why is Petra so interested in education?

Amy: Well, one of the inspirations for the idea was the British girl Tilly Smith. Tilly was ten at the time of the tsunami. She was on a beach in Thailand with her family. It was reported that when she saw the water disappear from the beach she remembered a geography lesson where her teacher had explained that this is what happens just before a tsunami. She screamed at her family and other people on the beach to get off the beach and to get to high ground. It's thought that Tilly saved around a hundred lives, all thanks to the education she received at school! Petra's known to have been very impressed by this.

Presenter: Wow, amazing! So tell us about the schools that the Happy Hearts Fund helps to create?

Amy: The new school buildings are claimed to be strong enough to survive another disaster. And they also have computer labs with new software and hardware. The idea is to give the students what they need to be able to look to the future with hope after everything that's happened to them. At the moment over 12,000 children are believed to be benefitting from the project.

Presenter: How does she manage to find the money for the Happy Hearts Fund?

Amy: Good point. Each school is said to cost around £110,000. So Petra has to work incredibly hard to raise the money. She uses her status as a supermodel to get support from big companies that work in the world of beauty and fashion. And she has connections with famous people who help out and she organises events to raise money. And, of course, local politicians and governments help out, too. Of course, the fact that Petra is known to have survived a natural disaster means that people take extra interest in her charity work.

Presenter: People must be so grateful for her work.

Amy: Yes, particularly because her organisation has become a specialist in helping out two or three months after a disaster strikes. Usually, when there's a flood or earthquake, there are lots of people helping immediately after. But then they leave the area. And at this stage local governments aren't usually ready yet to rebuild essential buildings. So the help from the Happy Hearts Fund is vital.

Presenter: So Petra's gone from suffering a major impact in her life to making a major impact on other survivors' lives.

Amy: Yes. She has an amazing amount of energy. She never stops travelling ... Above all, she loves what she does and really believes in it. As she says, when you make a child happy, you make yourself happy, too.

Presenter: Amy, thanks for telling us all about Petra Němcová, an example to us all.

Developing speaking p104

2b ▶ 42

1 one-quarter equals 25 per cent
2 20 per cent equals one-fifth
3 ten per cent equals one-tenth
4 66.6 per cent equals two-thirds
5 one-half equals 50 per cent
6 80 per cent equals four-fifths

Gateway to exams: Units 7–8

Listening p109

3 ▶ 43

Girl 1: Hey, look at this website.

Girl 2: Let's see. What is it?

Girl 1: Well, I'm doing this project for school about natural disasters and I've got to do something about hurricanes. But I've just found this website for a company that helps you to escape them – hurricanes, that is.

Girl 2: How? By helicopter or what?

Girl 1: Yes, you'd expect it to be a helicopter, wouldn't you? But it says there that they 'evacuate you in style'. It's basically a private jet company.

Girl 2: That must be expensive.

Girl 1: It doesn't say, but, yeah, it must be really expensive. The only good thing is that it says you can take small pets on the jet for free. It says that not only can you hire a plane to get out of the hurricane zone, they can also reserve five-star hotels for you, including transfer to the hotel by limousine!

Girl 2: Are you sure? It sounds more like the holiday of a lifetime than a rescue mission.

Girl 1: Hmm. Well that's exactly what their slogan is: 'Turn a disaster into a vacation'.

Girl 2: So, let's see if I understand. You live in a place like Florida where they often have hurricanes. You know a hurricane is on its way. Couldn't you just book a normal flight to get away? That'd be much cheaper.

Girl 1: Yes, but that's what happened to the man who started this company. The storm was on its way and he started to look for standard commercial flights out of the area for him and his family and they were all fully booked. So they got into their car and started driving, but the roads were blocked with so many people trying to get away that they just gave up and headed back. That's when he got the idea.

Girl 2: But it's not really fair, is it? It's OK if you're rich, but otherwise ...

Girl 1: I suppose if those people have got enough money to take a private luxury flight it'll probably leave more free spaces on normal flights. Hmm. It doesn't actually give prices, but it does say you have to pay a membership fee each year and then you have to pay for the flight separately. But the director of the company says he's sure that lots of people are going to pay to join.

Girl 2: Yeah, I'm sure that some people have got enough money for that. I read recently that when there were those forest fires in California, while most houses were completely destroyed one or two were still in perfect condition. The owners had enough money to pay a company to cover their houses in a special spray that slowed down the effects of the fire, and then the company sent special mobile units to put the fire out round the house.

Girl 1: Look. Now I've found another hurricane company. They promise to supply you with generator-produced electricity and fuel after a storm hits. So that if you have a business, you can keep it running despite the storm. Or another one that helps you to prepare an evacuation by boarding up all the windows of your house, emptying the fridge and doing anything else you need.

Girl 2: So, is it offering a brilliant service or is it just making money from death and destruction?

Girl 1: I don't know, but it does prove one thing.

Girl 2: What?

Girl 1: You can find anything on the Internet these days if you look hard enough.

Unit 9

Vocabulary p110

4 44

OK, first make sure the computer is plugged in and then switch it on. On my computer you have to press a button on the right. You don't need to keep pressing, just press once. Wait for the computer to start up. Mine usually takes a couple of minutes. Then click on the bottom right corner of the screen, where you can see the time and date. Just click once. Click the right button, not the left. Then you can see a calendar and a clock. It shows you where to change the day and time and you click there. It's really easy. Once you've got the day, date and time you want, just press 'accept'. Or you can click in the right corner again and the window on the screen closes. And that's all you have to do!

Listening p116

2, 3 and 4 46

Radio presenter:
So all this week we've been asking you, the listeners, to ring in with your tips for solving those typical everyday problems that we suffer with technology. And, as always, we've chosen the four best tips. So have a listen and see what you think.

Speaker 1:
Well, this may sound really stupid, but once I fell into a river. I was wearing all my clothes and had a backpack and everything. Anyway, when I got out of the water, suddenly my smartphone started to go crazy! It started vibrating because of the water. But last week I found out that I'm not the only one to get my phone wet. I read that 31% of people in Britain have damaged their smartphone because of water or other liquids! But there *is* something you can do when your phone gets wet. Take out the battery first. The problem is that there could be a short circuit if the battery stays in the mobile. Don't press any keys because that will just help the water to get right inside the phone. Then put the mobile phone in a bowl of dry rice, you know, straight from the packet. What happens is that the rice draws all of the water out of the device. You should leave the phone for between 24 and 48 hours. A simple trick, and cheap. Much cheaper than buying a new phone!

Speaker 2:
I like to follow tech blogs because they often have practical tips. I remember discovering a great tip a while ago on one of them. It might sound a bit strange, but believe me, it works. If you've got wi-fi in your house but the signal from the router isn't very strong, there's something you can do to make the signal much stronger. All you do is cover a piece of cardboard with silver foil, you know, the aluminium foil that you use to cover sandwiches and stuff.

Then make it into the shape of a dish. Put the dish next to your router and remember to point it in the direction that you want the signal to go in. Our router at home isn't very good, but this dish has made it much easier to pick up a good signal.

Speaker 3:
I remember staying at a friend's house once. I'd forgotten to bring a charger for my mobile with me, and my friend had a different charger. The battery was running out and I really wanted to be able to use my mobile on the journey back home, so that I could call my parents. I didn't know what to do. But then my friend gave me this great tip for when you really need a few more hours of life from your mobile battery. First of all, take the mobile out of your pocket. Body heat makes the chemical reactions in the battery go faster, so it uses it up more quickly. What you do then is take the battery out of the phone and put it in the fridge. It sounds unusual, but it's logical. The colder the battery is, the slower it'll use up all its energy.

Speaker 4:
I'm sure you're like me and you all like having a juice or coffee or something while you're using a laptop. But have you ever stopped to think how dangerous it can be? Suddenly your hand slips or your cat knocks over your glass and the drink goes all over the keyboard. What should you do in that situation? Well, the first thing to do is to stop using the laptop, obviously. Unplug it and take the battery out. At the very least, switch the laptop off. Then you should turn the laptop upside down, with the screen down, and leave it in that position. Don't forget to put a towel under it. Anyway, leave the laptop like that for 48 hours or more. It's essential that the laptop is upside down. It helps to get as much liquid out as possible. After a day or two, it should be dry. Then you'll probably need to take it somewhere where a professional can check how bad the damage is. But by switching everything off quickly and putting the laptop upside down you may have saved it!

Radio presenter:
So there you have it, four of the best tech tips. Tune in again next week for more Top Tips!

Developing speaking p118

3 47

Man: Well, it sounds quite sensible to me, that students should be allowed to take smartphones into class. They're a part of daily life now, after all. We take them everywhere. Why shouldn't kids take them into the classroom?

Woman: I'm not sure. I mean, yes, they're a part of daily life, but so are video games and I don't see why students should be playing computer games in class time. They can do that at the weekend.

Man: But you can learn to become an autonomous learner with a smartphone.

Woman: I'm not sure what you mean by that.

Man: What I mean is that you can learn how to find out information by yourself. You don't have to depend on the teacher to explain it to you. For example, you could connect to the Internet and use your phone as a dictionary in English lessons. Or you could connect to a map if you're studying geography. Do you see what I mean?

Woman: Mmm, yes. But take the example of the student using his phone to take a photo instead of copying the information down. I think that's just being lazy. In the end, students will forget how to write.

Man: Well, I think that's OK, if that's what they would do outside the classroom ...

Woman: Are you saying that students don't need to learn to write?

Man: No, that's not what I meant. I just think that a smartphone today is like a pen. It's an instrument that you can use for learning.

Woman: Yes, but the problem is that some students will do things with their phone that they shouldn't, like take photos or video teachers, or other students. Or they may use them to cheat in exams.

Man: In other words, you wouldn't trust the students to use their phones responsibly.

Woman: I'd trust most students, but, you know what it's like. There's always somebody who does something they shouldn't.

Unit 10

Vocabulary p122

6 49

Speaker 1:
Tomorrow is Friday the 13th and computer experts are warning people to be extra careful about protecting their PCs as from midnight. A particularly dangerous worm has already infected millions of computers worldwide, but experts think that the hackers will try to create more damage on Friday the 13th. The worm, called Conficker G, gets into your computer when you are online or via a USB connection. The aim of the worm is a mystery, but it is thought that it may be asked to take information about credit cards.

Speaker 2:
John Kitson is in the news again today, but this time his fans won't be so happy. At the weekend Kitson got two goals and helped his team to win the semifinal of the Carlton Cup. But today the controversial striker says that that is going to be his last match for current team Melchester United. The reason for this sudden decision seems to be a dramatic argument which the player had in training with Melchester manager Roy Hutchinson. Hutchinson refused to make any comment about the incident, or about Kitson's threat.

Speaker 3:
A 52-year-old man was arrested yesterday following police investigations into the construction industry. The man arrested is thought to have offered money to officials in exchange for permission to build a shopping centre on park land near the city centre. In the last few months, the police have received information about various illegal operations in the building sector where officials have given permission to build houses and flats in protected areas after receiving large quantities of money from anonymous sources.

Listening p128

2 and 3 51

Reporter 1: Hi. We're from *West Country News*. I wonder if you could tell us exactly what happened. You were on a train in Cornwall, weren't you?

Boy: Yes, I was. And there was this man opposite me. He was just sitting here reading a book most of the time. But then he opened his bag and all these pencils fell out.

Reporter 1: Were they just normal pencils?

Boy: Yeah, but I saw that he also had spray paints in his bag. The ones that graffiti artists use. Anyway, I just picked the pencils up for him and gave them back to him.

Reporter 2: I'd like to ask you what the man looked like.

Boy: Erm, he had long, fair hair and blue eyes. He wasn't young. I'd say he was in his 40s. His clothes certainly weren't very smart. I specially remember that his jacket was small and didn't go over his arms. And he had paint on his jeans. Oh, and he had a blue baseball cap that looked really old and dirty, too.

Reporter 1: He told you that his name was Arthur Street, didn't he?

Boy: That's right. He actually asked me if I knew who Arthur Street was.

Reporter 2: But you'd never heard that name before, had you? You didn't know that Arthur Street is the name that the famous artist Bootsy sometimes uses. In fact, you'd never heard of Bootsy either, had you? I *am* right in saying that, aren't I?

Boy: It was only when I got home that I found out. I looked him up on the Internet.

Reporter 2: I wonder what your reaction was when you found out how famous Bootsy is!

Boy: It was quite a shock actually, especially thinking about what he'd given me.

Reporter 1: Could you tell us exactly what that was?

Boy: Yeah, it was a picture of a superhero with a paintbrush in his hand. I think it's one of his most famous pictures, but I don't know where the original is.

Reporter 2: He signed the print, didn't he?

Boy: Yeah. He signed it and put the date. And then he added some flowers in different colours at the top. He actually said to me 'This will be worth about £20,000.' I didn't really believe that at first, which is why I looked him up on the Internet when I got home.

Reporter 1: Have you got any idea why he gave you the picture?

Boy: Just because I helped him to pick up his pencils, I think.

Reporter 2: Nobody is sure who Bootsy really is, are they? He keeps his real identity a mystery. Do you believe that it really was him, and that the picture is authentic?

Boy: I've just been reading different stories and theories about Bootsy – that he's a construction worker or that he was a rich student from Oxford. Another story I heard is that even his parents don't know what he does. They just think he's a successful decorator. There's even a story that Bootsy isn't one person, it's a group of artists who work together. Who knows? Maybe that's true. The man I met was definitely an artist – maybe he is one of a team of artists. But what we've decided to do now is ... my dad is going to take the picture and get some experts to examine it, and see what they say.

Reporter 1: Let's imagine that the experts say it really is a work by Bootsy. Do you know what you'd do? Would you sell it or keep it?

Boy: I suppose the value would go up in the future. But I wouldn't mind selling it. I mean, I think maybe he gave it to me so that I could get some money for it, you know, as a way of saying thank you.

Reporter 2: If you did sell it, can I ask what you'd do with the money?

Boy: That's easy. I'd probably spend about a thousand pounds and get a new laptop. And then I'd save the rest, I reckon.

Reporter 2: And if it isn't authentic? I *have* just heard that a spokesperson for Bootsy says that it wasn't him on the train. But, of course, everything Bootsy does seems mysterious so maybe he's saying it wasn't him just to confuse us all.

Boy: I don't know. Anyway, I didn't help the man on the train because I wanted something or expected a reward, so it wouldn't really change anything.

Reporter 1: Well, personally, I hope it is authentic and that you get the money. It's great to see somebody getting an immediate reward for a simple act of kindness. That isn't the sort of thing that happens every day, is it?

Boy: No, I s'pose not.

Grammar in context p129

9, 10b and 10c 52

1 Everybody likes the summer, don't they?
2 I'm right, aren't I?
3 We should use question tags, shouldn't we?
4 The news will be on soon, won't it?
5 We're going to be on TV one day, aren't we?
6 You read the news yesterday, didn't you?
7 She never comes late, does she?
8 We've got homework tonight, haven't we?

Developing speaking p130

3 and 4 54

I'd like to begin by saying that I agree with the statement. Let me explain why.

Firstly, when celebrities start out, they desperately want to be famous so that people love them and go to see their films or buy their records. They often do shocking things so that the whole world talks about them. However, when they become rich and famous, when they have their mansions and their sports cars, suddenly they don't want attention from the press.

There's no denying that it must be very annoying to have paparazzi following you all day long. But let's not forget that at the start of many celebrities' careers, it's the celebrity who is begging the press to come and take photos of them. You can't argue with the fact that a famous person's life isn't always fun because of the pressure from newspapers and magazines looking for stories. Having said that, celebrities are luckier than most people because they make lots of money and can live like kings.

To sum up, in my opinion, being followed by photographers when you go out is a small price to pay for all the fame and money that most celebrities receive.

Gateway to exams: Units 9–10

Listening p135

6 55

Reporter 1:

Hi. I'm from the *Enquirer*. I'd like to ask you why you were dressed up as Batman at the time. That isn't something that you do regularly, is it?

Shop owner:

No, no, it isn't. You see, last Saturday was International Free Comic Day. We've been celebrating it at our comic store for a few years now. We have one or two free comics for everybody who buys something at the

store. And just to make it more of a special event, the guys who work at the store, we dress up. Some of us are superheroes, some are villains. And some of the people who regularly come and buy in our shop were dressed up, too. There was a group of friends all dressed up as vampires and stuff.

Reporter 2:

Have you any idea how many people were in the shop at the time?

Shop owner:

Phew. Impossible to say because it was so busy. It's usually one of our busiest days. There were at least a hundred people, which is a lot for us because it's just a small shop.

Reporter 3:

You saw the thief on a camera, didn't you?

Shop owner:

That's right. I'd been watching him for a while. It was just the way he moved, and he had a bag with him that he was holding in a strange position. From time to time he was looking round. And he was in a section of the shop where we have some of our most expensive comics.

Reporter 3:

Was he young?

Shop owner:

No, he wasn't, he wasn't a teenager or anything, he was middle-aged, 30-something I would say. That wasn't unusual, though, we get people of all ages and types, it's not just young people who are into comics.

Reporter 4:

You'd never seen this guy before, had you?

Shop owner:

No, no I hadn't. We often get a lot of new people coming in on a day like that.

Reporter 1:

I wonder if you could tell us what exactly he was trying to steal.

Shop owner:

Sure. I suppose it's quite ironic because he was actually trying to take three or four Batman comics. They were collector's items, each one was worth between $150 and $200. So, you know, I wasn't just going to let him go. I went down to get a closer look at him, and I actually saw him put them into his bag.

Reporter 2:

Do you know if he was on his own?

Shop owner:

Yeah. I'd been watching for a while and I hadn't seen anyone else with him.

Reporter 1:

So, could you tell us how you stopped the man?

Shop owner:

Well, you know, now that I think back it was kind of funny, but not really at the time. I had my Batman costume on for the day. He's my favourite character. So I had the mask and cape and everything, and I just came behind him and said, 'Can I see what's inside your bag, please?' When

the guy turned round his eyes nearly popped out! He couldn't believe what he was seeing. But after that he became a bit aggressive. I mean, I know I was meant to be Batman, but I hate violence! Anyway, in the end he tried to push me away and get out of the store. I shouted out to people who were near the door not to let him pass. The thing is I was really worried because at first they didn't take me seriously because they thought we were acting, you know, that it was something we'd prepared as part of the celebrations. But I shouted again and told somebody to call the police. Then they started to believe me and stepped in his way. It was quite funny because there was a Spider-Man there, a Wonder Woman, a whole bunch of superheroes who just stood there.

Reporter 1:

And what did the shoplifter do then?

Shop owner:

I think he thought there were just too many superheroes to take on at the same time! He tried to say he was innocent, that it had been a mistake, but by that time the police were on their way.

Reporter 3:

I wonder what their reaction was when they came and saw what was going on.

Shop owner:

Oh, it took a while to convince them that it was serious and that it wasn't just some kind of publicity stunt. Afterwards, they were cool and they all wanted a photo with me. They thought it was hysterical to catch a thief and take him back to the police station thanks to the work of Batman. Oh, and we gave them a free comic each, too.

Workbook answer key

Unit 1

Vocabulary p4

1

Studying at university: assignment (n), coursework (n), degree (n), lecture (n/v), master's (n), notes (n), tutorial (n)

Life at university: become independent (v), extracurricular activity (n), hall of residence (n), student loan (n)

People: tutor (n), undergraduate (n)

Exams/Assessment: continuous assessment (n), mark (n/v), resit (v)

2

1 independent   2 continuous
3 assignments   4 tutorial   5 activity
6 residence

3

1 c   2 b   3 b   4 c   5 a   6 b   7 c

VOCABULARY EXTENSION p4

4

1 c   2 d   3 f   4 a   5 e   6 b

Reading p5

1

1 the course content and structure ✓
2 the cost of the fees ✓
3 opportunities to get work experience ✓
4 extracurricular activities ✓

2

2 D   3 A   4 B   5 D   6 E   7 A   8 E
9 C

3

1 ✓   2 ✓   4 ✓   5 ✓

4

1 drop out   2 close-knit   3 prestigious
4 placement   5 vocational

Grammar in context p6

1

a simple   b continuous   c simple
d simple   e continuous

2

1 is, complaining (e)   2 have (a)
3 understand (d)   4 'm doing (b)
5 start (c)

3

The library closes at 5.25 pm during university holidays.

They are constructing a new exhibition area.

They are extending the basement storage area.

The library opens 24 hours in term-time. The library opens at 9 am during university holidays.

Dr Maria Gurther and Frederick Johnson run the library.

4

1 applied   2 finished   3 discovered
4 seen   5 been working

5

a 2   b 4   c 1   d 5   e 3

6

a has, started   b has been studying
c has decided   d have told   e has been following   f has been going   g has been thinking

GRAMMAR CHALLENGE p6

7

1 've been living here for   2 is forever giving us   3 haven't finished my research yet   4 are always talking about   5 've already read   6 's been revising since

Developing vocabulary and listening p7

1

do	make
an assignment	an appointment
an exam	breakfast
homework	a decision
the housework	an excuse
the shopping	friends
someone a favour	a mistake
sport	a noise
well	a promise
	a suggestion

2

2 Nathan made a mistake.   3 Juliet did the housework.   4 Harry did a Spanish course.   5 Kate did well.   6 Lara made an excuse.   7 Ben did an assignment.

3

3 ✓   4 ✓

4

1 a   2 b   3 c   4 c   5 b   6 c

VOCABULARY EXTENSION p7

5

1 d   2 f   3 a   4 e   5 c   6 b

Grammar in context p8

1

1 Sorting out   2 to set up   3 Checking
4 to keep   5 walking   6 to cook
7 sharing   8 to take, forgetting   9 to do

2

a 6, 8, 9   b 2   c 4   d 7, 8   e 1, 3, 5

3

2 e   3 d   4 b   5 a

4

1 to meet   2 to do   3 cooking   4 to hand   5 walking   6 to go   7 to turn
8 borrowing

GRAMMAR CHALLENGE p8

5

1 ~~for keep fit~~ to keep fit   2 ~~doing~~ to do   3 ~~buy~~ buying   4 ~~I've been forgetting~~ I've forgotten   5 ~~text~~ to text   6 ~~I've done~~ I've been doing   7 ~~is finishing~~ finishes   8 ~~to become~~ becoming

Developing speaking p9

1

2 What is your favourite part of the day?   3 Is it easy to study where you live?   4 Do you prefer to be inside or outside [outside or inside]?   5 What would you like to do next summer?

2

1 F   2 T   3 F   4 T   5 F

3

1 watch   2 going   3 not stay
4 have   5 not staying   6 going out
7 not to go   8 to go

4

1 ~~going~~ go   2 ~~than~~ to   3 ~~I rather~~ I'd rather   4 ~~don't~~ not to   5 ~~to be~~ than [be]   6 ~~I prefer have~~ I'd prefer to have

Developing writing p10

1

2 formal   3 informal   4 informal
5 formal   6 informal   7 formal
8 formal   9 informal

2

What have you and your family been doing recently?

I'm also considering coming to study in your country. What do you think the advantages are for me doing that?

Maybe you could come and study here, or we could both go and study in Australia together! What would you prefer?

What kind of preparation for leaving school do you get?

Revision: Unit 1

Grammar p11

1
1 always make **2** are getting on
3 always **4** have **5** 'm revising
6 always pays

2
1 've walked **2** 's been waiting
3 Have, finished **4** 've already
seen **5** has been looking, still hasn't
found

3
1 sailing **2** to feed **3** talking **4** to
study **5** cycling

4
a 'm writing **b** replying **c** 've been
d go **e** have **f** 've handed
g 'm having **h** made **i** Living
j to move **k** 've been looking **l** had

Vocabulary p11

1
1 assessment **2** tutor **3** undergraduate
4 facilities **5** assignment **6** tutorial

2
1 degree **2** notes **3** coursework
4 grade, mark **5** resit **6** graduate
7 master's **8** extracurricular

3
1 make **2** do **3** make **4** make
5 do **6** do **7** make **8** do

Unit 2

Vocabulary p12

1
Suggested answers
Farmers: 1, 4, 6, 7, 11
Nurses: 1, 2, 4, 5, 8, 12
PAs: 3, 4, 5, 8, 10, 12
Firefighters: 1, 2, 4, 6, 8, 9, 11

2
1 negative **2** positive **3** negative
4 positive

3
a responsible **b** deal with **c** stressful
d get a promotion **e** experience
f training
Restaurant manager

4
2 e **3** b **4** a **5** d

VOCABULARY EXTENSION p12

5
1 job-share **2** perks **3** high-
powered **4** sick leave **5** deadlines

Reading p13

1
c

2
Jack: sheep shearing, Positive
Sheena: skyscraper window cleaner,
Positive

3
1 T **2** F **3** T **4** NM **5** F **6** T
7 NM **8** T

4
1 ✓ **2** ✓ **3** ✗ **4** ✓ **5** ✗

5
1 buckets **2** told off **3** scorching
4 backbreaking **5** stick with

Grammar in context p14

1
1 e **2** c **3** a **4** b **5** d

2
1 were waiting **2** was shining **3** went
4 got **5** was surfing **6** didn't have

3
a studied **b** was sitting **c** happened
d stopped **e** was doing **f** applied
g tried **h** cried **i** was travelling

4
4 ✓

5
a 3 **b** 2, 4 **c** 2, 4 **d** 1

6
1 We used to live in a small town.
2 I used to have a part-time job in a shop.
3 I'd go to work every Saturday. **4** I'd
start at nine in the morning. **5** I didn't
use to work late. **6** I didn't use to like my
job so I decided to leave.

GRAMMAR CHALLENGE p14

7
1 ~~didn't had~~ didn't have **2** ~~tryed~~
tried **3** ~~was read~~ was reading **4** ~~like
a fisherman~~ as a fisherman **5** ~~applied
at~~ applied for **6** ~~was travelled~~
travelled **7** ~~got up~~ get up **8** ~~works~~
worked **9** ~~didn't liked~~ didn't like **10** ~~is
work~~ is working **11** ~~didn't used~~ didn't
use **12** ~~is better than work~~ is better than
working

Developing vocabulary and listening p15

1
2 b **3** a **4** e **5** h **6** d **7** f **8** g

2
1 c **2** f **3** a **4** b **5** e

3
1 D **2** E **3** B **4** F **5** A

4
2 h **3** c **4** a **5** f **6** g **7** e **8** b

5
a set up **b** Draw up **c** Send out
d Stick to **e** drag on **f** Write down
g carry out **h** follow up

Grammar in context p16

1
1 C **2** C **3** S **4** both **5** S

2
1 been **2** been helping **3** been
travelling **4** made **5** been **6** been
learning

3
2 I was hungry because I hadn't eaten.
3 She was exhausted because she'd been
working since 5 am. **4** They were late
because they'd missed the bus. **5** My
teacher was annoyed because I hadn't
done my homework. **6** Everything was
white because it'd been snowing for
days. **7** I didn't recognise Sam because I
hadn't seen him for ages.

4
a went **b** 'd, finished **c** 'd been
studying **d** 'd, visited **e** 'd gone **f** 'd
stayed up **g** knocked **h** didn't wake up
i 'd been trying **j** drove **k** 'd forgotten
l had

GRAMMAR CHALLENGE p16

5
1 After he'd left, I did my
homework. **2** While I was working
in Argentina, I made some good
friends. **3** When I saw the advert, I
immediately decided to apply. **4** After
I'd earned some money, we went
travelling. **5** While I was staying in
Romania, I visited lots of interesting
places. **6** After we'd waited/'d been
waiting for two hours, the bus eventually
arrived.

Developing speaking p17

1

Asking for opinions	Agreeing	Disagreeing
What about you? What do you think?	That's a good idea. Yes, you're right.	I see what you mean, but … I suppose so, but …

2

2 relaxing   **3** learning a language
4 volunteering   **5** working

3

volunteering

4

What do you think about ...? ✓ What
about ...? ✓ Do you agree? ✓ Yes, I agree.
✓ Yes, you're right. ✓ That's a good idea. ✓
I think you're right. ✓ Maybe, but ... ✓
I suppose so, but ... ✓ I agree up to a
point. ✓

5

a you think   **b** up to a   **c** see what
d do you think   **e** suppose   **f** agree with

Revision: Units 1–2

Grammar p19

1

1 used to   **2** had already left   **3** were
you doing   **4** had forgotten   **5** would go

2

1 had been to   **2** used to be   **3** hadn't
been feeling   **4** didn't use to do
5 hadn't revised

3

1 b   **2** c   **3** c   **4** b   **5** a   **6** c

Vocabulary p19

1

1 outdoors   **2** nine to five   **3** employee
4 full-time   **5** well paid

2

1 is responsible for   **2** self-employed
3 overtime   **4** made redundant
5 sacked   **6** qualifications   **7** for

3

1 fill in   **2** turn down   **3** get
ahead   **4** take over   **5** keep at

4

1 skilled   **2** experience   **3** a lecture
4 a mistake   **5** note   **6** a graduate
7 an assignment

Gateway to exams: Units 1–2

Reading p20

1

all the points given, plus: to get a better
job with a higher salary, the course
structure is different, to enjoy the
extracurricular activities, because the
facilities are good

2

1 C   **2** C   **3** B   **4** A   **5** A   **6** B   **7** A
8 B

Use of English p20

3

1 used to do   **2** would phone   **3** had
been living   **4** didn't use to enjoy   **5** are
always having

Listening p21

4

1 E   **2** C   **3** F   **4** A   **5** B

COMMON MISTAKES p21

6

1 I'm considering going to university
next year.   **2** I'd like to study marketing,
but it depends on my grades.   **3** My
parents didn't use to learn English at
school.   **4** Daniel has been studying
in France for six months.   **5** I'd like
to find a well-paid job when I finish
my degree.   **6** Sara has written three
assignments so far this term.   **7** My
dad used to live at home when he
was a student.   **8** I'm interested in
finding work/a job in a bank or in an
office.   **9** When I went to London, my
friends had already been living there
for a year.   **10** It's difficult to live in
another country if you don't speak the
language.   **11** I often make mistakes
when I do my English homework.   **12** My
dad was made redundant after working in
the company for 20 years.

Unit 3

Vocabulary p22

1

1 platform   **2** tube   **3** motorway
4 luggage   **5** crew   **6** passenger
7 astronaut   **8** train   **9** traffic jam
10 vehicle   **11** rocket   **12** flight
Shaded words: future travel

2

	Car	Bus	Train	Plane	Spacecraft
get off		✓	✓	✓	
get into	✓				✓
get out of	✓				✓
board		✓	✓	✓	✓
take off				✓	✓
land				✓	✓

3

1 journey   **2** voyage   **3** trip   **4** travel

VOCABULARY EXTENSION p22

4

1 drop, off   **2** set off   **3** pick, up
4 gets in   **5** stop off   **6** see, off
7 get away   **8** get stuck

Reading p23

1

1 the Personal Rapid Transit system
2 private transport   **3** No, probably not.

2

1 B   **2** C   **3** G   **4** F   **5** A   **6** D

3

1 ✓   **4** ✓   **5** ✓

4

1 give up on   **2** cross   **3** go ahead
4 widespread

5

1 go ahead   **2** cross   **3** widespread
4 gave up on

Grammar in context p24

1

2 c   **3** a   **4** e   **5** b

2

2 P   **3** I   **4** I   **5** I

3

1 goes   **2** is playing   **3** 'm meeting
4 starts

4

1 ✓   **5** ✓   **6** ✓

5

2 What are you going to do/are you doing
next weekend?
3 Our flight leaves at 9.30 tomorrow
morning.
4 I'm going to study law at Bristol
University next year.

6

1 'm/am going to
2 won't/will not
3 leaves
4 'm/am playing

GRAMMAR CHALLENGE p24

7

1 F I going I'm going   **2** M will meet 'm
meeting   **3** F as soon as you will gets
home as soon as you get home   **4** S
begining beginning   **5** M grows will
grow   **6** S wan't won't   **7** F going be
going to be   **8** M is going to leave leaves

Developing vocabulary and listening p25

1

Prefix	Words
co-	operate, present, star, write
dis-	appeared
inter-	national
mis-	calculate, paid, understood, write
over-	booked, estimate, paid, populated, power, write
post-	graduate
re-	appeared, calculate, consider, paid, populated, title, write
sub-	standard, zero
super-	power, star
under-	estimate, graduate, paid, populated, write

2

2 That was irresponsible! 3 That's unbelievable! 4 That's unusual! 5 That's inconvenient! 6 That's impossible!

3

1 ✓ 3 ✓ 4 ✓ 6 ✓

4

1 low 2 lunar hotels 3 before 4 be completely 5 long-distance 6 virtual 7 rooms in houses

VOCABULARY EXTENSION p25

5

Suggested answers

2 unsure – I'm unsure about what I want to do in the future. 3 impatient – Don't be impatient. Dinner will be ready soon. 4 misbehave – Children often misbehave because they want attention. 5 incapable – My four-year-old nephew is incapable of sitting still for very long. 6 misinformed – I'm afraid you've been misinformed. The museum is closed today. 7 illegal – It's illegal to ride a motorbike without a helmet. 8 disobey – You should never disobey the law.

Grammar in context p26

1

will have done – future perfect simple – activities/states that will be finished before a particular point in the future

will be doing – future continuous – activities in progress at a particular point in the future

will have been doing – future perfect continuous – how long an activity has been in progress before a particular point in the future

2

1 at home 2 during 23rd March 3 complete five years as the team coach

3

1 Photo c a will have started school b will be studying lots of different school subjects
2 Photo e a will still be working in a shop b will have become a shop manager
3 Photo a a will have qualified as a chef b will have been managing a restaurant for about two years
4 Photo d a will have won her first big race b will be training for the next Olympics
5 Photo b a will have retired b will have been/will be travelling around the world for six months

GRAMMAR CHALLENGE p26

4

1 My brother is one of those people who will knows ... 2 For example, he's going to be go to university ... 3 In five years' time, he'll have been finished his course ... 4 In ten years' time he'll already be getting married ... 5 As soon as they will have enough money, ... 6 I know that when he retires, he will have been worked ... 7 I will have no idea ... 8 where I'll be doing in five years' time. 9 I hope I'll have doing a job .... 10 that I will enjoy ...

Developing speaking p27

1

First part: Compare the photographs
Second part: say what you think about the ways of travelling on holiday

2

Similarities	Differences
people travelling on holiday	1: travelling by plane, 2: travelling by bicycle
they have luggage with them	1: at an airport, 2: in the countryside
	1: they have big backpacks, 2: she has a small backpack

3

Yes

4

1 Both photographs show 2 In the first photograph 3 whereas in the second photograph 4 In both pictures 5 but one big difference between the photos 6 while 7 Another important difference is that 8 Compared with

Revision: Units 1–3

Grammar p29

1

1 am meeting 2 will rain 3 leaves 4 going to love 5 get

2

1 'll have finished 2 'll have been living 3 'll be sleeping 4 'll have been travelling

3

1 c 2 b 3 a 4 c

4

1 is having a party 2 've been doing yoga for 3 Greg had gone 4 will have started 5 had been working

Vocabulary p29

1

1 unlikely 2 irresponsible 3 unsuccessful 4 incomplete 5 underestimated

2

Across: 2 facilities 6 trip 8 degree 10 overtime 11 promotion
Down: 1 voyage 3 lecture 4 set up 5 fired 7 flexitime 9 board

Unit 4

Vocabulary p30

1

Suggested answers

	Must be	Must not be
a surgeon	patient	nervous
a teacher	assertive	bossy
a pilot	determined	insecure
a tour guide	polite	quiet, reserved
a diplomat	tactful	tactless
a journalist	assertive	narrow-minded
a security guard	determined	insecure

2

1 silly 2 brusque 3 modest 4 easygoing 5 tidy

3

2 big-headed 3 good-natured 4 bad-tempered 5 self-confident 6 hard-working

1 b 2 e 3 d 4 a 5 c 6 f

VOCABULARY EXTENSION p30

4

Suggested answers

self-reliant, self-centred, self-made good-hearted, good-humoured

hard-headed, hard-hearted
well-meaning, well-behaved, well-mannered, well-adjusted, well-spoken, well-read

Reading p31

1

c

2

1 b **2** c **3** a **4** b **5** a

3

1 F **2** O **3** F **4** O **5** O

4

1 smash **2** sparked **3** glow
4 from scratch **5** stunned

5

1 from scratch **2** smashed **3** glow
4 sparked **5** stunned

Grammar in context p32

1

2 *the* + adjective + *-est* **3** *more*
+ adjective + *than* **4** *the most* +
adjective **5** *more* + adverb + *than*
6 *the most* + adverb **7** *late, long, soon,
near, hard, early* **8** irregular adverbs (e.g.
good, bad)

2

2 the best **3** the most dramatically
4 more often **5** more carelessly
than **6** earlier than **7** more widely than
8 more energetically than **9** calmer,
better

3

4 Jane doesn't go jogging as often in the
winter as in the summer. **5** Jared doesn't
usually ride his bike as carelessly as he did
when he crashed it. **6** Peter didn't expect
to finish as early as he did. **8** Jarvis
doesn't play the piano as energetically as
Nina.

4

1 The sooner the better! **2** Better
late than never! **3** Better safe than
sorry! **4** This is going from bad to worse!

GRAMMAR CHALLENGE p32

5

3 Feliks solved the puzzle more quickly
than Erik. **4** Feliks was the fastest
contestant. **5** Yu solved the puzzle the
most slowly. **6** Erik was slower than
Feliks.

Developing vocabulary and listening p33

1

Adjectives	Nouns: things/ subjects/ ideas	Nouns: people
creative	creation	creator
electrical	electricity	electrician
political	politics	politician
scientific	science	scientist
Verbs		
direct	direction	director
employ	employment	employer, employee
invent	invention	inventor
compete	competition	competitor
educate	education	educator
profess	profession	professor, professional
operate	operation	operator
investigate	investigation	investigator
perform	performance	performer

2

1 -ness **2** -ist **3** -ment **4** -ence

3

1 b **2** c

4

1 F **2** NM **3** T **4** NM **5** NM **6** T
7 T **8** F

VOCABULARY EXTENSION p33

5

2 relationship = the way in which two
or more people or things are connected
to each other **3** friendship = a
relationship between two people who
are friends **4** motherhood = the state
of being a mother **5** neighbourhood
= a particular area of a city or
town **6** partnership = the position of
being one of two or more people who own
a company as partners **7** membership
= the fact of being a member of a club,
organisation or group **8** brotherhood =
a close group of people, usually used for
men

Grammar in context p34

1

2 a/an **3** the **4** 0 **5** the **6** the

2

a a **b** the **c** a **d** the **e** the **f** the
g 0 **h** 0 **i** 0 **j** the **k** a **l** the

3

1 e **2** d **3** f **4** b **5** c **6** a

4

1 too **2** enough **3** so **4** watch
5 that **6** such **7** so

GRAMMAR CHALLENGE p34

5

1 too **2** the **3** enough **4** so **5** an
6 0 **7** such **8** a

Developing speaking p35

2

1 disagree **2** not all children can be
geniuses; genius is something you are born
with; parents put pressure on children to be
exceptional

3

1 a **2** b **3** a **4** a **5** b **6** b **7** a

Revision: Units 1–4

Grammar p37

1

1 worst **2** as fast **3** most successful
4 more accurately **5** farther/further

2

1 such **2** so **3** enough **4** too

3

1 0 **2** a **3** the **4** 0, an

4

1 is too expensive (for me) **2** so
tired last night that **3** more and more
difficult **4** such a boring film that **5** not
tall enough

5

1 b **2** b **3** b **4** a **5** b **6** b

Vocabulary p37

1

1 self-confident **2** outgoing **3** broad-minded **4** bad-tempered **5** modest
6 tactful

2

a performer **b** confidence **c** scientist
d education **e** happiness

3

1 appearance **2** employment
3 unexpected **4** politician
5 rewrite

Gateway to exams: Units 3–4

Reading p38

1

1 stronger **2** flower **3** twelve **4** 11, 5

2

2 a **3** e **4** b **5** d

3

1 C **2** G **3** D **4** H **5** A **6** F **7** E
8 B

Use of English p39

4

a researchers **b** development
c scientists **d** performance
e difference **f** suggestion
g encouragement

Listening p39

5

1 unicycle **2** two and a half years
3 18,000 **4** 25 **5** Bag

6

1 F **2** NM **3** F **4** T **5** F

COMMON MISTAKES p39

8

1 By this time next year, he'll have finished / he'll be finishing his trip around the world. **2** Most people aren't brave enough to travel around the world alone. **3** I'm going to have a bath as soon as I get home. **4** This time next month, we'll be relaxing because we'll have finished all our exams. **5** Emily works harder than anyone else in class. **6** Our flight leaves at nine o'clock tomorrow morning. **7** The journey by train was too expensive so we decided to go by bus.

Unit 5

Vocabulary p40

1

Across: 2 change **3** value **5** bargain
8 interest **10** charges **12** debt
13 refund
Down: 1 waste **4** loan **6** receipt
7 account **9** sale **11** fee

2

1 a purse, a wallet, a pocket **2** No, it isn't. **3** an ATM/cashpoint **4** it's safer, you could earn interest **5** the bank **6** the date and time when a purchase was made, the item purchased, the price, the name and location of the shop (also the method of payment) **7** so people buy more things, to move excess stock **8** £3.15

3

a 3 **b** 7 **d** 4 **e** 6 **f** 2 **g** 5

VOCABULARY EXTENSION p40

4

1 on **2** paid for **3** in, by **4** out
5 up for **6** for **7** in **8** on

Reading p41

1

1 job **2** environment **3** evaluate

2

1 wanted to **2** didn't manage
3 positive

3

1 She wanted to work in a more stimulating and fulfilling way and to preserve the environment. **2** An energy company supplied free gas and electricity in return for research on their green products. **3** She made bartering agreements with a restaurant, a farm and a shop. **4** The shop was reluctant to get involved, but finally agreed; others were inspired and supportive. **5** Her relationships with the people around her became deeper.

4

1 F **2** O **3** O **4** O

5

1 sustainable **2** spare **3** buzz
4 carried on **5** fulfilling

Grammar in context p42

1

1 have to **2** should **3** has to
4 isn't allowed **5** has to
6 mustn't **7** shouldn't

2

Modal verb	Past form	Function of the past form
have to need to	had to needed to	express obligation and necessity in the past
needn't not have to not need to	needn't have didn't have to didn't need to	say that something happened but was not necessary
not have to not need to	didn't have to didn't need to	say something didn't happen because it wasn't necessary
ought to ought not to should should not	ought to have oughtn't to have should have shouldn't have	criticise a past action or say that it was a mistake

not be allowed to can't	wasn't/ weren't allowed to couldn't	say something was prohibited or not possible

3

2 shouldn't have eaten **3** couldn't go to the island (for three days) because it was **4** wasn't allowed to go in (the swimming pool) **5** ought to have closed **6** didn't need to hand in his / needn't have handed in his

GRAMMAR CHALLENGE p42

4

She shouldn't have/oughtn't to have gone to get her school bag ready. She should have/ought to have dried her jumper. She should have/ought to have put a new battery in her watch. She shouldn't/oughtn't to have watched the TV programme. She shouldn't/oughtn't to have worn flip-flops.

Developing vocabulary and listening p43

1

1 f **2** h **3** c **4** b **5** a **6** d

2

1 b **2** b **3** a **4** b **5** a **6** b

3

It operated without money, possibly because the Inca people dedicated their efforts to agriculture rather than economics.

4

a 1300s **b** indigenous **c** Peru **d** gold
e 12 **f** large **g** 40,000 **h** government
i worked **j** clothes **k** climate **l** states

VOCABULARY EXTENSION p43

5

1 e **2** b **3** c **4** d **5** a

Grammar in context p44

1

Possibility

0%	50%	100%
can't	could	must
	may	
	might	

2

1 can't **2** could, could **3** can't
4 must **5** could **6** must

3

1 might not **2** can't **3** can't **4** might not **5** can't **6** can't

4

Present modal	Past modal	Use this form when there is ...
must	must have (been)	1
mustn't	–	–
could	could have (been)	2
couldn't/ can't	couldn't/ can't have (been)	4
may	may have (been)	2
may not	may not have (been)	3
might	might have (been)	2
might not	mightn't have (been)	3

5

2 Ann may not have left yet.   **3** They can't have seen us.   **4** It must have been a mistake.   **5** John may have taken your coat.

GRAMMAR CHALLENGE p44

6

1 I'm sure he didn't.   **2** You haven't slept.   **3** There's no other explanation.   **4** He often calls in the evening.   **5** We've already got one.   **6** There aren't any lights on.   **7** Why didn't you?   **8** I suppose it's possible.   **9** It was too expensive.

Developing speaking p45

1

Similar: People want to withdraw money at a bank. **Different:** In picture 1, people are waiting in a queue inside the bank. In picture 2, someone is withdrawing money from an ATM machine outside a bank.

2

a show   **b** first   **c** whereas   **d** both   **e** difference   **f** second

3

c

4

Describing	Comparing	Speculating	Giving opinions	Fillers
at the top in the foreground on the left/ right	more convenient quicker	can't have could have I imagine might it looks as if	I'm not sure, but I think Personally,	Let me think

5

quicker ✓ more convenient ✓ Personally ✓ I think ✓ I mean ✓

6

1 on the right   **2** seem, imagine   **3** may have spent   **4** quicker, more, better   **5** reliable as   **6** my opinion   **7** Personally

Developing writing p46

1

You have bought an item of clothing. There is a hole in it. You live too far away to return it.

2

1 d   **2** b   **3** c   **4** a

4

1 Sir or Madam   **2** phrasal verbs, abbreviations, contractions   **3** longer, formal   **4** faithfully

Revision: Units 1–5

Grammar p47

1

1 a   **2** c   **3** b   **4** c   **5** c

2

1 must   **2** can't   **3** might   **4** can't   **5** may

3

1 had better see a   **2** may have left my bag   **3** are not/aren't allowed to   **4** do not/don't have to   **5** should not/ shouldn't have bought

4

a are opening   **b** an   **c** has had   **d** asking   **e** couldn't   **f** Having   **g** better   **h** opened   **i** were   **j** may   **k** to catch

Vocabulary p47

1

a current account   **b** bank fees   **c** overdraft   **d** interest   **e** pay   **f** cashpoint   **g** withdraw

2

1 sales, bargain   **2** receipt   **3** cut back   **4** came to   **5** pick up

3

1 refund   **2** journey   **3** illogical   **4** tactful   **5** assessment

Unit 6

Vocabulary p48

1

1 forehead   **2** chin   **3** throat   **4** chest   **5** lungs   **6** heart   **7** hip   **8** wrist   **9** thigh   **10** ankle   **11** heel   **12** toes

2

Injuries	Other health problems	Symptoms	Treatment
dislocate fracture sprain twist	addiction allergy heart disease	feel dizzy have a temperature	check-up injection medicine operation prescription take someone's blood pressure

3

2 a   **3** f   **4** d   **5** g   **6** e   **7** b

4

Suggested answers

1 take your temperature, take your blood pressure   **2** work out in a gym, have a balanced diet (avoiding fatty or processed food with too much salt and sugar)   **3** give you an injection, give you a prescription   **4** having a temperature, feeling dizzy, shivering   **5** twist, sprain, fracture, break, dislocate

VOCABULARY EXTENSION p48

5

1 heal   **2** aches   **3** sick   **4** injuries   **5** cure   **6** sore

Reading p49

1

1 c F   **2** a F   **3** b T   **4** d F

2

1 T   **2** T   **3** F   **4** T   **5** T   **6** F

3

2 ✓   **3** ✓

4

1 crave   **2** catch up   **3** posture   **4** trigger

Grammar in context p50

1

Conditional	Used for describing	Tense used in part of sentence with *if*	Tense used in other part of sentence
Zero	F	B	B
First	D	B	G
Second	A	E	C

2

1 F   **2** eat, make T   **3** doesn't burn, rub F   **4** put, stops O   **5** avoid, eat O   **6** swallow, takes F   **7** damage, sit O   **8** sleep, snore F

3

2 have, fall asleep   **3** goes, 'll feel   **4** would sleep, had   **5** sleep, do

4

1 as long as/providing/provided that
2 as long as/providing/provided that
3 unless   **4** unless   **5** in case   **6** in case

GRAMMAR CHALLENGE p50

5

1 I'll tell Paul if I~~'ll~~ see him.   **2** If you ~~would do~~ did more exercise, you'd be healthier.   **3** Your English won't improve ~~provided~~ unless you practise speaking.   **4** Take your umbrella in case it ~~will rain~~ rains.   **5** If Stephen were shorter, he ~~won't~~ wouldn't be such a good basketball player.   **6** You~~'d~~ 'll pass your driving test next week as long as you ~~didn't~~ don't panic.   **7** If you ~~won't~~ don't water these plants, they'll die.   **8** I won't apologise to Lisa unless she ~~doesn't apologise~~ apologises first.

Developing vocabulary and listening p51

1

1 the weather (N)   **2** in shape (P)   **3** out (N)   **4** on your feet (P)   **5** down with (N)   **6** of the world (P)

2

2 was feeling under the weather yesterday   **3** on top of the world   **4** if I see it, I black out   **5** to stay in shape

3

climbing ✓ surfing ✓ cycling ✓ swimming ✓ football ✓ yoga ✓

4

1 E   **2** F   **3** D   **4** A   **5** C

5

very ill	not well	getting better	very well
in a bad way	off colour run down	on the mend on the road to recovery up and about	a clean bill of health as right as rain as fit as a fiddle

6

1 b   **2** b   **3** a   **4** a   **5** b

Grammar in context p52

1

1 past simple, *have* + past participle
2 imaginary, past

2

1 d   **2** b   **3** c   **4** a   **5** f   **6** e

3

1 had trained, would have won   **2** would have written, hadn't been   **3** 'd known, wouldn't have ordered   **4** 'd asked, would have lent   **5** wouldn't have bought, hadn't given   **6** would have gone, hadn't had

4

2 I wasn't wearing/I hadn't put on/I hadn't worn a thick jumper   **3** hadn't lent my maths book to Tom   **4** he wouldn't tell jokes at parties   **5** I'd done some guitar practice this week   **6** he/she wouldn't phone me at dinnertime

GRAMMAR CHALLENGE p52

5

1 had   **2** had gone   **3** have woken   **4** knew   **5** would ask   **6** have   **7** hadn't eaten   **8** knew

Developing speaking p53

2

	Advantage	Disadvantage
basketball	team sport – good way to meet people	you need time for it, to practise and play matches
swimming	a good way to keep in shape you can do it at any time	it takes time to go to the pool, swim, get changed and have a shower
running	you can do it at any time you don't have to belong to a gym you can do it with a friend	you could get injured – sprain your ankle or pull a muscle
tennis	you can play it with a friend	you usually have to belong to a club, and that's quite expensive
skiing	it's exciting	it's expensive it's only for winter you have to travel to different places to do it

3

2 i   **3** c   **4** b   **5** d   **6** h   **7** a   **8** e   **9** g

4

1 b   **2** a   **3** b   **4** c   **5** a   **6** a

Revision: Units 1–6

Grammar p55

1

1 'll have to   **2** would look   **3** have   **4** would have become   **5** had been

2

1 wishes he were (was)   **2** provided (that) it's   **3** won't go skiing unless   **4** in case we have to

3

1 c   **2** b   **3** b   **4** d   **5** c   **6** d   **7** c

Vocabulary p55

1

1 lungs   **2** balanced   **3** sprain   **4** increases   **5** infection

2

1 e   **2** d   **3** f   **4** a   **5** b   **6** c

3

1 residence   **2** misunderstood   **3** receipt   **4** employer   **5** overtime   **6** improvement

Gateway to exams: Units 5–6

Reading p56

1

1 Uganda **2** Girls Power Micro-Lending Organisation (GIPOMO) **3** women to help them set up small businesses **4** four

2

1 T **2** T **3** F **4** NM **5** T **6** NM **7** F

Use of English p57

3

1 shouldn't have left **2** unless their parents can **3** ought to go to school **4** wish I hadn't spent **5** had better save some money **6** may open other businesses

Listening p57

5

a exercise **b** 40 **c** stomach **d** heart **e** blood **f** cold **g** Cousins **h** funny **i** sleep **j** relationships

COMMON MISTAKES p57

8

1 You should go to hospital ~~as long as~~ in case it's something serious. **2** I wish I ~~would be~~ were in shape, but I hate working out. **3** You ~~didn't need~~ didn't need to buy/needn't have bought this orange juice. We've already got some. **4** You ~~better~~ had better go to bed if you're coming down with a cold. **5** I had ~~temperature~~ a temperature yesterday and I ~~not~~ wasn't allowed ~~go~~ to go to school. **6** You ~~mustn't~~ can't be hungry. You've just eaten a big meal. **7** Could you take my ~~receipt~~ prescription to the chemist's and get me my medicine?

Unit 7

Vocabulary p58

1

a stage **b** lyrics **c** gig **d** crowd **e** track

2

1 b **2** d **3** f **4** a **5** c **6** e

3

1 download films **2** stream **3** live streams **4** peer-to-peer, file-sharing **5** mobile device **6** transfer **7** purchase

VOCABULARY EXTENSION p58

4

an act T, applause T, bestseller B, blurb B, chapter B, costume T, frame A, index B, interval T, sculpture A, self-portrait A, sketch A

Reading p59

1

1 b **2** c **3** a

2

1 F **2** T **3** T

3

1 A ticket sales company noticed a trend for more theatre sales to young people. **2** More participation in drama clubs and acting schools, more students studying theatre, and changes in the theatre. **3** Performances take place outside or in different locations, not in a theatre, and the audience participates in the performance. **4** It has managed to reinvent itself to appeal to modern audiences.

4

1 F **2** F **3** O **4** O

5

1 dying out **2** striking **3** commissioned **4** shift **5** engage

Grammar in context p60

1

1 one tense, stay the same **2** simple, perfect **3** could, would, should, might **4** true

2

2 Ollie, interesting **3** Mike, fantastic **4** Liam, amazing **5** Simon, great

3

2 Jimmy wanted to know if Bella had seen Green Day in concert. She told him she'd seen them two years before and she was going to see them again the following month. **3** Jimmy wanted to know who the drummer in Green Day was/is. She told him it was/is Tré Cool, who'd/'s been playing in the band since 1990, but it had been/was someone else before that. She'd forgotten his name. **4** Jimmy asked Bella if Green Day was/is her favourite band. She told him it wasn't/isn't, she liked/likes lots of different bands.

4

2 Jason Love said that he could have been a doctor, but there were/had been too many good shows on TV. **3** Leo Gallagher said he wished there was/had been a knob on the TV so you could turn up the intelligence. **4** Ann Landers said television proved/had proven that people would look at anything rather than each other. **5** Paddy Chayevsky said it was the menace that everyone loved to hate but couldn't seem to live without.

GRAMMAR CHALLENGE p60

5

1 c **2** d **3** a **4** e **5** b

Developing vocabulary and listening p61

1

P	A	G	E	T	U	R	N	E	R			
									D			
B	O	X	O	F	F	I	C	E	R			
L		S							A			F
O	U	T	C	O	M	E			W			E
C			R						B			E
K	M	A	R	K	E	T	P	L	A	C	E	
B					E				C			D
U				N		K			B			
S					P				A			
T	U	R	N	O	U	T			L			C
E						A	K					
R	S	O	U	N	D	T	R	A	C	K	Y	

1 blockbuster **2** drawback **3** soundtrack **4** page-turner **5** outcome **6** turnout **7** feedback **8** marketplace **9** box office **10** screenplay

2

1 songwriter **2** File-sharing **3** thought-provoking **4** fast-moving **5** brand-new

3

1 *Star Wars* **2** autographs **3** objects **4** 4th May

4

1 F **2** T **3** F **4** T **5** NM **6** F **7** T **8** T

VOCABULARY EXTENSION p61

5

2 folk festival **3** headphones **4** hotspot **5** street performer **6** stand-up comedian **7** tourist trap

Grammar in context p62

1

2 me **3** me/0 **4** 0 **5** me

2

verb + infinitive	agree, claim, offer, promise, refuse
verb + gerund	admit, advise, deny, recommend, regret, suggest
verb + object + infinitive	advise, ask, instruct, invite, order, recommend, remind, tell, warn
verb + preposition + gerund	apologise for, confess to, insist on, object to

verb + object + preposition + gerund	congratulate ... on, criticise ... for, warn ... against

3

1 recommended me to go
2 congratulated Freddie on performing
3 confessed to being   **4** refused to take   **5** suggested putting

4

1 not to spend so much time on his laptop   **2** to make another film soon   **3** for missing the penalty   **4** to bring some more water   **5** doing anything wrong   **6** Sam to send the package   **7** on having at least two hours of rehearsal time

GRAMMAR CHALLENGE p62

5

2 It instructs you to click on the 'new review' button to add your favourite artist or band.   **3** It suggests writing a concert review because it's getting more expensive to go to concerts, so your review can help others decide which gigs to go to and which to miss.   **4** It claims to give independent and free advice.
5 It reminds you to mention the atmosphere, the venue, cost of merchandise and how well organised it was as well as whether the band themselves lived up to your expectations.

Developing speaking p63

1

A book is better because ...	A film is better because ...
the plot is more detailed	there are special effects
you can use your imagination	there is a soundtrack
	they sometimes change the ending
	it's more sociable

2

1 a   **2** c

3

1 There's no, in my   **2** Take   **3** You can't, that   **4** instance   **5** but don't   **6** really do   **7** example of that   **8** at, for example   **9** I'm totally

4

Giving emphasis	Giving examples
Don't forget that ...	Just to give you an idea ...
I really do think that ...	... such as ...
You have to remember that ...	What about the case of ...?

Developing writing p64

1

A 3   **B** 1   **C** 4   **D** 2

2

1 introduction – released 2010, Facebook the most popular social networking website, millions of users   **2** basic plot – early 2000s at Harvard University, the birthplace of the website, friendships, jealousy, lawsuits   **3** your opinion about the film – loved it, convincing and believable storyline, not clichéd but gripping, true to life, Jesse Eisenberg amazing, has won awards   **4** your recommendation – hugely enjoyable, recommend to everyone

Revision: Units 1–7

Grammar p65

1

1 he would see Sam the next day
2 he hadn't seen the film the night before
3 when I normally finish(ed) work
4 if I had/have ever been to the museum
5 she might go for a swim today

2

1 b   **2** c   **3** b   **4** c   **5** a

3

1 refused to do the washing-up
2 congratulated me on passing my exams
3 invited me to go to a concert this weekend
4 confessed to taking the wallet
5 insisted on paying for the tickets

4

1 has met   **2** mustn't   **3** wasn't allowed to   **4** 'll be working   **5** 'd had

Vocabulary p65

1

a download   **b** mobile device   **c** live
d performance   **e** stars   **f** acting
g scenes

2

Adjective	Noun
brand-new	box office
fast-moving	feedback
thought-provoking	file-sharing
	page-turner
	soundtrack

3

1 box office   **2** feedback   **3** page-turner   **4** fast-moving   **5** soundtrack

4

1 curricular   **2** unskilled   **3** violinist
4 promotion   **5** disobeys

Unit 8

Vocabulary p66

1

Across: **4** forest fire   **6** avalanche
7 earthquake   **8** landslide
Down: **1** volcanic eruption   **2** tsunami
3 drought   **5** flood

2

a damage   **b** erupt   **c** destroyed
d refugees   **e** ash   **f** destruction
g evacuated   **h** survivors   **i** hurricanes
j torrential   **k** sweep across   **l** eruption

VOCABULARY EXTENSION p66

3

1 d   **2** e   **3** c   **4** f   **5** b   **6** a

Reading p67

1

b

2

1 d   **2** a   **3** c

3

1 F   **2** F   **3** O   **4** O   **5** F

4

1 drill   **2** overwhelming   **3** prone
4 bewildered   **5** imminent

5

1 imminent   **2** bewildered   **3** prone
4 drill   **5** overwhelming

Grammar in context p68

1

a action   **b** know   **c** obvious   **d** past participle   **e** are   **f** been   **g** is being   **h** was   **i** will be   **j** can be

2

1 is used   **2** ranges   **3** flows   **4** are formed   **5** were shown   **6** be warned
7 were vaccinated   **8** have been set up

3

a can be seen   **b** were covered   **c** have been built   **d** was slightly damaged
e was carried out
Other passives: The dams were built on the slopes, All four check dams were constructed.

4

2 I'm still owed some sponsorship money.
3 All students at the school were sent a letter.   **4** Customers who return faulty products are offered refunds.   **5** The scientists have been promised more funding.

GRAMMAR CHALLENGE p68

5

Suggested answers: The roof of the building has been blown away. The whole street has been affected. The taxi has been covered with debris. The trees have been damaged. The taxi has (probably) been destroyed.

Developing vocabulary and listening p69

1

agree with/to, apologise for, believe in, belong to, complain about, depend on, dream of, listen to, protect from, rely on, spend on, wait for

2

1 apologised for, complained about   **2** listened to, agreed with   **3** dream of, spend on   **4** belong to, waiting for   **5** believe in, depend on   **6** rely on, protect, from

3

a Rob and Paul   **b** Sri Lanka   **c** 17 and 15   **d** flip flops   **e** for Orphans

4

1 F   **2** T   **3** T   **4** NM   **5** F   **6** NM   **7** T   **8** F

VOCABULARY EXTENSION p69

5

1 e   **2** a   **3** d   **4** b   **5** g   **6** f   **7** c

6

a learn about   **b** heard about   **c** named after   **d** feel like   **e** covered with

Grammar in context p70

1

1 has was   **2** say said   **3** be been   **4** He It   **5** like that

2

2 It was thought that everything was made of fire, earth, air and water. Now it is known that there are over a hundred elements.   **3** It was thought that the Moon was a smooth ball. Now it is known that it has valleys and mountains.   **4** It was said that feelings came from your liver. Now it is said that they come from your heart.   **5** It was thought that having a bath once a month was enough. Now it is believed that we need to have a bath or shower every day.   **6** It was believed that kings were gods. Now it is known that they are only human.   **7** It was thought that our bodies constantly made new blood. Now it is known that the body circulates blood.

3

2 is (always) said that, is (always) said to be   **3** is known, are known to have lived   **4** is believed that, is believed to need   **5** has been claimed that, has been claimed to be

GRAMMAR CHALLENGE p70

4

2 to have escaped   **3** to have found   **4** to cause   **5** to have got

Developing speaking p71

1

2 a quarter   **3** three-quarters   **4** a tenth   **5** sixty-six per cent   **6** one in three

2

1 number of natural disasters   **2** floods   **3** volcanic eruptions   **4** windstorms   **5** droughts

3

1 It increased.   **2** in 1990   **3** between 2005 and 2010   **4** It fluctuated.   **5** between 1984 and 1989

4

Disasters related to the weather.

5

1 a gradual dramatic increase in the number of weather-related disasters   **2** the number doubled tripled   **3** The biggest decrease increase   **4** a fall rise in the number of windstorms   **5** a sharp steady increase in the number of floods   **6** the number of droughts stayed the same fell   **7** the number of geophysical disasters rose significantly fluctuated   **8** there was a big little change in the number of earthquakes

Revision: Units 1–8

Grammar p73

1

1 was   **2** being   **3** been   **4** Are   **5** have

2

1 was claimed that   **2** was believed to protect   **3** being carried   **4** to be mended   **5** were given

3

1 had been blown   **2** are being shown   **3** if I could find it   **4** we would have fun   **5** for arriving late and not calling

Vocabulary p73

1

1 avalanche   **2** drought   **3** refugee   **4** landslide   **5** flood

2

1 a   **2** c   **3** c   **4** b   **5** c

3

1 on   **2** dreamed   **3** apologise   **4** to   **5** believe

4

1 brand-new   **2** role   **3** eruption   **4** fire   **5** turn   **6** live

Gateway to exams: Units 7–8

Reading p74

1

b

2

1 b   **2** a   **3** b   **4** a   **5** b   **6** c

Use of English p74

3

a an   **b** was   **c** had   **d** in   **e** so   **f** will   **g** do   **h** does/should   **i** long

Listening p75

4

1 F   **2** T   **3** T   **4** NM   **5** F   **6** F   **7** T

COMMON MISTAKES p75

6

1 The careers of many artists have launched have been launched for by this website.   **2** I admit to spend spending too much money for on music and clothes.   **3** My brother offered lend to lend me £10 to go to the cinema.   **4** The latest Bond film it is thought is is thought to be the best.   **5** Dan apologised for be being late and promised not doing to do it again.   **6** Our teacher told said that/told us that he won't wouldn't be at school next week.   **7** Sarah accused me not to know of not knowing anything about music.
8 Fans complained to not be about not being informed that the concert cancelled was/had been cancelled.

Unit 9

Vocabulary p76

1

Computer and phone hardware	Internet or phone connection	Electrical household equipment
charger	coverage	dishwasher
device	network	microwave
flash drive	wireless	vacuum cleaner
headphones		washing machine
laser printer		
touch screen		
webcam		

2

1 plug   **2** touch screen   **3** flash drive   **4** network coverage   **5** devices   **6** wireless

3

2 D: digital camera   **3** B: satnav   **4** E: dropdown menu   **5** A: remote control

4

Suggested answers

2 recharge your phone 3 freezes, press the ESC key 4 upgrade it 5 install an anti-virus program 6 you can adjust it to make it quieter 7 delete files/documents that you don't need 8 disconnect your devices when you aren't using them 9 tap it gently

VOCABULARY EXTENSION p76

5

1 go 2 order 3 working 4 reboot 5 paste 6 drag 7 highlight

Reading p77

1

1, 2, 3, 5

2

1 G 2 C 3 A 4 E 5 B 6 H 7 F

3

1 3 2 2 3 3 4 1

4

1 avid 2 resources 3 address 4 immersed 5 brainchild

5

1 address 2 immersed 3 avid 4 resource 5 brainchild

Grammar in context p78

1

	Defining relative clauses	Non-defining relative clauses
for things	which, that	which
for people	who, that	who
for places	where	where
for times	when	when
for reasons	why	why
for possessions	whose	whose
use commas?	no	yes
can omit relative pronoun?	yes	no

2

a who b which c why d which e which f which g where h whose

3

Replaced: b, d, f
Omitted: c

4

2 There is a button on the side of the phone (which) you need to press. 3 That was the moment (when) I knew I wanted to be a doctor. 4 The people in my class whose exam results were good had revised very hard. 5 It would be good if someone invented something that would cure the common cold.

5

Suggested answers

1 Harry, who lives next to Jim, is the boy who won the prize. 2 Annie is going to the park, where she loves walking, to meet her best friend. 3 Paul gave me a box of chocolates to thank me for my help, which was kind of him. 4 Katie, who works at Stacey's shop, will lend the book to Stacey and then (she will lend it) to me. 5 We're going to take the train to Paris, which I love, and stay with my aunt for a couple of days. 6 My favourite uncle, who lives in Oxford, is visiting this weekend. 7 The class at my old school gave me a lovely necklace, which I wear all the time, as a leaving present.

GRAMMAR CHALLENGE p78

6

1 ~~that~~ where 2 ~~who~~ whose 3 ~~a device, which~~ a device which 4 ~~when~~ why 5 ~~that~~ who 6 ~~Rome where he's been twice before on~~ Rome, where he's been twice before, on 7 ~~that~~ which 8 ~~where~~ when

Developing vocabulary and listening p79

1

1 run on 2 print out 3 back up 4 scroll down 5 set up 6 pick up 7 pop up 8 go off 9 run out 10 zoom in

3

1 c 2 d 3 b 4 a

4

b 3 c 4 d 3 e 1 f 2 g 4 h 3 i 1 j 2

VOCABULARY EXTENSION p79

5

1 b 2 d 3 e 4 a 5 c

6

1 key in 2 free up 3 hack into 4 go down 5 hook up

Grammar in context p80

1

1 a 2 b 3 b 4 a 5 a

2

1 d 2 e 3 a 4 f 5 b 6 c

3

1 remembers washing 2 stop buying 3 remembered to make 4 stop to tie up 5 likes windsurfing 6 forget meeting

4

1 stop using your phone 2 like to switch off 3 remember leaving 4 forgot to download 5 stopped doing my homework 6 forgot taking my laptop

GRAMMAR CHALLENGE p80

5

1 falling 2 to buy 3 making 4 talking 5 to get up 6 going 7 to hand in 8 learning

Developing speaking p81

1

b N c N d Y e Y f N

2

The woman: Yes The man: Yes

3

1 M 2 M 3 W 4 W 5 M 6 W 7 W

4

1 Do you see what I mean? 2 Could you go over that again? 3 I don't understand what you're getting at. 4 No, that's not quite what I mean. 5 Are you with me? 6 If I understand you correctly 7 I'm not sure what you mean. 8 Are you following me?

5

a Are you with me? b I don't understand what you're getting at./I'm not sure what you mean. c If I understand you correctly d Do you see what I mean?

Developing writing p82

1

1 Introduction – the aim of the report 2 Use of computers 3 How useful they are 4 Conclusion

Revision: Units 1–9

Grammar p83

1

1 when 2 why 3 whose 4 where 5 who 6 which

2

1 that 2 who 3 where 4 whose 5 which

3

1 sailing 2 to feed 3 meeting 4 to be 5 to call

4

1 after/when I had finished reading 2 you (got) any idea why 3 eats more slowly than 4 are too full to eat 5 fill in this form

Vocabulary p83

1

1 remote control   **2** vacuum cleaner
3 flash drive   **4** keyboard   **5** charger

2

a streaming   **b** upgrade   **c** frozen
d pressing   **e** disconnect

3

1 up   **2** scroll   **3** up   **4** on   **5** go

4

1 d   **2** h   **3** f   **4** b   **5** g   **6** e

Unit 10

Vocabulary p84

1

1 B   **2** E   **3** C   **4** F   **5** A   **6** D

2

1 e   **2** i   **3** g   **4** j   **5** a   **6** h   **7** c
8 f   **9** b   **10** d   **11** k

3

1 cut   **2** key   **3** plea   **4** pledge
5 link   **6** PM   **7** probe   **8** riddle
9 spark   **10** wed   **11** aid   **12** back

4

Suggested answers

1 PM's wife pledges to attend Fashion
Week   **2** Library services cut sooner than
expected   **3** Soap opera star to wed
her producer (next year)   **4** Forest blaze
brought under control   **5** Althlete's gold
medal boosts national team

5

Wildlife officials probe bird deaths

VOCABULARY EXTENSION p84

6

1 daily   **2** fortnightly   **3** national
4 local   **5** monthly

Reading p85

1

1 c   **2** b   **3** a

2

A Teenager made to tidy up finds winning
lottery ticket   **B** Teen lottery winner left
with nothing

3

1 T   **2** F   **3** NM   **4** T   **5** F   **6** F
7 T   **8** T

4

Bringing out the best in people: His
father wants him to invest the money and
use it as a deposit to buy a house. He also
wants to help his younger brother to buy
a car. Ryan has no plans to quit his job or
stop his work with charity First Response …
'… I'm planning on donating some of the
winnings to them.' She bought houses and

cars for … her friends and family. '… now
I'm stronger.'

Bringing out the worst in people: But
far from making her happy, Callie fell into
depression. She didn't have a job and she
felt lonely and vulnerable. People would
act like her best friend but she didn't know
who to trust.

5

1 clear up   **2** broke   **3** give in   **4** put
away   **5** the high life

6

1 gave in   **2** put away   **3** the high
life   **4** clear up   **5** broke

Grammar in context p86

1

2 ✓   **3** ✓   **5** ✓   **6** ✓   **7** ✓

2

a were   **b** would   **c** going   **d** about
e was   **f** would

3

1 hadn't cleared   **2** wouldn't lose
3 had thrown   **4** didn't go   **5** would be
able   **6** hadn't met   **7** were/was

4

2 If I liked science-fiction films, I would
have seen the film on TV last night.   **3** If
I weren't busy, I would have gone to the
party last weekend.   **4** If I had studied
at school, it wouldn't be difficult to find a
job.   **5** If I spoke French, I would have
applied for that job.   **6** If I'd been born
in the US, I wouldn't need a visa to work
there.

GRAMMAR CHALLENGE p86

5

1 do   **2** was   **3** was to   **4** could
5 have flown   **6** were   **7** would be

Developing vocabulary and listening p87

1

1 Breaking news   **2** Holding a press
conference   **3** A turn of events   **4** Front-
page news   **5** A newsflash   **6** A news
update

2

1 b   **2** c   **3** a   **4** a   **5** b   **6** c

3

1 Customers clash in ice cream shop
drama   **2** Woman arrested for stealing
from blind man   **3** It pays to do the right
thing

4

Headline 3

5

1 b   **2** c   **3** c   **4** a   **5** c   **6** b

VOCABULARY EXTENSION p87

6

1 editor   **2** subeditor   **3** correspondent
4 contributor   **5** columnist   **6** reporter

Grammar in context p88

1

1 how old Joey is   **2** if he works
there every day   **3** if the customer
left quietly   **4** how the email became
public   **5** how Joey feels about being
famous   **6** what he is going to do now

2

Can I ask/Do you know/Have you got any
idea/I'd like to ask/I wonder …   **1** where
the fox was found   **2** … what the fox has
been nicknamed   **3** … how it entered the
building   **4** … who saw the fox   **5** how
you caught the fox   **6** where the fox is
now

3

1 won't he   **2** isn't it   **3** wasn't it
4 have you   **5** do we   **6** can you
7 wasn't it   **8** hadn't he

4

2 She was born in New York, wasn't
she?   **3** She isn't touring at the moment,
is she?   **4** She's made five albums so far,
hasn't she?   **5** She plays the piano very
well, doesn't she?   **6** She doesn't play the
guitar, does she?

GRAMMAR CHALLENGE p88

5

1 ~~does this cost~~ this costs   **2** correct
3 ~~isn't it~~ aren't they   **4** ~~could you~~ you
could   **5** correct   **6** ~~hasn't he~~ has he
7 ~~would you do~~ you would do   **8** ~~am I~~
aren't I

Developing speaking p89

2

You can read the news wherever you are.
Some online newspapers are free. It's
better for the environment.

3

1 There's no denying   **2** However
3 let's not forget   **4** I accept   **5** Having
said that   **6** let's not forget

Developing writing p90

1

1 c   **2** e   **3** f   **4** a   **5** b   **6** d

Revision: Units 1–10

Grammar p91

1

1 was going to   **2** was about to
3 going to   **4** would be   **5** to be

2

1 would be   **2** he had gone/went
3 would have kept   **4** weren't (wasn't)
5 wouldn't be

3

1 tell me how old you are   **2** you
could tell me which way it is to the
beach   **3** know why you became an
actor   **4** ask how much that laptop costs

4

1 will she   **2** didn't they
3 had he   **4** doesn't she

5

a returning   **b** who   **c** made   **d** had
e left   **f** to find   **g** up   **h** have visited
i did   **j** was

Vocabulary p91

1

1 weather forecast   **2** arts and
entertainment   **3** business and
finance   **4** showbiz/gossip   **5** health

2

1 e   **2** a   **3** c   **4** b   **5** d

3

1 breaking news   **2** front-page
news   **3** turn of events   **4** keep,
informed   **5** hold a press conference

4

1 b   **2** d   **3** a   **4** c

Gateway to exams: Units 9–10

Reading p92

1

A business   **B** technology

2

1 F   **2** T   **3** T   **4** F   **5** NM   **6** F
7 T   **8** NM   **9** F   **10** T

Use of English p93

3

Suggested answer

c moving

4

1 C   **2** D   **3** B   **4** B   **5** D   **6** B

Listening p93

5

1 b   **2** a   **3** c   **4** a

COMMON MISTAKES p93

8

1 The students, ~~that~~ who are from
London, stopped ~~to use~~ using their
phones.   **2** Have you got any idea why
~~did they do~~ they did it?   **3** I ~~was to~~ was
going to buy a new phone, but my parents
gave me one for my birthday.   **4** This
story made the headlines, ~~wasn't~~ didn't
it?   **5** Don't forget ~~backing~~ to back up
your documents every evening.

Workbook audioscript

Unit 1

Developing vocabulary and listening p7

3 and 4 ▶ 01

Presenter: Hi and welcome to today's Education Podcast. Not many students like doing exams, but some exams are more stressful than others. Here to tell us about one of the most difficult exams in the world is James Harding. James, what is this exam and where do students do it?

James: Well, it's called the Gaokao, or the Big Test and it's the exam that students do in China at the end of their final year at high school.

Presenter: How does it work?

James: Well, it takes place over two or three days, and includes exams in Chinese, maths and a foreign language, usually English, but it can also be Japanese, Russian or French. Then there are also separate exams for students who want to do a science degree. They do exams in physics, chemistry and biology, while arts students do exams in history, geography and political education.

Presenter: And why is it important?

James: Well, it basically decides which university a student can go to, like in other countries, but it can determine what kind of job they get in the future, too. So getting a good mark is incredibly important, not only for the student but for their whole family. There's enormous pressure on them to do well.

Presenter: And how do they prepare for these exams?

James: Well, the year before the exam, high schools often dedicate all their time to teaching for the exam, and there are specialised schools, too. Parents pay a lot of money for their kids to go to these schools and sometimes a parent takes time off work to help them study as well.

Presenter: So what are these specialised schools like?

James: They're incredibly strict. There's no free time to go swimming or play football, or do the things that teenagers normally do. Students have just one day off a month and it's quite normal to start the day at 5.30 in the morning and study until about 10 o'clock at night. There are no mobile phones, and there are even cameras in the classrooms to make sure they work hard.

Presenter: That's amazing! I can't imagine anything like that here.

James: No, exactly. Then about nine million students start this exam on the same day and it's like the whole country stops! Traffic stops near where the exams take place, and people don't listen to loud music or make a noise in case it disturbs them.

Presenter: How do these kids cope with the pressure?

James: Well, it's difficult and sometimes they're too tired or stressed to concentrate. There's some debate about the exam itself too because the students learn a lot of information, but they don't necessarily learn to think about things in a critical way. And the other thing is that they tend to specialise very early, so if they make a decision to study sciences, they can't change to a different subject.

Presenter: Really?

James: Yes. Some teachers want education to be broader instead of focusing on the exam.

Presenter: So do you think it will change in the future?

James: It is changing. The government has agreed to include more critical thinking in the exam and they're considering including other things in university entrance too, such as hobbies, and things like volunteering. So it is changing, slowly.

Presenter: OK, well, thanks for telling us about this exam, James. It's been very interesting.

James: Thank you.

Developing speaking p9

2 and 3 ▶ 02

Speaker A
Yes, I do. I often go with friends at the weekend. I'd rather watch films at the cinema than at home. I like science-fiction films and the special effects are more spectacular on a big screen than on a small screen. The only thing is that it's quite expensive where I live so I don't go every weekend. I like watching films on TV too, but I prefer going to the cinema.

Speaker B
Mmmm ... I think it's the evening. I'm not keen on getting up to go to school in the morning and I enjoy having free time in the evening after I've finished my homework. And I like going out with friends in the evening at weekends. I don't mind getting up early on Saturdays – I'd rather not stay in bed. But I still prefer the evenings.

Speaker C
No, it's actually quite difficult because I share a room with my younger brother. I've got a desk and a computer, but it's not ideal because he often comes in and disturbs me. I'd rather have my own room so that I can close the door and concentrate, but unfortunately that's not possible because we live in a small flat. I hope to have my own room when I go to university.

Speaker D
Well, I like spending time in my room at home because I can relax there and read and listen to music. But I spend most of the day at school so I prefer not staying inside all weekend, too. I usually go out with friends. We go shopping or go to the park and stuff like that. My parents would rather I stay at home and study, but I prefer going out at the weekend.

Speaker E
Well, next summer my parents want to go to Paris, but I'm not keen on going to museums and art galleries – I get bored easily – so I'd prefer not to go to a city. I'd prefer to go somewhere hot. I'd like to go to the beach and spend my time relaxing and swimming in the sea. Ideally, I'd like to go to Croatia. I've heard that the beaches are incredible there.

Unit 2

Developing vocabulary and listening p15

2 and 3 ▶ 03

Speaker 1:
In May I started to think about how to fill in my time during the coming summer. I had three months before going back to uni and I wanted to travel but also do something worthwhile. I'd been playing cricket on both my university and school teams for many years, and I wanted to use my talent to teach others so my choice of destination was limited to where people play cricket. I'd never been to Jamaica before and I wanted to go to a country where the people are as passionate about sport as I am. As soon as I arrived I was given a lot of responsibility. It was challenging at times, but I really feel that I developed as a coach and I experienced a culture quite different from my own.

Speaker 2:
I'd been travelling in Central America for a couple of months by the time I arrived in Panama and I wanted more contact with Spanish-speaking people to practise my Spanish before starting a course in German and Spanish at uni and I was lucky enough to find work as a reporter on a music

radio station, which meant collecting lists of music to add to the radio's database and writing reports about gigs and other music events. It was pretty boring most of the time, actually, but I kept at it for a few weeks. Although one day I got to replace a DJ on a live radio show at the last moment. This was really fun, especially as my friends had been listening and it gave them a big surprise. I definitely improved my Spanish, and I got some additional experience working in media, which I can add to my CV.

Speaker 3:

I travelled to Nepal by motorcycle, which was a long and difficult journey. I paid for the journey by working weekends in a restaurant. I'd been to developing countries before so I knew life there would be harsh, but the conditions in Nepal were the worst I'd ever seen. While I was there, I worked as a volunteer for a disaster relief agency, rebuilding a school that had been destroyed in an earthquake. We also managed to set up English classes for the younger kids before I left. I feel that I arrived as an inexperienced student, but left with a much better understanding of the difficulties people face in some countries. In the future I hope to find a job in a non-governmental organisation or charity.

Speaker 4:

I decided to volunteer on an international wildlife conservation project because I'd never done anything like it before. I was a bit nervous about joining a camp of people who had been together for a long time, but everyone was very friendly. We spent a lot of our time clearing large areas of land and making sure we removed anything that could be a danger to the animals. One of the most interesting experiences was watching all the different animals in the evening as they came to the water hole to drink together. It was an unforgettable sight. Nothing I did in Africa was directly related to my career now, but just the experience itself was a personal achievement for me.

Speaker 5:

I've always been interested in international history and culture, so the opportunity to go to Cambodia and work on a project on a famous archeological site was one I couldn't turn down. I'd been studying South-East Asian history at university, but Phnom Penh is a much more modern city than I had expected. On the first day, we learnt about the dig and where to look for signs of objects. We found lots of ancient objects, which was very exciting. I took over the job of making lists of things we found and even selecting what would go to museums all over the world! I gained responsibility and learnt a lot of new archeological techniques, and I also made some great friends. I definitely want to go back again sometime, it was an unforgettable experience.

Developing speaking p17

3 and 4 04

Examiner: I'd like you to imagine that you are looking into different options of how to spend time before university. Here are some ideas and a question for you to discuss. Talk to each other about how useful you think these ways of spending time are.

Boy: So, what do you think about learning a language?

Girl: Well, I think it's useful because languages are very important in most jobs these days.

Boy: That's true. What about working? I think that's useful too because it means that you earn money and get some work experience.

Girl: I suppose so, but it depends what type of work you do. If it's unskilled work, like working as a waiter or a shop assistant, it's not so useful. But if it's something that allows you to get ahead in your career, I think that's a good idea.

Boy: Yes, I agree. What about relaxing and having fun? I don't think that's useful at all. Do you agree?

Girl: I'm not sure. After studying hard for exams, it's probably necessary! But I think you're right. It's not very useful. What do you think about travelling?

Boy: I think it's a great idea, if you can afford to do it. It's a great way to learn about different cultures and you can relax and have fun at the same time.

Girl: Yes, you're right. I think you learn to be more independent when you travel and it's a good way to make friends.

Boy: So what about volunteering? I think that's useful, especially if you travel at the same time.

Girl: I agree with you. I think it's something that you can talk about when you go for interviews and you can learn some useful skills.

Examiner: OK! Now you have about a minute to decide which of the ways of spending time you think is the *most* useful.

Girl: Mmm ... perhaps learning a language because it's so important for finding a job these days.

Boy: I agree up to a point, but it depends how you learn. Sitting in a classroom isn't very exciting, and you can learn a language when you travel. Maybe travelling is more useful?

Girl: Maybe, but what about volunteering abroad? I think you can learn another language, learn new skills and travel all at the same time.

Boy: Yes, I think you're right. I think it's the most useful thing to do.

Gateway to exams: Units 1–2

Listening p21

4 05

Speaker 1:

I had a Saturday job in a shop all through secondary school *and* during the holidays. It wasn't well paid, but I kept at it because I wanted to earn my own money. It taught me to be responsible. Now I have my own business and I regularly employ 16- to 18-year-olds, but in my experience, only about 50% are prepared to work hard. They're often late and they're always getting their mums to phone me and say that they're sick. When they do come to work, I'm always catching them using their mobiles. If you ask me, life skills are more important than academic achievement, especially when it comes to finding a job.

Speaker 2:

My son has been applying for part-time jobs for months now in everything from shop work to cleaning. Nobody will take him because he hasn't got any experience. It's ridiculous! Young people can't get a job because they don't have experience, but they can't get experience because no one will give them a job. What are they supposed to do? My son is at college and he's prepared to work at any time his timetable allows. We put his availability on his application forms, but employers want people who can work during the week, too. So it's not that he doesn't want to work. He's constantly trying to find a job but without success!

Speaker 3:

At college and university I worked part-time three days a week and I did voluntary work to improve my chances of getting a job. This didn't have a negative effect on my grades. I think working and doing voluntary work means you won't end up unemployed. Plus, I had no choice because my parents aren't wealthy. I had to pay my own rent at university and I couldn't rely on my mum and dad. Degrees are so common nowadays that you have to set yourself apart with work experience, whether paid or voluntary. I've never been out of work since leaving university and I'm currently doing a master's while working full-time.

Speaker 4:

I think people are forgetting that times have changed. The demands on students to achieve academically are greater than ever before. It's not like in previous generations when you could fail exams and still get a job in one of the big industries.

Nowadays, you need qualifications *and* languages. I'm in my last year of school and hope to go to university next year. I have to do a lot of coursework as well as revise for exams so I often spend my weekends studying to keep up with it all. I'd rather concentrate on my studies now than work so that I have the best possible chance of getting a good job in the future.

Speaker 5:

If you ask me, too many young people are protected by their parents and not allowed to get life experience. The biggest decision they have to face is where to go out at the weekend or what new mobile to buy. Their parents finance their social life so it's no wonder that many have debts – they've never learnt to manage their finances! They study weird subjects like drama and psychology, and they're hardly ever at school. Personally, I think the school day should be longer. If they went to school from nine to five, it would be less of a shock when they actually started work.

Unit 3

Developing vocabulary and listening p25

3 and 4 ▶ 06

Presenter: Have you thought about your next holiday yet? The chances are you'll be spending it on a beach or visiting a nearby country. But what about your holiday in 20 or 30 years' time? Where will you be going on holiday then? Here to give us her predictions is Pippa West. So Pippa, what can you tell us about holidays of the future?

Pippa: Hello. Well, it'll come as no surprise if I tell you that a lot of us will be spending our holidays in space. At the moment, only a few rich people can afford it, but it's going to become much more common.

Presenter: So holidays on the Moon in other words.

Pippa: Well, the first step will be to go to Earth's low orbit, in other words 2,000 kilometres up, high enough to see the curve of the Earth and experience weightlessness. There'll be sky resorts up there. Then the next step will be to go to the Moon. There are already plans to use 3D printing to build lunar hotels for people to stay in.

Presenter: But people *have* been talking space travel for quite some time now.

Pippa: Exactly, but the other way to go of course is down, under the sea.

Presenter: Now that's more unusual.

Pippa: Well, it's not in fact. There's already a hotel in Dubai that has rooms under the sea. There are wonderful views through the windows of fish swimming and underwater life. At the moment it's very expensive. A room costs about 5,000 euros a night, but it'll get cheaper as more hotels are built.

Presenter: Are there plans to build more hotels then?

Pippa: Yes, in Fiji for example, they're going to build a complete underwater hotel, with a restaurant and gym and everything. They planned it some time ago and they hoped to finish it in 2008, but it was delayed, I think because they underestimated the time and the cost. I'm sure they'll have finished it by about 2025 though.

Presenter: And do you think people will want to go there?

Pippa: Yes, in fact, some people have already booked rooms. They'll have been waiting for their holiday about 15 years when they eventually get there!

Presenter: Oh dear! But what about hotels on land, for those of us who don't fancy being underwater? What are your predictions for these?

Pippa: Well, the general idea seems to be to reinvent hotels to make them much more comfortable and for a stay to be more personalised.

Presenter: What do you mean exactly?

Pippa: Well, one of the problems people have when they travel long distances is changing time zones, so the idea is to design hotel rooms to help travellers get over the discomfort of jet lag. There will be pillows that give you a massage to help you sleep, and showers that have vitamin D in the water.

Presenter: That sounds unbelievable!

Pippa: And then of course you won't have to worry about going to the gym, because in ten years' time, you'll be exercising in your room with your own virtual personal trainer.

Presenter: So soon?

Pippa: Yes, I mean, technology is advancing so fast now that things that seem improbable to us will be normal in a few years' time.

Presenter: OK so, what about alternatives to hotels. I know a lot of people prefer to rent an apartment when they go on holiday.

Pippa: Yes, there will be changes there, too. People are talking about an increase in so-called social travel.

Presenter: And what's that?

Pippa: It basically involves cooperation between ordinary people. So in about ten years' time, apparently, between five and ten per cent of us will be renting out our homes or rooms in our homes to travellers. It seems that people would rather get to know the locals than stay in a hotel.

Presenter: Interesting. Well, that's all we have time for now. Thanks, Pippa.

Developing speaking p27

3 and 4 ▶ 07

Teenage boy:

Both photographs show people travelling on holiday. In the first photograph the girls are probably travelling by plane, whereas in the second photograph the girl is cycling. In both pictures, the people have luggage, but one big difference between the photos is that the girls have got a lot of things with them, including toys and backpacks, while the cyclist has only one bag on her bike. Another important difference is that the girls seem relaxed and happy, perhaps because they're starting their holiday, but the cyclist is working hard to go up a hill on her bike. Perhaps she's on a cycling holiday because the countryside there is very beautiful.

I think they are both good ways of travelling on holiday. Travelling by plane is fast and comfortable. You can travel long distances and get to your destination quickly. Compared with flying, cycling is slow and it can be uncomfortable, especially if the weather is hot or it's raining. But I think it can be a good way to see the countryside. The girl in the picture is alone and there aren't a lot of other people around. She's doing exercise and getting fresh air at the same time so it's a healthy way to travel.

Unit 4

Developing vocabulary and listening p33

3 and 4 ▶ 08

Leo: Hey Jade, if you had a hidden talent, what would you like it to be?

Jade: Hidden talent? What are you talking about?

Leo: You know, like on that programme on TV.

Jade: The one where ordinary people find out they have a special talent?

Leo: Yes, that's the one.

Jade: Hmm ... good question. Maybe lie-detecting, that would be useful. Or the ability to learn languages like the boy who learnt Arabic. What about you?

Leo: I'm really interested in the idea of being a super-recogniser.

Jade: What's that?

Leo: Well, apparently some people have the ability to remember faces. They only see a person once, and that's enough for them to remember the face years later.

Jade: Was that on the show?

Leo: Yes, it was. They gave the candidates two tests. In the first test, the candidates had to identify celebrities from childhood photographs, people like Tom Cruise.

Jade: I don't think that would be too difficult to do.

Leo: No, but in the second test, they had to memorise computer-generated faces. At the beginning they saw these faces, then the faces were obscured so that you couldn't see them properly.

Jade: Were they able to do it?

Leo: Three people could. A graphics student, someone who works in an office and who also teaches swimming ...

Jade: Well, remembering faces is probably a good skill to have if you're a teacher.

Leo: Right, and the other was a Brazilian business student who used to live in a dangerous neighbourhood. He said recognising faces there could mean the difference between life and death!

Jade: Wow! So who was the best of these three?

Leo: Hold on. So they took these three people to a busy train station in London and then later, they had to identify 15 people who had been at the station. And they were all wearing identical clothes, by the way, so they really had to rely on faces.

Jade: I can't imagine anyone doing that. It's such a difficult thing to do!

Leo: I know, but these people could do it. They got one point for every face they remembered, and lost one point for every face they got wrong. The graphics student was the best. He got eight points.

Jade: Amazing! So why do you think this would be a useful skill to have?

Leo: Well, I was fascinated so I started to read online about these super-recognisers. There's a woman called Jennifer who can pass someone in a café once and remember them weeks later. And once she saw someone on the subway with grey hair and recognised her as a kid she saw a few times when she was young.

Jade: She'd be a good witness then, if she ever saw a crime.

Leo: Exactly. There's this other woman called Moira. She worked in a shop which was robbed and she was able to identify the thieves out of 200 photos and they were arrested. Now she works for the police, helping to identify criminals.

Jade: OK, I agree, that's a useful skill to have.

Leo: Apparently, the police are using super-recognisers to identify people on surveillance films. And another thing is that psychologists are using them to investigate the opposite problem – a thing called face blindness. It seems some people can't remember faces at all.

Jade: So for example, a mother goes to school to pick up her child and doesn't recognise him or her.

Leo: Exactly. Imagine that! Anyway, there's a test online to see if you're a super-recogniser. Do you want to try it?

Jade: Sure. Let's have a go.

Developing speaking p35

2 and 3 ▶ 09

I'd like to begin by saying that I disagree with this statement. Let me explain why. First of all, the definition of a genius is someone who is *more* intelligent and skilled than other people. So it's impossible for all children to be geniuses. There are only a few *real* child geniuses in the world.

Secondly, I think that a real genius is usually born with an exceptional talent. They may be very good at maths or art or science. Parents of geniuses often say that they notice their child is different when they are still very young. It isn't something you can learn.

What's more, I believe that parents sometimes put a lot of pressure on their children to be very good at something. They force them to learn, or to practise a musical instrument all the time because they want their child to be exceptional.

It's important to remember that geniuses aren't always successful in life. For example, they sometimes find it difficult to make friends. The point I'm trying to make is that there are more important things than being a genius.

To sum up, I think real genius is something you are born with, and parents shouldn't try to create a genius by putting pressure on their children to be exceptional.

Gateway to exams: Units 3–4

Listening p39

5 and 6 ▶ 10

Hannah: Now, like many teenagers, 19-year-old Ed Pratt has a dream to travel the world. That's not so unusual, you're thinking. Well, it's not, but what's unusual about this story is not only that Ed is making his dream come true, but he's doing it in a very extraordinary way. Sean Simmons is here to tell us about it.

Sean: Hi Hannah. That's right. This time tomorrow, Ed Pratt will be setting off on a trip of a lifetime. This Somerset teenager is going to travel around the world, not by car, not by train, and certainly not by plane. He's going to travel around the world ... by unicycle.

Hannah: I beg your pardon?

Sean: You heard me, Hannah. He's hoping to become the first person ever to circumnavigate the world on one wheel.

Hannah: That's unbelievable! And how long will this trip take, Sean?

Sean: Well, Ed predicts that it'll take at least two and a half years, but he says he's not going to rush. He's not trying to break any speed records, so when he gets to a place he likes, he'll stop for a few days. Or he'll stop if he gets injured or has a problem with the bike.

Hannah: Better to be safe than sorry, right? And where is he going exactly?

Sean: Well, his first stop is Weymouth, in the south of England. That's the only part of the trip that he's actually booked. He's catching a ferry from there tomorrow afternoon to France and from there, he'll cycle across Europe to Turkey, China and Australia. Then he's flying to San Francisco for the American leg and from there, back to Portugal and then home again. By the time he finishes this trip, he'll have cycled around 18,000 miles, that's nearly 29,000 kilometres.

Hannah: I hope he's fit!

Sean: Apparently, he's done some training, Hannah, but he reckons he'll get fitter as the trip progresses, and when he gets to China, he says he'll be stronger!

Hannah: So what are some of the challenges he faces, Sean?

Sean: Well, he'll be travelling alone, so, you know, that's always a risk, but he hopes to meet people along the way and maybe travel with them for a bit or stay at their place. Then of course, riding a unicycle isn't as easy as it looks. It's much harder than riding an ordinary bicycle, and it's slower too, so he's chosen his route to avoid too many hills. Apart from that, he'll be carrying everything he needs, his luggage if you can call it that, with him on his bike.

Hannah: Really? How is that going to work?

Sean: He's got special panniers, you know, bags attached to his bike, so he's taking a tent, a sleeping bag, a stove to cook on, a puncture repair kit and a few clothes. But if you can imagine, he'll be cycling with about 25 kilos in those panniers, so that's going to make things even more difficult.

Hannah: It sounds impossible to me! But is there any particular reason for this trip?

Sean: Yes, there is. Apart from the personal challenge, Ed is also raising money for a charity called 'School in a Bag'. It's a charity that distributes learning equipment, like exercise books, pens and pencils in a handy rucksack, to poor children, particularly orphans or children affected by disasters. He hopes that by the end of the journey, he'll have raised £7,500, that's over 10,000 euros. That will pay for about 500 bags.

Hannah: That's such a great story. We wish him the very best of luck. Thanks, Sean.

Unit 5

Developing vocabulary and listening p43

3 and 4 11

Presenter: Hello, and welcome to the history podcast. In today's society, money is a necessary part of living. We work to earn a salary, calculate how much we need to get by, set aside a certain amount for our old age and occasionally splash out on the things we really want. For most of us, money is central to our lives, and whether the currency is cows or cocoa beans, I think we can safely say that has always been the case. But today I'd like to take you back in time, back to the 1300s and to a small indigenous tribe living in the highlands of Peru. This was the origin of the great Inca Empire, which, in the 15th and 16th centuries, became the largest empire South America had ever known. It was a civilisation rich in food, textiles, cocoa and gold. But one of the many mysterious facts about the empire is that it operated without money. In fact, it may be the only advanced civilisation in history that had no money and no commerce of any kind. William Stevens has been studying the Inca for over 30 years.

William: Of course, we don't know exactly why the empire developed the way it did.

It may have been for many different reasons. But we know that the Inca Empire was very rich. It was so rich that it could afford to have hundreds of people who were specialised in agricultural techniques, and that might have been the key to their success. We know that they built farms on the side of mountains and chose crops that would grow in the temperatures at different altitudes. They had sophisticated irrigation methods to transport water where it was needed. In fact, we think that they were able to grow more food than they actually needed.

Presenter: So here we have a population of about 12 million people all living without money. There were no shops or markets, and without these, there was no buying or selling of goods. Yet this was a civilisation that built enormous pyramids and temples, and places like the great Machu Picchu. The cities were as large as any European city, and archeological remains show that they must have been cleaner, more organised and better places to live. All of this, connected by a system of roads that covered almost 40,000 kilometres, that's about three times the diameter of the Earth. So how did they do it?

William: From what we know, the government controlled everything. Instead of paying taxes in money, the Inca people worked for the state. In exchange for their work, they received all the necessities of life. That included food, tools and clothes and care for the elderly and the sick.

Presenter: But why did this rich and sophisticated culture develop without inventing money? This is one of the questions that scientists and historians who study the Incas are trying to answer. Lucy Roberts has written a book about it. She explains:

Lucy: We believe it could have been because the Inca people dedicated all of their efforts to agriculture rather than economics. This is a region with an unpredictable climate. The Wari, a previous civilisation, had already disappeared because of a lack of rain. The Inca knew that if they had another period like that they wouldn't be able to grow

food and that was a danger to their survival. So food was their money and the extra they produced allowed them to take control of other local states.

Presenter: Eventually, it wasn't the weather, but disease, brought to the continent by European invaders, that was their downfall. Still, the Inca people were able to develop one of the greatest empires in history ... without ever spending a cent!

Developing speaking p45

2 and 6 12

Let me think ... Both photographs show people at a bank, but in the first photograph, the people are inside the bank whereas in the second photograph, a man is using an ATM outside the bank. In both pictures people are withdrawing money, or maybe they're paying money into their account in the first picture. But one big difference is that in the first picture, there are people waiting in a queue to speak to a cashier. We can see them standing on the right and they seem a bit impatient. I imagine they've been waiting for a long time because the queue's quite long. The man in the second picture doesn't have to wait because he's using a machine. I think he must have been shopping, or maybe he's going to work because he's got a bag over his shoulder. He may have spent all his money and now he needs more.

3, 5 and 6 13

I think that machines are useful in some situations but not always. I mean, if you want to withdraw money at a bank, or buy a train or cinema ticket, it's much quicker to use a machine. But if you need advice or if you have a more complicated question, it's better to speak to a person because they can understand your situation. So I think it depends on what you need to do. Also, machines don't always work. I mean, they aren't as reliable as people because they can break down, or there could be a computer problem. So, in my opinion, machines are good for some customer services, but they shouldn't replace people completely. Personally, I like using machines because they're faster and more convenient, but sometimes I prefer to speak to a real person.

Unit 6

Developing vocabulary and listening p51

3 and 4 14

Speaker 1:

I recently ran a 12-hour ultra-marathon, but I didn't use to be fit. In fact, I'd avoid sport whenever I could, mostly because I was embarrassed at how slow I was. I had a pretty unhealthy lifestyle – I just ate junk food, slept and studied. Change didn't come fast. I signed up for a football club and I learnt a lot from our coach. He showed me how to do yoga and how to eat more healthily. One summer we started running to build up stamina and I became addicted. I've run 20 races since then so I guess I owe it all to my coach. If he hadn't encouraged me to run, I wouldn't have found a sport I really love.

Speaker 2:

Both of my parents are runners, which is probably what got me started. I first watched a race when I was about three. My dad is my coach now and I run about 50 kilometres a week and I travel to races at weekends. It's a lot, I know, but it isn't about keeping in shape. It's about pushing myself to the limit. People say I'm too young, that my body can't take the stress, but I'm getting faster and stronger all the time. I wish they'd change the age limit so I can run in all the races. I don't see why you have to be 18. I came fourth in my last half marathon, which shows I'm just as good as any adult. If I hadn't started too fast, I think I'd have won the race.

Speaker 3:

You may have read the story in the newspaper. I didn't have my running shoes, but I ran anyway. I was 10th out of over a thousand runners, even though I ran in my normal school shoes. I think I'd left my running shoes on the bus when we went on a school trip, but I didn't want to let that stop me. I admit I hadn't really trained for the race. I'd done a few short runs and a couple of long-distance ones, but I'm pretty fit anyway 'cos I go surfing and I do some cycling, too. No doubt I'd have done better if I'd trained, but I felt on top of the world when I finished. And all those journalists wouldn't have wanted to interview me if I'd run in proper running shoes.

Speaker 4:

I'd trained a lot for the race and I was in second place. We were coming to the end of the race and we were doing laps inside a stadium. Everyone was cheering so I felt pretty great. Then the girl in front of me fell. Maybe she was dehydrated or something, I don't know, but she blacked out for a second. I didn't even think twice. I just stopped running and helped her to her feet. We walked to the finishing line together and other runners passed us on the way. Of course, I wish I'd won the race, but there'll be others. People are calling me a hero now, but I'm not really. It was just the right thing to do.

Speaker 5:

I'd started running seriously when I was about 12 and people said I was the up-and-coming runner. I pushed myself even when I felt under the weather and wanted to stay at home. When I got injured, I just carried on. I went through a stage when I hurt everywhere. I think I put too much pressure on my knees and ankles because there was a point when I just stopped winning. If I'd

rested, my ankles would have got stronger, but I didn't want to get left behind. It was a hard decision, but in the end I had to stop competing. I do some climbing now and I go swimming because you don't need strong ankles for that. I wish I could run still, but I can't. I think I learnt my lesson, but it came a bit too late.

Developing speaking p53

2 and 3 ▶ 15

Examiner:	I'd like you to imagine you have a friend who wants to take up a new sport. Here are some sports for you to discuss. Talk to each other about the advantages and disadvantages of each sport for someone who doesn't have much time.
Boy:	OK. What do you think about basketball?
Girl:	Well, I think it's a good team sport, so if you want to make friends, it's a good way to meet people.
Boy:	I agree, but the problem with basketball is that you need a lot of time for it. I mean, you usually have to go to practice sessions during the week and then you play a match at the weekend so it's not really a good sport for someone who doesn't have much time.
Girl:	That's true. So what about swimming?
Boy:	I think it's a good way to keep in shape, and it's a sport you can do at any time.
Girl:	Maybe, but it takes a lot of time, you know? You have to go to the swimming pool, get changed, swim and have a shower afterwards. It's not very convenient.
Boy:	Yes, I see what you mean. Running is more convenient because you can do that at any time and you don't have to belong to a gym. You can go running in a park or on the beach if you live near a beach, and it's something you can do with a friend. What do you think?
Girl:	I'm not sure. A lot of people get injured when they go running. It's easy to sprain your ankle or pull a muscle.
Boy:	I suppose so, but as long as you wear good running shoes and do proper stretching exercises, it's OK.
Girl:	Mmm ... what about tennis?
Boy:	I think it's a good sport and you can play with a friend, but you usually have to belong to a club and that's quite expensive, at least where I live.
Girl:	Yes, you're right. I think skiing is exciting, but it's expensive,

too. And you can't do it all year. It's only for winter so I think you need to do another sport at the same time.

Boy:	I think you're right, and you have to travel to different places to do it and that takes time.

5 ▶ 16

Examiner:	Now you have a minute to decide which sport you think is best for your friend.
Boy:	What do you think?
Girl:	Well, I think that the best option is tennis. It might be expensive, but you can play when you want and it doesn't take much time.
Boy:	I see what you mean, but I think swimming might be a better choice because you can go to the swimming pool for a short time or for a long time. It's quite flexible.
Girl:	Maybe, but running is flexible, too. In my opinion, running is a better option because you don't need to go to the pool.
Boy:	Yes, I think you're right. I think running is a good choice.
Girl:	Let's choose running then.
Examiner:	Thank you.

Gateway to exams: Units 5–6

Listening p57

5 ▶ 17

Presenter:	We hear a lot these days about the things we should do to be healthy. We should eat a balanced diet, cut back on fatty and processed food and work out at the gym. But today, Laura Byatt has another tip for us, and this one is much more fun. She's here to tell us about the health benefits of laughter. Laura, why is laughing good for us?
Laura:	Well, believe it or not, there are lots of reasons. Some people say that laughing is a form of exercise. It's actually as good for you as working out. So if you don't have time to go to the gym or do any other physical activity, it gets your heart pumping and burns a similar number of calories as walking slowly. In fact, laughing for just 10 or 15 minutes a day burns up to 40 calories. I'm not saying that's an excuse to eat fast food, but every bit helps!
Presenter:	Laughing helps you to keep fit then.
Laura:	Exactly. It even helps to tone your muscles. When you're

laughing, you use the muscles in your stomach. They expand and contract, so if you want to have a flat stomach, you should try laughing.

Presenter: I didn't know that! And are there other ways that laughing is good for us?

Laura: Yes, there are. As I say, laughing gets your heart pumping, and it reduces the build up of fat and cholesterol in your arteries, so that means it's good for your heart. It reduces the risk of heart disease.

Presenter: So the saying that laughter is the best medicine is certainly true when it comes to protecting your heart.

Laura: That's right. And it reduces blood pressure, too. It helps to reduce stress, which is one of the causes of high blood pressure.

Presenter: So if you're feeling angry or stressed, it's a good idea to read a funny book or watch a comedy on TV. It'll make you laugh and so feel less stressed.

Laura: Yes, but there's actually another benefit which comes from being less stressed. When you're stressed, your body doesn't fight diseases well. So laughing makes your immune system function better, and helps to fight against diseases.

Presenter: Incredible. So the next time you feel under the weather, or you feel a cold coming on, try laughing. It might be better than taking pills or medicines!

Laura: I must tell you the story of Norman Cousins. Have you heard of him?

Presenter: I don't think so. How do you spell his name?

Laura: Cousins, that C-O-U-S-I-N-S. He used to be an editor for a news magazine. Anyway, he had a very serious and very painful disease that affected his bones. His doctors said that he would probably never recover. He tried all sorts of traditional medicines – injections and pills to relieve his symptoms, but nothing worked. So he left the hospital and went to a hotel, took some vitamin C and watched funny films and programmes on TV. He found that laughing allowed him to sleep, and he eventually recovered from his disease. If he hadn't laughed, he wouldn't have got better. He wrote a book about his experience and started laughter therapy, which some health centres now use to treat patients.

Presenter: That's an amazing story. I'm sure it doesn't happen for everyone though.

Laura: No, of course not, but even if a patient doesn't recover, laughing can help to relieve pain. It causes the body to release endorphins, you know, the chemicals that give us a good feeling, the same chemicals that are produced when you work out, or eat chocolate.

Presenter: I think we should also mention that laughing, apart from being good for our health, is also good for our relationships, isn't it? I mean, it's something we do with friends and family.

Laura: That's right. You know how infectious laughing is. When one person laughs, then another person starts laughing, and it creates a good feeling, it brings us together and makes us feel happy.

Presenter: So just to finish then, I think the message is clear. If we all laughed more, we would feel better, and we would be healthier, too.

Laura: Exactly.

Presenter: Thanks, Laura.

Unit 7

Developing vocabulary and listening p61

3 and 4 ▶ 18

Presenter: Since it first opened in 1977, the *Star Wars* film series has become a worldwide pop culture phenomenon. There are *Star Wars* theme parks, museums and, of course, video games. The series has produced millions of casual fans, and perhaps the biggest and most dedicated group of superfans ever known. With me today is one of these superfans, Dave Barnes. Dave, what is it about *Star Wars* that people love so much?

Dave: Well, it's just a great story, great heroes, great soundtrack. Everything about it is great.

Presenter: When did you first get interested in it?

Dave: I was just a kid when I saw the first film. I remember queuing outside the cinema, waiting to get in. It just had a tremendous impact on me. I was quite introverted at the time, I didn't have many friends and it was my escape, my way of dealing with things.

Presenter: And then you started collecting?

Dave: That's right. I collected anything that was to do with *Star Wars* – figures, I've got four or five hundred figures now, and autographs – probably hundreds of autographs.

Presenter: And are these things valuable now?

Dave: Some things are, but a lot of them I used to play with, so they were toys for me, and I've never had them valued. But the most important pieces aren't the ones that cost the most. If you spend two years trying to find someone who appeared in the film and then you talk to them, for maybe just two seconds, and get their autograph, that makes it more valuable, to me anyway.

Presenter: I'm not sure if everyone feels the same as you do.

Dave: No, I know some people hire private detectives to find people and then they try to get things cheap and sell them for lots of money. That's not really what it's about though.

Presenter: What do you mean exactly?

Dave: Well, it's about meeting people who were there, when the film was made. Like, there's one collector who was reading a book a few years ago, and this book claimed that George Lucas, the director, wanted to thank the president of 20th Century Fox for taking a risk on the film. So he invited the president to take a prop from the film, you know, as a thank-you present. Well, 30 years later, this collector called the president of 20th Century Fox and asked him if he still had the prop, and he did. So the guy explained that he was a big fan and the president agreed to sell it to him. And he flew all the way to the States to get it.

Presenter: That's amazing! That really is a superfan! And I know that there are lots of copies of the original props from the film, so you have to be careful, right?

Dave: Right. Some people spend years, and thousands of pounds building costumes and equipment. The funny thing is that the guy who made the original props admits picking up old things for hardly any money at all because they didn't have a big budget to make the film.

Presenter: But Dave, I know that it's not only about collecting things, is it? There are lots of other ways that people celebrate the

Dave: film. Can you tell us a bit about those?

Dave: Well, let me see. There was a couple who got married recently, and they're both *Star Wars* fans. So they had a *Star Wars* wedding. It was the bride, in fact, who insisted on having her father dress up as Darth Vader and walk her down the aisle. And they had Storm Troopers at the ceremony, and everything. You can go on special *Star Wars* holidays, where you visit all the locations where the film was made. Lots of fans make their own *Star Wars* films, too.

Presenter: Oh, yes. I've heard about those. People make their own sets and costumes and make films to post online.

Dave: That's right. And of course, we have our own special day. People have parties everywhere. They dress up in the costumes of their favourite character from the film. It's a lot of fun.

Presenter: What day is that?

Dave: It's May the 4th, you know "May the fourth be with you!"

Presenter: Of course, what else!

Developing speaking p63

2 and 3 ▶ 19

Boy: So, which do you think is usually better, the book or the film?

Girl: There's no doubt in my mind that the book is nearly always better. Take *The Hunger Games*, for example. I enjoyed the films, but the books were much better. They were real page-turners.

Boy: I agree. I usually like books more than films. But you can't deny that some film adaptations are good. For instance, *The Lord of the Rings* films were fantastic. I loved all the special effects.

Girl: Yes, the special effects *were* good, but there were a lot of changes to the plot. The books were much more detailed and the film left a lot of things out.

Boy: Yes, but don't forget that the books were very long. Whoever wrote the screenplay had to tell the story in a much shorter time.

Girl: Yes, that's true, but I like to imagine the characters and the places, not see them on the screen.

Boy: Maybe, but I really do think that the film is sometimes better than the book. You only have to think of *The Social Network*. The book was quite complicated, but the film was gripping.

Girl: I agree there are exceptions, and the acting and the soundtrack make a difference. A good example of

that is *Slumdog Millionaire*. Even though some of the actors weren't professionals, they all made the film seem very real, and I loved the music.

Boy: Exactly. And sometimes books are written after the film. Look at the *Transformers* books, for example.

Girl: That's true, but still, they're exceptions. Personally, I'm totally convinced that the book is nearly always better than the film.

Unit 8

Developing vocabulary and listening p69

3 and 4 ▶ 20

Presenter: Last week, we heard the story of Petra Němcová, and how she turned her experience of the 2004 tsunami in Thailand to good. Today, we have another story to tell you. This time, it involves two brothers, Rob and Paul Forkan. Here to tell us about them is our Asian correspondent Mike Shepherd. Mike, where were the boys when the tsunami hit?

Mike: Hi. They were in Sri Lanka at the time. You see, up until about four years before the tsunami hit, the Forkans were a normal family living in London. But the boys' parents had always dreamt of a different life so they sold their house and business and took Rob, Paul, and their younger brother and sister to live in India. There were two older sisters, but they stayed behind in London.

Presenter: So why were they in Sri Lanka then?

Mike: Well, after four years living and volunteering in Goa, the family went back to London with the idea of staying there, but they needed to go back to India to organise things. So the holiday in Sri Lanka was just a last family holiday before they went back to live in London for good.

Presenter: And what happened on that day, in 2004?

Mike: Well, it was about 8 o'clock in the morning. Rob and Paul were still in bed in their bungalow – the others were in another bungalow nearby – when Rob woke to see some water coming under the door. Then they heard a loud noise, a loud bang, and water poured into their room. They just had time to escape and climb onto the roof before the room was completely flooded.

Presenter: They must have been terrified!

Mike: I think they were, but they said the fact that they'd travelled a lot before meant they were able to stay calm while everyone else was panicking. Still, there was incredible destruction everywhere, trees torn up and buildings swept away.

Presenter: So what happened next?

Mike: Well, by chance, they saw a child in a tree, and luckily, it turned out to be their younger brother. So they were able to rescue him, and then a little later they found their sister. But they couldn't find their parents anywhere. Their sister was injured, so they had a difficult decision to make. They could wait to see if their parents turned up, or take her to a hospital. They both knew that their parents would want them to take their sister to a hospital, so they decided to leave. They didn't have any money or passports, but they managed to get a lift to the nearest city, and from there, they were eventually flown back home, back to London.

Presenter: That shows a lot of courage. How old were the boys at this time?

Mike: They were only teenagers. Rob was 17 and Paul just 15. When they got back home, they all went to live with one of their older sisters. And this is where the story gets even more incredible. During that time, someone mysteriously paid for an extension on the house, and also paid for books, beds, and so on. The boys later found out that a businessman in London had heard their story and had been so moved by it that he secretly decided to pay all their expenses.

Presenter: That's amazing! So what are the boys doing now?

Mike: Well, after travelling again for a while, Rob and Paul decided to set up a business together, selling flip flops. They'd worn flip flops all the time while they were in India, they said.

Presenter: That's a cool idea.

Mike: Yes. They wanted to do something they believed in, and they've been very successful, too. The business is thought to have a turnover of over a million pounds. They've also set up a charity called *Orphans for Orphans* which helps other children who've lost their parents. They give 10% of all the profits from their business to this charity. So far they've built a school in Sri Lanka and they're hoping to build schools in India and other places, too.

Presenter: That's really great!

Mike: But the boys still wear their flip flops. They even wore them to Buckingham Palace when they met Prince Harry. He had a good laugh about it apparently. They've written a book about their experience. It's called *Tsunami Kids: Our Journey from Survival to Success*. I recommend it.

Presenter: Well, that really is an incredible story, Mike. Thanks for telling us about it.

Mike: Thank you.

Developing speaking p71

4 and 5 21

Girl: Well, the graph shows that there has been a dramatic increase in the number of weather-related disasters in recent years.

Boy: Yes, in fact, the number tripled between 1980 and 2010. There were fewer than 150 weather-related disasters in 1980, but in 2005, there were nearly 450.

Girl: That's right. The biggest increase was in the number of storms.

Boy: Yes, and if we look at the pie charts, we can see a rise in the number of windstorms between 2012 and 2013, too.

Girl: There was a steady increase in the number of floods between 1980 and 2010, and the number rose between 2012 and 2013.

Boy: But the number of droughts fell.

Girl: At the same time, the number of geophysical disasters fluctuated between 1980 and 2010.

Boy: Yes, the pie charts show that there was little change in the number of earthquakes and volcanic eruptions between 2012 and 2013.

Girl: So it seems that disasters related to weather are the biggest problem we face at the moment. In particular, problems related to storms and floods.

Boy: That's right, because the number of geophysical disasters has stayed more or less the same.

Gateway to exams: Units 7–8

Listening p75

4 22

Boy: Hey, have you seen this website?

Girl: No, what is it?

Boy: It's a site where you can write music reviews and earn money doing it.

Girl: That sounds interesting. Where did you hear about it?

Boy: I was chatting to some friends at school, and complaining about not having much money ...

Girl: Well, if you didn't spend all your money on clothes and music!

Boy: Yes, I know, I know, they accused me of doing the same thing. But anyway, Greg told me about this site and suggested that I look at it. He said his cousin had written some reviews and got paid for it.

Girl: So how does it work?

Boy: Basically, all you need is an Internet connection. You register to become a member, and then you're sent a password. You log in at the site, listen to the music, and then you write your review.

Girl: So what kind of music do you write about?

Boy: It can be any kind of music. You don't get to choose. You just hit the play button and listen to whatever comes out.

Girl: And what's the point of it? I mean, apart from earning money for you. Do famous musicians really read these reviews?

Boy: It's not really intended for big stars, it's more for artists that are just starting out. They get the chance to get people listening to their music, and they get feedback on it.

Girl: Well, I guess that's useful.

Boy: Exactly, and the music with the best reviews is referred to scouts, you know, people who work for music companies. That means that they could be signed by a music company and get financing, and the site also has an influence on whether the music is played on radio stations.

Girl: OK, that sounds good, but do you really think you can write a review? Don't you need special training for that?

Boy: Not really. According to Greg, they just want to know what ordinary people think about the music, so you don't have to be an expert. And I've found this site here that tells you how to write a review.

Girl: Let me see ... right, so it says that you can comment on the tune, the voice, the lyrics, instruments ...

Boy: And it even gives you adjectives you can use. So the tune can be original, or memorable if it's good, or tuneless if it's bad.

Girl: And the lyrics can be thought-provoking, or confusing and repetitive. That's cool. So how much are you paid for writing these reviews?

Boy: About one dollar fifty per review.

Girl: Is it an American company then?

Boy: No, it's British. It was started in 2007 according to Greg, but I don't know who by.

Girl: But wait a minute, one dollar fifty, that's not very much money, is it. You'd have to write a lot of reviews to earn anything.

Boy: Well ... true, Greg warned me about that. It's not very much, but how much you get depends on how many reviews you write. If you write maybe ten an hour, you earn 15 dollars.

Girl: It seems like a lot of work to me.

Boy: Yes, but it's not just about the money. You're helping new bands to get started, and earning money for listening to music. It sounds like a good deal to me.

Girl: Well, good luck. Let me know how you get on.

Unit 9

Developing vocabulary and listening p79

3 and 4 23

Presenter:

OK, now you may remember last week we told you a story about a man who lost his mobile on the beach. And then his girlfriend got a call a week later from a fisherman who said he'd found it – inside a fish! Well, we started to wonder if any of you listeners had your own stories to tell about losing a mobile. And sure enough, it seems lots of you have.

Speaker 1:

Hi, this happened to me a few months ago. I was walking to college with a friend when I stopped to send a message and realised I didn't have my mobile. I couldn't find it anywhere. I searched everywhere and I thought, well somebody's stolen it. But anyway we decided to go back to the coffee shop where we'd been earlier to see if somebody had handed it in. Some girls were sitting on the sofa where we'd been sitting, but they said they hadn't seen it. So we were about to leave, when my friend decided to call my number and suddenly one of the girls jumped up and started screaming. It turns out she'd been sitting on my mobile and I had it set to vibrate, not to ring. She thought she was sitting on a mouse or something. I had to buy her another coffee, but at least I got my mobile back.

Speaker 2:

OK, so I've lost a few mobiles in fact. I dropped one in a river when I was taking a selfie, another disappeared from my hotel room when I was on holiday. I'd left it behind to charge and I didn't have my photos backed up so I lost all my holiday pics. But the worst time was a couple of years ago. I went out for a run one day with my tracksuit on and my new phone in the pocket. Anyway, I got back about an hour later, threw my clothes into the washing machine and went to have a shower. Then I realised that I'd forgotten to take my phone out of my pocket, so I rushed downstairs, just as the washing machine was finishing the cycle. I took my tracksuit out and my phone was there, but it was too late. I tried to dry it out, but it didn't work. It was a very expensive run that day!

Speaker 3:

So, I'm the sort of person that loses things all the time, and last month it was my phone. It was a Saturday, and I'd taken the bus into town and when I got off, I realised I didn't have it. I must have dropped it or something. So I went to the bus station and reported it missing and then went home and started to panic because I thought about all the information I had on it. Then I remembered downloading a finder app, so I went online and the location of the phone immediately popped up on the screen. The app lets you send a message so I sent one with my contact details and waited. Nothing happened, but I could see the phone was moving around town. Eventually, I got a call later that evening and went to pick up my phone, which was great, but I still don't know why the people who found it travelled around with it all day.

Speaker 4:

This isn't really a lost story, more of a found one, but anyway … this happened to my grandad. He'd never had a mobile before and he didn't want to buy a new one so he went to a market where they had second-hand phones and picked one up there. So anyway, when he got home, he charged the battery and turned on the phone. It wasn't password protected, and he looked in the contact information and saw the name of a famous footballer. I won't tell you who it was, but at first he thought it was just another person with the same name. Then he scrolled down and saw the names of other footballers in the same team. He could have called them, but he didn't. Instead he just called the manager of the team and returned the phone to him. It turns out that he'd forgotten to delete the contacts when he'd bought a new phone.

Developing speaking p81

2 and 3 24

Woman: Personally, I think it's true that technology has caused a generation gap, but not in a negative way.

Man: What do you mean by that?

Woman: I mean when we talk about a generation gap, we usually mean a conflict or problems between generations, you know, fighting about music or clothes or how to behave. I think technology has created differences, but not really problems.

Man: Sorry, I'm not sure I'm with you.

Woman: What I mean is that I think technology is developing so rapidly that there are differences between the devices and the media that kids use even if they're

only a few years apart. What's popular today is no longer popular tomorrow. So it's inevitable that there are differences between this generation and the previous one. I just don't believe that it causes problems.

Man: I see, but I think it's not only the devices that kids use nowadays, or which social network site is fashionable and which isn't. I think there is a difference between how generations view technology.

Woman: Are you saying that technology is more important for young people, that they can't imagine life without it?

Man: Yes, that's exactly what I mean. I think people of all generations use technology, but for older people it's something that's useful, convenient, but it's not essential. But for younger people, it's a priority.

Woman: That's true, but I think there have always been generation gaps. This is nothing new. And young people aren't using technology to rebel against their parents. It's just that it's something that they've always known. Do you get what I'm saying?

Man: Yes, I do, though I think that there are sometimes disagreements between kids and their parents about how much time they spend playing computer games, or when kids want to use their phone all the time, even when they're having dinner.

Woman: In other words, some parents don't understand how important technology is, and feel their kids rely on it too much.

Man: Yes, so in that sense there is a generation gap because of technology.

Unit 10

Developing vocabulary and listening p87

4 and 5 25

Presenter: Hi and welcome back. This is CNB News keeping you informed with the latest news and headlines from around the world.
Now we have a story that has turned one young man into something of a hero. The news of his simple act of kindness has been reported in both national and international news. Here to tell us about it is Chloe Lorrett. Chloe, you've been following the story, haven't you?

Chloe: Yes, Cole. It was a typical day here at an ice-cream parlour in downtown Minneapolis where 19-year-old Joey Prusak works. Joey was serving behind the counter like he does every day when he happened to see a woman steal 20 dollars from a blind customer. So Joey didn't think twice. He confronted the thief and asked her to return the money to its owner. And when she refused, he gave the customer 20 dollars out of his own pocket.

Presenter: And do you know how we got to hear the story, Chloe? Was it from the customer?

Chloe: No, and not from Joey either. There was another customer in the store that day who witnessed what happened, and she wrote an email to the store, praising Joey's actions. They put a copy of the letter on their noticeboard, photographed it and then posted it online. And as we now know Cole, the letter went viral.

Presenter: It sure did. So, I wonder if you could tell us what it said, Chloe. You've seen the letter, haven't you?

Chloe: I have, Cole. It explains that the customer saw a blind man, or partially sighted man, we're not sure, drop the 20 dollar bill on the ground while he was struggling to find his pocket and put away his change. An older woman, waiting in line to be served, picked it up. At first, the customer thought the woman was going to give it back to him. Instead, she put the money in her purse.

Presenter: And Joey asked her to give it back, didn't he?

Chloe: That's right. He politely asked her to return the money, but she insisted that *she'd* dropped it, even though everyone could see that wasn't the case. So Joey said he wasn't going to serve her and asked her to leave the store.

Presenter: Do you know if she went quietly?

Chloe: Apparently not. She was very angry in fact, but Joey stayed calm and the woman eventually left. Then Joey went over to the blind man, opened his wallet and gave the man another 20 dollar bill. He said it wasn't the same note, but it had the same value.

Presenter: And the act has caused quite a reaction, hasn't it?

Chloe: Yes, it has. Since it happened, Joey's been invited to appear on all sorts of news channels and TV shows. He even got a call from Warren Buffet, one of the richest men in the world and a shareholder in the company that owns the ice-cream parlour. He phoned to thank Joey and to congratulate him on what he'd done. He said Joey was a role model for all the other employees, and for people in general, and he's invited him to attend the next shareholder's meeting. He's going to fly him down to Texas for that.

Presenter: Well, I bet he got a surprise when he got *that* call. But that wasn't the only reward he got, was it Chloe?

Chloe: No, that's right. Apparently, Joey is a big fan of car racing. In fact, it's his favourite hobby, and he's been invited, with three guests, to go to the next big race. He'll be the personal guest of one of the top racing drivers there.

Presenter: That's great! And Chloe, have you got any idea how he's taking his sudden fame?

Chloe: He's quite surprised by it all, and very modest about what he did. When I asked why he gave the man the money, he said it just felt like it was the right thing to do.

Presenter: Well, Chloe, I think it was Martin Luther King Jr who said, 'It's always the right time to do the right thing.' Thanks for that. It's good to hear a positive story for a change. Now on …

...veloping speaking p89

2 and 3 26

I'd like to begin by saying that I agree with the statement. Let me explain why.

Firstly, the circulation of print newspapers is already decreasing. Most people nowadays prefer to read a newspaper on a mobile device because it's much more convenient. ʹou can read the news wherever you and although you have to pay a ʹription to some papers, others are ʹe.

There's no denying that reading an online newspaper can be annoying. Advertisements pop up on the screen, and sometimes you have to wait for articles to load. However, as Internet connections improve, it will become faster to load articles, and let's not forget that there are advertisements in print newspapers, too.

I accept that older people, who are more used to reading print newspapers, will continue to do so for a while. Having said that, I believe that it will become too expensive to produce print copies and they will eventually disappear. And let's not

forget that print newspapers are bad for the environment. Trees must be cut down to make paper, and too many people throw away old newspapers instead of recycling them.

To sum up, in my opinion print newspapers will be extinct by 2025 because more and more people read the news online and newspapers won't be able to afford to produce print copies.

Gateway to exams: Units 9–10

Listening p93

5 ▶ 27

Sister: Hey, what are you doing?

Brother: I'm just checking my page, why?

Sister: Do you think you're addicted to your phone?

Brother: No, why?

Sister: We watched this video in class today about some students who gave up using their phones for a week.

Brother: Why would anybody want to do that?

Sister: Well, they'd been talking about how much time they used their phones and their teacher suggested it.

Brother: OK.

Sister: Listen, this is interesting. Apparently, kids spend about six and a half hours a day in front of a screen. That's more than twice as much as they did 20 years ago.

Brother: Well, they didn't have smartphones then, so what else were they going to do?

Sister: I'd like to know how many hours you spend on your phone every day?

Brother: Maybe one or two …

Sister: You're kidding, aren't you? I know I spend more time than that. Apparently, girls spend more time on social media and boys use their phones more to play games.

Brother: That sounds right. You don't play games, do you?

Sister: Not much. Anyway, half the class volunteered to give up their smartphones for a week. They were given phones they could use for texting and phone calls, and £10 credit.

Brother: What about tablets?

Sister: I think they had to stop using computers too, for social media and games, I mean.

Brother: It must have been difficult.

Sister: It was. They made videos of themselves, so you kind of watch them going through it. It was really funny when they got their phones. One guy said he'd never read instructions before, and he had no clue even how to turn it on.

Brother: I don't think I'd know either.

Sister: Another said he always used his phone as an alarm, and the one he had was useless. He didn't know how to set it and it didn't go off.

Brother: Right.

Sister: And another girl said she couldn't stand being without music.

Brother: Yeah, that would be the worst thing for me. I don't think I could live without my music. I like to listen when I walk to school and back.

Sister: I know. But what was interesting was that at first they were completely lost. They didn't know what to do with themselves. But after a while, they actually liked it.

Brother: Why?

Sister: Well, they said they started to do other things instead. One girl visited a friend and usually they'd both be on their phones, but they watched TV and chatted. Another boy said that he'd started to read books and he'd never had time to do that before.

Brother: You read books, don't you?

Sister: Yes, but maybe I could read more. Then another girl said she'd got her homework done on time and hung out with her family more.

Brother: We're hanging out now, aren't we?

Sister: Yes, OK. And the other thing was that they'd all gone to bed earlier than usual, and got more sleep.

Brother: But I bet they were happy to get their phones back though, weren't they?

Sister: Yes, but they all said that they were going to stop using their phones so much. And the funny thing was, they said they felt happier without their phones.

Brother: So why are you telling me this?

Sister: I'm thinking of doing the same. I'm going to stop using my phone for a week.

Brother: Well, I hope you're not going to ask me to do the same because I'm not giving up my phone, all right?

Sister: OK, it was just a thought.

Brother: No way!

Macmillan Education Limited
4 Crinan Street
London N1 9XW

Companies and representatives throughout the world

ISBN 978-0-230-47098-9

This edition published 2016
First edition entitled *Gateway B2 Teacher's Book* published 2011

Designed by emc design ltd
Page make-up by Expo Holdings Sdn Bhd
Cover design by emc design ltd and Macmillan Publishers Ltd

The publishers would like to thank the staff and pupils at the following schools in Mexico and Spain for helping us so enthusiastically with our research for this second edition of Gateway: Concha Campos, IES Burgo de Las Rozas, Las Rozas, Madrid; Félix Gaspar, IES Las Encinas; Villanueva de la Cañada, Madrid; Cristina Moisen, IES Joaquín Turina, Madrid; Colegio Montessori Cuautitlán; Colegio Conrad Gessner; Colegio Erasmo de Rotterdam; Colegio Kanic, Centro Educativo Erich Fromm; Universidad Franco Mexicana; Centro Pedagógico María Montessori de Ecatepec; Instituto Cultural; Escuela Maestro Manuel Acosta; Liceo Sakbé De México.

The publishers would also like to thank all those who reviewed or piloted the first edition of Gateway: Benjamin Affolter, Evelyn Andorfer, Anna Ciereszynska, Regina Culver, Anna Dabrowska, Justyna Deja, Ondrej Dosedel, Lisa Durham, Dagmar Eder, Eva Ellederovan, H Fouad, Sabrina Funes, Luiza Gervescu, Isabel González Bueno, Jutta Habringer, Stela Halmageanu, Marta Hilgier, Andrea Hutterer, Nicole Ioakimidis, Mag. Annemarie Kammerhofer, Irina Kondrasheva, Sonja Lengauer, Gabriela Liptakova, Andrea Littlewood, María Cristina Maggi, Silvia Miranda Barbara Nowak, Agnieska Orlinska, Anna Orlowska, María Paula Palou, Marta Piotrowska, N Reda, Katharina Schatz, Roswitha Schwarz, Barbara Scibor, Katarzyna Sochacka, Joanna Spoz, Monica Srtygner, Marisol Suppan, Stephanie Sutter, Halina Tyliba, Prilipko, Maria Vizgina, Vladyko, Pia Wimmer, Katarzyna Zadrozna-Attia and Katarzyna Zaremba-Jaworska.

The author and publishers would like to thank the following for permission to reproduce their photographs:
Shutterstock/Artem Kovalenco pp11, 13, 17, 18, 19, back cover; Shutterstock/ively p11; Shutterstock/M.Stasy p12, back cover

Full acknowledgements for illustrations and photographs in the facsimile pages can be found in the Student's Book and Workbook.

Printed and bound in the UK by CLOC Ltd

2022 2021
17 16